Abstract

At the request of the U.S. Senate Committee on Finance, the U.S. International Trade Commission ("Commission") undertook an investigation to better understand the role of digital trade—domestic commerce and international trade conducted via the Internet—in the U.S. and global economies, as well as the effects of barriers and impediments to digital trade that impede U.S. access to global markets. The Commission's analysis provides findings at three levels: at the firm level, through 10 case studies; at the industry level, through a survey of U.S. businesses; and at the economy-wide level, using computable general equilibrium and econometric models. This analysis shows that digital trade contributes to economic output by improving productivity and reducing trade costs. Digital trade also contributes to the economy as a whole as it facilitates communication, expedites business transactions, improves access to information, and improves market opportunities for small and medium-sized enterprises (SMEs).

Digital trade's combined effects of increased productivity and lower trade costs are estimated to have increased U.S. real gross domestic product (GDP) by $517.1–$710.7 billion (3.4–4.8 percent), and increased U.S. aggregate employment by 0.0 to 2.4 million full-time equivalents (0.0 to 1.8 percent). These estimates of the effects of digital trade are not exhaustive, however, as other effects of digital trade were not captured in these findings. According to survey results, U.S. firms in digitally intensive industries sold $935.2 billion in products and services online in 2012, including $222.9 billion in exports; they purchased $471.4 billion in products and services online in 2012, including $106.2 billion in imports. Online sales by U.S. SMEs in digitally intensive industries totaled $227.1 billion in 2012. However, the Commission's analysis suggests that foreign trade barriers are having discernible effects on U.S. digital trade. According to the Commission's econometric estimates, removing these barriers would increase the U.S. real GDP by an estimated $16.7–$41.4 billion (0.1–0.3 percent).

Table of Contents

Abstract 1

Abbreviations and Acronyms 10

Executive Summary 13

Chapter 1 Introduction 27

    Objective 28

    Scope 29

        Definition of Digital Trade 29

        Industries Particularly Involved in Digital Trade 30

    Approach 31

        Firm-level Findings: Case Studies 32

        Industry-level Findings: Survey of U.S. Firms 32

        Economy-wide Findings: Quantitative Assessments 33

        Other Information Sources 34

    Organization of the Report 34

    Bibliography 36

Chapter 2 Digital Trade and U.S. Businesses: Domestic Operations and
International Trade 39

    Key Findings 39

    Results 40

    Estimate of Digital Trade in the U.S. Economy 41

        Online Sales of Products and Services 41

        Online Purchases of Products and Services 45

        International Trade 47

        Business Practices 50

        Advertising 54

        Online Advertisements 54

    Cyber Incidents 58

    Bibliography 61

Chapter 3 Broader Linkages and Contributions of Digital Trade to the U.S.
Economy 65

    Key Findings 65

    Analytic Approach and Data Sources 66

    Economic Benefits of Increased Productivity due to the Internet 67

        The Contribution of the Internet to Productivity 67

        Economy-Wide Implications of the Productivity Effects of the Internet 70

    Economic Benefits of Reduced International Trade Costs due to the Internet 72

    Simulations That Combine the Two Types of Effects 73

    Bibliography 76

Chapter 4 Barriers to International Digital Trade and Their Economic Effects 77

    Key Findings 77

    U.S. Firms' Assessments of Barriers to International Digital Trade 79

        Approach 80

        Localization Requirements 81

3

Market Access Limitations 86

Data Privacy and Protection Requirements 88

IPR Infringement 92

Uncertain Legal Liability 95

Censorship 97

Customs Requirements 99

Estimated Effects of Removing Digital Trade Barriers 100

Survey Results: Effects of Barriers on Sales Abroad 100

Survey Results: Barriers Rankings by Country 102

Estimated Economy-wide Effects of Removing Foreign Barriers to Digital Trade 102

Bibliography 105

Chapter 5 Case Studies: How Digital Trade Creates New Opportunities for Businesses and Consumers 109

Case Study 1: Enabling Independent Creators in the Content Industries 112

Challenges for SMEs within the Traditional Pre-Internet Industry Framework 113

Internet Technologies Are Lowering Barriers to Entry for SMEs 114

Bottom Line for Content Creators and Consumers 122

Case Study 2: Facilitating Greater Capacity Utilization in the Travel and Lodging Industry 124

Background 125

The Internet's Impact on the Direct Sales Channels 125

The Internet's Impact on Intermediary Sales Channels 126

The Internet's Impact on Capacity Utilization 127

The Internet and Private Capacity Utilization 128

Case Study 3: How the Internet Reduces Job Search Frictions and Lowers Unemployment 131

Case Study 4: Increasing Collaboration and Integration in Online Services—The Economic Contributions of Application Programming Interfaces 133

Benefits to Businesses from Using APIs 134

End-User (Consumer) Benefits 137

Challenges and Concerns 138

Bibliography 139

Chapter 6 Case Studies: The Rise of Big Data 151

Case Study 5: Data Analytics Innovations in the Insurance Industry 153

Competitive Drivers for Adopting Advanced Data Analytics in Insurance 154

Case Study 6: Machine-to-Machine (M2M) Communication Is Improving Production Processes 159

Benefits of M2M Communication 160

Examples of How Firms Use M2M Communication to Increase Efficiency 161

Risks and Vulnerabilities of the Internet of Things 163

Case Study 7: Digital Innovations in Agriculture 164

M2M Communications-based Packages Delivering Agricultural Solutions 165

Growing Use of Unmanned Aerial Vehicles (UAVs) 167

Online Privacy Considerations to Be Addressed 168

Case Study 8: Internet User Data Collection—Balancing Benefits with Privacy Concerns 169

Companies Use Many Tools to Collect and Aggregate Information about Internet Users' Activities Online 169

Internet User Data Collection Helps Digital Services Evolve and Become More Efficient ... 170

Internet Users' Concerns about Data Collected Online 173

Internet Companies Are Working to Maintain Their Users' Trust 175

Companies and Consumers Working Toward a Balance 176

Bibliography 178

Chapter 7 Case Studies: How the Internet Is Facilitating International Trade 191

Case Study 9: The Global Competitiveness of U.S. Internet Companies 191

Global Market Share and Competitiveness 192

Case Study 10: Facilitating SME Exports 201

Digital Intensity Is Tied to SME Growth and Export Performance 202

The Internet Lowers Marketing and Export Transaction Costs for SMEs 204

A Variety of Online Platforms and Services Make It Much Easier and Less Costly for SMEs to Export
.... 205

Secure and Convenient Payment Systems Promote SME Trade 206

The Growth of Mobile Devices Benefits SME Trade 207

Digital Communications and Cloud Computing Present Tremendous Export Opportunities for SMEs,
but Also Risks 208

Bibliography 209

Appendix A Request Letter 217

Appendix B Federal Register Notices 223

Appendix C Calendar of Hearing 233

Appendix D Summary of Positions of Interested Parties 237

Boxes

Box 4.1 Data security and national intelligence agencies' activities 91

Box 5.1 Crowdfunding enables entrepreneurs across industries 116

Box 5.2 Peer-to-peer rental companies: Growing pains 129

Box 6.1 Data collection inspired by Fukushima: An example of crowdsourcing and big data analytics in
the nonprofit sector 152

Box 6.2 How websites collect information from users 169

Box 7.1 How TaoBao overcame eBay in China 196

Box 7.2 Foreign Internet companies in the United States 197

Box 7.3 Specific limitations in China 199

Figures

Figure ES.1 How U.S. firms in digitally intensive sectors use the Internet, survey results 22

Figure 2.1 Online sales of digitally delivered products and services, by sector and firm size (billions $) . 42

Figure 2.2 Share of total firms that increased their online sales of digitally delivered products and
services during 2011–12, and expected growth of such sales during 2012–13, by sector 43

Figure 2.3 Online sales of physically delivered products and services, by sector and firm size (billions $)
.... 44

Figure 2.4 Share of total firms that increased their online sales of physically delivered products and services during 2011–12 and expected growth of such sales during 2012–13, by sector 45
Figure 2.5 Online purchases of digital products and services, by sector and firm size, 2012 (billions $)..47
Figure 2.6 Online purchases of physical products and services, by sector and firm size, 2012 (billions $) 47
Figure 2.7 Exports of products and services by sector and delivery mode, 2012 (billions $)....................48
Figure 2.8 Top regions for exports of products and services ordered online, by percentage of firms, 2012 49
Figure 2.9 Imports of products and services online by sector and delivery mode, 2012 (billions $) 50
Figure 2.10 Characteristics of Internet usage 51
Figure 2.11 Characteristics of Internet usage, by firm size...52
Figure 2.12 Business functions affected by the Internet 53
Figure 2.13 Percentage of firms advertising online, by sector, 2012 55
Figure 2.14 Online advertising as a share of total advertising, by sector, 2012 55
Figure 2.15 Share of firms with apps or mobile websites, by sector...57
Figure 2.16 Number of cyber incidents, by sector, 2012 59
Figure 2.17 Share of firms affected by cyber incidents, by type of impact 60
Figure 4.1 Firms' perceptions that localization requirements present an obstacle to digital trade, by sector and firm size..82
Figure 4.2 Firms' perceptions that market access limitations present an obstacle to digital trade, by sector and firm size..87
Figure 4.3 Firms' perceptions that data privacy and protection requirements present an obstacle to digital trade, by sector and firm size..89
Figure 4.4 Firms' perceptions that IPR infringement presents an obstacle to digital trade, by sector and firm size...93
Figure 4.5 Firms' perceptions that uncertain legal liability rules present an obstacle to digital trade, by sector and firm size..95
Figure 4.6 Firms' perceptions that censorship presents an obstacle to digital trade, by sector and firm size 97
Figure 4.7 Firms' perceptions that customs requirements present an obstacle to digital trade, by sector and firm size..99
Figure 4.8 Large firms' expected changes in sales abroad if foreign barriers removed, by sector 101
Figure 6.1 Interactive digital data transfer chain between the agricultural community and equipment166
Figure 7.1 Foreign revenues of selected U.S. Internet companies, 2002–13 194
Figure J.1 Cumulative growth of IT jobs by state between 2009 and 2013..331

Tables

Table ES.1 Digitally intensive industries and sectors covered 15
Table ES.2 Economy-wide effects of digital trade: Combined effects of enhanced productivity and lower trade costs..17
Table ES.3 Economy-wide effects of digital trade: Effects of removing foreign barriers to digital trade . 19
Table ES.4 U.S. firms' online sales and purchases, 2012 (survey results)..20
Table ES.5 U.S. firms' online sales and purchases, SMEs and large firms, 2012, survey results 21
Table ES.6 U.S. digital trade: Online international trade, 2012, survey results..21
Table ES.7 Sectors with the largest portions of firms that identified each barrier as a "substantial" or "very substantial" obstacle to digital trade, by firm size, survey results..23
Table 1.1 Digitally intensive industries and sectors...31
Table 3.1 Digital trade: Summary of methodology and data sources 67

Table 3.2 Reported impact of the loss of the Internet on productivity, by sector (percent in each range) 68

Table 3.3 Reported uses of the Internet, average measure of frequency by sector (scale from 1 to 5)...69

Table 3.4 Average marginal effects on productivity of not having the Internet for each of the uses of the Internet, based on the estimated logit model 69

Table 3.5 Economy-wide effects: Estimated effects of reported enhanced productivity due to the Internet in digitally intensive sectors, percent change...71

Table 3.6 Economy-wide effects: Estimated effects of reported reductions in international trade costs due to the Internet in digitally intensive sectors, percent change...73

Table 3.7 Economy-wide effects: Estimated combined effects of enhanced productivity and lower trade costs due to the Internet in digitally intensive sectors, percent change...............................74

Table 4.1 Sectors with the largest portions of firms that identified each barrier as a "substantial" or "very substantial" obstacle, by firm size 78

Table 4.2 Digital trade barriers ranking of countries, by percentage of firms that faced barriers............79

Table 4.3 Seven barriers to digital trade identified in the Commission's *Digital Trade 1* investigation....80

Table 4.4 Top locations where firms perceived that obstacles limited doing business online 83

Table 4.5 Effects of removing foreign barriers to digital trade on U.S. employment in digitally intensive industries; share of firms with effects in each of the ranges...103

Table 4.6 Economy-wide effects of removing foreign barriers to digital trade, percent change............103

Table 7.1 Top Web properties in leading economies 193

Table 7.2 Users, revenues, and average revenue per user (ARPU) for leading U.S. Internet companies195

Table F.1 Digitally intensive industries and selected NAICS codes 276

Table F.2 Minimum employee requirements by NAICS code 277

Table F.3 Composition of the 19 strata in the sampling frame 277

Table F.4 Sample selection and response rates 278

Table F.5 Adjustments to the sample size and number of respondents 279

Table F.6 Response rates by industry and stratum, (percent)...280

Table F.7 Determinants of survey participation 282

Table F.8 Detailed weighting for each stratum..283

Table G.1 Total sales and employees for digitally intensive industries 287

Table G.2 Sales and employees for digitally intensive industries, by size 287

Table G.3 Sales and employees for digitally intensive industries, by industry sector 288

Table G.4 Full-time employees in digitally intensive industries that work with online products or services 288

Table G.5 Full-time employees in digitally intensive industries that work with online products or services, by firm size 288

Table G.6 Full-time employees in digitally intensive industries that work with online products or services, by industry sector..289

Table G.7 Projected increase or decrease in number of full-time employees in digitally intensive industries that work with online products or services 289

Table G.8 Impact on firm productivity if firms did not have access to the Internet, by size (percentage of firms answering each option) 289

Table G.9 Impact on firm productivity if firms did not have access to the Internet, by industry sector (percentage of firms answering each option)...289

Table G.10 Firm total online sales, 2012..290

Table G.11 Firm total online sales, by firm size, 2012 290

Table G.12 Firm total online sales, by industry sector, 2012...291

Table G.13 Bundled Internet and non-Internet products or services, 2012..291

Table G.14 Bundled Internet and non-Internet products or services, by firm size, 2012 291
Table G.15 Bundled Internet and non-Internet products or services, by industry sector, 2012.............292
Table G.16 Firm total online purchases, 2012 292
Table G.17 Firm total online purchases, by firm size, 2012...292
Table G.18 Firm total online purchases, by industry sector, 2012 293
Table G.19 Savings/costs associated with switching to Internet-based services 293
Table G.20 Savings/costs associated with switching to Internet-based services, by firm size, 2012 293
Table G.21 Savings/costs associated with switching to Internet-based services, by industry sector, 2012
....293
Table G.22 Total spending on Internet-based services, 2012...294
Table G.23 Total spending on Internet-based services, by firm size, 2012 294
Table G.24 Total spending on Internet-based services, by industry sector, 2012................................294
Table G.25 Total spending on traditional advertising, 2012...294
Table G.26 Total spending on traditional advertising, by firm size, 2012...294
Table G.27 Total spending on traditional advertising, by industry sector, 2012 295
Table G.28 Total spending on Internet advertising, 2012...295
Table G.29 Total spending on Internet advertising, by firm size, 2012 295
Table G.30 Total spending on Internet advertising, by industry sector, 2012......................................295
Table G.31 Online purchases of products or services imported, 2012..296
Table G.32 Online purchases of products or services imported, by firm size, 2012.............................296
Table G.33 Online purchases imported, by industry sector, 2012..296
Table G.34 Exported online sales of digitally delivered products or services, 2012.............................296
Table G.35 Exported online sales of digitally delivered products or services, by firm size, 2012 296
Table G.36 Exported sales of digitally delivered products or services, by industry sector, 2012............297
Table G.37 Online sales of physically delivered products or services exported, 2012 297
Table G.38 Online sales of physically delivered products or services exported, by firm size, 2012........297
Table G.39 Online sales of physically delivered products or services exported, by industry sector, 2012
....297
Table G.40 Localization requirements as a barrier to digital trade, percent response by sector and firm
size 298
Table G.41 Mean response to localization requirements as a barrier to digital trade...........................298
Table G.42 Market access limitations as a barrier to digital trade, percent response by sector and firm
size 299
Table G.43 Mean response to market access limitations as a barrier to digital trade 299
Table G.44 Privacy and data protection requirements as a barrier to digital trade, percent response by
sector and firm size...300
Table G.45 Mean response to privacy and data protection requirements as a barrier to digital trade .300
Table G.46 IPR infringement as a barrier to digital trade, percent response by sector and firm size.....301
Table G.47 Mean response to IPR infringement requirements as a barrier to digital trade 301
Table G.48 Uncertain legal liability as a barrier to digital trade, percent response by sector and firm size
....302
Table G.49 Mean response to uncertain legal liability as a barrier to digital trade 302
Table G.50 Censorship as a barrier to digital trade, percent response by sector and firm size 303
Table G.51 Mean response to censorship as a barrier to digital trade..303
Table G.52 Compliance with customs requirements as a barrier to digital trade, percent response by
sector and firm size...304
Table G.53 Mean response to compliance with customs requirements as a barrier to digital trade 304

Abbreviations and Acronyms

Acronyms	Terms
ADA	Application Developers Alliance
APEC	Asia-Pacific Economic Cooperation
API	application programming interface
AUVSI	Association for Unmanned Vehicle Systems International
B2B	business-to-business
B2C	business-to-consumer
BEA	Bureau of Economic Analysis (U.S. Department of Commerce)
BLS	Bureau of Labor Statistics (U.S. Department of Labor)
BSA	Business Software Alliance
CAD	computer-aided design
CBO	U.S. Congressional Budget Office
CBPR	cross border privacy rules
CD	compact disc
Census	Census Bureau (U.S. Department of Commerce)
CGE	computable general equilibrium (economic model)
DMCA	Digital Millennium Copyright Act
DVD	digital video disc or digital versatile disc
e-book	electronic book
e-commerce	electronic commerce
EC	European Commission
EU	European Union
FAA	U.S. Federal Aviation Administration
FCC	U.S. Federal Communications Commission
FDI	foreign direct investment
FTC	U.S. Federal Trade Commission
FTEs	full-time equivalent (workers)
GDP	gross domestic product
GDS	global distribution systems
GPS	global positioning system
GTAP	Global Trade Analysis Project
IAB	Interactive Advertising Bureau
ICT	information and communications technology
IIPA	International Intellectual Property Alliance
IMF	International Monetary Fund
IP	Internet protocol
IPR	intellectual property rights
ISP	Internet service providers
IT	information technology
M2M	machine-to-machine
Mbps	megabits per second

Acronyms	Terms
MPAA	Motion Picture Association of America
NAICS	North America Industry Classification System
NSA	U.S. National Security Agency
NRI	Networked Readiness Index (World Economic Forum)
OBA	online behavioral analysis
OECD	Organisation for Economic Co-operation and Development
OES	Occupational Employment Survey (U.S. Department of Labor, Bureau of Labor Statistics)
OTA	online travel agent
PII	personally identifiable information
R&D	research and development
RFP	request for proposals
SBA	U.S. Small Business Administration
SME	small and medium-sized enterprise
TCP	transmission control protocol
TV	television
UAV	unmanned aerial vehicle
UBI	usage based insurance
USDOC	United States Department of Commerce
USITC	U.S. International Trade Commission
USTR	U.S. Trade Representative
VoIP	Voice over Internet protocol
WEF	World Economic Forum
WIOD	World Input-Output Database

Executive Summary

This is the second of two reports on digital trade—domestic commerce and international trade conducted via the Internet—prepared by the U.S. International Trade Commission (USITC or Commission) at the request of the U.S. Senate Committee on Finance (Committee).[1] The reports' overall aims are to help the Committee better understand the role and contributions of digital trade in the U.S. and global economies, and to clarify the effects of diverse barriers to digital trade that impede U.S. access to global markets.

This report defines digital trade as U.S. domestic commerce and international trade in which the Internet and Internet-based technologies play a particularly significant role in ordering, producing, or delivering products and services.[2] The report focuses on U.S. industries particularly involved in digital trade, or digitally intensive industries (described in more detail below). It estimates the value and contribution of digital trade to the U.S. economy by applying a global trade model and by analyzing data from a survey of U.S. firms conducted by the Commission. It also describes major barriers to digital trade and their effects based on survey results. This report further provides 10 case studies that highlight the importance of digital trade for U.S. industries.

Main Findings

Economy-wide Effects of Digital Trade: Model Results

Digital trade, through the combined effects of the Internet in enhancing productivity and lowering international trade costs in certain digitally intensive industries, has resulted in an increase in U.S. gross domestic product (GDP) of 3.4–4.8 percent ($517.1–$710.7 billion in 2011).[3] U.S. real wages were higher by 4.5–5.0 percent, and U.S. total employment was higher by 0.0 to 2.4 million full-time equivalents (FTEs).[4] If the effects of enhanced productivity and

---

[1] For the Commission's first report on digital trade, see USITC, *Digital Trade in the U.S. and Global Economies, Part 1*, 2013 (hereafter *Digital Trade 1*).

[2] This report uses a broader definition of digital trade than that used for *Digital Trade 1* to reflect input from public comments the Commission received during the course of these investigations. The Commission defined digital trade more narrowly in *Digital Trade 1* as "commerce in products and services delivered over digital networks." That definition excluded commerce in most physical goods, such as goods ordered online and physical goods that have a digital counterpart such as hard copy books and software, music, and movies sold on CDs or DVDs.

[3] The data base for the global trade model used for this report, Version 9 (pre-release) of the Global Trade Analysis Project (GTAP), uses sector-level bilateral trade flows with a 2011 baseline, the most recent year available.

[4] The ranges in the estimates are the result of two different scenarios concerning assumptions about the responsiveness of labor supply to changes in wages that are analyzed; these scenarios are described in more detail below and in chapter 3. FTEs are employees on full-time schedules plus employees on part-time schedules converted to a full-time basis. Thus, two employees working half-time schedules equal one FTE. This measure facilitates the comparison of employees regardless of their schedules.

lower international trade costs due to the Internet in non-digitally intensive sectors were also quantified, the economy-wide estimates would likely be larger.

The removal of foreign barriers to digital trade to digitally intensive industries would result in an estimated 0.1–0.3 percent increase in U.S. GDP (a $16.7–$41.4 billion increase in 2011). U.S. real wages would be 0.7–1.4 percent higher, and U.S. total employment would be higher by 0.0 to 0.4 million FTEs in 2011.

Digital Trade and U.S. Businesses: Survey Findings[5]

U.S. digitally intensive firms sold $935.2 billion in products and services and purchased $471.4 billion in products and services over the Internet in 2012. An estimated $296.4 billion (30.6 percent) of these online sales and $49.3 billion (10.5 percent) of these online purchases consisted of products and services delivered over the Internet (i.e., not delivered physically or in person).

In 2012, online sales by digitally intensive small and medium-sized enterprises (SMEs) were $227.1 billion, or about one-fourth of total online sales, and online purchases by SMEs were $162.2 billion, or about one-third of total online purchases. Sales and purchases by both SMEs and large firms are more likely to have been delivered physically or in person than digitally delivered.

U.S. digitally intensive firms use the Internet most frequently for internal communications and to order products and services. Survey estimates also showed that losing access to the Internet would reduce productivity by 15 percent or more for more than 40 percent of digitally intensive firms.

Most exports and imports ordered online are delivered physically or in person—not digitally. Digitally intensive firms exported $222.9 billion and imported $106.2 billion in products and services ordered online in 2012.

Barriers to International Digital Trade: Survey Findings

Localization requirements, market access limits, data privacy and protection requirements, intellectual property rights infringement, uncertain legal liability rules, censorship, and customs measures in other countries all present obstacles to international digital trade.

Removal of these foreign barriers to digital trade would boost U.S. sales abroad, although not all sectors would necessarily benefit equally. Large firms in the content, digital communications, retail, and other services sectors expected that sales abroad would increase more from the

---

[5] The Commission conducted a survey of nearly 10,000 U.S. firms in digitally intensive industries in November 2013. Survey results are presented in chapters 3 and 4 of the report.

removal of trade barriers than firms in finance and manufacturing. Large firms also generally expected higher gains than did SMEs, according to the survey results.

Firms most frequently identified Nigeria, Algeria, and China as countries where barriers to digital trade precluded doing business or where they faced barriers. By contrast, Australia, the United Kingdom, and Italy were the locations where firms least frequently felt that they faced digital trade barriers or that barriers precluded them from doing business.

Digitally Intensive Industries

For this report, the Committee requested that the Commission conduct a survey of U.S. firms in industries particularly involved in digital trade. The digitally intensive industries of the U.S. economy, as defined in this report, comprise more than 140,000 firms in the sectors shown in table ES.1.

Table ES.1 Digitally intensive industries and sectors covered

Industry	Sectors covered
Content	Publishing, including newspapers, periodicals, books, directory and mailing lists, and other publishers; motion picture and sound recording, including video and music production and distribution; broadcasting except Internet (see digital communications below); and news syndicates.
Digital communications	Software publishing; data processing, hosting, and related services; Internet publishing and broadcasting, and Web search portals.
Finance and insurance ("finance")	Establishments primarily engaged in financial or insurance transactions and/or in facilitating these transactions.
Manufacturing	Chemicals, printing, industrial machinery, metalworking machinery, engines, computers and electronics, power, distribution, specialty transformer, relay and industrial control, transportation equipment, and medical equipment and supplies.
Retail trade	Retail sales in motor vehicles and parts, furniture, electronics and appliances, and clothing through non-store retailers.
Selected other services ("other services")	Accounting; architectural services; engineering services; graphic design; computer programming; computer systems design; marketing consulting services; media buying agencies; travel arrangement and reservation services; couriers and express delivery services.
Wholesale trade	Distribution of motor vehicles and parts, computers, electrical equipment, and clothing through business-to-business electronic markets.

Source: Compiled by Commission staff. The selection of industries and sectors covered is described in more detail in appendix F.

Report Highlights

This report examines digital trade from three perspectives: the economy-wide level, using computable general equilibrium (CGE) and econometric models;[6] the industry level, through a survey of U.S. businesses; and the firm level, through 10 case studies. Because the Internet is so pervasive, however, available data do not capture all of the economic activities it facilitates; all of its contributions to productivity, employment, growth, and trade; as well as its broader impacts on individuals, firms, and society as a whole.

---

[6] The specific CGE model used for this analysis is the Global Trade Analysis Project (GTAP) model. GTAP is a global trade model that takes into account the links between all of the sectors in each country and the pattern of trade flows among the countries. The GTAP model is described more fully in appendix H.

Economy-wide Effects of Digital Trade

The economy-wide effects of digital trade on the U.S economy were estimated by assessing two impacts attributed to the Internet—higher productivity, and lower costs for trading products and services across borders—as well as the potential impact of removing foreign barriers to trade associated with U.S. digitally intensive industries.[7] The CGE model was used to measure digital trade's effects on U.S. GDP, U.S. wages, and U.S. employment (in FTEs).

The model-based estimates in this report reflect the net economic effects of digital trade's contributions to the U.S. economy. They include digital trade's benefits, in terms of job and revenue gains in booming digitally intensive sectors; they also include the associated downsizing of other parts of the broader U.S. economy as scarce resources and limited budgets are reallocated.

The combined economy-wide effects of enhanced productivity and lower international trade costs in certain digitally intensive industries due to digital trade resulted in an estimated increase of 3.4 to 4.8 percent in U.S. GDP ($517.1–$710.7 billion in 2011).

Enhanced productivity and lower trade costs from use of the Internet in digitally intensive industries have linkages and contributions to the U.S. economy as a whole:

Higher productivity in certain digitally intensive industries due to the Internet increases output in these industries while lowering costs of producers and therefore prices to consumers. These gains in digitally intensive industries spill over to the rest of the economy and lead to economy-wide effects. Higher demand for workers in the digitally intensive industries drives up wages in the labor market, draws workers from other sectors of the economy, and can also increase aggregate employment as more workers are brought into the labor force. The productivity-based reductions in costs translate into lower prices for consumers, and this increases the purchasing power of their wages.

Reduced international trade costs in digitally intensive industries due to the Internet have a broader impact on the economy. These reductions in trade costs lower the prices of inputs for producers and the prices of final goods for consumers. They increase the purchasing power of wages and the purchasing power of aggregate income (measured by GDP).

---

[7] As described in further detail in chapters 3 and 4 and in appendix H of this report, data obtained from the survey were used to provide estimates of effects of the Internet on U.S. productivity and the potential employment effects of the removal of foreign barriers to digital trade. These estimates, in turn, were used in the CGE model. To reduce the burden on survey respondents, the Commission's survey did not ask for information on trade costs. Instead, the Commission used an econometric model to estimate what the effects would be on the trade costs of U.S. imports and exports in digitally intensive industries if the United States and its trading partners did not use the Internet; these trade cost effects were then used in the GTAP model to estimate the effects for the broader U.S. economy of reductions in trade costs due to the actual use of the Internet in digitally intensive industries.

Effects of enhanced productivity and lower trade costs. The combined economy-wide effects of enhanced productivity and lower costs of trading goods across borders that result from digital trade in certain digitally intensive industries resulted in an estimated 3.4 to 4.8 percent increase in U.S. GDP ($517.1–$710.7 billion in 2011), as shown in table ES.2. The range of these estimates is a result of two different scenarios concerning assumptions about the responsiveness of labor supply to changes in wages. One scenario (a fixed labor force scenario) corresponds to an economy with a relatively tight labor market, and the other scenario (a flexible labor force scenario) corresponds to an economy with some slackness in the labor market.

Table ES.2 Economy-wide effects of digital trade: Combined effects of enhanced productivity and lower trade costs

Economic outcomes	Estimated effects[a]	
	Fixed labor force (Column A)	**Flexible labor force (Column B)**
Increase in U.S. real GDP[b]	$517.1 billion	$710.7 billion
	3.4 percent	4.8 percent
Increase in U.S. real wages	5.0 percent	4.5 percent
Increase in U.S. aggregate employment[b]	No change[c]	2.4 million FTEs[d]
	0.0 percent	1.8 percent

Source: Modeling results from Commission analysis.
Notes:

[a]Column A (fixed labor force) assumes that the aggregate labor force is fixed and thus does not respond to changes in real wages; that is, the aggregate labor supply elasticity is equal to zero. Column B (flexible labor force) assumes that the aggregate labor force responds to changes in real wages and the aggregate labor supply elasticity is equal to 0.4. These elasticity values are from a 2012 U.S. Congressional Budget Office (CBO) study described in more detail in chapter 3.

[b]GDP and employment levels are based on levels in 2011, the base year used in the model; see White House, *Economic Report of the President*, March 2014.

[c]The assumption that the aggregate labor force is fixed implies that there is no change in net aggregate employment although workers in the labor force may move from contracting sectors to expanding sectors.

[d]The assumption that the aggregate labor force is flexible implies that net aggregate employment increases in response to higher wages due to enhanced productivity and lower trade costs in expanding sectors.

Average U.S. real wages were higher by an estimated 4.5–5.0 percent, and U.S. total employment was higher by 0.0 to 1.8 percent (0.0 to 2.4 million FTEs in 2011) due to the enhanced productivity and lower trade costs in digitally intensive industries from digital trade. The net effect on employment could be zero (with increased employment in some industries offset by reductions in others) if wage increases associated with increased productivity take place in an economy with a relatively tight labor market, i.e. with few potential workers ready to enter the market, to take jobs, or to increase their hours. The net effect on employment would be positive in an economy with some slackness in the labor market (due to relatively low employment), with workers ready to enter the labor force, to take jobs, or to increase their hours.

It should be noted that, as this analysis focuses on digitally intensive industries, these are not exhaustive estimates of the effects of digital trade on the economy as a whole.[8] If the effects of enhanced productivity and lower international trade costs due to the Internet in non-digitally intensive sectors were also quantified, the economy-wide estimates would likely be larger.

In addition, there are other ways Internet technologies benefit producers and consumers and contribute to digital trade that could not be quantified for the model. For example, the Internet has allowed firms to improve logistics management, manage supply chains more efficiently, introduce more efficient business practices, increase market intelligence, gain greater access to more markets and customers, and develop additional channels for service delivery. These developments associated with the application of Internet technologies remain potentially important areas for future analysis of the impact of digital trade.[9]

The removal of foreign barriers to digital trade in digitally intensive industries would result in an estimated increase of 0.1–0.3 percent ($16.7–$41.4 billion) in U.S. GDP in 2011.

Removing foreign barriers to digital trade would increase U.S. employment in digitally intensive industries which, in turn, would benefit the U.S. economy as a whole. As shown in table ES.3, the removal of barriers would trigger an estimated 0.1 to 0.3 percent increase (a $16.7–$41.4 billion increase at 2011 levels) in U.S. GDP, a 0.7–1.4 percent increase in U.S. real wages, and a 0.0 to 0.3 percent increase in U.S. total employment. Digitally intensive firms surveyed estimated that their sales abroad would be positively affected by the removal of foreign barriers. This was particularly true for large firms in the wholesale trade and the digital communications sectors, both of which estimated increased sales of between 5 and 15 percent.

The Internet helps lower job search costs, benefiting overall U.S. employment.

As job search has moved online, job search costs and the time it takes job seekers to find prospective employers have fallen. An econometric analysis used to assess the relationship between a country's Internet usage and its unemployment rate estimated that the U.S. unemployment rate in 2012 was about 0.3 percentage points lower than it would have been if Internet usage rates in 2012 had been the same as in 2006 (when they were lower).

---

[8] For this investigation the Commission was requested to focus on selected industries particularly involved in digital trade, i.e., firms in digitally intensive industries, although other effects of digital trade are likely in non-digitally intensive industries.

[9] For a discussion of the economic effects of the use of Internet technologies in the broader economy, see USITC, *Digital Trade 1*, 2013, chapter 3 and appendix F.

Table ES.3 Economy-wide effects of digital trade: Effects of removing foreign barriers to digital trade

	Estimated effects[a]	
Economic outcomes	Fixed labor force (Column A)	Flexible labor force (Column B)
Increase in U.S. real GDP[b]	$16.7 billion	$41.4 billion
	0.1 percent	0.3 percent
Increase in U.S. real wages	1.4 percent	0.7 percent
Increase in U.S. aggregate employment[b]	No change[c]	0.4 million FTEs[d]
	0.0 percent	0.3 percent

Source: Modeling results from Commission analysis.
Notes:

[a]Column A (fixed labor force) assumes that the aggregate labor force is fixed and thus does not respond to changes in real wages; that is, the aggregate labor supply elasticity is equal to zero. Column B (flexible labor force) assumes that the aggregate labor force responds to change's in real wages and the aggregate labor supply elasticity is equal to 0.4. These elasticity values are from a 2012 CBO study described in more detail in chapter 3.

[b]GDP and employment levels are based on levels in 2011, the base year used in the model; see White House, Economic Report of the President, March 2014.

[c]The assumption that the aggregate labor force is fixed implies that there is no change in net aggregate employment although workers in the labor force may move from contracting sectors to expanding sectors.

[d]The assumption that the aggregate labor force is flexible implies that net aggregate employment increases in response to higher wages due to the removal of foreign barriers to digital trade in expanding sectors.

Digital Trade and the U.S. Economy: Survey Results

The Commission sent questionnaires to nearly 10,000 firms in digitally intensive industries in November 2013. The survey's response rate was nearly 41 percent, and 80 percent of the more than 3,600 responding firms were SMEs.[10] The survey asked companies how they use the Internet in their domestic operations and how the Internet has changed their business operations, as well as what their experiences have been with foreign barriers and impediments to digital trade. Some questions asked firms to distinguish between what they sell online ("online sales") and what they order or purchase online ("online purchases"). The survey also asked firms to indicate how these online sales or purchases were delivered—either online (e.g., as software downloaded or services performed online) or physically/in person (e.g., goods physically delivered or services provided face to face).

In 2012, U.S. firms in digitally intensive industries sold nearly $1 trillion in products and services over the Internet, and they purchased nearly $500 billion of products or services online. Most of those online sales and purchases were delivered physically or in person— not online.

Online sales by U.S. firms in digitally intensive industries were estimated to be $935.2 billion in 2012 (table ES.4). An estimated $296.4 billion (30.6 percent) of these online sales consisted of products and services delivered over the Internet (i.e., not delivered physically/in person). The

---

[10] SMEs are broadly defined in this report as organizations with at least 10 but less than 500 employees.

Table ES.4 U.S. firms' online sales and purchases, 2012 (survey results)

Economic activity	Value	Mode of delivery	Leading sectors
Online sales	$935.2 billion		
		Delivered online: $296.4 billion (30.6 percent)	Digital comm.: $114.7 billion (38.7 percent) Finance: $49.9 billion (16.7 percent)
			Manufacturing: $295.7 billion (46.3 percent)
		Delivered physically/in person: $638.8 billion (66.0 percent)	Retail: $163.7 billion (25.6 percent) Wholesale: $88.4 billion (13.8 percent)
Online purchases	$471.4 billion		
		Delivered online: $49.3 billion (10.5 percent)	Other services: $12.2 billion (24.7 percent) Finance: $11.7 billion (23.7 percent)
		Delivered physically/in person: $422.2 billion (89.6 percent)	Manufacturing: $157.4 billion (37.3 percent) Retail: $87.7 billion (20.8 percent)

Source: USITC calculations of weighted responses to the Commission questionnaire.

top two sectors delivering products and services over the Internet were digital communications ($114.7 billion) and finance and insurance ("finance") ($49.9 billion). An estimated $638.8 billion of total online sales (66.0 percent) transacted online were of products and services delivered physically/in person, primarily in the manufacturing ($295.7 billion), retail ($163.7 billion), and wholesale ($88.4 billion) sectors.

Online purchases of products and services by firms in digitally intensive industries totaled $471.4 billion in 2012. An estimated $49.3 billion (10.5 percent) of these online purchases were of products and services delivered online. The top two sectors purchasing products and services online that were delivered online were selected other services ("other services") ($12.2 billion) and finance ($11.6 billion). An estimated $422.2 billion of total online purchases (89.6 percent) were of products and services delivered physically/in person, led by manufacturing ($157.4 billion) and retail ($87.7 billion).

SMEs in digitally intensive industries accounted for relatively small shares of online sales and online purchases in 2012. Sales and purchases by both SMEs and large firms are more likely to have been delivered physically or in person than digitally delivered.

Online sales by SMEs totaled $227.1 billion in 2012, or almost one-fourth of total online sales by firms in digitally intensive industries, while large firms accounted for about three-fourths of online sales, valued at $708.1 billion (table ES.5). Online sales by both SMEs and large firms were more likely to have been delivered physically/in person than digitally delivered.

Online purchases by SMEs totaled $162.2 billion in 2012, or about one-third of total online purchases by firms in digitally intensive industries, while large firms accounted for nearly two-thirds of online purchases, valued at $309.2 billion. As was the case for online sales, online purchases by both SMEs and large firms were more likely to have been delivered physically/in person than digitally delivered.

Table ES.5 U.S. firms' online sales and purchases, SMEs and large firms, 2012, survey results

Economic activity		Total	SMEs	Large firms
Online sales		$935.2 billion	$227.1 billion (24.3 percent)	$708.1 billion (75.7 percent)
	Delivered online		$67.6 billion	$228.8 billion
	Delivered physically/in person		$159.5 billion	$479.3 billion
Online purchases		$471.4 billion	$162.2 billion (34.4 percent)	$309.2 billion (65.6 percent)
	Delivered online		$22.5 billion	$26.7 billion
	Delivered physically/in person		$139.7 billion	$282.5 billion

Source: USITC calculations of weighted responses to the Commission questionnaire.

Online international trade is a relatively small component of U.S. exports and imports of both digitally and physically delivered products and services.

Firms in digitally intensive industries exported $222.9 billion in products and services ordered online in 2012, and imported products and services ordered online valued at $106.2 billion (table ES.6). The manufacturing sector was the leading exporter and importer of products and services ordered online, with $86.5 billion in exports and $50.7 billion in imports.

Most exports and imports ordered online by U.S. digitally intensive firms are delivered physically/in person. An estimated 40.6 percent of U.S. exports sold online ($90.6 billion) were delivered digitally in 2012, and 59.3 percent were delivered physically/in person ($132.3 billion). Just 6.2 percent of U.S. imports purchased online ($6.6 billion) were delivered digitally in 2012, and 93.7 percent ($99.6 billion) were delivered physically/in person.

Table ES.6 U.S. digital trade: Online international trade, 2012, survey results

Online activity	Value	Delivered digitally	Delivered physically/in person
U.S. exports	$222.9 billion	$90.6 billion (40.6 percent)	$132.3 billion (59.3 percent)
U.S. imports	$106.2 billion	$6.6 billion (6.2 percent)	$99.6 billion (93.7 percent)

Source: USITC calculations of weighted responses to the Commission questionnaire.

Internal communications and online ordering of products and services are the leading ways U.S. firms in digitally intensive sectors use the Internet.

Most U.S. firms surveyed reported they use the Internet for internal communications, ordering physical products and services, and business-to-business communications (figure ES.1). Firms also reported they use the Internet for supply chain management and market research. Large firms were more likely to report these uses of the Internet than SMEs—possibly because large firms are more likely than SMEs to have large networks of suppliers and other service providers that can benefit from the use of the Internet for these functions.

Figure ES.1 How U.S. firms in digitally intensive sectors use the Internet, survey results

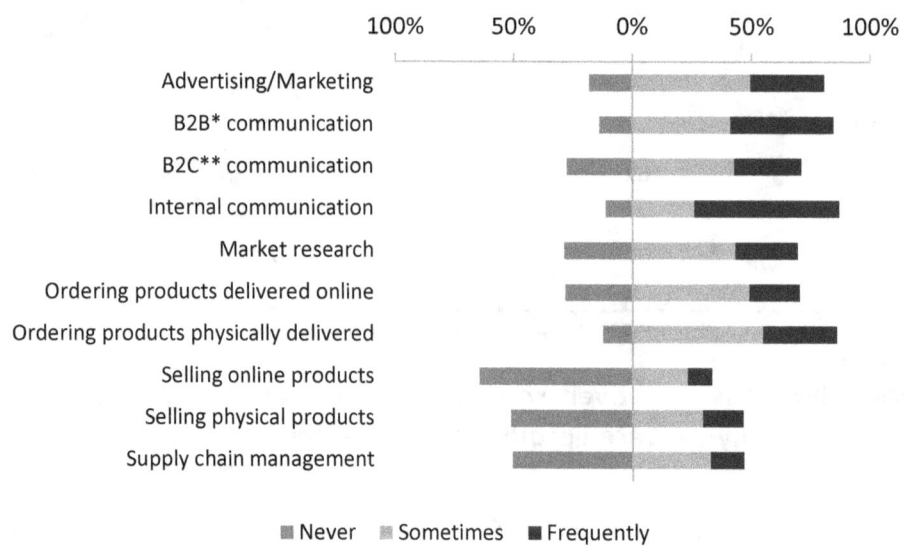

Source: USITC calculations of weighted responses to the Commission questionnaire.
Note: *B2B- business to business, **B2C- business to consumer.

Barriers to International Digital Trade and their Economic Effects

A wide range of barriers present obstacles to international digital trade, although perceptions of the barriers' severity vary by sector and firm size.

Based on survey responses, localization requirements, market access limits, data privacy and protection requirements, intellectual property rights (IPR) infringement, uncertain legal liability rules, censorship, and customs measures in other countries all present obstacles to international digital trade by U.S. firms in digitally intensive industries.[11]

Firms' perceptions of the severity of these barriers vary by sector and firm size. Based on survey estimates, table ES.7 shows the top groups that perceived each barrier to be a "very substantial or substantial" obstacle to trade. Large firms in the digital communications sector and SMEs in the finance sector were the most likely to view localization, data privacy and protection, uncertain legal liability, and censorship as "substantial or very substantial" obstacles to digital trade. Large firms in the content sector and SMEs in digital communications had the highest percentages that viewed IPR infringement as a "substantial or very substantial" obstacle. By contrast, large firms and SMEs in the retail sector had the largest portions that viewed customs requirements as "substantial or very substantial" obstacles.

---

[11] These barriers and impediments to international digital trade were identified in *Digital Trade 1* based on consultation with industry participants and experts at the Commission's March 2013 hearing and in fieldwork.

Table ES.7 Sectors with the largest portions of firms that identified each barrier as a "substantial" or "very substantial" obstacle to digital trade, by firm size, survey results

Barrier	Large firms	SMEs
Localization requirements	Digital communications (34%)	Finance (21%)
Market access limitations	Wholesale (24%)	Finance (23%)
Data privacy and protection requirements	Digital communications (34%)	Finance (20%)
IPR infringement	Content (34%)	Digital communications (27%)
Uncertain legal liability	Digital communications (18%)	Finance (24%)
Censorship	Digital communications (12%)	Finance (8%)
Compliance with customs requirements	Retail (14%)	Retail (39%)

Source: USITC calculations of weighted responses to the Commission questionnaire.

Removal of foreign digital trade barriers would boost U.S. sales abroad.

Firms expected that their sales abroad would be positively affected by the removal of foreign barriers to digital trade. Large firms in the content, digital communications, retail, and other services sectors estimated higher gains in sales abroad from the removal of trade barriers than firms in finance and manufacturing, according to survey results. Large firms also generally expected higher gains than SMEs. For example, the mean response for large digital communications firms was that sales abroad would increase by 5–15 percent while SMEs believed sales would increase by less than 5 percent if foreign barriers to digital trade were removed.

U.S. firms ranked several emerging markets highest in barriers to digital trade.

U.S. digitally intensive firms most frequently identified Nigeria, Algeria, and China as countries where barriers to digital trade precluded them from doing business or where they faced barriers. By contrast, Australia, the United Kingdom, and Italy were the countries where firms least often felt that they faced digital trade barriers or that barriers precluded them from doing business.

Case Studies

This report features 10 case studies that describe key trends in the emergence of digital trade, including how Internet technologies affect businesses' and consumers' cost structures, purchasing decisions, and innovation, and the extent to which the Internet facilitates international trade. The case studies are grouped into three themes—new business opportunities, big data, and global competitiveness and SMEs:

New Business Opportunities

The first four focus on how the Internet-based economic activity has created new or improved business opportunities—and sometimes disrupted older business models—in a number of areas:

- As illustrated in the first case study, "Enabling Independent Creators in the Content Industries," the Internet has provided new opportunities for independent creators to compete with large businesses in producing content such as music, films, and books. This case study also describes how Internet technologies lower barriers to entry for SMEs, promote new opportunities for content creators, and benefit consumers. It shows that while the Internet-based business environment may be creating more opportunities for content creators, these new opportunities do not necessarily mean that more creators will meet with traditional commercial success.

- The second case study, "Facilitating Greater Capacity Utilization in the Travel and Lodging Industry," shows how Internet technologies increase consumer welfare by enabling consumers to bypass traditional "middlemen" or brokers, such as travel agents, and make their own travel plans. The Internet has allowed airlines and hotels to utilize their capacity more fully, while saving the consumer money. This new business model, however, has greatly disrupted the travel agency business. The case study also discusses how individuals are now able to become product or service providers by renting their unused or underused assets (such as a spare bedroom, car, power tools, etc.) using Web sites and mobile apps to create peer-to-peer "sharing companies." While peer-to-peer transactions were not unknown before the Internet, the Internet has helped this segment of the economy quickly expand—to the point of now challenging some established business models.

- The third case study, "How the Internet Reduces Job Search Frictions," explains how Internet tools have improved the efficiency of the labor market. Job seekers and potential employers now interact directly on job websites and via social media networks, often bypassing recruiters, to fill jobs faster and at lower costs. This case study also discusses the Commission's econometric analysis that estimated that the U.S. unemployment rate in 2012 was almost 0.3 percent points lower than it would have been if Internet usage rates in 2012 had failed to rise from their 2006 level.

- As discussed in the fourth case study, "Increasing Collaboration and Integration in Online Services," online service providers also collaborate, creating tools—called application programming interfaces (APIs)—that allow third parties to build off their core services. APIs permeate the Internet and are central to the operations behind mobile apps. Use of APIs allows small firms to benefit from the use of larger platforms, and also lets large online service providers benefit by having a network of smaller companies creating custom tools that link their core services to an ever-broader range of business types and models.

Big Data

The next four case studies focus on the massive amounts of data currently available over the Internet, and the different ways companies and consumers use this data to develop innovative products and services and to enhance productivity:

- The fifth case study, "Data Analytics Improving Services in the Insurance Industry," focuses on how business can harness the vast amounts of data generated online. It explains how insurers collect large sets of data from various sources over the Internet, analyze it, and then use it to more accurately price risk, often allowing insurers to charge their customers lower premiums. In subsectors such as health and automobile insurance, insurers are pioneering usage-based insurance, in which insurers employ customer-specific usage data to price risk specific to individual customers.

- Another major use of data draws on the so-called "Internet of Things," which involves collecting data from machines for a variety of uses. The sixth case study, "Machine-to-Machine (M2M) Communication Is Improving Production Processes," explains how these data are used in manufacturing, and how new technologies allow manufacturers to collect environmental and performance information wirelessly from their machines to increase efficiency and find cost savings.

- The increasing role of M2M communication economy-wide is highlighted in the seventh case study, "Digital Innovations in Agriculture," which examines the application of M2M communication technology from a non-industrial perspective. It describes how farmers use the technology, often with the help of remote data analytics centers, to track their machinery, soil and weather conditions, and crop growth, increasing yields and farm efficiency. This Internet-based "precision farming" may become particularly useful to farmers as they face economic uncertainty from changing weather conditions and volatile market prices.

- The pervasiveness of the Internet in the economy makes issues related to data security and data privacy important to both consumers and companies that collect data. The eighth case study, "Internet User Data Collection Enables the Evolution of Digital Services and Increases Efficiencies of Exchange," examines the use of and risks associated with online user data collection. It describes some of the ways companies collect and use consumer data online and how companies can benefit from these data. It also discusses some of the consumer privacy concerns associated with online user data collection.

Global Competitiveness and SMEs

The final two case studies look at the Internet and international digital trade, including from the perspective of U.S. SMEs:

- The ninth case study, "The Global Competitiveness of U.S. Internet Companies," describes the worldwide presence of U.S. Internet companies, which currently dominate most major markets except Russia and China. As the case study explains, foreign companies can sometimes compete with U.S. companies when they focus on local expertise and language, but this appears to occur only in large markets. In these instances, local government regulations often play a role in making local firms more competitive.

- The final case study, "Facilitating SME Exports," describes how SMEs have leveraged the Internet to compensate for their size disadvantages and lower their trade costs. It details various ways the Internet is making it easier for SMEs to export and to connect with customers and suppliers globally. Digital trade has enabled SMEs to overcome many of the impediments associated with exporting that traditionally only larger firms could manage. In addition, operating online has allowed worldwide consumer demand to fuel demand for SME exports of products and services. These factors have made the Internet a critical sales channel for U.S. SMEs.

Chapter 1
Introduction

U.S. companies have pioneered the development of digital trade—broadly defined in this report as domestic commerce and international trade conducted using Internet-based technologies. The Internet now reaches, and indeed has transformed, virtually all sectors of the U.S. economy by facilitating communication, speeding business transactions, improving access to information, or simply bringing more convenience to daily activities. These Internet-based activities contribute to economic output by raising productivity and cutting costs, especially in sectors particularly involved in digital trade.[12] The emergence of digital trade has changed the way both domestic and international commercial activities are conducted, radically altered some industries, and paved the way for new business models and participants.

U.S. providers of Internet-based services and online content rank among the most familiar names in markets worldwide. In recent years, however, the global landscape of Internet-based economic activity has changed. Internet penetration appears to be peaking in the United States, with almost 81 percent of the U.S. population already having access to the Internet by 2012.[13] Accessing the Internet is increasingly being done through wireless devices such as smartphones and tablets.[14] Internet use is expanding more rapidly in emerging markets such as China, India, and—albeit more recently—sub-Saharan Africa. Growth in the number of Internet users who speak Arabic, Russian, Chinese, Portuguese, and Spanish now vastly outpaces growth in the number of English-language Internet users worldwide.[15] Indeed, the world's fastest Internet connection speeds—which may reflect a country's readiness to more fully engage in Internet-

---

[12] For further discussion of the transformational effects of the Internet, see OECD, "Measuring the Internet Economy," 2013.

[13] Internet penetration is the number of Internet users as a share of the population. World Bank, "Internet Users" (accessed April 18, 2014).

[14] OECD, "The App Economy," 2013.

[15] At yearend 2011, the top 3 Internet languages (by number of users) were English, Chinese, and Spanish. There were 565 million English language Internet users worldwide at yearend 2011, 510 million Chinese language users and 165 million Spanish language users. Between 2000 and 2011, the number of Arabic language Internet users increased by 2,501 percent; Russian, 1,826 percent; Chinese, 1,479 percent; Portuguese, 990 percent; Spanish, 807 percent; and English, 301 percent. The Internet was created using Latin characters—specifically, characters conforming to the American Standard Code for Information Interchange (ASCII). Beginning in 2010, non-Latin characters (as well as Latin characters with diacritical marks like the accent, cedilla, and umlaut) were cleared for use for entire Internet address names, reflecting the growth of an increasingly non-English-using Internet. ICANN, "First Non-Latin Domain Names Go Online," May 6, 2010; Miniwatts Marketing Group, "Internet Users, Population and Facebook Statistics for Africa," 2012; Miniwatts Marketing Group, "Top 10 Languages Used in the Web," 2012.

enabled ("digital") trade—are not in the United States.[16] According to the World Economic Forum's 2014 Networked Readiness Index, the United States ranks seventh globally in terms of its preparedness to benefit from the Internet-driven economy.[17] These trends indicate that U.S. Internet companies are likely to face stronger competition globally as other countries develop their own Internet markets and industries, while foreign companies will likely continue to increase their presence in the U.S. market.

In recent years, Internet-enabled economic activity in the United States has been a catalyst for overall economic growth, job creation, enhanced productivity, innovation, and increased market opportunities for small and medium-sized enterprises (SMEs). If digital trade is to remain a catalyst, more information is required so that both experts and the public can understand the role of digital trade in the economy here and abroad, as well as the steps needed to ensure that world markets remain open to that activity. Like its predecessor—*Digital Trade in the U.S. and Global Economies, Part 1* (hereafter *Digital Trade 1*)—this report aims to respond to these pressing needs.

Objective

As discussed in *Digital Trade 1*, the Internet is widely considered a fundamental infrastructure for businesses, governments, and individuals. Because the Internet is so pervasive, however, available business and economic statistics do not capture all of the economic activities that are facilitated by or occur via the Internet. Nor do available data fully measure the Internet's contributions to economic productivity, employment, economic growth, and international trade. It is also a formidable challenge to assess the broader impacts of the Internet—including the innovative economic activities the Internet has made possible—on individuals, SMEs, and society as a whole.[18]

Like *Digital Trade 1*, this report was requested by the U.S. Senate Committee on Finance (Committee) to assist the Committee in better understanding the role and contributions of

---

[16] At yearend 2013, the Republic of Korea (Korea) ranked as the country with the fastest average Internet connection speed, at 21.9 megabits per second (Mbps), followed by Japan (12.8 Mbps), the Netherlands (12.4 Mbps), Hong Kong (China) (12.2 Mbps), and Switzerland (12.0 Mbps). The United States ranked 10th, with an average Internet connection speed of 10.0 Mbps. The situation for cellphones was somewhat different: a Russian mobile provider had the fastest average connection speed at 8.9 Mbps, followed by a U.S. provider at 8.5 Mbps. Akamai, "State of the Internet," 4th quarter, 2013, 17.

[17] Ranked ahead of the United States were Finland, Singapore, Sweden, the Netherlands, Norway, and Switzerland. The Networked Readiness Index is composed of a mixture of quantitative and survey data designed to assess a country's ability to benefit from the information and communications technologies that drive Internet-based economic activity. World Economic Forum, "The Global Information Technology Report, 2014," 2014, 3.

[18] For more information on the challenges of measuring economic activity linked to the Internet, see USITC, *Digital Trade in the U.S. and Global Economies, Part 1*, 2013, chapters 4 and 6. The Organisation for Economic Co-operation and Development (OECD) is working to create global standards for measuring the global digital economy in a comparable way across countries; see OECD, "Measuring the Internet Economy," 2013. A review of recent literature on measuring the economic effects of the Internet is provided in appendix I of this report.

digital trade in the U.S. and global economies.[19] *Digital Trade 1* outlined U.S. and global digital trade activities; discussed the shortcomings in the available data on digital trade; outlined potential approaches for further assessing the role of digital trade in the U.S. economy; and identified notable barriers and impediments to digital trade. The present report, in accordance with the Committee's request, (1) estimates the value of U.S. digital trade and the potential growth of this trade, and highlights key trends and implications for U.S. businesses and employment; (2) provides insights into the broader linkages and contributions of digital trade to the U.S. economy, including effects on consumer welfare, output, productivity, innovation, business practices, and job creation; (3) presents case studies that examine the importance of digital trade to selected U.S. industries, including the impact of digital trade on SMEs; and (4) examines the effect of notable barriers and impediments to digital trade on selected industries and the broader U.S. economy.

Scope

Definition of Digital Trade

As mentioned above, this report defines digital trade as U.S. domestic commerce and international trade in which the Internet and Internet-based technologies play a particularly significant role in ordering, producing, or delivering products and services. This definition was adopted to capture the wide variety of economic activities that are facilitated by or occur via the Internet.[20] As reported in *Digital Trade 1*, however, there is no standard or generally accepted definition for "digital trade."[21]

This report uses a broader definition of digital trade than that used for *Digital Trade 1* to reflect input from public comments the Commission received during the course of these investigations. The Commission defined digital trade more narrowly in *Digital Trade 1* as "commerce in products and services delivered over digital networks." That definition excluded commerce in most physical goods, such as goods ordered online and physical goods that have a digital counterpart such as hard copy books and software, music, and movies sold on CDs or DVDs. As the Commission reported in *Digital Trade 1*, input from the public on that definition received at the March 7, 2013, hearing in Washington, DC and in written submissions expressed a wide range of views about that definition, including (1) comments that supported the definition; (2) comments that said the requirement that products and services be delivered over digital networks was overly restrictive and recommended that a broader definition be used; and (3) comments that said the definition was insufficient to capture the value of all of

---

[19] See appendixes A and B, respectively, for the request letter from the Committee and the *Federal Register* notices associated with this investigation.

[20] The Internet is a digital networking technology. There are other types of digital networking technologies, such as computer-to-computer data exchange systems over proprietary digital networks, some of which predate the Internet. This report focuses primarily on the Internet and Internet-based technologies.

[21] *Digital Trade 1* also reported that there are no standard or generally accepted definitions for similar terms, such as "Internet economy," "digital economy," and "e-commerce." USITC, *Digital Trade 1*, 2013, 1-2.

the diverse activities that occur over the Internet such as intra-company activities.[22] During the course of this investigation, the Commission received an additional public comment concerning the scope of the definition of digital trade recommending that the Commission make additional efforts to more comprehensively evaluate the contribution of copyright-intensive goods and services to digital trade.[23] The broader definition of digital trade used in this report reflects these concerns raised by U.S. industries.

Industries Particularly Involved in Digital Trade

The Committee requested that part of the analysis in this report focus on industries particularly involved in digital trade. Just as there is no standard definition for digital trade, there is no standard way to classify the industries that are especially engaged in it. Digital products are not separately categorized by type, as physical goods are.[24] A recent report by the Organisation for Economic Co-operation and Development (OECD) highlighted some of the challenges of identifying digital industry categories. Most available industrial classification systems are too broad to identify relevant digital trade-related activities, and even when such categories can be identified, the corresponding datasets often are not available.[25] However, *Digital Trade 1* described several possible ways to measure the degree to which firms in a given industry category have adopted Internet technologies in their businesses—their "digital intensity."[26] Some of the more useful indicators of digital intensity cited in that report were the proportion of online sales (e-commerce) to total sales; the share of total input purchases that are information technology (IT)-related; the proportion of employees in IT digital occupations; and the share of total IT spending directed to cloud services.[27]

To pinpoint the industries particularly involved in digital trade for this report,[28] the Commission identified industry sectors corresponding to (1) selected industry associations with a high apparent concentration of digitally intensive firms, and/or (2) categories within the North American Industry Classification System (NAICS) having a similar apparent concentration, based

---

[22] USITC, *Digital Trade 1*, 2013, 1-3, box 1-1.

[23] Written submission to the USITC, International Intellectual Property Alliance, March 21, 2014, 2.

[24] USITC, *Digital Trade 1*, 2013, 4-1.

[25] OECD, "Measuring the Internet Economy," 2013, 22–23.

[26] USITC, *Digital Trade 1*, 2013, 3-2 to 3-5.

[27] Computing services, such as running a program and storing data, are most often thought of as being performed using data stored on a local device such as a personal computer or laptop. With cloud computing, computing services—such as email, running mobile apps and business software programs, data storage, and other computing and data processing services—are performed on a server (a large computer that provides data to other computers) in a different location and accessed on demand via the Internet. For additional information, see USITC, *Digital Trade 1*, July 2013, 2-27 to 2-32.

[28] This report focuses on the role of digital trade in the private sector. E-government, or use of the Internet and Internet-based technologies by national, state, and local governments to deliver services and for public administration, is beyond the scope of this report.

on the digital intensity criteria just mentioned. Those seven digitally intensive industries are shown in table 1.1.[29]

Table 1.1 Digitally intensive industries and sectors

Industry	Sectors covered
Content	Publishing, including newspapers, periodicals, books, directory and mailing lists, and other publishers; motion picture and sound recording, including video and music production and distribution; broadcasting except Internet (see digital communications below); and news syndicates.
Digital communications	Software publishing; data processing, hosting, and related services; Internet publishing and broadcasting, and Web search portals.
Finance and insurance ("finance")	Establishments primarily engaged in financial or insurance transactions and/or in facilitating these transactions.
Manufacturing	Chemicals, printing, industrial machinery, metalworking machinery, engines, computers and electronics, power, distribution, specialty transformer, relay and industrial control, transportation equipment, and medical equipment and supplies.
Retail trade	Retail sales in motor vehicles and parts, furniture, electronics and appliances, and clothing through non-store retailers.
Selected other services ("other services")	Accounting; architectural services; engineering services; graphic design; computer programming; computer systems design; marketing consulting services; media buying agencies; travel arrangement and reservation services; couriers and express delivery services.
Wholesale trade	Distribution of motor vehicles and parts, computers, electrical equipment, and clothing through business-to-business electronic markets.

Source: Compiled by Commission staff. The selection of industries and sectors covered is described in more detail in appendix F.

Approach

As requested by the Committee, this report is based on publicly available information and economic data and on statistical estimates based on weighted responses by U.S. firms to the Commission's survey. Other qualitative information was developed through public hearings, written submissions, and interviews with industry representatives. This report also draws on information collected for, and the findings reported in, *Digital Trade 1*.

The Commission used multiple approaches to provide the requested information on digital trade and the effects of foreign barriers and impediments to digital trade. The Commission's analysis of digital trade provides findings at three levels: at the firm level, through 10 case studies; at the industry level, through a survey of U.S. businesses; and at the economy-wide level, using computable general equilibrium (CGE) and econometric models.[30] These three approaches are described below.

---

[29]Throughout this report, firms in digitally intensive industries are also referred to as "digitally intensive firms" or "firms."

[30] CGE models use economic theory and economic data to estimate how an economy might react to changes in policy, technology, or other external factors. Econometric models estimate the statistical relationships between economic variables, and how changes in one or more variables correlate with changes in another variable.

Firm-level Findings: Case Studies

To more fully illustrate the importance of digital trade to digitally intensive industries, the Commission prepared 10 case studies. The case studies provide a qualitative analysis of the ways in which the Internet affects U.S. businesses' and consumers' cost structures, purchasing decisions, and innovation, and the extent to which the Internet facilitates international trade. The case studies examine how the Internet is changing business dynamics; how firms are leveraging the Internet and the data it can generate to derive insights that innovate or improve products, services, and production processes across industries; and how the Internet is facilitating international trade, especially for SMEs. The selected case studies confirm the study's findings from industry-level and economy-wide analyses, as discussed below.

Industry-level Findings: Survey of U.S. Firms

In November–December 2013, the Commission conducted a survey of U.S. firms to examine the effects of digital trade on the seven digitally intensive industries in the U.S. economy listed above. In all, these sectors are estimated to comprise more than 140,000 U.S. firms of all sizes. To collect information for the survey, the Commission sent questionnaires to a stratified random sample of nearly 10,000 of these firms.[31] The questionnaires asked firms how they use the Internet and how the Internet has changed their business practices, sales, and productivity. The questionnaires also asked firms about their experiences with foreign barriers and impediments to digital trade. The survey had a response rate of nearly 41 percent. Of the more than 3,600 companies that responded, 80 percent were SMEs.

Survey responses were used to form an estimate of trade and the economic activities for the seven digitally intensive industries. Once the responses were compiled, Commission staff weighted results to ensure that they accurately represented the population surveyed. Staff also used relative standard errors (RSEs) to gauge the precision of the weighted results.[32] Appendix F provides more detailed information about the Commission's survey methods.

---

[31] In a stratified sampling process, the survey population is first divided into distinct strata (categories), and then organizations (in this case, the business entities selected for the survey) were independently selected from each stratum. By choosing strata that contain relatively homogenous organizations, stratified sampling can produce statistical estimates with lower standard errors than simple random sampling, in which all organizations in the survey population have the same probability of selection. For a description of the Commission's stratified sampling process for this survey, see appendix F.

[32] The Commission weighted results to reflect the sampling strategy and to correct for potential non-response bias. Throughout this report, all estimates based on calculations of weighted responses to the Commission's questionnaire were examined to determine their precision. The RSE is a measure of the precision of these estimates. RSEs are discussed in more detail in the context of the Commission's survey findings in chapters 2 and 4 of this report.

Economy-wide Findings: Quantitative Assessments

The Commission used multiple approaches to estimate digital trade's potential economy-wide effects and economic contributions, as well as the effects of foreign barriers on digital trade. To assess the effects of enhanced productivity and the removal of foreign barriers to digital trade, a computable general equilibrium (CGE) model was used. Such a model measures the net economic effects of any changes in either trade policy or other economic activity taking into account the broader linkages in an economy. The specific CGE model used for this analysis is the Global Trade Analysis Project (GTAP) model, described more fully in appendix H. The approaches used are summarized below:

- **Effects of enhanced productivity:** The GTAP model was used to estimate the economy-wide effects of Internet-based productivity improvements on U.S. gross domestic product (GDP), wages, and aggregate employment. This analysis used estimates from weighted responses to the Commission's survey on the impact of the Internet on productivity as an input for the model.

- **Effects on international trade costs:** The GTAP model was used to estimate the economy-wide effects of Internet-based reductions in international trade costs on U.S. GDP, wages, and aggregate employment. These reductions in international trade costs can stem from the improvements in communications technologies and easier access to information brought about by the Internet and Internet-based technologies. For this approach, the Commission used an econometric model to estimate the effects of the Internet on reducing trade costs. This estimate of reduced costs was then used as an input for the GTAP model.

- **Combined effects on productivity and trade costs:** The GTAP model was used to estimate the combined economic effects of both the productivity improvements and the reduced costs that stem from the use of the Internet on U.S. GDP, wages, and aggregate employment. These are not exhaustive estimates of the effects of digital trade on the economy; additional effects of digital trade are addressed elsewhere in the report using other approaches.[33]

- **Effects of removal of foreign barriers to digital trade:** The GTAP model was used to estimate the economy-wide effects of the removal of foreign barriers to U.S. digital trade on U.S. GDP, wages, and aggregate employment. This analysis used weighted responses to the Commission's survey on the impact of the removal of foreign barriers on firms' employment in the United States as an input for the model.

---

[33] For example, the Commission also used an econometric model to analyze the effects of Internet usage on improved job search and unemployment. As job search has moved online, job search costs and the time it takes job seekers to find prospective employers has fallen. The model provides estimates of the effects of the Internet on reducing unemployment.

Other Information Sources

The Commission held public hearings for this investigation in Washington, DC, on March 7, 2013 (in conjunction with the investigation for *Digital Trade 1*), and in Moffett Field, CA, on September 25, 2013. Witnesses for both hearings included representatives of academic institutions, nongovernmental organizations, industry, and trade associations.[34] Written submissions were provided by a diverse group of industry and trade association representatives.[35] The Commission also conducted in-person and telephone interviews with industry and academic representatives.

In addition to the survey results, the Commission used publicly available economic and trade data, including the World Input-Output Database (WIOD), the World Bank's World Development Indicators, and the International Monetary Fund's World Economic Outlook survey series.

Organization of the Report

This report contains seven chapters. The main body of the report is preceded by a detailed table of contents, a list of acronyms and abbreviations used in the report, and an executive summary.

Chapter 2 presents the findings from the Commission's survey of U.S. firms in digitally intensive industries with respect to the role of digital trade in the U.S. economy. It reports how firms use the Internet, how the Internet affects their business and their ability to do business, and the extent to which they conduct international trade using the Internet.

Chapter 3 discusses the economy-wide effects of digital trade and the linkages and contributions of digital trade to the U.S. economy. It gives quantitative estimates of the economy-wide benefits both of increased productivity from digital trade and of reduced trade costs from use of the Internet in international trade.

Chapter 4 examines the effects of notable foreign barriers and impediments to doing business across borders over the Internet. In *Digital Trade 1,* the Commission listed a number of measures reported to be most problematic for firms in this regard. Chapter 4 builds on the discussion in *Digital Trade 1* by describing the obstacles to digital trade that U.S. firms identified in the Commission's survey and through follow-up interviews with firms. This chapter also provides quantitative estimates of the economy-wide effects of removing barriers to digital trade in key U.S. export markets.

---

[34] See appendix C of this report for a list of participants in the September 25, 2013, hearing in Moffett Field, CA. See appendix C of *Digital Trade 1* for a list of participants in the March 7, 2013, hearing in Washington, DC.
[35] See appendix D for summaries of positions of interested parties received for this report. Appendix D of *Digital Trade 1* summarizes the positions of interested parties that were received before that report was published.

Chapters 5, 6, and 7 present ten case studies that examine the importance of digital trade to selected U.S. industries. The case studies draw on examples of firms of all sizes in various digitally intensive industries to describe the impact of digital trade. The case studies in chapter 5 present several examples of how the Internet is changing business dynamics by creating new or improved business opportunities and sometimes disrupting older business models. The case studies in chapter 6 take multiple approaches to discuss how firms are leveraging the Internet and the data it can generate to derive insights that lead to innovative products, services, and production processes across industries. The case studies in chapter 7 examine the global competitiveness of U.S. Internet companies as well as describe some of the ways the Internet is facilitating cross-border trade, particularly for SME exports.

Finally, technical information about the Commission's survey methodology, including a copy of the survey, additional survey data, technical information on the CGE and econometric models that were used, and a literature review that updates the review provided in *Digital Trade 1*, are provided in the appendixes.

Bibliography

Akamai. *State of the Internet Report* 6, no. 4 (fourth quarter 2013). http://www.akamai.com/dl/akamai/akamai-soti-q413.pdf?WT.mc_id=soti_Q413.

Boston Consulting Group. The Connected World: The $4 Trillion Opportunity, March 2012.

———. The Connected World: The Digital Manifesto—How Companies and Countries Can Win in the Digital Economy, January 2012.

Economist. "Arabic and the Internet: Surfing the Shabaka," April 12, 2014.

Kahn, Robert E., and Vinton G. Cerf. "What Is the Internet (And What Makes It Work)," December 1999. http://www.cnri.reston.va.us/what_is_internet.html.

Internet Corporation for Assigned Names and Numbers (ICANN). "First Non-Latin Domain Names Go Online." News release, May 6, 2010. http://www.icann.org/en/news/press/releases/release-06may10-en.pdf.

McKinsey Global Institute. Internet Matters: The Net's Sweeping Impact on Growth, Jobs, and Prosperity. McKinsey & Co., May 2011.

Meltzer, Joshua. "Supporting the Internet as a Platform for International Trade: Opportunities for Small and Medium-sized Enterprises and Developing Countries." Brookings Institution. Global Economy and Development Working Paper No. 69, February 2014.

Miniwatts Marketing Group. "Internet Users, Population and Facebook Statistics for Africa, 2012 Q2 June 30, 2012." Internet World Stats, 2012. http://www.internetworldstats.com/stats1.htm.

———. "Top Ten Languages Used in the Web (Number of Internet Users by Language)," May 31, 2011. Internet World Stats, 2012. http://www.internetworldstats.com/stats7.htm.

Organisation for Economic Co-operation and Development (OECD). "The App Economy." OECD Digital Economy Papers, No. 230, December 16, 2013.

———. "Measuring the Internet Economy: A Contribution to the Research Agenda." OECD Digital Economy Papers, No. 226, July 12, 2013.

U.S. International Trade Commission (USITC). *Digital Trade in the U.S. and Global Economies, Part 1* (*Digital Trade 1*). USITC Publication No. 4415. Washington, DC: USITC, July 2013. http://www.usitc.gov/publications/332/pub4415.pdf.

World Bank. "Internet Users." World Development Indicators database. http://data.worldbank.org/indicator/IT.NET.USER.P2 (accessed April 18, 2014).

World Economic Forum. "The Global Information Technology Report 2014: Rewards and Risks of Big Data," 2014. http://www3.weforum.org/docs/WEF_GlobalInformationTechnology_Report_2014.pdf.

Zinnov. "The Rise of Asian Powerhouses," June 2013. http://zinnov.com/download.php?file=226.

Chapter 2
Digital Trade and U.S. Businesses: Domestic Operations and International Trade

This chapter presents key findings from the Commission's digital trade survey about U.S. companies' domestic operations, along with basic information about the level of their involvement with international trade. As explained below, all data presented in this chapter are weighted estimates. Additional survey findings are presented in chapter 3 (the contributions of the Internet to productivity) and chapter 4 (the impact of foreign barriers to trade).

Key Findings

- In 2012, online sales by firms in digitally intensive industries36 totaled nearly $1 trillion in products and services. Large firms accounted for approximately 75 percent of online sales.

  - About one-third ($296.4 billion) of these sales consisted of products and services delivered over the Internet. The top two sectors delivering products and services over the Internet were digital communications ($114.7 billion) and finance and insurance ($49.9 billion).

  - In 2012, $638.8 billion of sales transacted online were of products and services delivered physically or in person. The leading sector making such sales was manufacturing ($295.7 billion), followed by retail trade ($163.7 billion) and wholesale trade ($88.4 billion).

- In 2012, online purchases of products and services by digitally intensive firms totaled $471.4 billion. Just $49.3 billion (10.5 percent) of the purchases were delivered online. An estimated $422.2 billion (89.5 percent) of these purchases were of products and services delivered physically or in person.

  - Finance and insurance and selected other service firms purchased the most products and services delivered over the Internet, with $11.6 billion and $12.2 billion, respectively.

---

[36] As discussed in chapter 1, the following digitally intensive industries are the focus of this report: content; digital communications; finance and insurance ("finance"); manufacturing; retail trade ("retail"); selected other services ("other services"); and wholesale trade ("wholesale"). A more detailed description of the sectors included in each is provided in chapter 1. Firms in digitally intensive industries are also referred to as "digitally intensive firms" or "firms."

- o Firms in the manufacturing sector purchased more products and services over the Internet that were delivered physically than any other sector, with $157.4 billion purchased.

- Firms in digitally intensive industries exported $222.9 billion in products and services ordered online, and imported more than $106.2 billion. Manufacturing was the leading importer and exporter of products and services ordered online, with $86.5 billion in exports and $50.7 billion in imports.

- Most firms in digitally intensive industries use the Internet to communicate internally, to order physical products and services, and to conduct business-to-business communication. Firms also use the Internet for supply chain management and market research, but this is much more common in large companies than in SMEs.

- Digitally intensive firms spent 41 percent of their advertising dollars on Internet-based advertising in 2012.

- Over 50 percent of digitally intensive firms have an official company page on at least one social network, but few pay for advertising on such sites. Only one-fifth of digitally intensive firms have their own mobile app or mobile website.

- Approximately 10 percent of digitally intensive firms experienced at least one cyber incident in 2012.[37]

Results

This section presents the results of the survey. As noted in chapter 1, the survey's response rate was nearly 41 percent, and 80 percent of the more than 3,600 responding firms were SMEs. The results below are given in terms of estimated response by industry sector, by firm size, and by both size and sector.[38]

---

[37] In the questionnaire, a cyber incident was defined as "an electronic attack that harmed the confidentiality, integrity, or availability of your organization's network data or systems."

[38] As explained in chapter 1, questionnaire responses were compiled and weighted to ensure that the reported results accurately represented the population surveyed. The results were weighted to account for the sampling strategy and to correct for potential non-response bias. All estimates based on calculations of weighted responses were examined to determine their precision. The relative standard error (RSE) is a measure of the precision of these estimates that describes how widely the estimates are distributed around a mean. More specifically, an RSE is defined as the standard error of a particular estimate divided by the estimate itself, expressed as a percentage. A smaller RSE indicates a more precise estimate. Unless otherwise noted, estimates presented in this report have RSEs below 50 percent (0.5), which indicates that the standard error of the estimate is less than half of its magnitude. In cases where the survey produced an estimate that is particularly relevant to the reader but has less precision (i.e., a higher RSE), an annotation to that effect is provided for that estimate. Appendix F provides additional information about the Commission's survey methods.

This section presents estimates of domestic digital trade, imports, and exports among digitally intensive sectors of the U.S. economy.[39] First, it gives results on online sales as a whole; then, by industry and firm size; and finally, by sector. This chapter then examines international trade by industry.

Online Sales of Products and Services

The Commission's estimates show that total online sales of products and services for either all digitally intensive sectors totaled $935.2 billion in 2012, or about 6.3 percent of U.S. GDP. About 30 percent of total online sales of products or services in 2012, $296.4 billion, were delivered online. This includes all Internet transactions for which the product or service was delivered digitally regardless of payment method, ranging from music or video downloads to online tax preparation. Less than 13 percent of firms with online sales of digitally delivered products or services experienced an increase in those sales from 2011. Nearly two-thirds of all sales of products or services ordered online were delivered physically or in person. This includes all transactions online for which the product or service was received in person, including everything from ordering parts online to reserving a rental car. The value of these transactions was over $638.8 billion in 2012. Less than 18 percent of firms, however, experienced an increase in such sales from 2011. Bundled online sales of physical and digital products and services[40] were a fraction of other sales at an estimated $32.4 billion in 2012.[41]

Large firms accounted for $708.1 billion (75.7 percent) of total online sales in 2012, with sales by SMEs accounting for $227.1 billion (24.3 percent). Over 20 percent of large firms also experienced growth in digitally delivered online sales over 2011–12 and expected growth from 2013 to 2014, while only 13 percent of SMEs increased these sales during 2011–12. Similarly, online sales of physically delivered products increased for over 26 percent of large firms from 2011 to 2012 and expected an increase in such sales in 2013, while only about 17 percent of SMEs increased their sales of physically delivered products during 2011–12.

Digital communications, which comprises software, Internet publishing, and other digitally intensive industries, led the other sectors surveyed in the largest estimated sales of products

---

[39] There are currently very little data publicly available concerning the size and scope of such sales. The U.S. Census Bureau estimates U.S. e-commerce through its "E-Stats" report, but does not differentiate between items (products and services) delivered online, and those physically delivered. Further, these data look only at domestic shipments, and do not separately examine international trade. The U.S. Department of Commerce also publishes estimates of "digitally deliverable" services trade, but could not differentiate between those services that were actually delivered digitally and those that were not. Meltzer, "Supporting the Internet as a Platform," February 2014, 4; Nicholson and Noonan, "Digital Economy and Cross-Border Trade," January 27, 2014; U.S. Census Bureau, "E-Stats," May 23, 2013.

[40] This included antivirus software with updates, hardcover books and e-books, DVD purchases and downloads, and other such products or services (whether Internet based or not) for which the sales value cannot be disaggregated.

[41] USITC calculations of weighted responses to the Commission questionnaire (question 3.1B).

and services delivered online in 2012, at $114.7 billion (figure 2.1). The digital communications industry has been growing in recent years because of rising demand for online content and services by both individual and commercial consumers.[42] Large firms accounted for the majority (92 percent) of these sales by value. The next leading sector was finance and insurance, which had estimated online sales of $49.9 billion in 2012 and was more evenly divided between large firms and SMEs (59 and 41 percent respectively). Given the growth of e-commerce in financial and insurance services, this result was also not unexpected. *Digital Trade 1* highlighted some of the Internet's impacts on this sector; in addition, the case study in chapter 6 of this report on advanced data analytics in the insurance industry describes ways that the industry is collecting, analyzing, and using digital records to offer new products and services.[43]

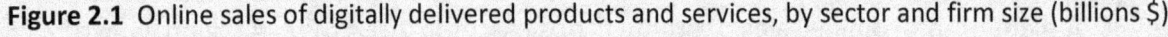

Figure 2.1 Online sales of digitally delivered products and services, by sector and firm size (billions $)

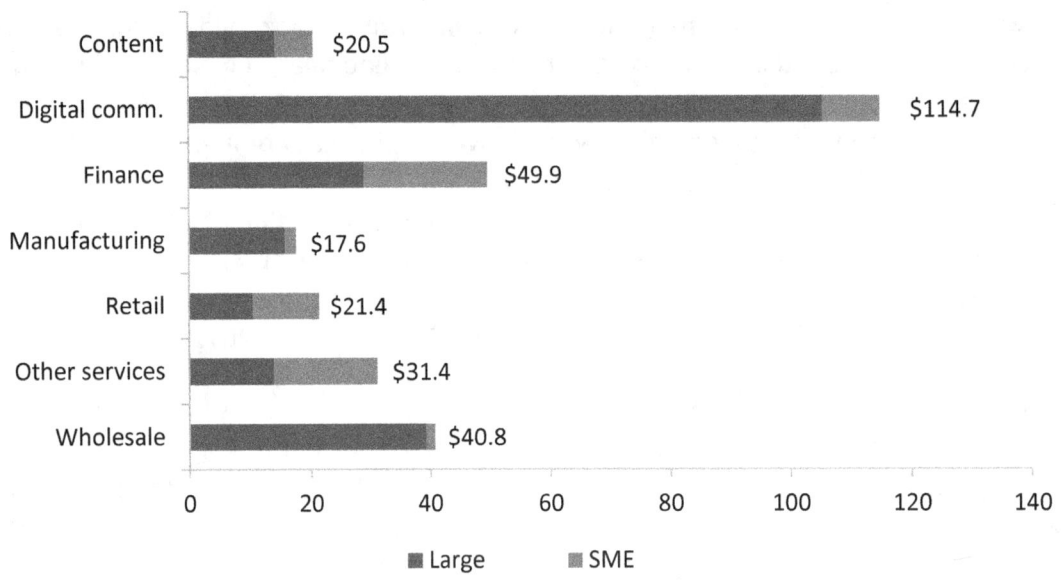

Source: USITC calculations of weighted responses to the Commission questionnaire (question 3.1a.1).

Overall, online sales grew for firms in both the content and digital communications sectors in 2011–12 and were expected to grow in 2013–14 as well (figure 2.2). This growth likely reflects

---

[42] USITC, *Digital Trade 1,* 2013, chapter 2. Additionally, it was noted that every company is now a software user, and many are also developing software themselves as the barriers to entry into software development are decreasing. Industry representative, interview by USITC staff, San Francisco, CA, May 1, 2014.

[43] *Digital Trade 1* also noted that the Internet has become an important source in which customers can gather information before buying insurance products. Further, U.S. customers prefer online banking for their account services, and a relatively standard set of online banking options are now offered by all types of financial services firms. USITC, *Digital Trade 1,* 2013, 3-16 and 4-24.

Figure 2.2 Share of total firms that increased their online sales of digitally delivered products and services during 2011–12, and expected growth of such sales during 2012–13, by sector

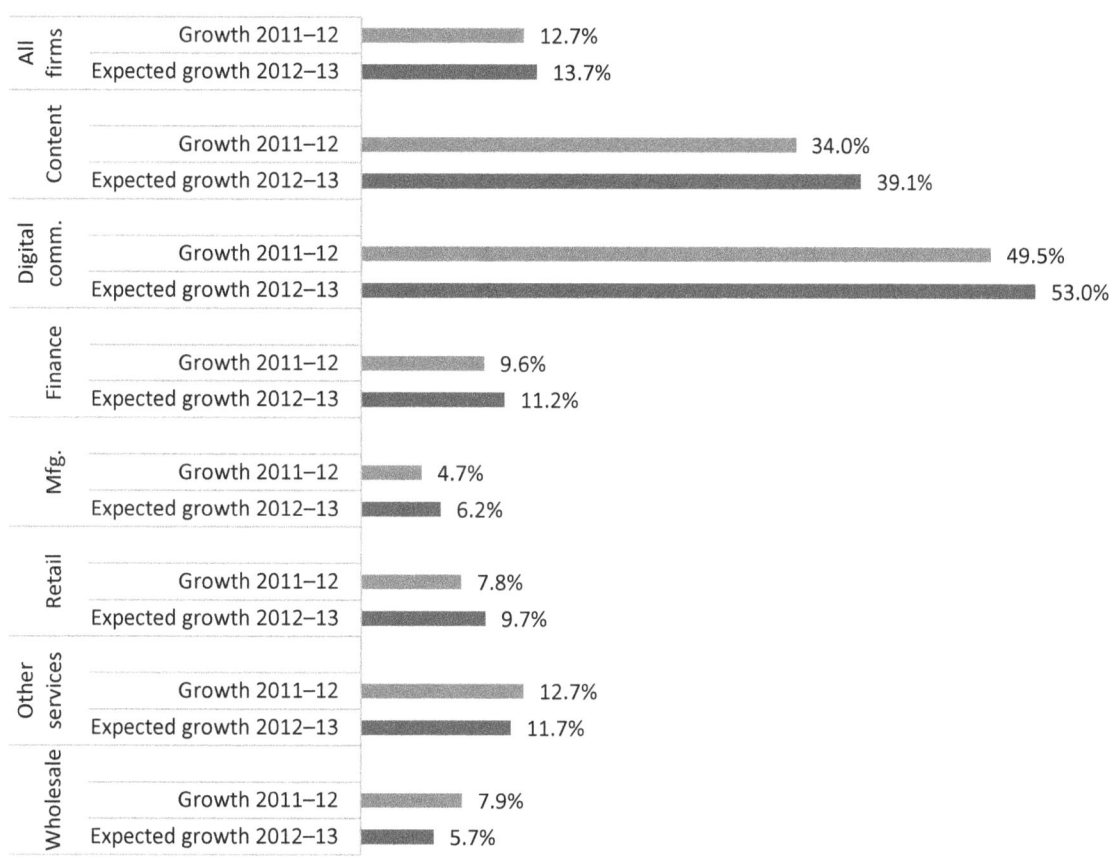

Source: USITC calculations of weighted responses to the Commission questionnaire (3.1a.2).

the increasing importance of online offerings in both sectors. For example, music industry sales grew in 2012 for the first time since 1999, primarily due to increasing digital sales.[44]

Online sales of products and services delivered physically or in person totaled $638.8 billion, with manufacturing accounting for nearly half of such sales. The manufacturing, retail trade, and wholesale trade sectors had the largest values of online sales that were physically delivered. This was especially the case for large firms (figure 2.3). This is unsurprising, as the manufacturing sector had by far the largest value of physically delivered sales, and a large number of manufacturing firms use the Internet and other digital networks to sell their products to consumers and other businesses. In all but two sectors, an estimated 15 percent or more of firms experienced increased online sales of physical products from 2011 to 2012 and

---

[44] Pfanner, "Music Industry Sales Rise," February 26, 2013; industry representative, telephone interview by USITC staff, March 25, 2014. As reported in *Digital Trade 1*, music is now a predominantly digital industry. USITC, *Digital Trade 1*, 2013, 2-15.

Figure 2.3 Online sales of physically delivered products and services, by sector and firm size (billions $)

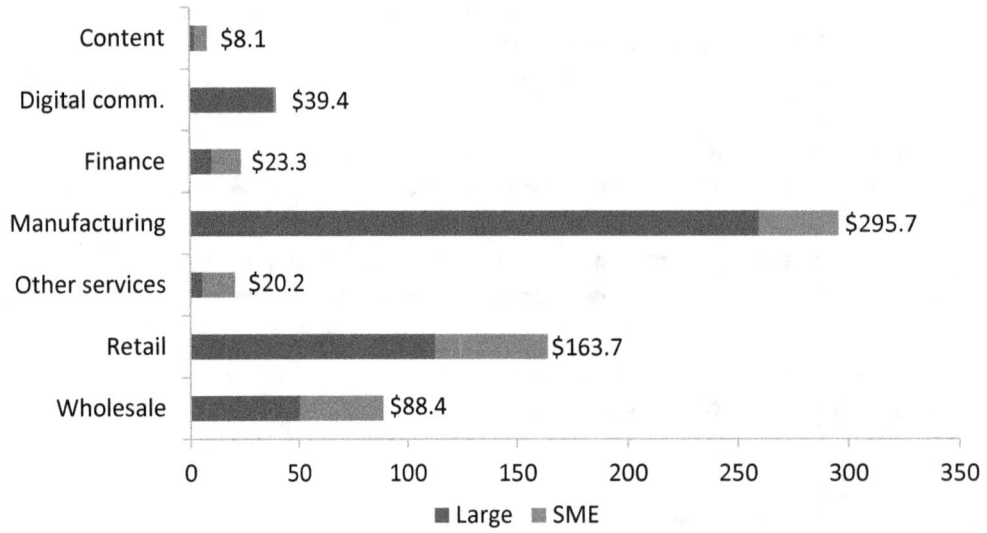

Source: USITC calculations of weighted responses to the Commission questionnaire (question 3.1a.2).

anticipated growth in 2013 (figure 2.4). The exceptions were the finance and other services sectors, which typically do not sell physical products.

Figure 2.4 Share of total firms that increased their online sales of physically delivered products and services during 2011–12 and expected growth of such sales during 2012–13, by sector

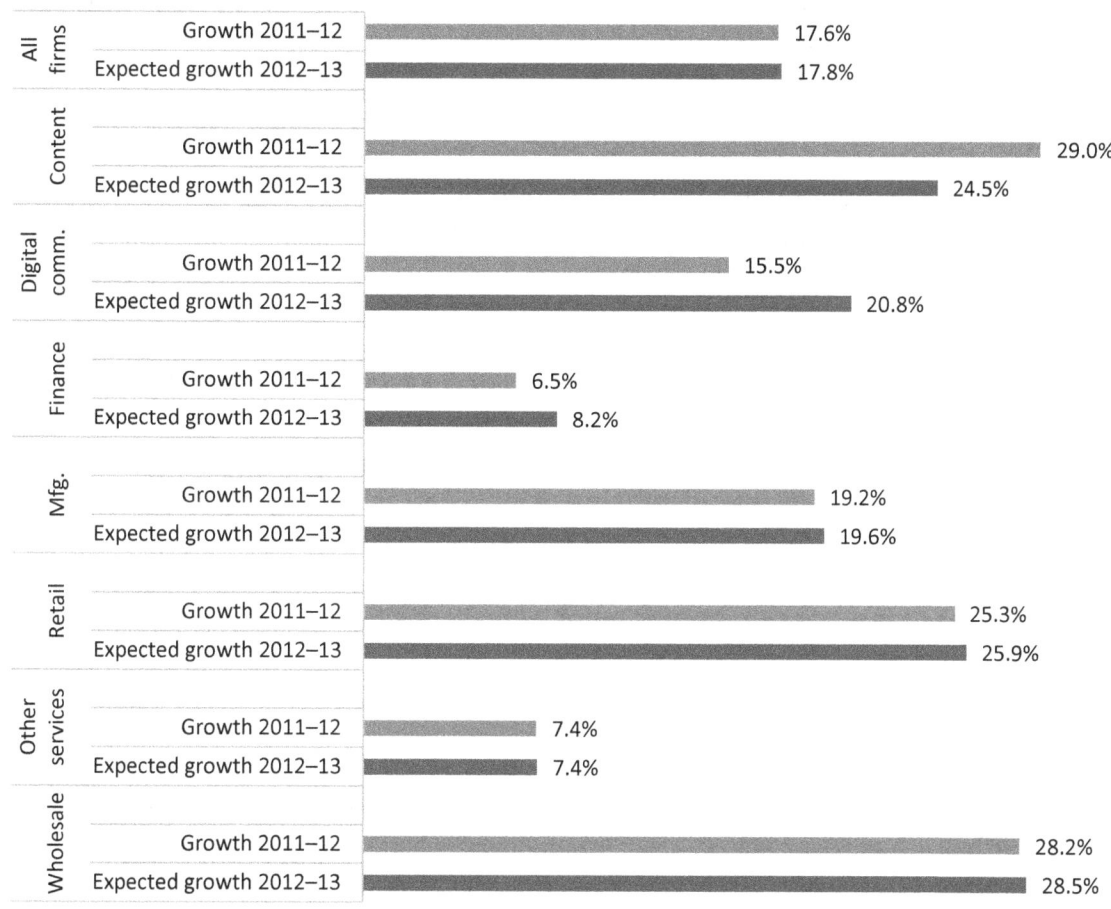

Source: USITC calculations of weighted responses to the Commission questionnaire (question 3.1a.2).

Online Purchases of Products and Services

Online purchases by digitally intensive firms were estimated to have been nearly $472 billion, with $422.2 billion in physical purchases and $49.3 billion in digital purchases made online in 2012.[45] Estimated online purchases of physically delivered products were thus more than eight times larger than estimated digitally delivered purchases. This is similar to the pattern noted above—that online sales of physically delivered products were higher than online sales of digitally delivered products and services. Further, nearly one-third of firms increased online purchases of physically delivered products and services from 2011 to 2012, which is more than

---

[45] In the survey, the figures for online purchases are likely smaller than those for sales because a significant percentage of sales went to consumers and/or firms in sectors or industries not included in the survey. Moreover, a number of respondents were unable to distinguish between online purchases and other purchases.

the portion of firms that increased digitally delivered purchases. More firms anticipated an increase for physically delivered purchases ordered online in 2013 as well.[46]

The online purchasing patterns of SMEs were like those of large firms in some ways, but not all. Estimated values of digitally delivered purchases of products and services in 2012 were fairly close for large firms and SMEs, at an estimated $26.7 billion and $22.5 billion, respectively. However, large firms ordered physically delivered products online at roughly twice the value of SMEs ($282.2 billion compared to $139.7 billion). Roughly 22 percent of all firms increased their online purchases of digitally delivered products and services over the 2011–12 period and expected another increase for 2013–14. Furthermore, about 30 percent of all firms increased their online purchases of physically delivered products in 2011–12 and expected another increase in 2013.[47]

Large firms and SMEs had divergent shares of firms experiencing growth in their online purchases in 2011–12 and having future expectations of growth for 2013 for both products and services delivered online and those delivered physically or in person. Products and services purchased and delivered online increased for more than 28 percent of large firms during 2011–12, and more than 29 percent of these firms expected growth to continue from 2012 to 2013, while only 22 percent of SMEs experienced or expected such growth. For physically delivered products and services ordered online, 40 percent of large firms' purchases increased in 2011 to 2012, and also were expected to increase in 2013–14, while only 32 percent of SME firms increased their purchases from 2011 to 2012, and 31 percent expected growth in such purchases from 2012 to 2013.

Digitally delivered online purchases in finance and insurance and in selected other services had the largest value in 2012, at $11.7 and $12.2 billion respectively (figure 2.5). However, the digital communications sector was estimated to have the highest increase in digitally delivered online purchases in 2011–12, as well as the highest expected increase in 2013.[48]

Large firms in manufacturing and SMEs in retail had the highest value of online purchases of physically delivered products (figure 2.6). However, the digital communications sector again had the highest estimated level of firms increasing online purchases from 2011 to 2012 as well as expected increases from 2012 to 2013.[49]

---

[46] USITC calculations of weighted responses to the Commission questionnaire (question 3.1A).
[47] Ibid (question 3.3.1).
[48] Ibid (questions 3.3.1 and 4.1).
[49] Ibid (question 3.3.2).

Figure 2.5 Online purchases of digital products and services, by sector and firm size, 2012 (billions $)

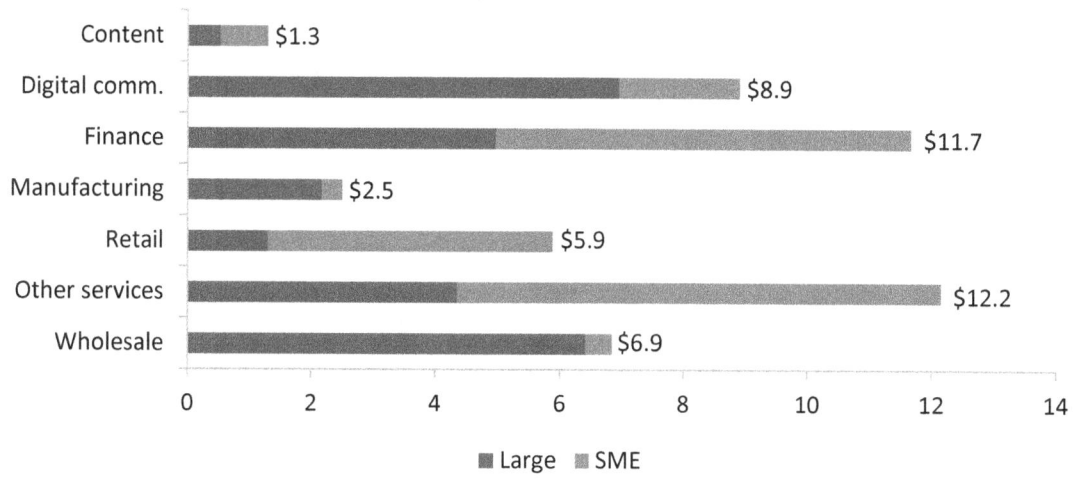

Source: USITC calculations of weighted responses to the Commission questionnaire (question 3.3.1).

Figure 2.6 Online purchases of physical products and services, by sector and firm size, 2012 (billions $)

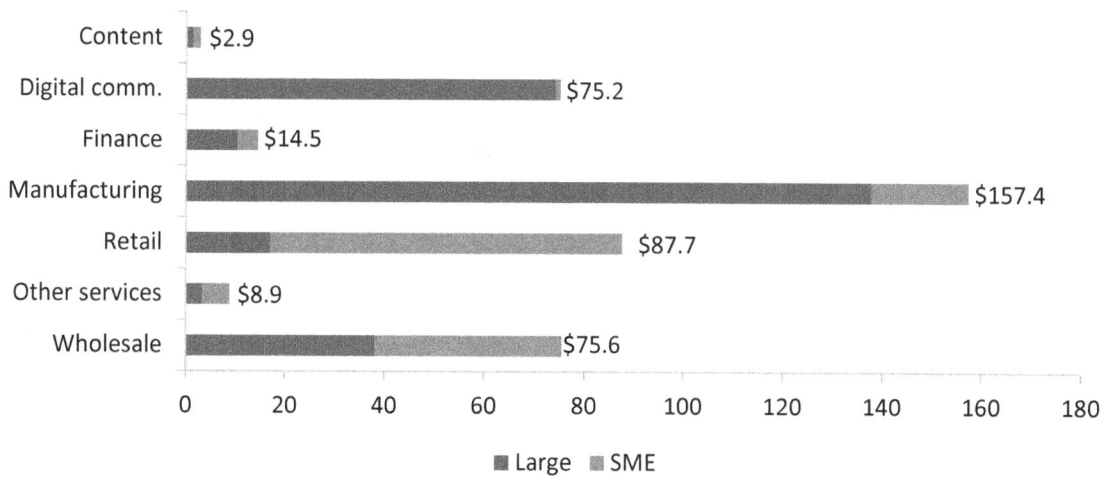

Source: USITC calculations of weighted responses to the Commission questionnaire (question 3.3.2).

International Trade

As reflected in the survey, online international trade was a relatively small component of U.S. imports and exports of both digitally and physically delivered products and services. According to Commission estimates, firms in digitally intensive industries exported a total of $222.9 billion in products and services ordered online in 2012. The top two sectors for exports of products and services ordered online were manufacturing ($86.5 billion or 38.8 percent) and digital communications ($58.9 billion or 26.4 percent).[50] Large firms made up 92 percent of exports of products and services ordered online (figure 2.7 and tables G.34, G.35, G.37, and G.38).

Figure 2.7 Exports of products and services by sector and delivery mode, 2012 (billions $)

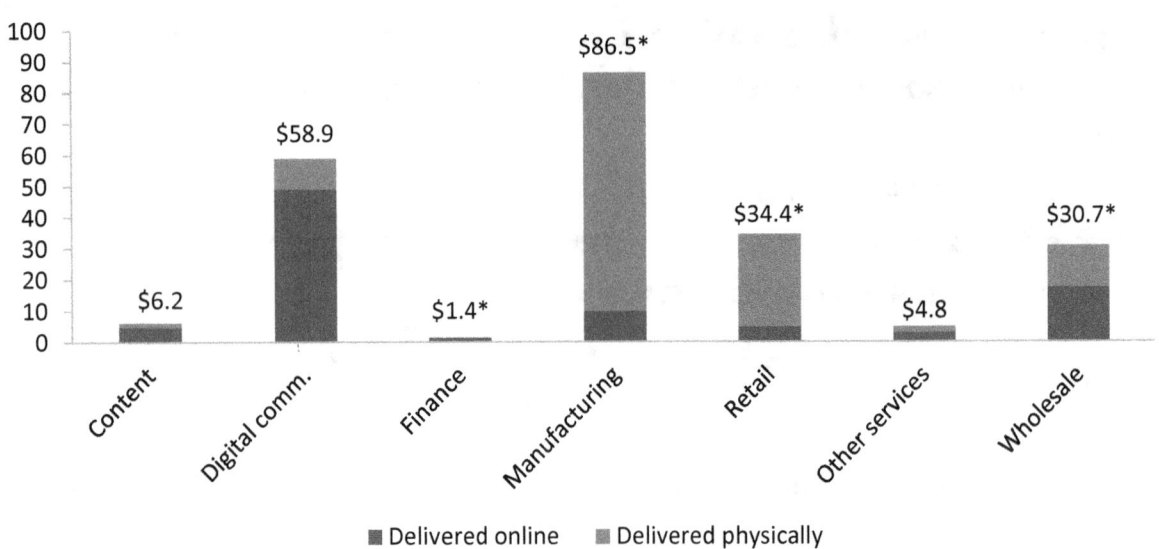

Source: USITC calculations of weighted responses to the Commission questionnaire (questions 3.1, 4.2, and 4.4).
Note: For those sectors with an asterisk next to the total, the RSE for the export calculation was greater than 0.5.

An estimated $90.6 billion (40.6 percent) of these exports were of products or services delivered online. By far, the largest sector for exports of products and services ordered and delivered online was digital communications at $49.1 billion. The remaining 60 percent (over $132 billion) of those exports were of products or services delivered physically.

The top destinations for both digitally and physically delivered U.S. exports that were ordered online—meaning that 10 percent or more of firms had these specific destination regions—were North America, primarily Canada; the European Union, notably the United Kingdom; and the Asia-Pacific region, principally Australia and China (figure 2.8).[51]

---

[50] International trade in digitally delivered products may be underestimated because of the difficulty of tracking the exchange of immaterial bits and bytes. As discussed in *Digital Trade I*, due to the way servers operate, digital information does not necessarily travel directly between two transacting parties. Instead, third-country host servers or way stations may be involved. USITC, *Digital Trade 1*, 2013, 4-23.

[51] USITC calculations of weighted responses to the Commission questionnaire (question 4.3).

Figure 2.8 Top regions for exports of products and services ordered online, by percentage of firms, 2012

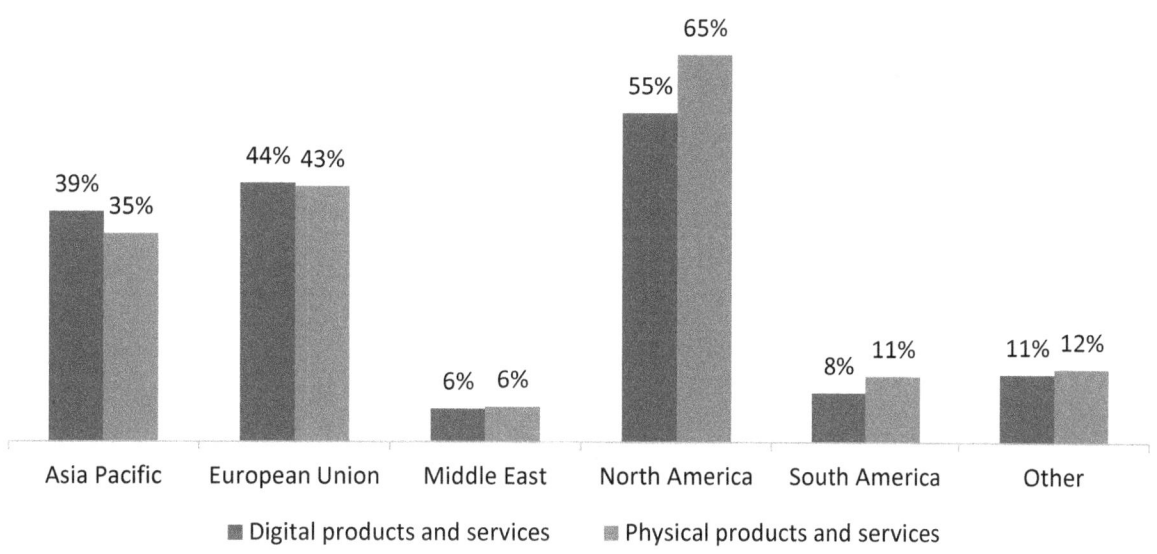

Source: USITC calculations of weighted responses to the Commission questionnaire (question 4.3).

The value of imports ordered online by firms in digitally intensive industries was $106.2 billion, with just $6.6 billion (6.2 percent) consisting of imports both ordered and delivered online. Firms in manufacturing ($50.7 billion), digital communications ($23.4 billion), and retail trade ($17.7 billion) had the largest shares of digitally and physically delivered imports that had been ordered online in 2012 (figure 2.9). Large firms imported 74 percent of products and services ordered online by digitally intensive firms in the United States (table G.32). Despite the relatively small role of exports and imports of online international trade, U.S. Internet companies are leading global providers for certain Internet products and services. A case study in chapter 7 of this report describes the global competitiveness of U.S. Internet companies.

Figure 2.9 Imports of products and services online by sector and delivery mode, 2012 (billions $)

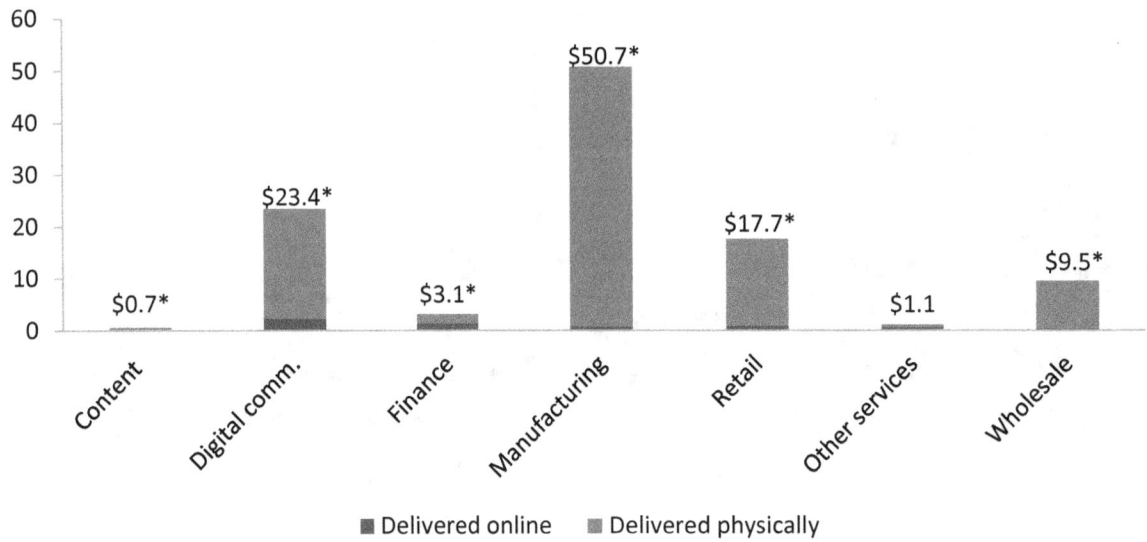

Source: USITC calculations of weighted responses to the Commission questionnaire (question 3.3 and 4.1).
Note: For those sectors with an asterisk next to the total, the RSE for the import calculation was greater than 0.5.

Business Practices

The Internet[52] has improved the way that many industries do business. Firms are gradually moving an increasing number of business activities online. The Internet offers ways for firms to network and collaborate, helps small firms reach a larger audience, and creates new opportunities for international trade.[53] The cost of some Internet services and tools can be relatively high, but a majority of firms nonetheless are using the Internet for various business functions.

Firms in digitally intensive industries use the Internet for an array of services, sales, and customer interactions. Majorities of both large and small firms use the Internet at least some of the time for advertising and marketing, communication (including business-to-business communication, communication with customers, and internal communication[54]), market research, and ordering both physical and digital products online. A majority of large firms use the Internet for supply chain management.[55] Less frequently, firms of all sizes use the Internet

---

[52] "The Internet" here refers to both the Internet proper and other digital networks, such as electronic data interchanges (EDI).

[53] Meltzer, "Supporting the Internet as a Platform," February 2014; USITC, *Digital Trade 1*, 2013, chapter 4.

[54] Examples of Internet tools used for businesses' internal communication include email, VoIP, instant messaging, and videoconferencing.

[55] Supply chain management activities that use the Internet include automated procurement, automated sales, and business collaboration with suppliers and partners online.

to sell both online and physical (or in-person)[56] forms of their products and services. In responding to the survey, firms wrote in other uses that they made of the Internet, including banking, content streaming, research, operating software-as-a-service and Web portals, regulatory compliance, client claim processing and invoicing, and entertainment.[57] A case study in chapter 5 of this report describes how businesses are harnessing the collaborative power of the Internet infrastructure through the use of application programming interfaces—links that allow one software program to interact with another software program—to create new online tools that facilitate communication among businesses, and between firms and their customers.

Businesses most commonly reported using the Internet for internal communication (such as for email, instant messaging, and videoconferencing), ordering physically delivered products or services, and business-to-business communication (figure 2.10). Among large firms, almost

Figure 2.10 Characteristics of Internet usage

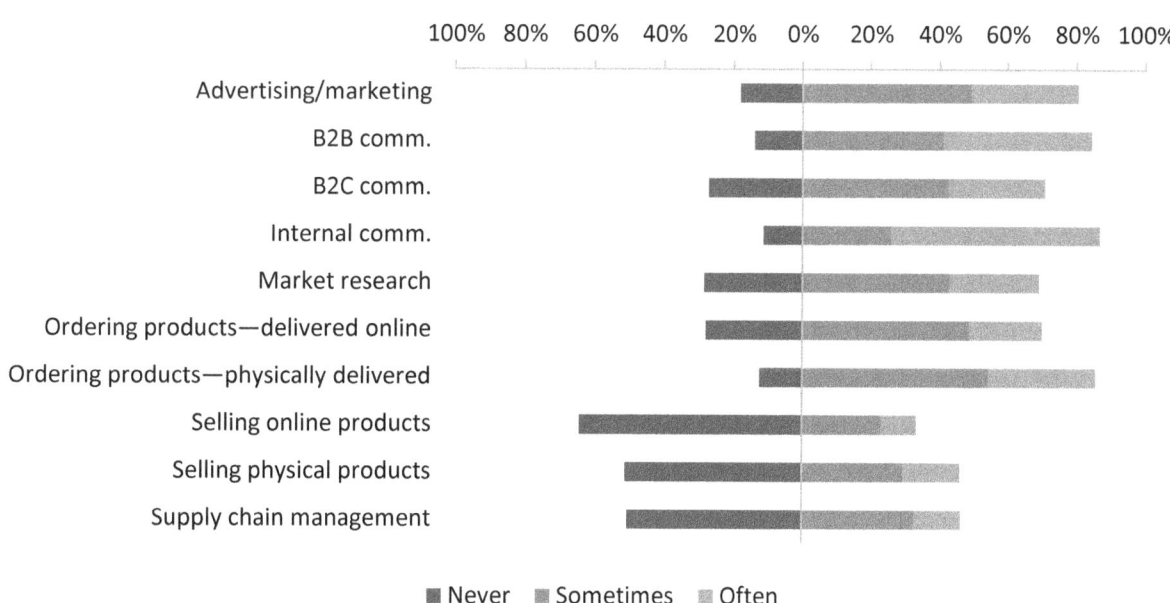

Source: USITC calculations of weighted responses to the Commission questionnaire (question 2.1).
Note: B2B refers to business to business, and B2C refers to business to consumer.

74 percent use the Internet to order products or services that are delivered online, while 70 percent of SMEs do so. Although majorities of firms across all digitally intensive industries use the Internet for internal and external communication, large firms are particularly inclined to do so. Almost all large firms (98 percent) use the Internet for internal communication, communication with other firms (91 percent), and to communicate with customers (70 percent). Similarly, most SMEs (87 percent) use the Internet for

---

[56] Physical, or in-person, forms of products and services includes any product or service not delivered over the Internet or some other digital network, but instead delivered in a store, via mail, or through personal means (e.g., a consultant giving advice face to face).
[57] USITC calculations of weighted responses to the Commission questionnaire (question 2.1).

internal communication, to communicate with other firms (84 percent), and to communicate with customers (71 percent).[58] A case study in chapter 6 of this report describes the increasing use of the Internet in machine-to-machine communication—in both manufacturing and agricultural settings equipment is increasingly being connected to the Internet to optimize production and monitor equipment.

Large firms and SMEs use the Internet for communicating with consumers—e.g., buying and selling products and services online—at similar rates. However, as previously noted, large firms are more prone to use the Internet for internal communication, market research, and supply chain management (figure 2.11).[59] Both supply chain management and market research may be more valuable to large or complex firms, as such firms tend to be spread out geographically. Large firms may also have more need than SMEs for digital forms of internal communication.

Figure 2.11 Characteristics of Internet usage, by firm size

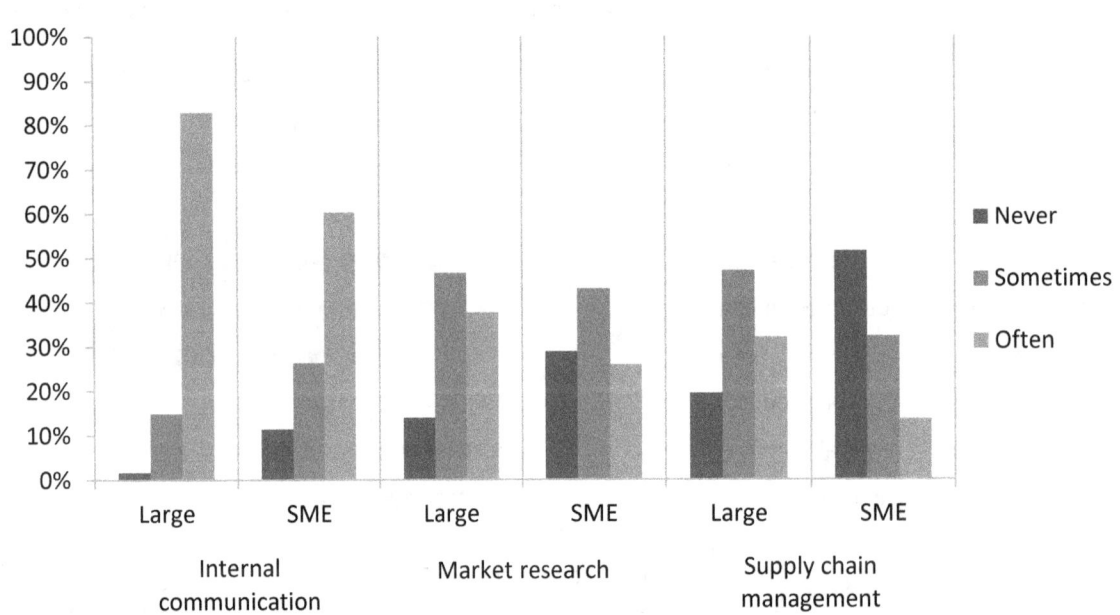

Source: USITC calculations of weighted responses to the Commission questionnaire (question 2.1).

The Internet has helped firms in other ways. For instance, more than 80 percent of digitally intensive firms use the Internet to process data and information, and improve interactions with customers and suppliers. Also, most firms use the Internet to enter new businesses or markets, expand their current markets, and reduce non-inventory costs (figure 2.12). Across digitally intensive sectors including digital communications, wholesale trade, retail trade, and large finance and insurance firms, the Internet has also enhanced firms' ability to match competitor offerings. Some firms also wrote in that the use of the Internet has helped them by providing

---

[58] USITC calculations of weighted responses to the Commission questionnaire (question 2.1).
[59] Ibid.

easy access to postal services, bolstering research opportunities, streamlining travel, improving recruiting, and facilitating contact with difficult-to-access customers.[60] A case study about independent creators in the content industries in chapter 5 of this report describes some of the ways the Internet helps SMEs bypass traditional "middlemen" to directly reach customers and even to obtain financing through "crowdfunding."

Figure 2.12 Business functions affected by the Internet

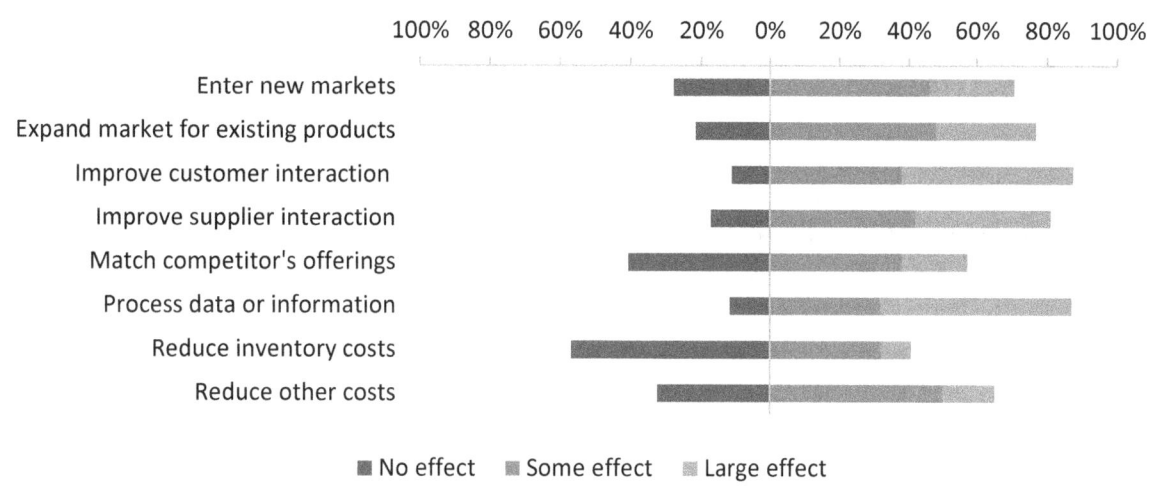

Source: USITC calculations of weighted responses to the Commission questionnaire (question 2.2).

Organizations across industries have replaced some traditional IT services and other services with services provided over the Internet. Software-as-a-service, online business services, and other online data, content, and computing services are growing increasingly widespread and can lead to a variety of efficiency improvements for firms.[61] SMEs across all sectors spent on average $92,000 on Internet-based services in 2012; large firms, $4.5 million on average.[62] Indeed, nearly two-thirds of large firms and over 39 percent of SMEs have replaced at least some traditional services with Internet-based services, particularly in finance and insurance, content, digital communications, and selected other services.[63] Firms were most likely to use online software and communication services to replace traditional services. Approximately one-third of all firms also used online infrastructure services, online computing platform services, and online non-bank payment processing to replace traditional services.[64] In general, larger

---

[60] USITC calculations of weighted responses to the Commission questionnaire (question 2.2).
[61] USITC, *Digital Trade 1,* 2013, chapter 2.
[62] USITC calculations of weighted responses to the Commission questionnaire (question 3.5).
[63] Ibid (question 3.4A).
[64] USITC calculations of weighted responses to the Commission questionnaire (question 3.4C). Further discussion of these services and their uses by consumers and firms can be found in chapters 2 and 3 of *Digital Trade 1*.

firms and firms in the digital communications, finance and insurance, and content industry sectors were more likely to replace traditional services with Internet-based services.[65]

Internet-based services can lead to cost savings for firms. Among firms that replaced traditional services with Internet-based services, nearly 71 percent of large firms and over 65 percent of SMEs expected cost savings from the switch. Small firms expected average annual savings of roughly $70,000; large firms, of over $1.5 million. Firms that anticipated additional costs rather than savings from switching from traditional services to Internet-based services estimated average annual costs of about $24,000 for SMEs and over $500,000 for large firms.[66]

Advertising

The Internet has had a significant impact on advertising, a tool used in all sectors to find customers and promote business. Across all industries, firms use both traditional and online advertising and outreach to interact with their target audiences.[67] In addition to Internet-based advertisements, companies can also use Internet-based means to interact directly with customers via mobile applications ("apps"), mobile websites, and social media. Approximately half of all firms use at least one social network to connect with customers, and 20 percent of all firms had an app or mobile website.[68] Overall, digital communications and content firms were the most likely to use Internet-based marketing, but most firms indicated that they do so to some extent.

Online Advertisements

Digital advertising has unique benefits. Advertising on the Internet allows firms to target specific consumer interests and searches, and, in many cases, to pay only when potential customers are identified (e.g., via pay-per-click advertising).[69] Also, some forms of Internet advertising can be delivered with lower implementation costs than traditional advertising.[70] Furthermore, because clicks and views can be tracked, online advertising gives firms more information about users and more opportunities for data analytics.[71]

A majority of firms in digitally intensive industries use the Internet for advertising, and many firms stated that the Internet improved interactions with customers. SMEs were more likely to spend money on online advertising, with 64 percent of SMEs and 50 percent of large firms advertising products and services online in 2012. The digital communications and retail trade

---

[65] USITC calculations of weighted responses to the Commission questionnaire (question 3.4A).

[66] Ibid (question 3.4B).

[67] Chapter 2 of *Digital Trade 1* discusses online advertising and its role in content distribution, social media, customer service, and other aspects of the U.S. economy.

[68] USITC calculations of weighted responses to the Commission questionnaire (question 3.9 and 3.10).

[69] *Economist,* "Internet Advertising: The Ultimate Marketing Machine," July 6, 2006.

[70] Burton, "A Marketer's Guide to Understanding the Economics of Digital," 2009.

[71] Burton, "A Marketer's Guide to Understanding the Economics of Digital," 2009; USITC, *Digital Trade in the U.S. and Global Economies, Part 1,* 2013. Data analytics are further discussed in the chapter 5 of this report.

sectors were most likely to use online advertising, while other services firms were least likely to do so (figure 2.13).[72]

Figure 2.13 Percentage of firms advertising online, by sector, 2012

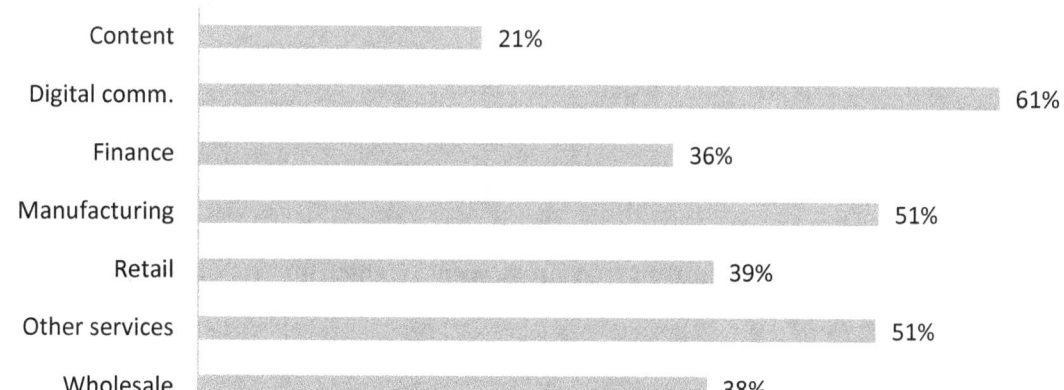

52%	69%	46%	46%	70%	41%	45%
Content	Digital comm.	Finance	Manufacturing	Retail	Other services	Wholesale

Source: USITC calculations of weighted responses to the Commission questionnaire (question 3.7).

On average, an estimated 41 percent of all advertising for firms in digitally intensive industries was Internet-based in 2012. This number was much lower in the content sector, where only 21 percent of advertising was online rather than in traditional channels. In contrast, the digital communications, manufacturing, and other selected services sectors all spent more than half of their advertising dollars on online advertising in 2012 (figure 2.14).[73] These shares may be lower for some firms if online marketing is less costly per advertisement than traditional advertising.

Figure 2.14 Online advertising as a share of total advertising, by sector, 2012

Sector	Share
Content	21%
Digital comm.	61%
Finance	36%
Manufacturing	51%
Retail	39%
Other services	51%
Wholesale	38%

Source: USITC calculations of weighted responses to the Commission questionnaire (question 3.6 and 3.7).

---

[72] USITC calculations of weighted responses to the Commission questionnaire (question 3.7).
[73] USITC calculations of weighted responses to the Commission questionnaire (questions 3.6 and 3.7).

Internet advertising still takes a smaller share of most firms' advertising budgets than more traditional advertising. Currently, search advertising and display and banner advertising are the highest-revenue areas of Internet advertising, but mobile and digital video have increased more rapidly than all other types of online advertising in recent years.[74] Increases in mobile and digital video advertising may be due in part to the fact that in the United States, consumers spent more than 34 hours on their smartphones per month in 2013, up from 28 hours per month in 2012.[75] Despite this growth, traditional advertising remains dominant: television advertising revenues were $74.5 billion in 2013, and newspaper, magazine, and radio revenues combined for another $48 billion in the United States in 2013.[76] This, too, matches with consumer use patterns: during the month of December 2013, Nielsen estimates that an average U.S. consumer spent 185 hours watching television.[77]

Social Networks

Social networks play a large role in consumers' lives, but 57 percent of large digitally intensive firms and 81 percent of SMEs do not pay for advertising on any social networks. Thirty-seven percent of large firms advertise on one to five social networking sites, and 16 percent of small firms do. Firms in the digital communications and retail trade sectors were most likely to have some social media advertising presence, while firms in manufacturing, selected other services, and wholesale trade sectors were least likely to advertise on social networking websites.[78]

Many firms use multiple social networks to connect with customer bases and get the company name out in the public sphere. While 7 percent of large digitally intensive firms have only one official page or account on one social networking site, 47 percent have an official account on two to five social networks. Similarly, 19 percent of small firms have an account on one social networking site, and 30 percent have an official page or account on two to five social networks. The three sectors that tend to be "consumer facing"[79]—content, digital communications, and retail trade—had the largest shares of firms with social media accounts. The finance and insurance, manufacturing, and wholesale sectors had fewer firms with a social media presence.[80] A case study in chapter 5 describes how the use of social media networks for marketing, promotion, and advertising has benefited SMEs in particular by lowering their costs for reaching potential customers.

Social network advertising by firms is expected to gain further ground in the coming years. A Duke University, McKinsey, and American Marketing Association survey of chief marketing officers (CMOs) at U.S. companies indicated that firms across industries currently spend an

---

[74] PricewaterhouseCoopers, "IAB Internet Advertising Revenue Report," April 2014.

[75] Nielsen, "How Smartphones Are Changing Consumers' Daily Routines," April 24, 2014.

[76] PricewaterhouseCoopers, "IAB Internet Advertising Revenue Report," April 2014.

[77] Nielsen, "How Smartphones Are Changing Consumers' Daily Routines," April 24, 2014.

[78] USITC calculations of weighted responses to the Commission questionnaire (question 3.8).

[79] Consumer-facing firms are firms that sell products and services directly to private individuals; in contrast, firms that are not consumer facing often sell to consumers through a middleman or only sell to other firms.

[80] USITC calculations of weighted responses to the Commission questionnaire (question 3.9).

average of 7 percent of their marketing budget on social media, with the highest shares in the communications and media, services, and technology industries.[81]

Apps

Even among firms in digitally intensive industries, providing a mobile app or mobile website is far from universal, particularly among SMEs. Fifty percent of large firms and 9 percent of SMEs provide an app or website intended specifically for use on a smartphone or tablet. Firms that have apps or mobile websites are particularly likely to be in content, digital communications, or finance and insurance (figure 2.15); a majority of large retailers use apps or mobile websites as well.[82] SMEs may be less likely to use apps and mobile sites because these tools can be costly, though cost estimates vary greatly, depending on the size and complexity of the app required.[83]

Figure 2.15 Share of firms with apps or mobile websites, by sector

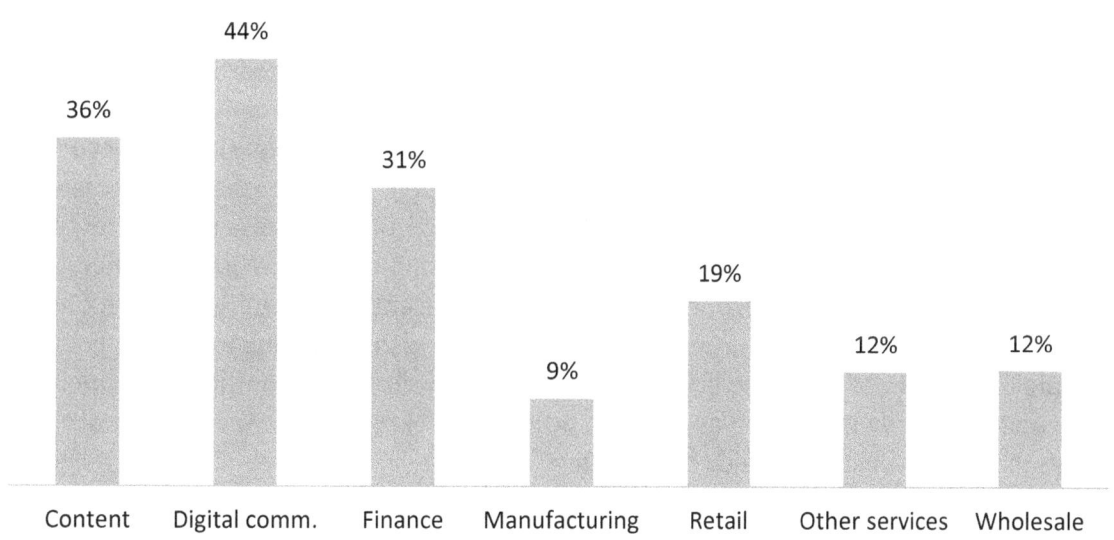

Source: USITC calculations of weighted responses to the Commission questionnaire (question 3.10).

---

[81] Duke University, McKinsey, and the American Marketing Association, "CMO Survey: Report of Results," February 2014.

[82] USITC calculations of weighted responses to the Commission questionnaire (question 3.10).

[83] Estimates for the minimum cost of developing an app vary, likely due to different definitions of what a "barebones app" consists of; however, 54 percent of respondents in an app development industry survey indicated that initial development costs for an app average between $25,000 and $100,000. 24 percent indicated that average initial development for an app costs more than $100,000. AnyPresence, "The State of Mobile Readiness 2013," 2013.

Cyber Incidents

While increasing use of the Internet carries a number of potential benefits to U.S. firms, it can also lead to increased risks. McKinsey and the World Economic Forum (WEF) recently reported that despite cyber protections placed by firms and governments, a majority of firms do not feel fully prepared to face cyber incidents. The McKinsey-WEF study estimates that cyber issues could cause as much as a $3 trillion loss to potential global GDP.[84]

The vast majority (85 percent) of firms in digitally intensive industries were not aware of any cyber incidents[85] at their firm in 2012. Another 9 percent experienced between one and nine cyber incidents in that year.[86] Types of firms that were most likely to experience cyber incidents were larger firms, firms that did not have a chief privacy officer, and firms that traded with multiple foreign countries.[87] In 2012, 76 percent of large firms experienced zero incidents, while 15 percent experienced between 1 and 9 cyber incidents, and another 3 percent of large firms experienced 10 or more cyber incidents. In contrast, only 10 percent of SMEs had any cyber incidents in 2012.[88]

In the digital communications sector, 22 percent of firms were estimated to have experienced cyber incidents in 2012, compared to only 7 percent of retail and 9 percent of wholesale firms (figure 2.16).[89] However, many firms do not discover that they have experienced a cyber incident until months or even years after the incident occurs,[90] and attackers are increasingly using third-party vulnerabilities that may not be easily identified to access firms' internal networks. Examples of hard-to-detect third-party vulnerabilities include building management systems connected to internal corporate networks or unintentional employee downloads of malicious software via fake restaurant menus.[91] Firms are also becoming increasingly vulnerable to even more subtle attacks, like the recent Heartbleed vulnerability in OpenSSL.[92] Heartbleed has already been used as an entry point for hackers to obtain confidential information from at least one major corporation.[93]

---

[84] WEF with McKinsey & Company, Risk and Responsibility in a Hyperconnected World, January 2014.

[85] In the questionnaire, a cyber incident was defined as "an electronic attack that harmed the confidentiality, integrity, or availability of your organization's network data or systems."

[86] USITC calculations of weighted responses to the Commission questionnaire (question 3.11).

[87] USITC calculations of weighted responses to the Commission questionnaire (questions 1.5, 3.11, and 5.6).

[88] USITC calculations of weighted responses to the Commission questionnaire (question 3.11).

[89] Ibid.

[90] Verizon RISK Team, "2013 Data Breach Investigations Report," 2013.

[91] Perlroth, "Hackers Lurking in Vents and Soda Machines," April 7, 2014.

[92] Heartbleed is a flaw in OpenSSL, a tool that many firms use to encrypt their websites and digital presence. It can be used to reveal unprotected information in the memory of a system connected to the tool, such as passwords, usernames, and other information that may be essential to firm security. For many sites, the vulnerability has now been fixed. OpenSSL, "TLS Heartbeat Read Overrun (CVE-2014-0160)," April 7, 2014; Yadron, "Massive OpenSSL Bug 'Heartbleed' Threatens Sensitive Data," April 8, 2014.

[93] Perlroth, "Heartbleed Internet Security Flaw Used in Attack," April 18, 2014; Anand, "Heartbleed: Why Companies Are Clueless About Security," April 16, 2014.

Figure 2.16 Number of cyber incidents, by sector, 2012

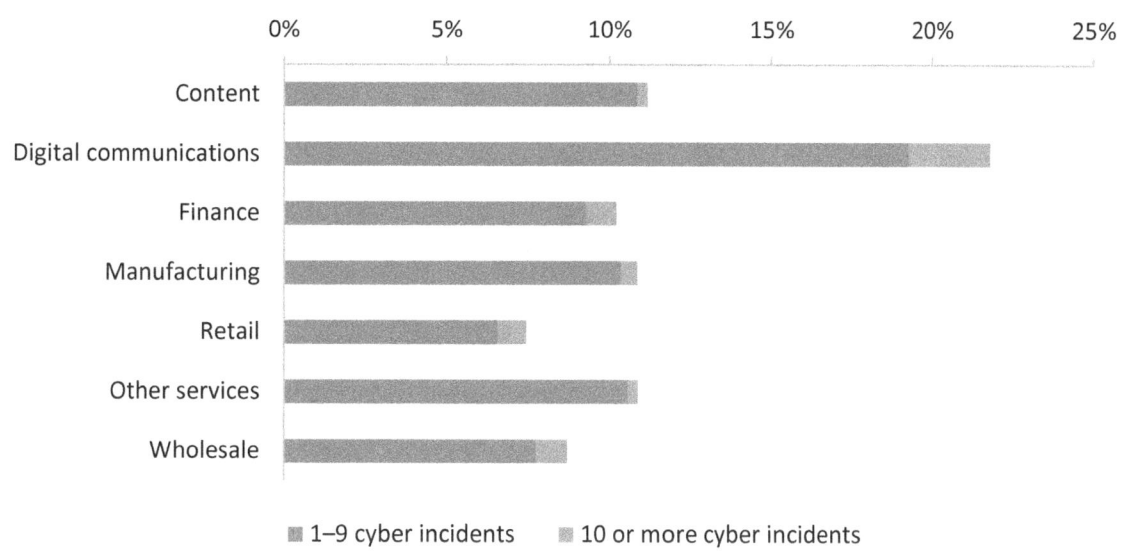

Source: USITC calculations of weighted responses to the Commission questionnaire (question 3.11).

Firms experiencing cyber incidents were affected in a number of negative ways. The most common effects for these firms were information losses and financial losses, followed by compromise of brand or reputation and loss of customers (figure 2.17). [94] SMEs were more likely to suffer financial losses and customer losses than large firms, who faced more information losses, thefts of intellectual property rights, and compromise of brand or reputation.[95] Cyber incidents can also have legal implications. For example, a U.S. District Court recently ruled that the Federal Trade Commission can pursue cases against firms that have compromised customer data by having security vulnerabilities.[96]

Reported negative impacts of cyber incidents varied somewhat by sector. Almost 43 percent of digital communications firms with cyber incidents had their brand or reputation compromised as a result. For content and wholesale trade firms, intellectual property theft was a major form of damage. Finance and insurance, retail trade, and manufacturing firms were particularly likely to suffer from financial losses due to cyber incidents.[97]

---

[94] USITC calculations of weighted responses to the Commission questionnaire (question 3.15).

[95] Ibid.

[96] Hattem, "Court: Feds Can Punish Hacked Companies," April 7, 2014.

[97] Other specific negative effects of cyber incidents on firms in digitally intensive industries included compromised financial information, computer damages, downtime or website incidents, fraud, and lost productivity. USITC calculations of weighted responses to the Commission questionnaire (question 3.12).

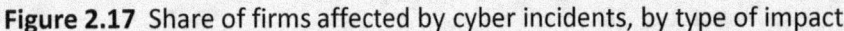

Figure 2.17 Share of firms affected by cyber incidents, by type of impact

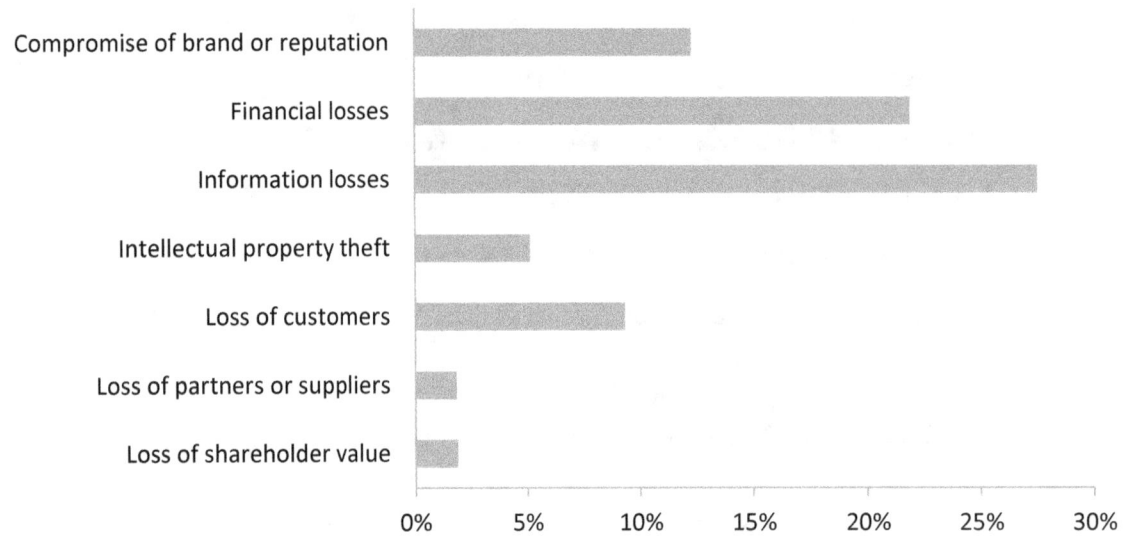

Source: USITC calculations of weighted responses to the Commission questionnaire (question 3.12).

An estimated 41 percent of firms' most serious cyber incidents in 2012 came from some form of hacker, while another 40 percent of firms experienced a cyber incident of unknown origin. A small minority of firms (less than 5 percent) also listed business partners, suppliers, current/former employees, and the government or law enforcement as the source of their most serious cyber incident. SMEs were more likely to have had a cyber incident that was perpetrated by a hacker, while large firms were less likely to know the source of a cyber incident. Similarly, many firms did not know the country of origin for serious cyber incidents, though firms did list the United States, China, Russia, and the EU, among other large trading partners, as attack sources.[98] A Symantec report on Internet security found that globally, the United States was by far the most frequent source of malicious cyber activities, followed by China, members of the EU, India, and Russia.[99]

Data privacy concerns are often linked to concerns about Internet security. Websites often collect Internet user data information. A case study in chapter 6 of this report describes how some companies collect data about individual Internet users, the value to consumers of the services enabled by that data collection as well as consumers' concerns about data collection, and the value to the companies that collect that data.

---

[98] USITC calculations of weighted responses to the Commission questionnaire (question 3.13). Industry representatives explained that with virtual private networks, attacks by groups rather than individuals, and other anonymizing methods of attack, it is becoming very difficult to identify the real geographic source of a cyber incident. Industry representatives, telephone interviews by USITC staff, March 20, 2014, and March 27, 2014.
[99] Symantec Corporation, "2014 Internet Security Threat Report," April 2014.

Bibliography

Anand, Priya. "Heartbleed: Why Companies Are Clueless about Security." MarketWatch, April 16, 2014. http://www.marketwatch.com/story/heartbleed-why-companies-are-clueless-about-security-2014-04-15.

AnyPresence. "The State of Mobile Readiness 2013." AnyPresence, 2013. http://www.anypresence.com/Mobile_Readiness_Report_2013.php.

Burton, Joe. "A Marketer's Guide to Understanding the Economics of Digital Compared to Traditional Advertising and Media Services." American Association of Advertising Agencies, 2009. https://ams.aaaa.org//eweb/upload/catalog/pdfs/mg18.pdf.

Dilworth, Dianna. "How Much Does It Cost to Make an Android App?" MediaBistro, May 7, 2012. http://www.mediabistro.com/appnewser/how-much-does-it-cost-to-make-an-android-app_b22641.

Dokoupil, Tony. "iPhone App Store Developers Aren't Getting Rich." *Newsweek,* March 13, 2010. http://www.newsweek.com/iphone-app-store-developers-arent-getting-rich-81195.

DragonRAD. "How Much Does a Mobile App Cost?" http://dragonrad.com/mobile-app-development-costs (accessed April 7, 2014).

Duke University, McKinsey, and the American Marketing Association. "CMO Survey: Report of Results," February 2014. https://faculty.fuqua.duke.edu/cmosurveyresults/The_CMO_Survey-Results_by_Firm_and_Industry_Characteristics-Feb-2014.pdf.

Economist. "Internet Advertising: The Ultimate Marketing Machine." Economist, July 6, 2006. http://www.economist.com/node/7138905.

Hattem, Julian. "Court: Feds Can Punish Hacked Companies." *The Hill,* April 7, 2014. http://thehill.com/blogs/hillicon-valley/technology/202857-court-says-feds-can-punish-companies-for-hacks.

Crew. "How Much to Make an App?" http://howmuchtomakeanapp.com (accessed April 7, 2014).

Meltzer, Joshua. "Supporting the Internet as a Platform for International Trade: Opportunities for Small and Medium-sized Enterprises and Developing Countries." Brookings, February 2014. http://www.brookings.edu/research/papers/2014/02/internet-international-trade-meltzer.

Nicholson, Jessica R., and Ryan Noonan. "Digital Economy and Cross-Border Trade: The Value of Digitally Deliverable Services." U.S. Department of Commerce. Economics and Statistics Administration. ESA Issue Brief #01-14, January 27, 2014.

Nielsen.com. "How Smartphones are Changing Consumers' Daily Routines around the Globe," April 24, 2014. http://www.nielsen.com/us/en/newswire/2014/how-smartphones-are-changing-consumers-daily-routines-around-the-globe.html.

OpenSSL. "TLS Heartbeat Read Overrun (CVE-2014-0160)." OpenSSL Security Advisory, April 7, 2014. https://www.openssl.org/news/secadv_20140407.txt.

Perlroth, Nicole. "Hackers Lurking in Vents and Soda Machines." *New York Times,* April 7, 2014. http://www.nytimes.com/2014/04/08/technology/the-spy-in-the-soda-machine.html.

———. "Heartbleed Internet Security Flaw Used in Attack." *New York Times,* April 18, 2014. http://bits.blogs.nytimes.com/2014/04/18/heartbleed-internet-security-flaw-used-in-attack.

Pfanner, Eric. "Music Industry Sales Rise." *New York Times,* February 26, 2013. http://www.nytimes.com/2013/02/27/technology/music-industry-records-first-revenue-increase-since-1999.html?_r=0.

PricewaterhouseCoopers. "IAB Internet Advertising Revenue Report: 2013 Full Year Results," April 2014. http://www.iab.net/media/file/IAB_Internet_Advertising_Revenue_Report_FY_2013.pdf.

Hurd, Mary. "How Much Does It Cost to Develop an App?" *User Manual* blog, Fueled.com, October 31, 2013. http://fueled.com/blog/how-much-does-it-cost-to-develop-an-app.

Stetler, Mark. "How Much Does It Cost to Develop a Mobile App?" AppMuse, September 24, 2013. http://appmuse.com/appmusing/how-much-does-it-cost-to-develop-a-mobile-app.

Symantec Corporation. *2014 Internet Security Threat Report.* Volume 19, April 2014. http://www.symantec.com/security_response/publications/threatreport.jsp.

U.S. Census Bureau. "E-Stats." May 23, 2013. https://www.census.gov/econ/estats/2011reportfinal.pdf.

U.S. Department of Commerce (USDOC). Bureau of Economic Analysis (BEA). "Gross Domestic Product." National Economic Accounts, March 27, 2014. https://www.bea.gov/newsreleases/national/gdp/2014/pdf/gdp4q13_3rd.pdf.

U.S. International Trade Commission (USITC). *Digital Trade in the U.S. and Global Economies, Part 1*. Publication No. 4415. Washington, DC: USITC, August 2013. http://usitc.gov/publications/332/pub4415.pdf.

Verizon RISK Team. "2013 Data Breach Investigations Report." Verizon, 2013. http://www.verizonenterprise.com/resources/reports/rp_data-breach-investigations-report-2013_en_xg.pdf.

World Economic Forum (WEF) with McKinsey & Company. *Risk and Responsibility in a Hyperconnected World*, January 2014. http://www.mckinsey.com/insights/business_technology/risk_and_responsibility_in_a_hyperconnected_world_implications_for_enterprises.

Yadron, Danny. "Massive OpenSSL Bug 'Heartbleed' Threatens Sensitive Data." *Wall Street Journal,* April 8, 2014. http://online.wsj.com/news/articles/SB10001424052702304819004579489813056799076.

Chapter 3
Broader Linkages and Contributions of Digital Trade to the U.S. Economy

In the request for this report, the Commission was asked to provide a report offering insights into digital trade's broader linkages with and contributions to the U.S. economy, including its effects on consumer welfare, output, productivity, and job creation. This chapter provides a quantitative assessment of the impact of digital trade on these facets of the broader U.S. economy.

Following a summary of key findings, the second section lays out the analytic approach used in framing the analysis this chapter, as well as the underlying data sources. The third section of this chapter quantifies the economy-wide benefits of increases in productivity due to the Internet, by incorporating data from the Commission's survey into the GTAP model. The fourth section quantifies the economy-wide benefits of reduced trade costs due to the Internet, based on an econometric model of international trade and GTAP simulations. The fifth section quantifies the combined effects of the increases in productivity and the reductions in international trade costs.

Key Findings

- Data from the Commission's survey indicate that the Internet improves productivity in certain digitally intensive sectors of the economy by 7.8–10.9 percent. The productivity gains are due primarily to the use of the Internet in business-to-business communications and in internal communications.

- Digital trade, through the effects of the Internet in enhancing productivity in digitally intensive sectors, increases U.S. real gross domestic product (GDP) by an estimated 3.4–4.5 percent (or $515.1–$671.0 billion), increases U.S. real wages by 3.6–4.0 percent, and increases U.S. aggregate employment (in full-time equivalents (FTEs))[100] by 0.0 to 1.4 percent (or 0.0 to 2.0 million FTEs) over the counterfactual scenario in which the Internet is absent.

- The econometric model of international trade flows and trade costs indicates that the Internet significantly reduces the trade costs of U.S. imports and exports in digitally intensive sectors, by about 26 percent on average.

---

[100] FTEs are employees on full-time schedules plus employees on part-time schedules converted to a full-time basis. Thus, two employees working half-time schedules equal one FTE. This measure facilitates the comparison of employees regardless of their schedules.

- Digital trade, through the effects of the Internet in lowering international trade costs in digitally intensive sectors, increases U.S. real GDP by an estimated 0.0 to 0.3 percent (or $1.6–$38.8 billion), increases real wages by 0.9 percent, and increases U.S. aggregate employment by 0.0 to 0.3 percent (or 0.0 to 0.5 million FTEs).

- Digital trade, through the combined effects of the Internet in enhancing productivity and lowering international trade costs in digitally intensive sectors, increases U.S. real GDP by an estimated 3.4–4.8 percent (or $517.1–$710.7 billion), increases real wages by 4.5–5.0 percent, and increases U.S. aggregate employment by 0.0 to 1.8 percent (or 0.0 to 2.4 million FTEs). If the effects of enhanced productivity and lower international trade costs due to the Internet in non-digitally intensive sectors were also quantified, the economy-wide estimates would likely be larger.

Analytic Approach and Data Sources

To assess the role and contributions of digital trade, it is important to consider the many ways that the U.S. economy can benefit from the development and application of new Internet-based technologies that make digital trade possible. The Internet increases productivity and creates new marketing opportunities at home and abroad, as indicated in the responses to the Commission's digital trade survey. Digital trade reduces transaction costs and expands international commerce, as indicated in econometric analysis discussed in this chapter. Although the growth of digitally intensive industries draws workers and resources from other sectors of the economy, it can be an important source of net aggregate job creation, as indicated in the economic simulations discussed in this chapter. In addition, increasing Internet usage may also help reduce labor market search costs, as is discussed in more detail in one of the case studies in chapters 5–7 of this report.

This chapter applies traditional tools for measuring net economic effects—econometric models and computable general equilibrium (CGE) models—though it applies them in a relatively new context.[101] Any measure of the economic contribution of digital trade should account for the net effects. It should not only count the benefits, in terms of the jobs and revenues in booming digitally intensive sectors, but also count the associated downsizing of other parts of the broader U.S. economy, as scarce resources and limited budgets are reallocated. The model-based estimates in this chapter apply this netting concept.

The analysis of economy-wide effects in this chapter uses several kinds of economic models and data, depending on the particular issue. The chapter uses an econometric logit model to analyze data from the Commission's digital trade survey and to quantify the effects of Internet-based business practices on productivity on the industries particularly involved in digital trade. It uses an econometric gravity model to quantify the effects of the Internet on international trade costs of U.S. exports and imports in digitally intensive sectors of the economy.

---

[101] These tools are described briefly in this chapter and in more detail in appendix H.

The analysis of international trade costs is based on public data sources, including the World Input-Output Database (WIOD), the World Bank's World Development Indicators, and the International Monetary Fund's World Economic Outlook. The chapter uses CGE models to estimate the economy-wide consequences of these increases in productivity and reductions in international trade costs.[102] Table 3.1 summarizes the different methodologies and sources of data. Chapter 6 of *Digital Trade 1* summarized the literature on the economic effects of digital trade and the Internet. Appendix I in this report updates that literature review.

Table 3.1 Digital trade: Summary of methodology and data sources

Methodology	Data sources
Econometric model to quantify the effects of Internet use on productivity	Weighted responses to USITC survey
CGE model to quantify the economy-wide effects of increased productivity	GTAP data base; sector-level compilation of data from USITC survey
Econometric model to quantify the effects of the Internet on international trade costs	WIOD international input-output tables; World Development Indicators; World Economic Outlook; other public datasets
CGE model to quantify the economy-wide effects of the reduction in international trade costs	GTAP data base; econometric estimates of the reductions in international trade costs

Source: Compiled by the Commission.

Economic Benefits of Increased Productivity due to the Internet

The Commission's survey indicates that access to the Internet contributes substantially to the productivity of U.S. firms in digital industries. This section quantifies the economy-wide implications by incorporating data from the survey into the GTAP model. The simulations in the GTAP model indicate that productivity improvement due to the Internet increases U.S. real GDP by 3.4–4.5 percent (or $515.1–$671.0 billion), U.S. real wages by 3.6–4.0 percent, and U.S. aggregate employment by 0.0 to 1.4 percent (or 0.0 to 2.0 million FTEs).[103]

The Contribution of the Internet to Productivity

The Commission's survey specifically asked firms how their productivity would change if, hypothetically, they did not have access to the Internet. Table 3.2 reports the survey results for five digitally intensive sectors: communications,[104] wholesale and retail trade (trade), manufacturing, finance and insurance (finance), and selected other services (services). The hypothetical reductions in productivity if the Internet were *not* available can be used as a measure of the actual productivity benefits of Internet access. More than 40 percent of firms in

---

[102] The specific CGE model used is the Global Trade Analysis Project (GTAP) model, described more fully in appendix H. The simulations use version 9 (pre-release) of the GTAP database, with a 2011 base year. The CGE model was also used to estimate the economy-wide effects of reducing foreign barriers to digital trade. This analysis is presented in chapter 4 as part of the discussion of notable foreign barriers to digital trade.

[103] These ranges represent alternative assumptions about the responsiveness of labor force participation to changes in real wages, as explained below in footnote 11 and as part of the discussion of table 3.5.

[104] Communications is an aggregation of the digital communications and content sectors.

Table 3.2 Reported impact of the loss of the Internet on productivity, by sector (percent in each range)

Sector	Productivity decrease greater than 15 percent	Productivity decrease less than 15 percent	No change in productivity	Productivity increase less than 15 percent	Productivity increase greater than 15 percent
Communications	67.2	27.6	3.8	0.5	0.9
Finance	54.0	30.1	15.0	0.4	0.6
Trade	46.2	34.7	15.7	3.0	0.5
Services	60.7	24.6	12.6	1.2	1.0
Manufacturing	43.6	37.9	15.4	2.1	1.1

Source: USITC compilation of weighted responses to the Commission questionnaire.
Note: As explained in chapter 1, survey responses were compiled and weighted to ensure that the reported results accurately represented the population surveyed. Appendix F provides additional information about the Commission's survey and reporting methods.

each of the five sectors responded that loss of access to the Internet or other digital networks would reduce their productivity by 15 percent or more. For the communications sector, the share of the responding firms was slightly above 67 percent.

One section of the Commission's survey focused on firms' Internet-related business practices, asking specifically how often they use the Internet for 10 different tasks. The firms rated their frequency of use on a scale from 1 (never) to 5 (always). Table 3.3 reports the average value of this frequency measure for each use by sector. The frequencies of the different uses vary across the five sectors, though internal communications and business-to-business communications are the most frequent in almost all of the sectors.

Each firm's response to these questions can be correlated with its estimate of the effects of losing access to the Internet on its productivity (table 3.2) to provide a deeper understanding of *how* Internet access contributes to productivity. Table 3.4 reports the findings of an econometric logit model that quantifies the contribution of each of the 10 uses of the Internet (in table 3.3).[105] The dependent variable in the model is equal to one if the firm estimates a decline in productivity of 15 percent or more and is equal to zero otherwise, and the independent variables are the survey measures of the frequency of a firm's use of the Internet. The table reports the estimated average marginal effects on productivity of not having the Internet for each of the listed uses of the Internet, based on the logit model. The marginal effect of a particular use is defined as the increase in the probability of a 15 percent or greater decline in productivity due to not having the Internet for each additional point in the scale of

---

[105] A logit model is a type of regression designed to explain binary (rather than continuous) economic outcomes – in this case, whether the firm estimates a decline in productivity of 15 percent or more. Appendix H provides further details about this econometric model.

Table 3.3 Reported uses of the Internet, average measure of frequency by sector (scale from 1 to 5)

Use of the Internet	Communications	Finance	Trade	Services	Manufacturing
Advertising and marketing	3.5	2.7	3.0	2.7	2.6
Business-to-business communications	3.3	3.3	2.9	3.4	3.4
Business-to-consumer communications	3.2	2.7	2.7	2.6	2.4
Internal communications	3.7	4.0	3.4	3.8	3.7
Market research	2.7	2.7	2.5	2.6	2.6
Ordering products and services that are delivered online	2.6	2.6	2.2	2.7	2.2
Ordering products and services that are physically delivered	2.6	2.8	3.0	3.0	3.0
Selling online products or services	2.5	1.6	1.7	1.6	1.4
Selling physical products or services	2.2	1.5	2.4	1.7	2.2
Supply chain management	1.8	1.7	2.2	1.8	2.3

Source: USITC compilation of weighted responses to the Commission questionnaire.
Note: As explained in chapter 1, survey responses were compiled and weighted to ensure that the reported results accurately represented the population surveyed. Appendix F provides additional information about the Commission's survey and reporting methods.

Table 3.4 Average marginal effects on productivity of not having the Internet for each of the uses of the Internet, based on the estimated logit model

Use of the Internet	Estimated effect of not having the Internet (point estimate x 100)	Standard error x 100
Advertising and marketing	3.0	1.3*
Business-to-business communications	4.8	1.3*
Business-to-consumer communications	1.1	1.2
Internal communications	2.7	1.3*
Market research	1.6	1.2
Ordering products and services that are delivered online	3.6	1.4*
Ordering products and services that are physically delivered	1.6	1.4
Selling online products or services	3.6	1.4*
Selling physical products or services	3.2	1.2*
Supply chain management	2.9	1.2*

Source: USITC staff econometric analysis of weighted responses to the Commission questionnaire.
Note: An asterisk indicates that the point estimate is significantly different from zero at the 5 percent level. As explained in chapter 1, survey responses were compiled and weighted to ensure that the reported results accurately represented the population surveyed. Appendix F provides additional information about the Commission's survey and reporting methods.

the frequency of the particular use. For example, if the frequency of use of the Internet in business-to-business communications rose from 3 to 4, then this would increase the probability of a large negative productivity effect by 4.8 percentage points.

According to this analysis, as shown in table 3.4, business-to-business communications rank as making the largest marginal contribution to the productivity benefits of the Internet. Selling and ordering online products or services tie as the second largest contributors to productivity. In all, seven of the uses of the Internet contribute significantly to the probability of a large productivity effect: advertising and marketing, business-to-business communications, internal communications, ordering products and services that are delivered online, selling online products and services, supply chain management, and selling physical products or services.

Economy-Wide Implications of the Productivity Effects of the Internet

A CGE model can translate the firm's productivity effects in table 3.2 into economy-wide effects on U.S. labor markets and GDP. GTAP's CGE model provides the framework for doing so. GTAP is a global trade model that takes into account the linkages between all of the sectors in each country and the pattern of trade flows among the countries.

The GTAP simulations for this study reduce the productivity levels in the most digitally intensive countries as if the Internet were not available by the amount of the productivity effects in the survey. Again, calculating the difference between the actual current situation and the hypothetical "no Internet" scenario makes it possible to estimate the Internet's (positive) effects on several important economic outcomes.[106]

The GTAP model traditionally assumes that there is a fixed number of workers in the labor force in each country and that all workers in the labor force are employed.[107] The simulations in this report extend the GTAP model by assuming a flexible labor force. That is, the model allows the number of workers in each country's labor force to rise with a rise in real wages and to fall with a fall in real wages. However, the simulations retain the traditional assumption that all workers who enter the labor force are employed. This extension of the model allows for adjustments in aggregate employment in each country.[108] The size of these adjustments depends on the responsiveness of aggregate labor supply in each country to the simulated changes in real wages. The Congressional Budget Office recently completed a synopsis of the peer-reviewed academic literature on the responsiveness of the aggregate labor supply to changes in after-tax wages.[109] The results of McClelland and Mok (2012) provide parameter values for the flexible labor force extension of the GTAP model.[110] The authors conclude that the aggregate labor supply elasticity for the total population in the United States ranges from 0.0 to 0.4.[111]

---

[106] The point estimates of the percentage reduction in productivity in the absence of Internet access are 11.57 percent for the communications sector, 10.27 percent for the finance sector, 8.90 percent for the manufacturing sector, 8.80 percent for the trade sector, and 10.41 percent for the other digital services sector. The details of these calculations are described in appendix H.

[107] By adopting this assumption, the GTAP model does not try to simulate aggregate employment effects.

[108] However, it does not allow the model to simulate changes in the unemployment rate, since the GTAP model assumes that the labor markets clear and there is no unemployment. The effect of the Internet on job search costs and frictional unemployment are addressed separately in chapter 5, using an econometric model that is separate from the GTAP model.

[109] The studies that were reviewed use survey data and tax return data to quantify the effect of after-tax wages on the decision to work and on a worker's number of hours.

[110] See McClelland and Mok, "A Review of Recent Research on Labor Supply Elasticities," 2012.

[111] The aggregate labor supply elasticity is defined as the percentage change in the quantity of labor supplied for every 1 percent increase in real wages. McClelland and Mok report separate elasticities for labor force participation and for hours worked for different demographic groups within the U.S. population. Since the GTAP model does not differentiate between different demographic groups and does not disaggregate labor inputs into hours and numbers of workers, the GTAP simulations use McClelland and Mok's total elasticity estimates (the sum of the participation elasticity and the hours elasticity) for the total U.S. population.

Table 3.5 reports the simulated increases in real GDP, real wages, and aggregate employment in the United States as a result of the productivity benefits of the Internet, as well as the simulated increase in output in each of the five digitally intensive sectors. The estimated effects reported in table 3.5 the results of two different simulations that correspond to the high and low ends of this range.

Table 3.5 Economy-wide effects: Estimated effects of reported enhanced productivity due to the Internet in digitally intensive sectors, percent change

Economic outcomes	Fixed labor force	Flexible labor force
U.S. real wages	4.0	3.6
U.S. aggregate employment (FTEs)	0.0	1.4
U.S. real GDP	3.4	4.5
U.S. production, by sector		
Communications	4.7	5.8
Finance	6.5	7.7
Trade	5.3	6.5
Services	4.5	5.7
Manufacturing	4.1	5.1

Source: GTAP model and weighted responses to the Commission questionnaire.
Note: Appendix F provides additional information about the Commission's survey and reporting methods. Estimates are based on sector-level bilateral trade flows with a 2011 baseline, the most recent year available in the GTAP data base.

- The first column of estimates in the table assumes that the aggregate labor force is fixed, it does not respond to changes in real wages, and the aggregate labor supply elasticity is equal to zero. This is the traditional assumption in GTAP simulations, and it is the low end of the range of aggregate labor supply elasticities in McClelland and Mok (2012).

- The second column of estimates in the table assumes that the aggregate labor force responds to changes in real wages and the aggregate labor supply elasticity is equal to 0.4. These estimates supplement the simulation based on the traditional fixed labor force assumption. They correspond to the high end of the range of aggregate labor supply elasticities in McClelland and Mok (2012).

It reports that the estimated increase in U.S. real GDP due to the productivity benefits of the Internet ranges from 3.4 to 4.5 percent.[112] The estimated increase in U.S. real wages ranges from 3.6 to 4.0 percent, and the estimated increase in U.S. aggregate employment ranges from 0.0 to 1.4 percent.[113]

There are several caveats that apply to these survey-based simulations. First, there may be productivity benefits of the Internet in other, less digitally intensive sectors of the economy, but they are not quantified in this simulation, since they are outside of the scope of the Commission's survey. If it were possible to include the productivity benefits in these other

---

[112] Real GDP is a measure of consumers' purchasing power and economic welfare. It is calculated as the ratio of consumer income to the consumer price index in the country.

[113] All estimates of job effects based on the GTAP models are calculated by applying the percentage change in employment in the model to total civilian employment in the United States in the baseline year. The details of these calculations are reported in appendix H.

sectors, it could increase the estimated effects on the U.S. economy. Second, the survey did not cover all NAICS codes within the five digitally intensive GTAP sectors. If it were possible to narrow the application of the productivity shocks to exactly match the scope of the survey, this could reduce the estimated effects on the U.S. economy.

Economic Benefits of Reduced International Trade Costs due to the Internet

The Internet also contributes to the broader U.S. and global economies by reducing the costs of trading goods and services across borders. All else being equal, there will be lower trade costs and more international commerce in products that are delivered via the Internet or with the assistance of Internet-based technologies.[114] While it is generally accepted that the Internet and other improvements in communications technologies have contributed to globalization trends, it is challenging to quantify these contributions.

This section estimates the economy-wide benefits of the reductions in international trade costs due to the Internet. First, it presents an econometric model of trade in digitally intensive sectors of the economy. The model includes the countries' Internet usage rates as one of the potential determinants of international trade costs. The econometric analysis finds that trade costs of U.S. imports and exports in these sectors would be significantly higher—on average 26 percent higher—absent the Internet. These changes in trade costs are incorporated into a GTAP model.

The traditional modeling framework for estimating the determinants of trade costs is the gravity model.[115] In order to focus on more digitally intensive sectors of the economy, the gravity model is applied to sector-level data for the financial intermediation, machinery, post and telecommunications, wholesale trade, and renting of machinery and equipment and other business activities sectors of World Input-Output Database (WIOD). The model uses sector-level bilateral trade flows in 2011 and national production and expenditure measures at the same level of disaggregation from the WIOD.

International trade costs for these digitally intensive sectors depend on the Internet usage rates of the two countries and traditional gravity model factors. Examples of gravity model factors are country size (using sector-level measures of expenditure and production), distance between the two countries, the existence of a free trade agreement between the countries, and the existence of a common border between the countries. The econometric estimates indicate that

---

[114] This chapter focuses on how the Internet facilitates international trade, for example by reducing communications costs. It does not address the effects of foreign barriers to digital trade, which are addressed at length in chapter 4.

[115] While basic gravity models have been in use since the 1960s, there have been significant advances in theory and methodology over the past 15 years stemming from Anderson and van Wincoop's "Gravity with Gravitas," 2003 and the extensive literature that followed. Baier and Bergstrand, "Bonus Vetus OLS," 2009 provide a relatively simple method for estimating complex non-linear gravity models of trade costs and aggregate bilateral trade flows. The details of this model appear in appendix H.

the Internet reduces trade costs of U.S. exports and imports in these digitally intensive sectors by 26 percent on average, ranging from a low of 3 percent to a high of 38 percent depending on the current level of Internet usage in the trade partner.

These reductions in trade costs contribute to the broader U.S. economy. Table 3.6 reports a set of GTAP simulations of these broader economic effects, again for the two alternative assumptions about the response of the labor force to changes in real wages. The simulations estimate that the reductions in trade costs in the digitally intensive sectors increase U.S. real GDP by 0.0 to 0.3 percent (or $1.6–$38.8 billion), increase U.S. real wages by 0.9 percent, and increase U.S. aggregate employment by 0.0 to 0.3 percent (or 0.0 to 0.5 million FTEs).[116]

Table 3.6 Economy-wide effects: Estimated effects of reported reductions in international trade costs due to the Internet in digitally intensive sectors, percent change

Economic outcomes	Fixed labor force	Flexible labor force
U.S. real wages	0.9	0.9
U.S. aggregate employment (FTEs)	0.0	0.3
U.S. real GDP	0.0	0.3
U.S. production, by sector		
Communications	2.4	2.6
Finance	1.6	1.8
Trade	0.0	0.3
Services	3.2	3.4

Source: GTAP model and weighted responses to the Commission questionnaire.
Note: Appendix F provides additional information about the Commission's survey and reporting methods. Estimates are based on sector-level bilateral trade flows with a 2011 baseline, the most recent year available in the GTAP data base.

Simulations That Combine the Two Types of Effects

Finally, the Commission considered the combined effects of enhanced productivity (analyzed in table 3.5) and reduced trade costs due to the Internet (analyzed in table 3.6). By estimating the combined effects, the simulation is able to capture the interactions between the two types of effects on the broader U.S. economy. Table 3.7 reports this final group of GTAP simulations, again for the two alternative assumptions about whether the labor force is fixed or adjusts in response to changes in real wages. According to the simulations, the combined effects increase U.S. real GDP by 3.4–4.8 percent (or $517.1–$710.7 billion), increase U.S. real wages by 4.5–5.0 percent, and increase U.S. aggregate employment by 0.0 to 1.8 percent (or 0.0 to 2.4 million

---

[116] The simulations quantify the effects of the Internet on trade costs only in digitally intensive service sectors. Adding the effects on trade costs in other sectors could increase the total effects on the broader U.S. economy.

Table 3.7 Economy-wide effects: Estimated combined effects of enhanced productivity and lower trade costs due to the Internet in digitally intensive sectors, percent change

Economic outcomes	Fixed labor force	Flexible labor force
U.S. real wages	5.0	4.5
U.S. aggregate employment (FTEs)	0.0	1.8
U.S. real GDP	3.4	4.8
U.S. production, by sector		
Communications	7.3	8.7
Finance	8.2	9.9
Trade	5.3	6.8
Services	8.0	9.5
Manufacturing	0.1	1.2

Source: GTAP model and weighted responses to the Commission questionnaire.
Note: Appendix F provides additional information about the Commission's survey and reporting methods. Estimates are based on sector-level bilateral trade flows with a 2011 baseline, the most recent year available in the GTAP database.

FTEs).[117] These combined effects are slightly larger than the sum of the percentage increases in the separate simulations reported in tables 3.5 and 3.6. The difference between the combined effects on real GDP and the sum of the separate effects on real GDP indicates that there is a small positive interaction between the two types of effects: the benefits of the increase in productivity are magnified (slightly) by the reduction in international trade costs.

It is important to keep in mind that the combined effects in table 3.7 are not an exhaustive estimate of the effects of digital trade on the broader U.S. economy. They are a combination of two types of effects—enhanced productivity and lower trade costs due to the Internet in digitally intensive sectors—that are straightforward to quantify, given the survey and econometric evidence available and the GTAP simulation framework.[118] Other economic effects of the Internet on digital trade, including an increase in product diversity and the boom in capital expenditures on information technology are not addressed in these estimates and remain potentially important areas for future analysis. *Digital Trade 1* provided an overview of the economic effects of the use of Internet technologies in the broader economy and highlighted some of the ways Internet technologies benefit producers and consumers, although the Commission was not able to quantify these effects for the GTAP model in this second

---

[117] The estimates of the effects on GDP are similar in magnitude to estimates in the literature of the contribution of the Internet to U.S. GDP. For example, McKinsey Global Institute estimates that the Internet accounted for 3.8 percent of U.S. GDP in 2009, and OECD estimates that the Internet accounts for 3.2 percent of U.S. business services value added in 2011. See McKinsey, *Internet Matters*, May 2011; OECD, "Measuring the Internet Economy," 2013. However, the methodologies in the literature are very different. They generally use an expenditure approach to sum the value of all Internet and Internet-supporting activities. Appendix I provided a more extensive review of the literature. In contrast, this chapter has quantified the contributions to real GDP based survey-based and model-based estimates of the effects on productivity and the efficiency of international trade. It quantifies how digitally intensive sectors are linked to the rest of the U.S. economy.

[118] For this investigation the Commission was requested to focus on selected industries particularly involved in digital trade, i.e., firms in digitally intensive industries, although other effects of digital trade are likely in non-digitally intensive industries as well.

report.[119] Moreover, if the effects of enhanced productivity, lower trade costs, or other economic effects due to the Internet in non-digitally intensive industries were also quantified, then the economy-wide estimates would likely be larger.

---

[119] The Internet has had many economic effects that impact digital trade, such as improved logistics management, more efficient supply chain management, more efficient business practices, improved market intelligence, greater access to more markets and customers, and additional channels for service delivery. For further information on how Internet technologies benefit producers and consumers and the competitive rationales for adopting Internet technologies in various industry sectors, see USITC, *Digital Trade 1*, 2013, chapter 3 and appendix F.

Bibliography

Anderson, James, and Eric Van Wincoop. "Gravity with Gravitas: A Solution to the Border Puzzle." *American Economic Review* 93, no. 1 (2003): 170–92.

Baier, Scott, and Jeffrey Bergstrand. "Bonus Vetus OLS: A Simple Method for Approximating International Trade-Cost Effects Using the Gravity Equation." *Journal of International Economics* 77 (2009): 77–8.

McClelland , Robert, and Shannon Mok. "A Review of Recent Research on Labor Supply Elasticities." U.S. Congressional Budget Office Working Paper Series, No. 2012-12, 2012.

McKinsey Global Institute (McKinsey). Internet Matters: The Net's Sweeping Impact on Growth, Jobs, and Prosperity. McKinsey & Co., May 2011.

Organisation for Economic Co-operation and Development (OECD). "Measuring the Internet Economy: A Contribution to the Research Agenda." OECD Digital Economy Papers, No. 226, July 12, 2013. http://dx.doi.org/10.1787/5k43gjg6r8jf-en.

U.S. International Trade Commission (USITC*). Digital Trade in the U.S. and Global Economies, Part 1 (Digital Trade 1).* USITC Publication No. 4415. Washington, DC: USITC, July 2013. http://www.usitc.gov/publications/332/pub4415.pdf.

Chapter 4
Barriers to International Digital Trade and Their Economic Effects

This chapter examines key barriers and impediments to international digital trade, and estimates their economic effects on U.S. digitally intensive industries and on the U.S. economy as a whole.[120] The Commission, through a survey, asked firms to report the extent to which impediments identified in the Commission's first digital trade investigation[121] constitute a trade obstacle for them and to assess the effects of these obstacles on their sales and employment.[122] This chapter presents and analyzes the survey results, and provides qualitative information from firm interviews and the Commission's hearing to contextualize these results. The chapter concludes by discussing the results of a CGE modeling analysis that examines the economy-wide benefits of a reduction in foreign barriers to digital trade for U.S. employment, wages, and GDP based on information collected in the Commission's survey and GTAP simulations.[123]

Key Findings

- Based on survey responses, localization requirements, market access limitations, data privacy and protection requirements, intellectual property rights (IPR) infringement, uncertain legal liability rules, censorship, and customs measures in other countries all present obstacles to digital trade.[124]

- Perceived barriers to digital trade vary by industry sector and firm size. Large firms in digital communications and SMEs in finance had the highest percentages that viewed localization, data privacy and protection, uncertain legal liability and censorship as "substantial or very substantial" obstacles to digital trade. Large firms and SMEs in the retail sector had the largest portions that viewed customs requirements as "substantial or very substantial" obstacles. By contrast, large firms in the content sector and SMEs in

---

[120] As discussed in chapter 1, the following digitally intensive industries are the focus of this report: content; digital communications; finance and insurance ("finance"); manufacturing; retail trade ("retail"); selected other services ("other services"); and wholesale trade ("wholesale"). A description of the economic activities included in each is provided in chapter 1.

[121] USITC, *Digital Trade 1*, 2013, chapter 5.

[122] Other findings from the Commission's survey are presented in chapters 2 and 3.

[123] The use of GTAP in this investigation is discussed in more detail in chapter 3 and appendix H.

[124] As explained in chapter 1, survey responses were compiled and weighted to ensure that the reported results accurately represented the population surveyed. The results were weighted to account for the sampling strategy and to correct for potential non-response bias. All estimates based on calculations of weighted responses were examined to determine their precision. No estimates reported in this chapter fell below the relative standard error (RSE) threshold of 50 percent (0.5) that has been applied throughout the report. Appendix F provides additional information about the Commission's survey and reporting methods.

digital communications had the highest percentages that viewed IPR infringement as a "substantial or very substantial" obstacle (table 4.1).

- Digitally intensive firms most frequently identified Nigeria, Algeria, and China as locations where they had decided not to do business because of digital trade barriers, or where they had faced barriers. By contrast, Australia, the United Kingdom, and Italy were the locations where firms least often felt that they faced barriers or that barriers precluded them from doing business (table 4.2).

- Removal of foreign digital trade barriers would boost U.S. exports and sales abroad, though not all sectors would necessarily benefit equally. Large firms in the content, digital communications, retail, and other services sectors believed that they had more to gain in sales abroad from the removal of trade barriers than firms in finance and manufacturing, according to the survey results. Large firms also generally believed that they had more to gain than SMEs. For example, the mean response for large digital communications firms was that sales abroad would increase by 5–15 percent while SMEs believed sales would increase by less than 5 percent if foreign trade barriers were removed.

- Based on the survey results and GTAP simulations, the Commission estimates that removing barriers would increase U.S. real GDP by 0.1 to 0.3 percent (or $16.7–$41.4 billion), increase U.S. real wages by 0.7 to 1.4 percent, and increase U.S. aggregate employment by 0.0 to 0.3 percent (or 0.0–0.4 million FTEs).

Table 4.1 Sectors with the largest portions of firms that identified each barrier as a "substantial" or "very substantial" obstacle, by firm size

Barrier	Large firms	SMEs
Localization requirements	Digital communications (34%)	Finance (21%)
Market access limitations	Wholesale (24%)	Finance (23%)
Data privacy and protection requirements	Digital communications (34%)	Finance (20%)
IPR infringement	Content (34%)	Digital communications (27%)
Uncertain legal liability	Digital communications (18%)	Finance (24%)
Censorship	Digital communications (12%)	Finance (8%)
Compliance with customs requirements	Retail (14%)	Retail (39%)

Source: USITC calculations of weighted responses to the Commission questionnaire (question 5.1).

Table 4.2 Digital trade barriers ranking of countries, by percentage of firms that faced barriers

Country	Percentage	Country	Percentage	Country	Percentage
Nigeria	46.9	Venezuela	24.0	Malaysia	18.3
Algeria	46.7	South Korea	23.6	Chile	18.1
China	42.8	Argentina	23.2	Philippines	18.1
Bangladesh	38.8	Mexico	22.9	Sweden	17.8
Russia	37.0	Colombia	22.8	Netherlands	17.7
Pakistan	36.4	Greece	21.8	Switzerland	17.6
Paraguay	33.7	Canada	21.4	Israel	17.4
Romania	33.7	South Africa	20.7	Norway	16.9
Vietnam	31.8	Turkey	20.4	Peru	16.8
Ukraine	30.7	Czech Republic	20.2	Taiwan	16.7
Brazil	29.4	Germany	20.2	France	16.6
India	27.5	Singapore	19.6	Belgium	16.5
United Arab Emirates	26.4	Portugal	19.5	Austria	16.0
Indonesia	25.8	Poland	19.4	Spain	15.9
Saudi Arabia	25.5	Japan	19.1	Australia	15.7
Egypt	25.4	Thailand	18.6	United Kingdom	15.5
				Italy	13.9

Source: USITC calculations of weighted responses to Commission's questionnaire (questions 5.6, 5.7 and 5.8).

U.S. Firms' Assessments of Barriers to International Digital Trade

The chapter begins by presenting survey results on obstacles to doing business across borders over the Internet. To provide a context for these results, the chapter also draws on additional information sources, including follow-up telephone interviews of firms that responded to the barriers section of the survey and were interested in giving more details, as well as testimony and submissions from the Commission's hearing.[125]

---

[125] These interviews were conducted in February–May 2014. Commission staff contacted survey respondents who reported that barriers presented obstacles to digital trade to find out if they would be interested in providing additional details; about 40 firms volunteered to do so. Unlike the questionnaire results, this information is anecdotal and is not based on a random sample. Thus, it cannot be assumed to represent the views of a broader population.

Approach

The barriers section of the survey draws on information developed as part of the Commission's first digital trade investigation, which identified seven barriers to international digital trade (table 4.3).[126]

Table 4.3 Seven barriers to digital trade identified in the Commission's *Digital Trade 1* investigation

Barrier	Description
Localization requirements	Government measures that favor domestic digital industries, products, or services at the expense of those from other countries, including: • Requirements that data servers or other infrastructure be located in-country; • Requirements that firms use a certain amount of local content, for example, to qualify for government procurement preferences or subsidies; and • Requirements to comply with country-specific standards rather than internationally accepted standards
Market access limitations	Other government measures that limit foreign firms' access to markets, including restrictions on investment, trading rights, distribution rights, or other core business functions
Data privacy and protection requirements	Government measures that regulate the movement of personal data or other sensitive information across borders
IPR infringement	The infringement of intellectual property rights associated with digital products or services, including copyright, patent, trademark, or trade secret infringement
Uncertain legal liabilities	Unclear laws governing the legal obligations of firms involved in digital trade, including the responsibilities of Internet intermediaries for the activities of others
Censorship	Government measures or practices that suppress information that can be accessed or viewed on the Internet
Customs measures	Customs measures that are unclear or overly complicated

Source: USITC, *Digital Trade 1,* 2013, chapter 5.

The survey results presented in this chapter are based on the responses of firms with some involvement in international digital trade, unless otherwise indicated. These firms were considered to be the most likely to have relevant information about barriers to such trade.[127] The survey asked firms to rate each potential barrier on a five-point scale running from 1, "not an obstacle," to 5, "a very substantial obstacle."[128] It also asked firms to identify the top three countries where they experienced each barrier. Firms were further asked to estimate, if possible, the impact on sales and employment in the United States and abroad if all obstacles to doing business across borders and over the Internet were removed.[129] The survey also asked

---

[126] The identified barriers appeared to have strengths and limitations as a basis for the barriers section of the survey. On the strengths side, firms seemed to have found them sufficient to describe the problem; they reported few other barriers, despite multiple opportunities to do so in the survey. More challenging was that some firms apparently were guided by their own definitions of barriers rather than those in the survey. Moreover, even as defined in the survey, some barriers were overlapping in nature; examples of particular overlap areas are described in the relevant sections below. See appendix F for a further discussion of caveats and limitations.

[127] Firms involved in international digital trade were those who provided an answer to questions about international imports or exports over the Internet (4.1, 4.2 or 4.4) or who identified customers outside of the United States in response to question 5.6. Using these criteria, 53 percent of responding firms had some involvement in international digital trade, and 47 percent did not. USITC calculations of weighted responses to questions 4.1, 4.2, 4.4 and 5.6.

[128] Appendix G contains data tables summarizing all responses to question 5.1, by sector and firm size.

[129] Commission questionnaire (questions 5.1–5.5).

firms to list the countries in which they have customers; where they face any of the seven obstacles; and where they have decided not to do business because of obstacles.[130]

All estimates based on calculations of weighted responses to the Commission's survey have been examined to determine their precision. Differences in mean responses, by sector and firm size, also have been analyzed for statistical significance. Only statistically significant differences are reported in the text.[131]

Localization Requirements

Survey Results

Firms perceive localization barriers to international digital trade differently, depending on sector and firm size.[132] Eighty-two percent of large firms and 52 percent of SMEs in the digital communications sector felt that localization requirements presented obstacles, figure 4.1.[133] The highest percentages of large firms that felt that localization barriers were "substantial or very substantial" obstacles were in digital communication (34 percent) and content (27 percent), though 20 percent of large firms in retail and 19 percent of large firms in the finance sector also believed them to be "substantial or very substantial" obstacles. Of SMEs, 21 percent of firms in finance, 16 percent of firms in the other services sector, and 15 percent of digital communications firms believed localization requirements to be "substantial or very substantial" obstacles.

The estimated mean responses of large firms by sector range from "minor" to "somewhat of an obstacle," while SME means are in the "minor obstacle" range across all sectors.[134] Statistical analysis of the variance in the means shows significant differences in how firms perceived the severity of each obstacle by sector and firm size. In the content and digital communications sectors, for example, large firms believed localization requirements to be a more substantial barrier than SMEs did.[135] Within large firms, firms in digital communications believed

---

[130] These questions (5.6–5.8), as well as the one on the U.S. employment effects of barriers (5.5), have been used as inputs into the modeling described at the conclusion of the chapter.

[131] Appendix F provides additional information about the Commission's survey methods.

[132] Localization requirements are defined broadly in the survey as measures designed to protect, favor, or stimulate domestic industries, service providers, or intellectual property at the expense of those from other countries. Commission questionnaire, Definitions ¶5. This definition is adapted from that used by the USTR. USTR, "Localization Barriers to Trade" (accessed April 10, 2014).

[133] Notwithstanding the survey's definition, in practice, firms had different interpretations of the term "localization requirements." Some did not limit their definition to government policy measures or practices, but instead interpreted the term to include the business need to localize products to make them attractive in other markets. Industry representatives, telephone interviews by USITC staff, March 7 and 10, 2014.

[134] See appendix G, table G.41.

[135] This result is consistent with two findings in chapter 2: that the share of large firms that conduct international digital trade is greater than the share of SMEs that do so, and that the value of large firms' trade is substantially higher. See the "International Trade" section in chapter 2.

Figure 4.1 Firms' perceptions that localization requirements present an obstacle to digital trade, by sector and firm size

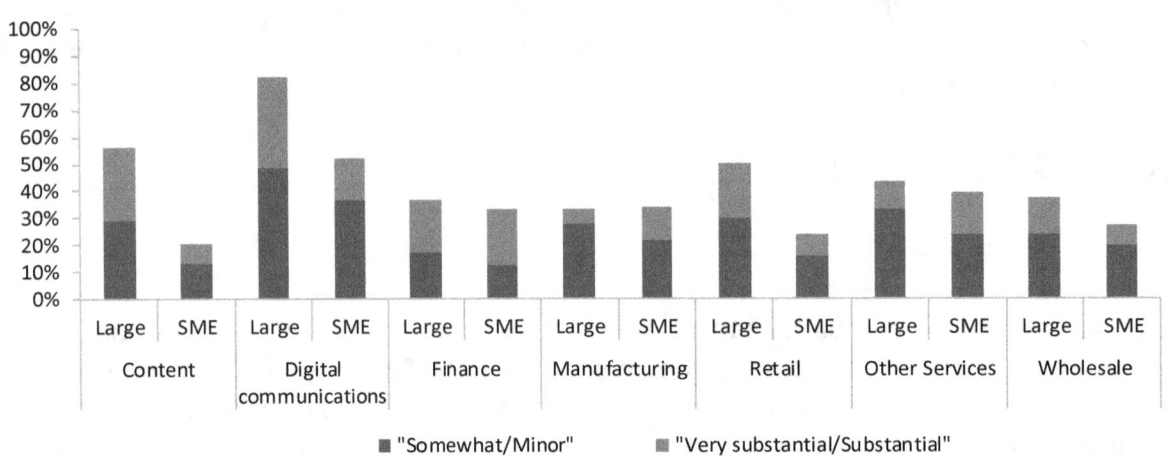

Source: USITC calculations of weighted responses to the Commission questionnaire (question 5.1).

localization to be a more substantial obstacle than those in finance, manufacturing, services, and wholesale.[136]

Across all sectors, large firms and SMEs felt that China and the EU were two of the top three locations where they experienced localization barriers. Large firms also identified Brazil, while SMEs identified Canada, as top locations for these barriers (table 4.4). The qualitative evidence described below sheds light on these survey results.

---

[136] SMEs had lower variance in their responses than large firms.

Table 4.4 Top locations where firms perceived that obstacles limited doing business online

Obstacle	Large firms Country (top 3 descending)	SMEs Country (top 3 descending)
Localization requirements	China	Canada
	EU	EU
	Brazil	China
Market access limitations	China	China
	Brazil	Canada
	EU	Mexico
Data privacy and protection requirements	EU	Canada
	China	China
	Canada	EU
IPR infringement	China	China
	EU	Canada
	Russia	Mexico
Uncertain legal liability	China	China
	EU	EU
	Brazil	Canada
Censorship	China	China
	EU	Canada
	Russia	EU
Compliance with customs requirements	China	Canada
	EU	Mexico
	Brazil	EU

Source: USITC calculations of weighted responses to the Commission questionnaire (question 5.2).

Concerns about Requirements for the Local Storage of Data or Local Servers

In follow-up interviews, firms across sectors reported substantial concerns about laws requiring that servers or certain types of data be located in-country.[137] Large firms, in particular, raised concerns about Brazil's consideration of legislation that would have required Internet companies to store local users' data within the country.[138] Firms also noted concerns about the difficulties of complying with local data-storage requirements proposed or in place in India, China, Malaysia, Taiwan, and Vietnam.[139] Firms further reported concerns about laws requiring that certain personal data be stored and accessed only in Canada, as well as other localization issues there.[140]

---

[137] Industry representatives, telephone interviews by USITC staff, March 10, 18, 19, and 20, and April 23, 2014; industry representative, email message to USITC staff, April 3, 2014; industry representatives, interviews by USITC staff, May 2, 2014. See also Chander and Le, "Breaking the Web," March 2014, 4.

[138] Industry representatives also expressed relief when this particular language was withdrawn in March of 2014. Industry representatives, telephone interviews by USITC staff, March 19 and 20, and April 23, 2014.

[139] Industry representatives, telephone interviews by USITC staff, March 10, and April 10 and 23, 2014; industry representatives, interviews by USITC staff, May 2, 2014; Chander and Le, "Breaking the Web," March 2014, 24.

[140] Industry representatives, telephone interviews by USITC staff, March 10 and 20, and April 10, 2014; USTR, "Canada," 2014, 54; USITC, *Digital Trade 1*, 2013, 5-4. Data protection measures may also give rise to requirements for local data storage, as discussed below in the section on data privacy and protection.

In general, firms reported that compliance with local data-storage requirements can be expensive, time-consuming, and disruptive to business planning and operations.[141] They also stated their perception that such requirements do not improve data security, which is often the officially stated purpose of this type of measure. Firms argue, for example, that data that are only stored in Brazil will be lost in the event of a security breach; however, data that are encrypted and stored based on global best practices are more likely to be secure.[142]

More fundamentally, local data-storage requirements reportedly conflict with the underlying design of the Internet as a "global network for interconnecting computers without regard for national borders."[143] At the Commission's hearing, representatives of IBM and eBay (including its subsidiary PayPal) stated that the ability to move data around the world is critical to the success of their businesses, as well as that of their large and small customers.[144] Moreover, companies that rely on the Internet have developed a host of new business models premised on the rapid and efficient movement of data across borders, subject to reasonable security and access controls.[145] The Internet of Things, for example, is premised on communications moving between devices or machines located anywhere in the world, with the goal of optimizing performance.[146] According to industry representatives, local data-storage requirements undermine valuable new business models, and can even implicate safety if communications do not occur efficiently and in real time.[147]

Concerns about Local-Content Requirements and Preferences for Local Firms and Standards

Firms that distribute digital content—for example, through the licensing of movies and television shows for streaming and downloading—also raised concerns about preferences for local firms. According to the testimony of the Motion Picture Association of America (MPAA),

---

[141] One study finds that it is more expensive to build a data center in Brazil (about $61 million on average) than in other Western Hemisphere countries, including the United States ($43 million) and Chile ($51 million). Moreover, operating a center in Brazil reportedly is more expensive as well because of high electricity costs and taxes. Chander and Le, "Breaking the Web," March 2014, 36–37; see also industry representatives, telephone interviews by USITC staff, March 20, April 1, and April 23, 2014; and industry representatives, interviews by USITC staff, San Francisco, May 1, 2014.

[142] Industry representative, telephone interview by USITC staff, March 20, 2014; industry representatives, interviews by USITC staff, May 2, 2014; Chander and Le, "Breaking the Web," March 2014, 32.

[143] Chander and Le, "Breaking the Web," March 2014, 4; see also industry representatives, interviews by USITC staff, May 2, 2014.

[144] USITC hearing transcript, September 25, 2013, 41 (testimony of Anick Fortin-Cousens, IBM Corporation) and 236 (testimony of David London, eBay).

[145] Industry representatives, telephone interviews by USITC staff, March 10 and 18, 2014.

[146] Similarly, "location independence" reportedly is a core aspect of cloud computing. Berry and Reisman, "Policy Challenges," May 2012, 18 (citing Mell and Grance, "The NIST Definition of Cloud Computing," September 2011). For additional information on the Internet of Things, see USITC, *Digital Trade 1*, 2013, box 3.1, 3-6.

[147] For example, a cross-country Boeing 737 flight reportedly generates many terabytes of data, which are used to monitor, analyze, and improve aircraft performance. National Board of Trade, "No Transfer, No Trade," January 2014, 11; industry representatives, telephone interviews by USITC staff, March 10 and 18, 2014. The Internet of Things, as well as some of the challenges associated with data security, is discussed in more detail in chapter 5.

local-content requirements or quotas initially arose in the physical marketplace in order to support local cultural interests, given that countries had only a limited number of screens, channels, and viewing hours. Such measures are less relevant in the online marketplace, where "shelf space" is essentially unlimited.[148] Notwithstanding, industry representatives noted that in developing and developed countries alike, including Brazil, China, France, and Canada, these types of restrictions are impeding online business.[149]

Firms also reported that government procurement preferences and other support for local firms may be localization barriers to international digital trade. Firms in the digital communications sector, for example, noted the difficulty of competing with large players in China, which receive substantial support from the government and from domestic banks and, thus, are able to offer their product at very low prices.[150] Brazil, India, and China also reportedly have government procurement preferences in place for firms in the information and communications technology (ICT) sector with indigenously developed technology. These preferences, too, are believed to affect foreign firms' ability to compete in the market.[151]

Firms further noted that countries can implicitly require local content by modifying technical requirements and standards to preserve markets for domestic firms; Japan and China were cited as examples of this type of localization barrier.[152] Requirements in India for duplicative in-country certification of the electronics devices that online retailers offer for sale also were identified as localization barriers.[153]

Concerns about Conflicting Financial and Payment Processing Regulations

Firms across industry sectors also raised concerns about the difficulty of complying with conflicting financial regulations, citing these, too, as a type of localization barrier.[154] In the highly regulated finance and insurance sectors, for example, firms noted that even within the United States, federal and state limits on the scope of their online and offline activities are substantial; simply serving U.S. customers who do business or travel abroad can raise even

---

[148] USITC hearing transcript, September 25, 2013, 209–10 (testimony of John McCoskey, MPAA); industry representative, telephone interview by USITC staff, March 20, 2014; and industry representatives, interviews by USITC staff, Los Angeles, CA, June 4, 2014.

[149] Industry representative, telephone interview by USITC staff, March 20, 2014; USITC hearing transcript, September 25, 2013, 209–10 (testimony of John McCoskey, MPAA); MPAA, "Comments," October 22, 2013.

[150] Industry representatives, telephone interviews by USITC staff, March 10 and April 3, 2014; Ragland et al., "Red Cloud Rising," March 22, 2014, 26 (the presence of Chinese national champion corporations in the cloud computing area may put foreign firms at a competitive disadvantage).

[151] USTR, "Brazil," "India," and "China," 2014; BSA I The Software Alliance, "Powering the Digital Economy," January 2014, 6–7.

[152] Industry representative, telephone interview by USITC staff, March 10 and 20, 2014; industry representatives, interviews by USITC staff, May 2, 2014; and BSA I The Software Alliance, "Powering the Digital Economy," January 2014, 6–7.

[153] Industry representative, telephone interview by USITC staff, March 19, 2014; and BSA I The Software Alliance, "Powering the Digital Economy," January 2014, 6–7.

[154] Industry representatives, telephone interviews by USITC staff, March 10 and April 1 and 3, 2014.

more difficult compliance challenges.[155] Taking the additional step of reaching out to foreign customers increases regulatory complexity to a degree that is generally feasible for only the very largest entities in these sectors to deal with, according to industry representatives.[156]

Similarly, firms in sectors that rely on cross-border financial transactions, including those in the digital communications and wholesale and retail trade sectors, noted the costs and difficulties inherent in measures that require a local presence for payment processing.[157] Taiwan, Turkey, China, and India were cited as examples of markets with difficult local-presence requirements for payments.[158] One firm noted that setting up a local entity to process payments in India, and then complying with related local tax and accounting issues, took more than a year.[159] As eBay stated at the Commission's hearing: when sellers and merchants are required to maintain a physical presence for payment processing, it is a "big obstacle" to online trading.[160]

Market Access Limitations

Survey Results

Firms view market access limitations to digital trade differently depending on sector and firm size, as shown in figure 4.2. Seventy-five percent of large firms and 44 percent of SMEs in the digital communications sector viewed market access limitations as an obstacle to digital trade. The businesses most commonly indicating market access limitations as "substantial or very substantial" barriers were large wholesale firms (24 percent) and SME finance firms (23 percent). Seventeen percent of large digital communications firms viewed market access limitations as a "substantial or very substantial" barrier, along with 16 percent of large retail firms and 14 percent of large finance firms. Fifteen percent of SME digital communications firms believed market access limitations are "substantial or very substantial" barriers to trade, as did 10 percent of SME services firms.

---

[155] For example, U.S. anti-money-laundering requirements that financial institutions "know their customers" and track movements of monies are complex when multiple countries are involved. Industry representative, telephone interview by USITC staff, March 28, 2014.

[156] Industry representative, telephone interviews by USITC staff, March 28 and April 23, 2014; see also Commission questionnaire, narrative responses to question 5.1(8) (other).

[157] Industry representatives, telephone interviews by USITC staff, March 10 and 18, and April 1, 2014. The ease of online payment processing also is an important facilitator of SME trade. See chapter 5 of this report ("Facilitating SME Trade").

[158] Industry representatives, telephone interviews by USITC staff, April 1 and 23, 2014; industry representatives, interviews by USITC staff, San Francisco, April 30, 2014.

[159] Industry representative, telephone interview by USITC staff, April 1, 2014.

[160] USITC hearing transcript, September 25, 2013, 241 (testimony of David London, eBay). Localization requirements overlap with market access limitations, particularly in the area of restrictions on foreign direct investment (FDI), as set forth in the following section.

Figure 4.2 Firms' perceptions that market access limitations present an obstacle to digital trade, by sector and firm size

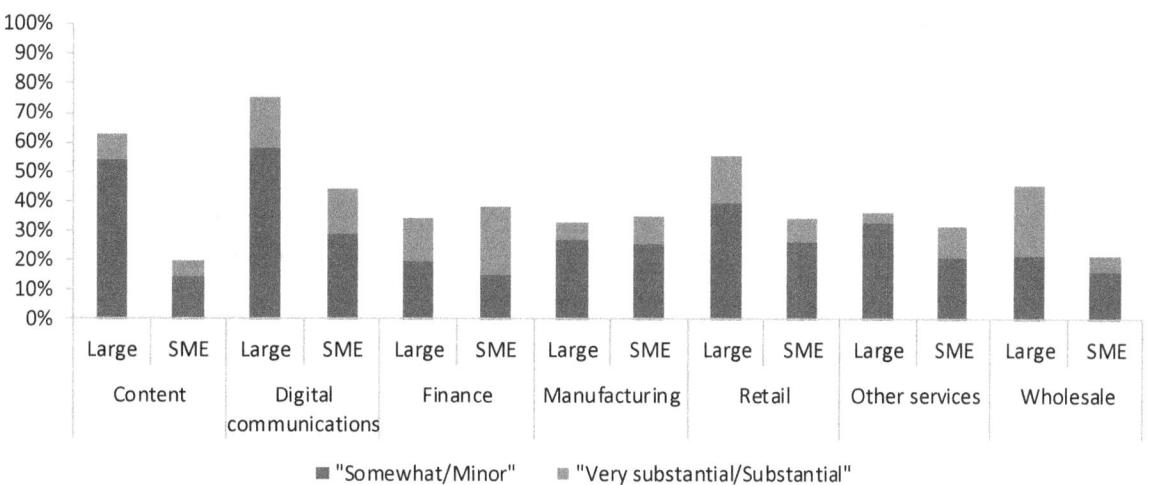

Source: USITC calculations of weighted responses to the Commission questionnaire (question 5.1).

Estimated mean ratings of market access limitations ranged from "minor obstacle" to "somewhat of an obstacle" for large firms while SME means all were in the "minor obstacle" range.[161] There were significant differences in ratings between large and small firms in different sectors. For example, in the content and digital communications sectors, large firms believed that market access limitations were a greater obstacle than SME firms did. Within large firms, those in the digital communications and content sectors tended to view market access limitations as a greater obstacle than those in the manufacturing and other services sectors.

Across all sectors, large firms and SMEs believed that China was the world's top location for market access barriers. Large firms also identified Brazil and the EU, and SMEs listed Canada and Mexico, as top locations for market access barriers (table 4.4).

Particular Concern about Market Access Barriers in China

U.S. industry and government representatives describe market access limits as substantial obstacles to digital trade, particularly those in China.[162] A December 2013 report issued by USTR said that "China's Internet regulatory regime is restrictive and non-transparent and impacts a broad range of commercial services activities conducted via the Internet."[163] The report noted that China is rapidly developing a wide range of online businesses, including retail websites, search engines, online advertisements, audio-video services, Web domain

---

[161] See appendix G, table G.43.

[162] Industry representatives, telephone interviews by USITC staff, March 20, April 10 and 23, 2014; and USTR, "2013 USTR Report to Congress," December 2013, 129.

[163] USTR, "2013 USTR Report to Congress," December 2013, 129.

registration, electronic trading, and online gaming, but characterized the Chinese market as dominated by domestic firms, due mostly to restrictions imposed on foreign companies' activities.[164]

Similarly, representatives of large firms in the digital communications, retail, and wholesale trade sectors told the Commission that foreign companies generally are not able to obtain Internet service provider (ISP) licenses in China, but must instead partner with a domestic company holding a license. [165] This, some said, raises intellectual property and other operational concerns. Firms that operate in China through local partners also expressed concerns about the opacity of the governing rules, and said that "it doesn't take much to get into real trouble" very quickly.[166] According to testimony at the Commission's hearing, large, non-Chinese Internet retailers operating in China also have difficulties in maintaining ownership of key intellectual property assets, such as domain and brand names. Instead, they must go through "corporate law gymnastics" to control these assets.[167] As a result, many leading U.S. Internet companies currently have no, or extremely limited, business operations in China.[168]

By contrast, market access concerns in Mexico and Canada, as described by some firms in follow-up interviews, may be less substantial. Some firms noted that they listed these locations as problematic because they were the first countries to which they had expanded (or were considering expanding), not because the barriers seemed more prevalent than in other locations.[169]

Data Privacy and Protection Requirements

Survey Results

Figure 4.3 shows firms' views on whether data privacy and protection requirements present an obstacle to digital trade. [170] Seventy-nine percent of large firms and 51 percent of SMEs in digital communications felt that data privacy and protection requirements presented an obstacle. The shares of total firms that perceived these requirements to be a "substantial or very substantial" obstacle were highest for large firms in the digital communications (34percent), content (23 percent), and finance sectors (23 percent), as well as SME finance

---

[164] Ibid.

[165] Industry representative, email message to USITC staff, April 3, 2014; industry representatives, telephone interviews by USITC staff, March 19 and 24, and April 23, 2014; industry representatives, interviews by USITC staff, San Francisco, April 30, 2014; industry representatives, interviews by USITC staff, May 2, 2014.

[166] Industry representatives, telephone interviews by USITC staff, March 18 and 20, 2014.

[167] USITC hearing transcript, September 25, 2013, 195 (testimony of Lee Cheng, Newegg, Inc.).

[168] USITC hearing transcript, September 25, 2013, 51–52, 195 (testimony of Markham Erickson, The Internet Association); industry representative, email message to USITC staff, April 3, 2014; industry representative, telephone interview by USITC staff, April 23, 2014. See also chapter 5 (case study on the global competitiveness of U.S. Internet companies).

[169] Industry representatives, telephone interviews by USITC staff, April 1 and 7, 2014.

[170] The survey defined data privacy and protection requirements as "laws that regulate the movement of personal data across borders." Commission questionnaire, definitions ¶1.

Figure 4.3 Firms' perceptions that data privacy and protection requirements present an obstacle to digital trade, by sector and firm size

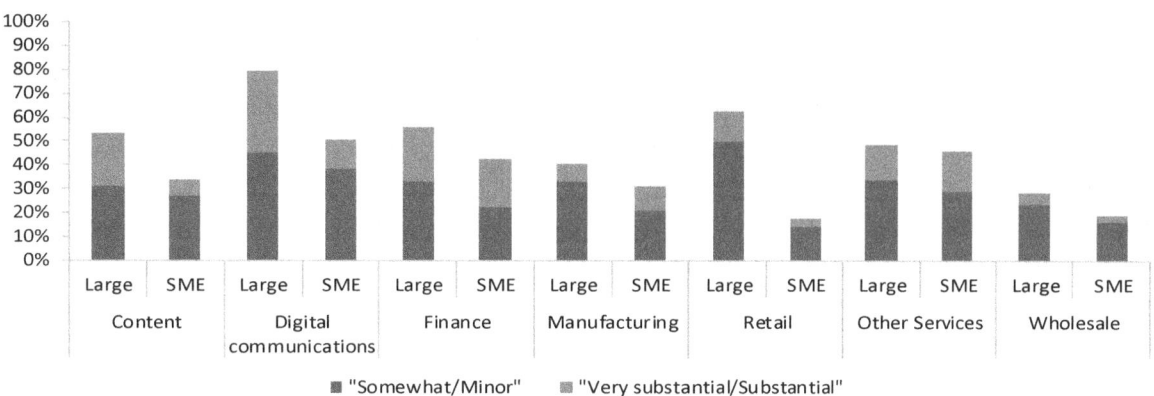

Source: USITC calculations of weighted responses to the Commission questionnaire (question 5.1).

firms (20 percent). By contrast, only 12 percent of SME digital communications firms believed that privacy and data protection requirements presented a "substantial or very substantial" obstacle.

Mean responses ranged from "minor obstacle" to "somewhat of an obstacle" for large firms, and were all in the "minor obstacle" range for SMEs.[171] There were significant differences in views about data privacy and protection requirements between large and small firms in different sectors. Within sectors, large firms in digital communications and retail found data privacy and protection requirements to be more of an obstacle than small firms in those sectors. Within large firms, those in the digital communications sector found data privacy and protection requirements to be a more substantial obstacle than firms in the manufacturing, other services, and wholesale sectors. Across industry sectors, large firms and SMEs believed that the top three locations for data privacy and protection-related barriers were the EU, China, and Canada (table 4.4).

Particular Concern about EU Data Protection Requirements

Firms across industry sectors reported that complying with data privacy and protection laws can be difficult as laws vary among countries, creating unpredictability and extra costs.[172] Many industry representatives state that instead of relying on often burdensome and conflicting legal requirements, privacy governance should emphasize organizational accountability and

---

[171] See appendix G, table G.45.

[172] USITC, *Digital Trade 1*, 2013, 5-8; National Board of Trade, "No Transfer, No Trade," 2014, 15; industry representatives, telephone interviews by USITC staff, March 7 and 18, 2014.

enforceable codes of conduct; representatives also advocate for privacy and data protection requirements that are interoperable.[173]

EU data protection regulations are considered by experts and industry representatives to be among the strictest and most difficult to comply with in the world.[174] Moving data out of the EU is forbidden unless the destination country has "adequate" protection, which in practice has meant protection equivalent to that provided in the EU; only a handful of countries have met this standard.[175] Although the European Commission has not found the U.S. privacy framework to be adequate, U.S. firms that certify compliance with the Safe Harbor Framework developed by the U.S. Department of Commerce and the European Commission, and that are subject to the enforcement jurisdiction of the Federal Trade Commission (FTC), are allowed to process data in the United States on EU citizens.[176] Certain sectors, including finance and insurance, are not subject to FTC jurisdiction and thus cannot rely on the Safe Harbor Framework.[177]

While industry representatives stated that the Safe Harbor Framework is critical to moving data between the United States and the EU, they also reported that substantial difficulties remain.[178] For example, the circumstances under which an Internet Protocol (IP) address or a cookie identifier will be treated as identifiable personal information, and thus subject to heightened data protection requirements, reportedly vary across EU member states.[179] Many firms use IP addresses to keep track of unique visits, to better understand visitors' interactions with their site, or to protect against fraud on sites that include customer reviews.[180] Similarly, cookies may be used on websites and stored on a visitor's computer to enable a unique recognition on the next visit.[181] Uncertainty about how to comply with the requirements around IP addresses and cookies reportedly creates problems for firms in many industry sectors.[182] Moreover, some firms noted that they cannot rely on Safe Harbor processes to transfer data because of

---

[173] USITC, hearing transcript, September 25, 2013, 43 (testimony of Anick Fortin-Cousens, IBM); USITC, hearing transcript, September 25, 2013, 26 (testimony of Jon Potter, Application Developers Alliance); industry representatives, telephone interviews by USITC staff, March 6 and 7, 2014; and U.S. Chamber of Commerce and Hunton & Williams, "Business Without Borders," May 2014, 30–32. The White House also has recently highlighted the importance of clarifying firms' obligations and building interoperability among different countries' frameworks. Executive Office of the President, "Big Data," May 2014, 21.

[174] National Board of Trade, "No Transfer, No Trade," 2014, 15; industry representative, telephone interviews by USITC staff, March 18, 19, and 21, and April 10, 2014.

[175] USITC, *Digital Trade 1*, 2013, 5-10; National Board of Trade, "No Transfer, No Trade," 2014, 15.

[176] The Safe Harbor Framework, which regulates the way that U.S. companies handle the personal data of European citizens, is described in the Commission's first digital trade report. USITC, *Digital Trade 1*, 2013, 5-10.

[177] Alternative approaches to compliance with EU data protection rules include model contracts and binding corporate rules. USITC, *Digital Trade 1*, 2013, 5-10.

[178] Industry representatives, telephone interviews by USITC staff, March 23 and April 1, 2014.

[179] Baker and Matyjaszewski, "The Changing Meaning of 'Personal Data,'" April 2011.

[180] Case study 8 in chapter 6 includes a more detailed examination of the data protection tensions surrounding the collection of customer data.

[181] USITC, hearing transcript, September 25, 2013, 37 (testimony of Jim Cook, Mozilla) ("At the end of the day digital technologies are built around identifying unique customers and unique customer IDs, and tracking those customer IDs for their interests, and using this unique customer data to deliver a better experience"); USITC, hearing transcript, September 25, 2013, 25 (testimony of Jon Potter, Application Developers Alliance) (applications publishers rely on the analysis of customer data from around the world to review and improve their products).

[182] Industry representatives, telephone interviews by USITC staff, March 18, 21, and 24, and April 10, 2014.

customer concerns, inasmuch as strict privacy regulators in some EU countries have found that Safe Harbor compliance does not satisfy data protection requirements.[183]

Firms in the finance sector also reported that European privacy laws can be especially difficult to navigate, particularly since the Safe Harbor Framework is not available.[184] For example, the rules governing the type of consent that a bank must obtain to use its customers' information reportedly are complicated and differ by jurisdiction; thus, customers in some countries may be able to opt out of having their checks processed by service providers in third countries, an option that is extremely difficult to address in business planning.[185]

The differences between U.S. and EU privacy and data protection viewpoints have led some EU government representatives and firms to support the creation of a European cloud. France, for example, has promoted a "sovereign cloud" through investments and ownership interests in local cloud computing firms.[186] Similarly, Deutsche Telekom AG, Germany's largest phone company, is advocating for EU-wide statutes requiring that electronic transmissions between EU residents stay within the territory of the EU, in the name of stronger privacy protection.[187] Information about surveillance activities allegedly undertaken by the U.S. National Security Agency (NSA) has been cited in support of these arguments (box 4.1).

Box 4.1 Data security and national intelligence agencies' activities

Information disclosed by Edward Snowden about NSA activities, and particularly Snowden's assertion that the NSA had obtained access to private user data within the systems of Google, Facebook, Apple, and other Internet giants, was just coming to light when the Commission's first digital trade report was published.[188]

Government and industry representatives, particularly those outside of the United States, noted the potential competitive fallout for U.S. firms from the Snowden information. As the European Commissioner for the Digital Agenda stated: "It is often American providers that will miss out, because they are often the leaders in cloud services. If European cloud customers cannot trust the United States government, then maybe they won't trust U.S. cloud providers either. If I am right, there are multibillion-euro consequences for American companies."[189]

---

[183] Industry representatives, telephone interviews by USITC staff, March 18 and 23, and April 3, 2014; industry representative, email message to USITC staff, April 3, 2014; industry representatives, interviews by USITC staff, San Francisco, May 1, 2014.

[184] Industry representatives, telephone interviews by USITC staff, March 10 and 28, 2014.

[185] Industry representative, telephone interview by USITC staff, March 28, 2014.

[186] Chander and Le, "Breaking the Web," March 2014, 12; industry representative, telephone interview by USITC staff, March 19, 2014.

[187] USTR, 2014 Section 1377 Review, 2014, 5.

[188] See, for example, Greenwald and MacAskill, "NSA PRISM Program," June 6, 2013.

[189] Traynor, "European Firms Could Quit U.S. Internet Providers," July 4, 2013.

Similarly, some business surveys suggested an increased reluctance on the part of foreign businesses to entrust data to U.S. cloud services and technology providers, and U.S. firms reported that the NSA disclosures had made it more difficult for them to do business abroad.[190]

While industry representatives say it is too early to quantify the economic effects on U.S. firms, they suggest that those effects may be substantial. One report projected a loss to U.S. cloud computing firms in the range of $21.5 to $35 billion over the next three years, based on industry survey responses.[191] A respondent to the Commission's survey asserted that its most serious cyber incident in 2012 was attributable to the activities of U.S. government intelligence or law enforcement agencies rather than foreign sources.[192]

According to testimony at the Commission's hearing, U.S. technology firms in the business-to-business area have been particularly affected by the disclosures, including being closed out of new business opportunities at the request-for-proposals (RFP) stage.[193] For example, a recent Canadian government RFP for information technology and email services reportedly prohibited contracting companies from allowing data to go outside of Canada because of national security concerns.

It appears that many factors—including uncertainty about the size and scope of U.S. surveillance practices and how they compare to those of other countries; whether the United States will change NSA practices in ways that enhance transparency and consumer trust; and the impact of technological improvements on data security—are likely to affect outcomes for U.S. firms. One source characterized the NSA surveillance disclosures as a "wake-up call" to U.S. Internet firms about the importance of improving encryption strategies.[194] Microsoft, Google, Yahoo, and others reportedly are in varying stages of completing the encryption of all information flowing between their data centers, and expect to use these improved capabilities to gain competitive advantages.[195]

IPR Infringement

Survey Results

As figure 4.4 shows, firms have varying views about barriers to digital trade caused by IPR infringement.[196] Seventy-five percent of large firms and 50 percent of SMEs in digital communications believed that it presented an obstacle to digital trade. The belief that IPR infringement presented a "substantial or very substantial" obstacle to digital trade was most prevalent among large firms in the content sector (34 percent), large retail firms (29 percent), and SMEs in the digital communications sector (27 percent). Figure 4.4 also shows a marked

---

[190] Kerry, "Why NSA Overreach Is Bad," January 15, 2014; Peer1 Hosting, "The Impact of the NSA," January 14, 2014, 1; Cloud Security Alliance, "CSA Survey Results," July 2013. See also industry representatives, interviews by USITC staff, San Francisco, April 30 and May 1, 2014.

[191] Castro, "How Much Will PRISM Cost?" August 2013, 3.

[192] Commission questionnaire, response to question 3.1.

[193] USITC, hearing transcript, September 25, 2013, 79–80 (testimony of Anick Fortin-Cousens, IBM Corporation).

[194] Bailey, "Google, Facebook, Twitter Bolster Digital Defenses," December 6, 2013.

[195] Ibid.

[196] IPR infringement was defined to include the violation of copyrights, patents, trademarks, and trade secret rights. Commission questionnaire, definitions ¶4. The term "piracy" generally refers to the infringement of copyrights and "counterfeiting" to the infringement of trademarks.

Figure 4.4 Firms' perceptions that IPR infringement presents an obstacle to digital trade, by sector and firm size

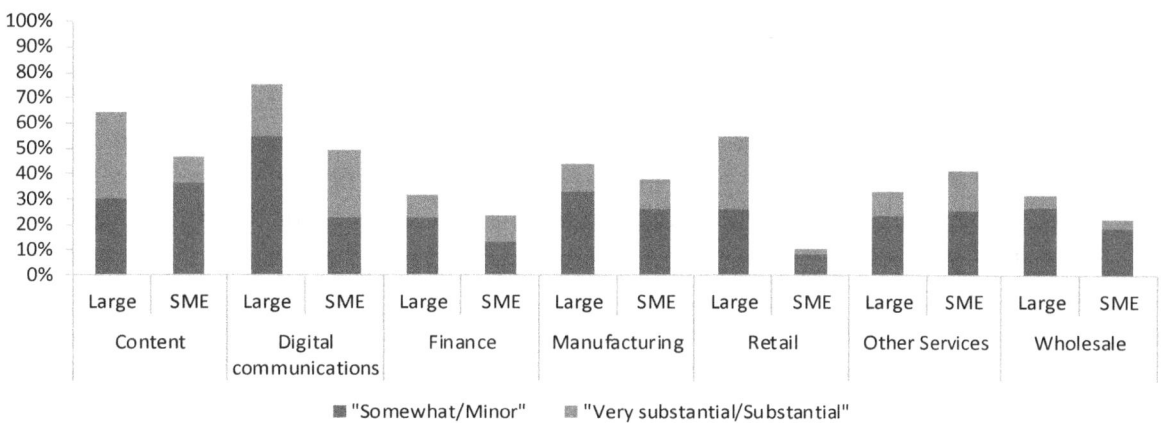

Source: USITC calculations of weighted responses to the Commission questionnaire (question 5.1).

contrast in the percentage of large retail firms that perceived IPR infringement as an obstacle, compared to SMEs in the same sector: 55 percent of large retail firms considered IPR infringement to be an obstacle (including those who saw it as a "somewhat or minor" obstacle), while only 11 percent of SME retail firms shared that view.

This contrast is reflected in the estimated mean responses, where there was a significant difference between large retail firms' mean response ("somewhat of an obstacle") and SME retail firms' mean response ("not an obstacle").[197] Perceptions varied by sector as well: large firms in the retail, digital communications, and content sectors considered IPR infringement to be a more substantial obstacle than those in the finance and wholesale trade sectors.[198]

Large firms and SMEs across industry sectors believed that China was the top location for IPR infringement-related obstacles to digital trade. Large firms further identified the EU and Russia, and SMEs Canada and Mexico, as top locations for this type of barrier (table 4.4).

Particular Concern about Infringement Online

While IPR infringement in general is reported as a problem for firms across sectors, industry representatives noted several widespread practices as particularly problematic in the online environment. These included the copying or misuse of a firm's branding assets—for example, through the unauthorized use of photos and videos depicting the branded product; "cybersquatting" on domain names associated with a brand or firm by persons who represent

---

[197] See appendix G, table G.47.

[198] Among SMEs, responses ranged from "somewhat of an obstacle" to "not an obstacle." Firms in retail believed the obstacle to be significantly less substantial than firms in content, digital communications, manufacturing, and other services.

themselves as partners or distributors but are not; rerouting of legitimate content and viewers to false sites; and the online infringement of all types of copyrighted content (including movies, music, software, and books and journals).[199]

The International Intellectual Property Alliance (IIPA) offered the following description of practices affecting the content industries and their consequences:

> Unauthorized downloading or streaming of a motion picture, for example, often sourced to a single illegal camcording incident, can decimate box office sales and harm subsequent release windows. Online and mobile piracy threatens the viability of licensed platforms, and erodes the capacity of artists, musicians, filmmakers, performers and songwriters to earn a living from their craft. Online piracy of entertainment software continues at prolific rates, facilitated by sites that link to infringing copies stored on cyberlockers or through peer to peer-to-peer (P2P) networks. Book and journal publishers are harmed by sites that provide and deliver unauthorized digital copies of medical and scientific journal articles on an illegal subscription basis, as well as sites that traffic in illegally obtained subscription login credentials, and increasingly face online piracy of trade books (fiction and non-fiction) and academic textbooks. Infringing software of all types is also prevalent on online sites, which constitutes a major source for unlicensed software for both consumers and business enterprises.[200]

Firms also expressed concerns about theft of trade secrets and patent infringement. To protect trade secrets, industry representatives stated that they must be careful about how they communicate sensitive information online to employees and partners in other countries.[201] In particular, firms reported that they take substantial precautions to guard against cyber threats.[202] With regard to patents, firms in the finance sector said that they seek patent protection for their software and business methods, but that this protection is not harmonized across countries or even within the United States.[203] As a result, they said, firms must be cautious to ensure that they do not stumble and violate a patent filed here or abroad and that their own intellectual property is protected from infringement.[204]

---

[199] Industry representatives, telephone interviews by USITC staff, March 18, 19, 20, 23, 24, and 26, and April 7, 2014; industry representatives, interviews by USITC staff, San Francisco, CA, April 30, 2014; industry representatives, interviews by USITC staff, May 2, 2014; and industry representatives, interviews by USITC staff, Los Angeles, CA, June 5, 2014. See also USITC, hearing transcript, September 25, 2013, 216 (testimony of Pavan Arora, Aptara, Inc.).

[200] IIPA, written submission to the USITC, March 21, 2014, 6.

[201] Industry representatives, telephone interviews by USITC staff, March 20 and 21, 2014.

[202] Cybersecurity issues are discussed in chapter 2.

[203] Industry representative, telephone interview by USITC staff, March 28, 2014; industry representatives, interviews by USITC staff, May 2, 2014.

[204] Industry representative, telephone interview by USITC staff, March 28, 2014. Industry representatives also raised concerns at the Commission's hearing about the high cost of abusive patent litigation in the United States, particularly cases involving software or business methods patents. USITC, hearing transcript, September 25, 2013, 170–76 (testimony of Lee Cheng, Newegg, Inc.); USITC, hearing transcript, September 25, 2013, 245, 330 (testimony of Martin Scott, Rambus, Inc.).

Retailers, digital communications firms, and content firms all said that infringing physical and digital products are widely available online, particularly on Chinese websites, and that international sales are undermined by the dilution of authorized brand names and the need to compete with infringing copies.[205] They reported that it can be extremely difficult to trace back the sources of online IPR infringement in order to pursue legal action.[206] SME representatives further expressed the view that, on a practical level, there is little they can do to address widespread infringement, as they lack the resources to go after all infringers.[207]

Uncertain Legal Liability

Survey Results

As figure 4.5 shows, firms in a number of sectors, particularly in digital communications, view uncertain legal liability rules as another barrier to digital trade.[208] The majority of large firms in the content and digital communications sectors viewed such rules as presenting some kind of barrier (57 percent and 69 percent, respectively), though most saw the problem as "somewhat of an obstacle" or "a minor obstacle." Among SME firms, those in finance were most likely (at 24 percent) to perceive uncertain legal liability rules as a barrier to digital trade.

Figure 4.5 Firms' perceptions that uncertain legal liability rules present an obstacle to digital trade, by sector and firm size

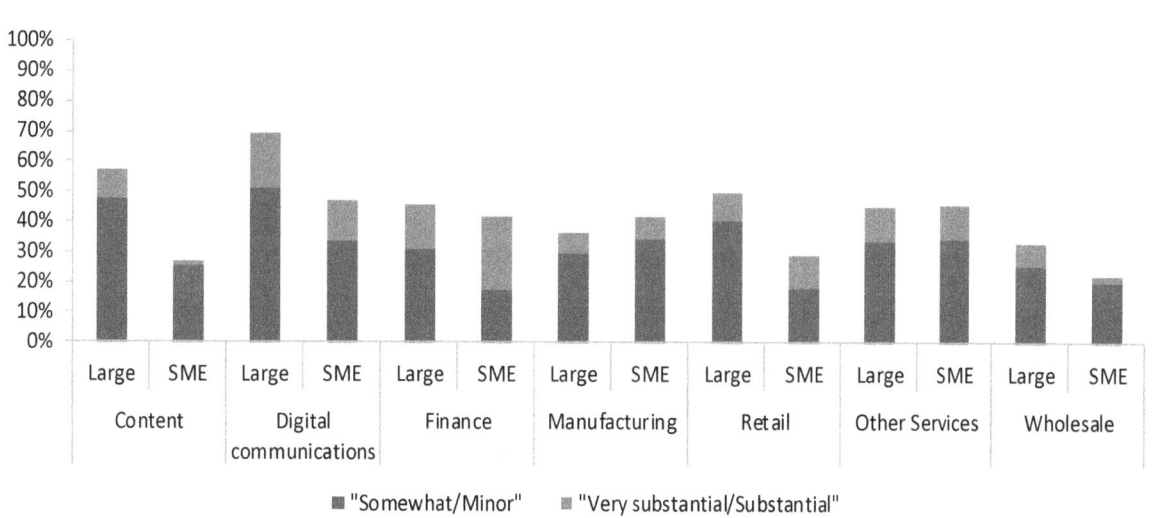

Source: USITC calculations of weighted responses to the Commission questionnaire (question 5.1).

---

[205] Industry representatives, telephone interviews by USITC staff, March 19, 24, and 26, 2014; industry representatives, interviews by USITC staff, May 2, 2014.
[206] Industry representative, telephone interview by USITC staff, March 27, 2014.
[207] Industry representative, telephone interview by USITC staff, March 24 and 26, 2014.
[208] This potential barrier was not defined in the questionnaire.

The mean response for large firms across all sectors, with the exception of digital communications, and for SMEs across all sectors, with the exception of finance, was that uncertain legal liability rules were a "minor obstacle."[209] Large digital communications firms and SMEs in the finance sector viewed them as "somewhat of an obstacle."

Across all sectors, large firms and SMEs identified China and the EU as top locations for uncertain legal liability rules. Large firms also noted Brazil, while SMEs identified Canada as top locations for this barrier (table 4.4).

Particular Concern about Uncertain Legal Liabilities for Internet Intermediaries

Large firms and SMEs in the digital communications sector particularly highlighted the importance of clear legal frameworks to govern the rights and responsibilities of Internet intermediaries and others online.[210] For example, witnesses at the Commission's hearing described the importance of the United States' fair use exception to copyright liability, which gives Internet firms a legal basis to scan the Web, make a copy for indexing purposes, and then make that copy available for search, all without committing copyright infringement.[211] They also cited section 230 of the Communications Decency Act and the safe harbor provisions of the Digital Millennium Copyright Act as protecting intermediaries from improper liability and providing space for innovation.[212]

Industry representatives report, however, that these types of clear legal frameworks are less available in other countries. For example, firms in the digital communications sector stated that German courts have gone beyond provisions of the European Commission's e-commerce directive, which requires providers to block illegal content when they have actual knowledge of its illegality, to require them to take additional "technically reasonable" steps to ensure that infringing content does not reappear.[213] Industry representatives stated that the required steps are unclear and the penalties for violation are substantial.[214] Similarly, digital communications firms report that unclear or unduly strict legal liability for Internet intermediaries in China,

---

[209] See appendix G, table G.49.

[210] Industry representatives, telephone interviews by USITC staff, March 18 and 19, and April 10 and 23, 2014; industry representative, email message to USITC staff, April 3, 2014.

[211] USITC, hearing transcript, September 25, 2013, 17 (testimony of Markham Erickson, The Internet Association); USITC, *Digital Trade 1*, 5-17 to 5-19.

[212] USITC, hearing transcript, September 25, 2013, 17–19 (testimony of Markham Erickson, The Internet Association); USITC, hearing transcript, September 25, 2013, 238 (testimony of David London, eBAY, Inc.) ("to protect the free flow of information, governments must provide certainty to intermediaries by ensuring that they will not be held liable for the actions of their users.").

[213] Industry representative, email message to USITC staff, April 3, 2014; industry representative, telephone interview by USITC staff, April 30, 2014.

[214] Industry representative, email message to USITC staff, April 3, 2014; industry representative, telephone interview with USITC staff, April 30, 2014. See also Sternbug and Schruers, "Modernizing Liability Rules," July 2013 (summarizing cases in Belgium, Denmark, France, Germany, and Italy, in which Internet intermediaries have been held liable for activities of users of their systems in situations that go beyond the requirements of the e-Commerce directive).

Russia, and India present substantial barriers to access in these markets.[215] Uncertain legal liability can also overlap with firms' concerns about censorship, as explained below.

Censorship

Survey Results

Figure 4.6 shows firms' views on censorship as an obstacle to digital trade. While 49 percent of large content firms viewed censorship to be an obstacle of some kind, large digital communications firms were the most likely to believe that censorship presents a "substantial or very substantial" obstacle, at 12 percent. Only low percentages of SMEs perceived censorship to be a "substantial or very substantial" obstacle. Mean responses were similarly low, ranging from "not an obstacle" to "minor obstacle" across sectors and firm sizes.[216] There were significant differences in responses between firms in the content and digital communications sectors and firms in the finance, manufacturing, other services, and wholesale sectors. Large firms and SMEs across industry sectors perceived that China and the EU were top locations for censorship-related barriers (table 4.4).

Figure 4.6 Firms' perceptions that censorship presents an obstacle to digital trade, by sector and firm size

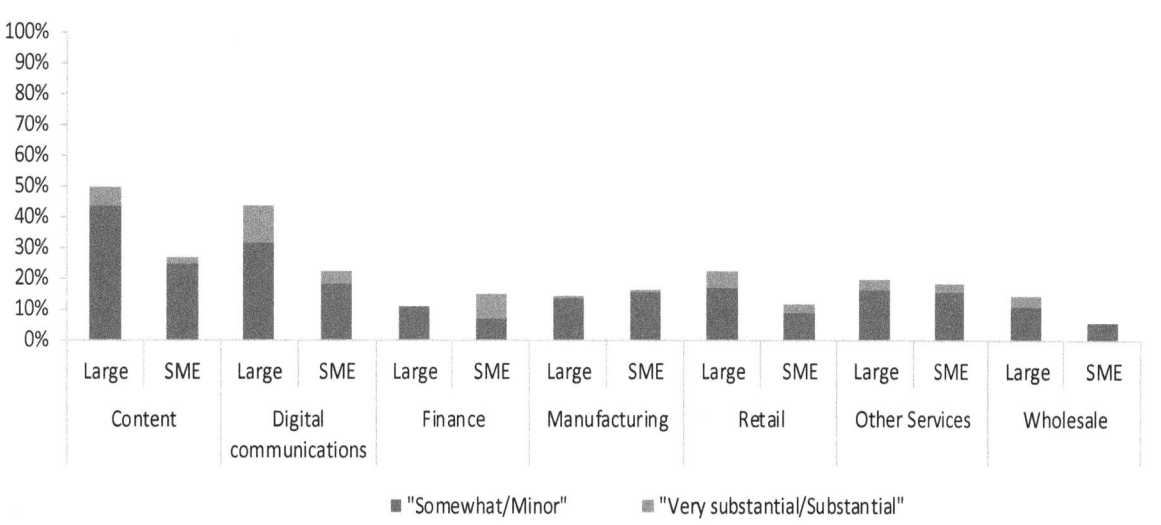

Source: USITC calculations of weighted responses to the Commission questionnaire (question 5.1).

---

[215] Industry representatives, telephone interviews by USITC staff, March 19, April 10 and 23, 2014); industry representative, email message to USITC staff, April 3, 2014.
[216] See appendix G, table G.51.

Chinese Censorship Practices Considered Particularly Problematic

The *Digital Trade 1* report described a variety of methods reportedly used by the Chinese government to control online information, and also highlighted the censorship of Internet tools and content in other countries.[217] In this investigation, industry representatives added to this information. For example, they noted that Chinese authorities have a history of using technical means to block content, including blocking sites by IP address, blocking and filtering URL and search engine results, and blocking virtual private networks.[218] Industry representatives assert that although targeted content has included political content, pornography, and some social networking sites, the rules are opaque.[219] They report that the lack of clarity in the censorship rules is sometimes used against foreign firms and to the advantage of domestic ones.[220] Moreover, although China has blocked many popular English sites and services over the years—including the *New York Times*, Bloomberg, *The Guardian,* Facebook, Picasa, Twitter, Tumblr, Google+, Foursquare, Hulu, YouTube, Dropbox, LinkedIn, and Slideshare[221]—more recently, industry representatives have noted a tendency of the "Great Firewall" to slow down or degrade some foreign services rather than block them outright.[222]

While China was the location that many firms cited as posing the most serious barriers, firms also listed other countries, including Russia, Saudi Arabia, Egypt, Turkey, Vietnam, and the United Arab Emirates, as imposing substantial censorship-related barriers.[223] Several firms also cited a strong privacy focus in Germany and other EU countries as a problem. Privacy rules may require Internet intermediaries to take down content that might affect the reputation of an individual or business, including content that would be protected as free speech in the United States.[224]

---

[217] USITC, *Digital Trade 1*, 2013, 5-20 to 5-22.

[218] Industry representative, email message to USITC staff, April 3, 2014.

[219] Industry representative, telephone interview by USITC staff, March 18 and 19, 2014; industry representative, email message to USITC staff, April 3, 2014.

[220] Industry representatives, telephone interviews by USITC staff, March 18 and 19, 2014; industry representatives, interviews by USITC staff, May 2, 2014.

[221] Freedom House, "China," 2013; Whatblocked.com website, http://whatblocked.com/ (accessed April 17, 2014).

[222] Industry representatives, telephone interviews by USITC staff, April 10, 2014; USITC, hearing transcript, September 25, 2013, 210 (testimony of John McCoskey, MPAA) (censorship barriers, such as those in Vietnam and China, erode the consumer experience and the competitiveness of the U.S. industry).

[223] Industry representatives, telephone interviews by USITC staff, March 18, 2014; industry representative, email message to USITC staff, April 3, 201; industry representatives, interviews by USITC staff, May 2, 2014.

[224] Similar issues are raised by the recent opinion of the European Court of Justice in *Google Spain v. Agencia Española de Protección de Datos*, Case C-131/12 (Luxembourg, May 13, 2014). The court's decision required Google to take down search results containing public-records information about an individual on the grounds that the results violated the individual's privacy rights. Ford, "Will Europe Censor This Article?" May 13, 2014; industry representative, telephone interview by USITC staff, March 21, 2014.

Customs Requirements

Survey Results

Figure 4.7 shows firms' perceptions on how much compliance with customs regulations operates as an obstacle to digital trade across firm sizes and sectors. Large retail firms tended to view customs requirements as an obstacle, with 39 percent viewing them as a "substantial or very substantial" obstacle, and 26 percent viewing them as "somewhat" of an obstacle or a "minor" obstacle. The majority of large digital communications and wholesale firms also believed that customs requirements presented an obstacle (61 percent and 54 percent, respectively), though only 12 percent of digital communications firms and 8 percent of wholesale firms believed that they present a "substantial or very substantial" obstacle. At 48 percent, manufacturing SMEs were the most likely among all SME firms to see customs requirements as impeding digital trade to some degree. SMEs in the retail sector were most apt to view customs requirements as a "substantial or very substantial" obstacle, though at a much lower rate (14 percent) than their large-firm counterparts.

Figure 4.7 Firms' perceptions that customs requirements present an obstacle to digital trade, by sector and firm size

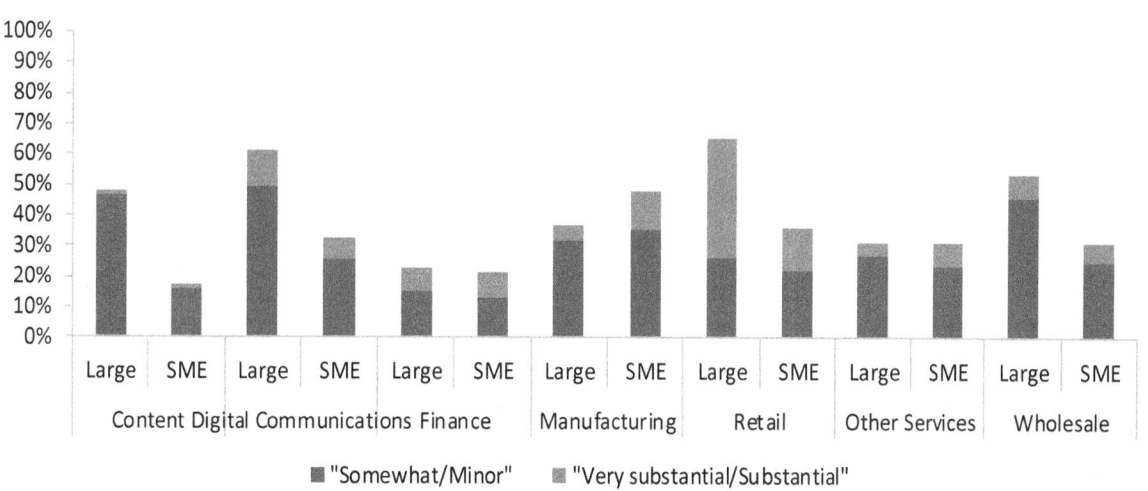

Source: USITC calculations of weighted responses to the Commission questionnaire (question 5.1).

Mean responses varied by firm size and sector, from "minor" to "somewhat of an obstacle" for large firms and from "not an obstacle" to "minor obstacle" for SMEs.[225] Both large and SME retail firms had relatively high means. Large retailers' mean response of "somewhat of an obstacle" was significantly higher than any other large firm's mean response, while SME retailers' and SME manufacturers' mean responses were higher than the mean responses of

---

[225] See appendix G, table G.53.

SMEs in content and digital communications. Across industry sectors, large firms identified China, the EU, and Brazil as top locations for customs-related barriers while SMEs identified Canada, Mexico and the EU (table 4.4).

Lack of Transparency and Low Thresholds for Customs Requirements as Particular Concerns

While the Internet has provided many small businesses with their first access to global customers, it has also required SMEs to confront the often complex world of customs and logistics.[226] As noted in the *Digital Trade 1* report, when countries' customs rules set low thresholds for import values—the transaction amounts for which a firm must file customs paperwork and pay duties—customs requirements can impede even the smallest sales. Raising such thresholds can be a straightforward way to facilitate Internet-enabled trade.[227]

Industry representatives reported that one of the biggest customs challenges is the unpredictability that results from regular changes in rules and procedures and the fact that government actions can be punitive when violations are found, notwithstanding the lack of clear notice.[228] They said that improving the transparency and interoperability of customs processes, as well as postal and express delivery services, could have large benefits for trading firms, particularly SMEs.[229]

Estimated Effects of Removing Digital Trade Barriers

Survey Results: Effects of Barriers on Sales Abroad

The Commission's survey asked firms to estimate the effect of removing foreign barriers to digital trade on the firms' sales and employment.[230] Figure 4.8 shows large firms' expected changes in sales abroad if foreign barriers were removed, by sector.[231] A number of large firms—22 percent of those in content, 24 percent of those in digital communications, and 25 percent of those in the wholesale sector—expected that that their sales abroad would increase by 15 percent or more if foreign barriers to digital trade were removed. Moreover, the majority of large firms in content, digital communications, retail, services, and wholesale expected that their sales abroad would increase to some degree if trade barriers were removed. The majority of those in finance and manufacturing, however, did not expect to see

---

[226] USITC, hearing transcript, September 25, 2013, 238 (testimony of David London, eBAY, Inc.).

[227] USITC, *Digital Trade 1*, 2013, 5-23.

[228] Industry representatives, telephone interviews by USITC staff, March 7 and 26, and April 23, 2014.

[229] USITC, hearing transcript, September 25, 2013, 238 (testimony of David London, eBay, Inc.).

[230] Firms estimated relatively minor effects on employment, and these effects are described in the CGE modeling analysis below. Also, firms across industry sectors generally reported that the removal of foreign barriers would not affect their domestic sales. USITC calculations of weighted responses to the Commission questionnaire (question 5.4).

[231] To simplify the data presentation, SME responses are not included in Figure 4.8. They are included in appendix G, table G.54, and in the calculation of mean responses in appendix G, table G.55.

Figure 4.8 Large firms' expected changes in sales abroad if foreign barriers removed, by sector

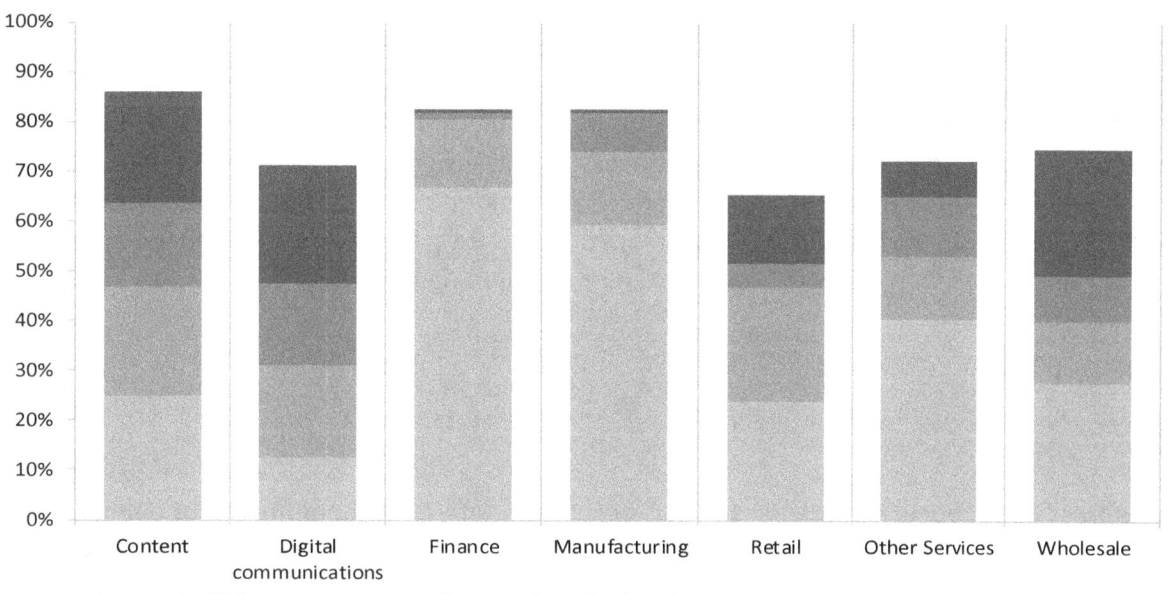

Source: USITC calculations of weighted responses to the Commission questionnaire (question 5.4).
Note: Columns do not sum to 100 percent because "unknown" responses are excluded.

any change in sales. Large content, digital communications, and retail firms had significantly higher means than SMEs in their respective sectors, meaning that large firms estimated that their sales would increase by more than the amount estimated by SMEs in the same sectors.[232]

In follow-up interviews, firms generally stated that these responses were "educated guesses."[233] Some large firms noted that major markets, particularly China, were largely closed because of digital trade barriers and that the opening of these markets could be expected to have substantial positive effects on sales abroad.[234] By contrast, other firms' estimates were commensurate with their current levels of international business. For example, firms that did little business overseas did not predict a substantial change in the event that barriers were removed; rather, they anticipated incremental improvements in the longer term.[235] Some firms stated that resources that are currently being expended to address barriers could be dedicated to new business opportunities, thus increasing domestic employment as well as sales abroad.[236]

---

[232] "Unknown" responses were taken out of the analysis of mean responses to achieve more continuity in the impact variable. The questionnaire defined a range between a decrease of 15 percent or more to an increase of 15 percent or more; taking the "unknown" out of the equation provides a more accurate picture. Appendix G, table G.55.

[233] Industry representatives, telephone interviews by USITC staff, March 20 and April 7, 2014.

[234] Ibid., March 20, and 21, and April 10, 2014.

[235] Ibid., March 23 and 28, and April 7, 2014.

[236] Ibid., March 19 and 20, and April 3 and 10, 2014.

Survey Results: Barriers Rankings by Country

The Commission's survey also provides the basis for a ranking of the digital trade policy environment, by country. [237] Firms were asked to identify all countries in which they have customers and face barriers, as well as all countries in which they decided not to do business at all because of barriers. [238] Table 4.2 ranks 49 countries based on firms' answers to these questions. The countries with the highest barriers scores—Nigeria, Algeria, and China—are those where firms most frequently faced barriers or decided not to do business because of barriers. By contrast, Australia, the United Kingdom, and Italy are where firms least frequently faced barriers or felt that barriers precluded them from doing business. [239]

Estimated Economy-wide Effects of Removing Foreign Barriers to Digital Trade

This final section reports a modeling analysis of the economy-wide benefits of removing foreign barriers to digital trade, based on information collected in the Commission's survey and GTAP simulations. [240] Key findings from this analysis are that removing the foreign barriers would increase U.S. employment in the digitally intensive sectors by 0.4–0.9 percent, depending on the sector, and would increase aggregate U.S. employment by 0.0 to 0.3 percent (or 0.0–0.4 million jobs). [241]

Firms surveyed reported that they faced obstacles to digital trade in many key export markets and that removing these obstacles would increase their U.S. employment. Table 4.5 is a summary of the weighted responses of firms in five aggregated sectors represented in the GTAP

---

[237] The barriers ranking of countries was calculated based on these responses of all firms, not just those involved in digital trade, in order to capture information from firms that were precluded from trading because of barriers.

[238] This barrier ranking is distinct from the description of the results of question 5.2, which requested that firms identify the top 3 locations where they experienced each particular barrier. The barriers ranking questions provide information about all barriers experienced across all countries, including barriers that precluded doing business at all, on a country-by-country basis. The EU was not an option in these questions.

[239] There are various broad measures of countries' digital policy environments. For example, the Networked Readiness Index (NRI) uses data from the World Economic Forum's Executive Opinion Survey, software piracy rates, and the World Bank's Doing Business indicators to quantify a country's ability and willingness to take advantage of ICT. The first pillar of the NRI, which scores political and regulatory environments by tracking laws relating to information technology, judicial independence, intellectual property protection, and contract enforcement, overlaps with the barriers portion of the Commission's questionnaire, although its consideration of political, judicial, and regulatory environmental factors is broader. See Bilbao-Osorio et al., *Global Information Technology Report 2013*, 31. See also The Boston Consulting Group, *The Connected World*, February 2014 (measuring inhibitors to participating in the Internet economy or "e-friction" based on infrastructure, industry, individual, and information-related factors the limit the availability of the Internet and online content).

[240] The Commission's use of GTAP in this investigation is discussed in more detail in chapter 3. However, there are different closure assumptions in the simulations in this chapter. Specifically, employment in the digitally intensive sectors in the United States is treated as an exogenous variable of the model, and tariffs faced by U.S. exports of the digitally intensive products are treated as endogenous variables of the model.

[241] The details of the CGE model and these simulations are described in appendix H.

Table 4.5 Effects of removing foreign barriers to digital trade on U.S. employment in digitally intensive industries; share of firms with effects in each of the ranges

Sector	Employment decrease greater than 5 percent	Employment decrease less than 5 percent	No change in employment	Employment increase less than 5 percent	Employment increase greater than 5 percent
Communications	0.01	0.65	87.86	6.40	5.07
Finance	0.00	0.64	94.69	1.37	3.30
Trade	0.75	1.31	87.47	7.17	3.30
Other services	1.77	0.25	86.16	4.37	7.45
Manufacturing	0.55	1.06	86.00	8.96	3.42

Source: USITC compilation of responses to Commission questionnaire (question 5.5).

model.[242] The table reports the shares of firms with an effect in each of five ranges, based on extrapolation from the survey responses to the population as a whole.

The employment effects in these digitally intensive industries have implications for the broader U.S. economy. The estimated increase in employment in the digitally intensive industries would draw resources, including workers, from other parts of the economy, but may also result in a net increase in aggregate employment. The removal of foreign barriers to digital trade would also increase real GDP and real wages in the United States according to modeling results.

The GTAP model translates the sector-specific employment effects from the survey into changes in real GDP, real wages, aggregate employment, and sector-level production in the United States. The simulations take the sector-specific effects on U.S. employment as given, and estimate the magnitude of foreign barriers that they imply. The simulations also estimate how workers move from other sectors in the economy. Table 4.6 reports the results for two alternative assumptions about the response of the labor force to changes in real wages.[243]

Table 4.6 Economy-wide effects of removing foreign barriers to digital trade, percent change

Economic outcomes	Fixed labor force	Flexible labor force
U.S. real wages	1.4	0.7
U.S. aggregate employment	0.0	0.3
U.S. real GDP	0.1	0.3
U.S. sectoral production		
Communications	0.8	0.6
Finance	0.4	0.3
Trade	0.5	0.4
Other services	0.9	0.8
Manufacturing	0.6	0.5

Source: GTAP model and USITC calculations of responses to Commission questionnaire.
Note: Appendix F provides additional information about the Commission's survey and reporting methods. Estimates are based on sector-level bilateral trade flows with a 2011 baseline, the most recent year available in the GTAP data base.

---

[242] These sectors are communications, which includes the digital communications and content sectors; finance, which includes insurance; trade, which includes the wholesale and retail trade sectors; other services; and manufacturing.
[243] These alternative assumptions about labor force flexibility are discussed in chapter 3.

The simulations estimate that removing the barriers will increase U.S. real GDP by 0.1–0.3 percent (or $16.7–$41.4 billion), would increase U.S. real wages by 0.7–1.4 percent, and would increase U.S. aggregate employment by 0.0 to 0.3 percent (or 0.0 to 0.4 million full-time equivalents).

Bibliography

Bailey, Brandon. "Google, Facebook, Twitter Bolster Digital Defenses in Wake of NSA Revelations." *San Jose Mercury News,* December 6, 2013. http://www.mercurynews.com/business/ci_24672504/google-facebook-twitter-bolster-digital-defenses-wake-nsa.

Baker, William B., and Anthony Matyjaszewski. "The Changing Meaning of 'Personal Data.'" International Association of Privacy Professionals, April 2011. https://www.privacyassociation.org/resource_center/the_changing_meaning_of_personal_data.

Berry, Renee, and Matthew Reisman. "Policy Challenges of Cross-Border Cloud Computing." *Journal of International Commerce and Economics* 4, no. 2 (2012): 1–38. http://www.usitc.gov/journals/jice2012no2.htm.

Bilbao-Osorio, Beñat, Soumitra Dutta, and Bruno Lavin, eds. *The Global Information Technology Report 2013: Growth and Jobs in a Hyperconnected World.* World Economic Forum, 2013. http://www3.weforum.org/docs/WEF_GITR_Report_2013.pdf.

BSA | The Software Alliance. "Powering the Digital Economy: A Trade Agenda to Drive Growth." January 2014. http://digitaltrade.bsa.org/pdfs/DTA_study_en.pdf.

Castro, Daniel. "How Much Will PRISM Cost the U.S. Cloud Computing Industry?" Information Technology and Innovation Foundation, August 5, 2013.

Chander, Anupam, and Uyen P. Le. "Breaking the Web: Data Localization vs. the Global Internet." UC Davis School of Law Working Paper 2014-1, March 12, 2014. To be published under the title "Data Nationalism" in *Emory Law Journal* 64 (forthcoming 2014).

Cloud Security Alliance. "CSA Survey Results," July 2013.

Executive Office of the President. "Big Data: Seizing Opportunities, Preserving Values." Washington, DC: White House, May 2014. http://www.whitehouse.gov/sites/default/files/docs/big_data_privacy_report_may_1_2014.pdf.

Ford, Matt. "Will Europe Censor This Article?" *Atlantic,* May 13, 2014. http://www.theatlantic.com/international/archive/2014/05/europes-troubling-new-right-to-be-forgotten/370796/.

Freedom House. "China." *Freedom on the Net 2013,* 2013. http://www.freedomhouse.org/report/freedom-net/2013/china#.U1E0M_IdVg0.

Galexia Consulting. *2013 BSA Global Cloud Computing Scorecard: A Clear Path to Progress.* BSA|The Software Alliance, 2013. http://cloudscorecard.bsa.org/2013/assets/PDFs/BSA_GlobalCloudScorecard2013.pdf.

Greenwald, Glenn, and Ewen MacAskill. "NSA PRISM Program Taps into User Data of Apple, Google and Others." *Guardian*, June 6, 2013.

International Intellectual Property Alliance. Written submission to the U.S. International Trade Commission in connection with inv. no. 332-540, *Digital Trade in the U.S. and Global Economies, Part 2,* March 21, 2014.

Kerry, Cameron. "Why NSA Overreach Is Bad." *Politico Magazine,* January 15, 2014.

Peer1 Hosting. "The Impact of the NSA on Hosting Decision Makers." Presentation, January 14, 2014. http://go.peer1.com/rs/peer1/images/Peer1-Report-NSA-Survey-NA.pdf.

Motion Picture Association of America, Inc. (MPAA). "MPAA Comments Regarding the 2014 National Trade Estimate Report on Foreign Trade Barriers (Docket: USTR 2013-0027)," October 22, 2013.

National Board of Trade (Kommerskollegium). *No Transfer, No Trade: The Importance of Cross-Border Data Transfers for Companies Based in Sweden.* January 2014. http://172.16.3.34:9090/progress?pages&id=4278491920&fileName=Tm9fVHJhbnNmZXJfTm9fVHJhZGVfd2ViYi5wZGY=&url=aHR0cDovL3d3dy5rb21tZXJzLnNlL0RvY3VtZW50cy9kb2t1bWVudGFya2l2L3B1Ymxpa2F0aW9uZXIvMjAxNC9Ob19UcmFuc2Zlcl9Ob19UcmFkZV93ZWJiLnBkZg==&serv=2&foo=2.

Ragland, Leigh Ann, Joseph McReynolds, Matthew Southerland, and James Mulvenon. "Red Cloud Rising: Cloud Computing in China." Center for Intelligence Research and Analysis, September 2013 (revd. March 22, 2014).

Sternbug, Ali, and Matt Schruers. "Modernizing Liability Rules to Promote Internet Trade." Computer & Communications Industry Association Research Paper, July 2013. http://www.ccianet.org/wp-content/uploads/2013/09/CCIA-Liability-Rules-Paper.pdf.

The Boston Consulting Group. *The Connected World: Greasing the Wheels of the Internet Economy.* February 2014. https://www.icann.org/en/system/files/files/bcg-internet-economy-27jan14-en.pdf.

Traynor, Ian. "European Firms 'Could Quit U.S. Internet Providers over NSA Scandal.'" *Guardian*, July 4, 2013. http://www.theguardian.com/world/2013/jul/04/european-us-internet-providers-nsa.

U.S. Chamber of Commerce and Hunton & Williams. "Business Without Borders." May 2014. https://www.huntonprivacyblog.com/files/2014/05/021384_BusinessWOBorders_final.pdf.

U.S. Department of Commerce (USDOC). Bureau of Economic Analysis (BEA). *Survey of Current Business,* October 2013.

———. "Quarterly Survey of Transactions in Selected Services and Intellectual Property with Foreign Persons," 2011. http://www.bea.gov/surveys/pdf/be125_web.pdf.

United States International Trade Commission (USITC). *Digital Trade in the U.S. and Global Economies, Part 1 [Digital Trade 1].* USITC Publication 4415. Washington, DC: USITC, July 2013.

United States Trade Representative (USTR). "Canada." *2014 National Trade Estimate Report on Foreign Trade Barriers.* Washington, DC: USTR, 2014.

———. *2014 Section 1377 Review.* Washington, DC: USTR, 2014. Washington, DC: USTR, 2014.

———. 2013 USTR Report to Congress on China's WTO Compliance. Washington, DC: USTR, 2013.

———. "Localization Barriers to Trade." http://www.ustr.gov/trade-topics/localization-barriers (accessed April 10, 2014).

Chapter 5
Case Studies: How Digital Trade Creates New Opportunities for Businesses and Consumers

This and the following two chapters describe key trends in the emergence of digital trade, including how digital technologies affect businesses' and consumers' cost structures, purchasing decisions, and innovation, and the extent to which the Internet facilitates international trade.[244] These three theme-based chapters present 10 case studies to illustrate the diverse effects of the Internet on specific industry sectors. These specific industry sectors include entertainment media ("content"), travel and tourism, software, insurance, manufacturing, agriculture, and online services/marketing.[245] In addition, several case studies focus on small and medium-sized enterprises (SMEs). Many of the insights and observations described extend beyond the specific context in which they are presented, reflecting the importance of the Internet economy-wide.

The four case studies in this chapter examine how the Internet is changing business dynamics, sometimes subtly, and sometimes disruptively. In chapter 6, four case studies investigate how industries are leveraging the Internet by harnessing "big data" to derive insights that improve products, services, and production processes across industries. In chapter 7, the international component of digital trade is considered, with two case studies illustrating how the Internet is facilitating foreign direct investment and cross-border trade.[246] Together, these case studies highlight the benefits of Internet innovations to businesses and consumers alike, balanced against challenges posed by regulatory uncertainty, intellectual property protection needs, privacy issues, and shifting competitive landscapes.

The four case studies in this chapter illustrate how the Internet has changed the way business is conducted, radically altering some industries and paving the way for new business models and participants.[247] Beyond serving as a retail platform for the distribution of digital and physical

---

[244] This chapter will often refer to "Internet technologies" to represent the types of digital products and services developed and offered by Internet companies such as Google, Facebook, and Amazon, which enable other companies and users to navigate or leverage the Web.

[245] All of these industries are "users" of digital products and services that incorporate Internet-based technologies into various aspects of their business models. Most, with the exception of manufacturing and agriculture, are also "producers" of digital products and services because they interact with customers online, provide online content, or provide enabling Internet technology.

[246] These themes emerged through USITC hearing testimony, discussions with industry, and independent research.

[247] McKinsey, *Perspectives on Digital Business,* January 2012, 8. For further discussion of the disruptive power of digital technology, see McKinsey Global Institute, "Disruptive Entrepreneurs: An interview with Eric Ries," April 2014.

products and services, Internet technologies have created new or improved business opportunities throughout the value chain.

The following list gives examples of ways that Internet technologies are changing the economics of business, and provides a few illustrations of how U.S. companies are applying Internet technologies. The Internet facilitates:

- Alternative methods of financing, such as "crowdfunding" (Kickstarter, Crowdfunder) [248]

- Less costly access to business infrastructure through cloud computing (Amazon, Rackspace, Salesforce) [249]

- Launching of new business ideas through mobile apps (Apple's App Store, Google Play)[250]

- More ways to generate ideas and innovation through crowdsourcing (Procter & Gamble)[251]

- Collection and analysis of data for product/service improvement (IBM, Microsoft) [252]

- Increasingly targeted advertising (Google Adwords, Facebook)

- Consumer-to-consumer promotion of goods and services through social media (Facebook, Twitter)

- Reduced information asymmetries for consumers via online ratings, reviews, and price comparisons (Yelp, Expedia)

- More efficient matching of buyers with sellers through search technology (Google, Yahoo)

---

[248] "Crowdfunding" refers to collaborative funding online, where small contributions from numerous individuals can finance a particular project. See case study 1.
[249] USITC hearing transcript, September 25, 2013, 146 (testimony of Jim Cook, Mozilla).
[250] USITC hearing transcript, September 25, 2013, 22 (testimony of Jon Potter, App Developers Alliance).
[251] For example, Procter & Gamble has a new "open innovation" Web platform to tap external intellectual property created at SMEs, universities, and other research settings, and to coordinate collaboration with scientists and engineers globally. Submissions of innovations received through the platform have been successfully commercialized, benefiting both Procter & Gamble and its innovation partners. See www.pgconnectdevelop.com; industry representative, email message to USITC staff, April 7, 2014.
[252] This is discussed in greater detail in chapter 6.

- Instant access to global customer bases through e-commerce platforms (eBay, Amazon)[253]

The adoption of these Internet technologies has been a disruptive process, causing some companies to contract and shed jobs as they transition to more digitally oriented business models. At the same time, it has allowed other companies to become more efficient, grow, and reach new markets, and still others to emerge as start-ups, entering the market armed with an innovative idea and an Internet connection. The Internet has lowered barriers to entry for a number of industries, allowing SMEs more options and a greater ability to reach consumers. Concurrently, consumers enjoy an abundance of choices, more information about the quality and pricing of these choices, and potentially lower prices due to increased competition brought about by new entrants.

The following four case studies provide examples of how the Internet is changing the economics of business:

- Case study 1: *Enabling independent creators in the content industries*. A key characteristic of the Internet is its democratizing power—that is, its ability to empower individuals and SMEs to participate in digital trade on a more even footing with large businesses. This empowerment is explored in the context of the creative content industries in a case study that examines the new ways Internet technologies are enabling SMEs and individual writers, musicians, and filmmakers to reach their audiences.

- Case study 2: *Encouraging greater capacity utilization in the travel and lodging industry*. This case study focuses on the travel and lodging industry to examine how Internet technologies allow consumers to make their travel plans directly online, working to the detriment of travel agents, but also allowing the industry to improve capacity utilization. The Internet's efficiency-enhancing ability to match supply with demand is also giving rise to the "sharing economy," where ordinary individuals can become product or service providers by renting out their unused assets.

- Case study 3: *How the Internet reduces job search frictions and lowers unemployment*. Widespread use of Internet tools has improved the efficiency of the labor market, often enabling job seekers to bypass recruiters and access firms directly. As a result, Internet use has had an impact on reducing frictional unemployment—the portion of unemployment that is linked to job search costs. This case study includes the Commission's estimates of the reduction in unemployment rates caused by increased Internet use for the United States and other major markets.

- Case study 4: *Increasing collaboration among online services via application programming interfaces (APIs)*. Many companies have embraced models that allow third parties to build upon their core services and software platforms to develop new

---

[253] USITC hearing transcript, September 25, 2013, 16, 147 (testimony of Markham Erickson, Internet Association, and Jim Cook, Mozilla).

digital products and services, often helping small firms compete with larger ones in the process. The burgeoning use of APIs demonstrates how the ability to link simple software instructions from many different sources can facilitate a more collaborative and integrated business environment. APIs enable companies to open themselves up to third-party ideas and innovation, while giving app developers a platform for improving on existing products or creating new ones.

Case Study 1: Enabling Independent Creators in the Content Industries

In the current digital era, there are more ways than ever to create, collaborate, and connect with peers and potential customers. Within the creative content industries, Internet phenomena such as crowdfunding (described below), social media, and e-commerce have altered the conventional industry value chain and created more opportunities for creators—often individuals or SMEs—to reach their audiences. Although this discussion will focus primarily on the film, music, and book publishing industries, the trends discussed here extend to a multitude of creative endeavors that collectively compose the "content" or "entertainment and media" industries.[254] Indeed, the same technologies that are enabling small and independent media creators to flourish in new ways are also enabling entrepreneurs across a wide swath of industries in other sectors.

Increasingly embraced as a common business platform, the Internet is being leveraged by well-established industry "middlemen," such as film studios, record labels, and publishing houses, as well as individual content creators. In fact, more and more individual creators are finding that Internet technologies may allow them to sidestep the intermediaries that traditionally controlled the supply chain.[255] Consumers, in turn, are increasingly empowered to act as curators of content, playing a greater role in determining what content is produced and ultimately becomes successful.

This case study begins with a brief overview of the challenges creators faced within the traditional, pre-Internet industry framework. It then identifies the ways Internet technologies are enabling small and independent creators to participate at key stages of the creative industry supply chain—financing, production, distribution, and marketing and promotion. To facilitate the discussion, the terms "creator" or "artist" will be used here to refer to those producing original copyrightable works, such as filmmakers, musicians, and writers.

---

[254] For a discussion of the growth of digitally delivered content and digitally oriented business models in the content industries, see USITC, *Digital Trade in the U.S. and Global Economies, Part 1* (hereafter *Digital Trade 1*), 2013, 2-5 to 2-21.

[255] In the early days of the Internet, copyright infringement, enabled by the ease of digital replication and distribution, had a devastating effect on commercial content creators and related copyright holders, particularly in the music and video industries. Copyright infringement continues to be a paramount concern for rights holders and licensed digital-distribution platforms, which must compete against unlicensed services. International Intellectual Property Alliance, written testimony to the USITC, March 21, 2014; USITC, hearing transcript, September 25, 2013, 132 (testimony of Markham Erickson, representing the Internet Association).

Challenges for SMEs within the Traditional Pre-Internet Industry Framework

In the past, all three of the creative industries discussed here shared several characteristics that made entry and subsequent commercial success by SME content creators difficult.[256] Traditionally, content middlemen such as film studios, record labels, and publishing houses played a central role in their respective industries, controlling virtually every aspect of the supply chain through vertical integration and sheer economies of scale.[257] The functions of these intermediaries varied somewhat according to industry, but typically included scouting talent, providing financing and access to sophisticated equipment, editing and creative advice, physical replication of creative products, marketing and promotion, and distribution to brick-and-mortar retailers.[258] Effectively, the middleman played a curator or gatekeeper function. Often this was the case both in reality, because the middleman controlled the supply chain, and from the perspective of the consumer, who might view the middleman as conferring a stamp of legitimacy, quality, or talent.

Consequently, emerging content creators wanting to break into the music, movie, or book publishing industries had two choices: (1) gain acceptance by one of the established industry players; or (2) secure contracts with smaller, specialized entities, such as home video distributors, independent ("indie") record labels, or local publishers.[259] Before the Internet, if artists could not sign with an entity through these options, their creative work had little chance of reaching consumers. The high cost of manufacturing and reproducing physical products, and the limitations on time and space for self-promotion and sales, made it almost impossible for smaller content creators to be discovered and reach broad audiences.[260] SME creators lacked the resources of major media intermediaries, as well as their relationships with movie theatres, radio stations, and retailers. Since the physical (as opposed to the digital) world has constraints on the amount of seats a movie theater can hold, a radio station's spectrum and airtime, the room on a bookseller's shelf, etc., SMEs had very few options.

At the same time, the odds were against a particular creator signing a deal with a major intermediary. The costs of professionally producing, distributing, and marketing a creative product—tasks undertaken by the intermediary—tended to be very high compared to the cost of developing a creative idea, meaning that the supply of potential creative works far exceeded the number an intermediary was able to fund and bring to market.[261] In addition, because most

---

[256] Vogel, Entertainment Industry Economics, 2011, 47–49.

[257] Amobi, "Movies and Entertainment," December 2013, 20–21; Vogel, *Entertainment Industry Economics*, 2011, 47–49.

[258] For a discussion of each industry in turn, see Cameron and Bazelon, "The Impact of Digitization on Business Models," 2011; Vogel, *Entertainment Industry Economics*, 2011.

[259] Vogel, *Entertainment Industry Economics*, 2011, 49–51, 114–15; Amobi, "Movies and Entertainment," December 2013, 20–21, 25; Rochette, "Publishing and Advertising," December 2013, 14–15; 30–31.

[260] Vogel, *Entertainment Industry Economics*, 2011, 258–262; Amobi, "Movies and Entertainment," December 2013, 19–21; Rochette, "Publishing and Advertising," December 2013, 37–39; Rich Bengloff (President, A2IM), telephone interview by USITC staff, March 25, 2014.

[261] Vogel, Entertainment Industry Economics, 2011, 44.

traditional media companies depended on "hits" for a large part of their revenue stream, much of their focus was placed on producing content that would appeal to the widest possible audience (or to the "tyranny of the lowest-common-denominator fare"), leaving out most niche content creators.[262] As a result, from the perspective of SMEs with no industry track record or representation, intermediaries' decisions about which creative works to accept and finance seemed subjective and unpredictable.[263] Even for content creators fortunate enough to sign a deal with a major intermediary, the majority of contracts were structured so that artists would relinquish most of their creative rights, as well as being financially responsible for most or all of the initial investments made by the movie studio, record label, or book publisher.[264]

Internet Technologies Are Lowering Barriers to Entry for SMEs

Digital distribution may represent the biggest change to the traditional content industry supply chain, but it has paved the way for other changes as well. Internet technologies such as crowdfunding for financing; social media for advertising and promotion; and ratings and recommendations technology to aid discovery of new artists all represent forces disrupting the traditional industry model. The changes have been characterized as deemphasizing the gatekeeper role of established middlemen.[265] As mentioned above, artists, consumers, and new Internet platforms are combining to function in roles previously reserved exclusively for traditional content intermediaries such as record labels, film studios, and publishing houses.

Financing

The Internet phenomenon known as crowdfunding has emerged as an alternate means of financing creative endeavors, allowing artists to raise money directly from their fans

---

[262] Vogel, *Entertainment Industry Economics*, 2011, 49–50, 365; Christopherson, "Hollywood in Decline?" 2013, 150–51.

[263] For instance, the highly successful feature films *Star Wars* and *Raiders of the Lost Ark* were shopped around to several studios before Twentieth Century Fox and Paramount, respectively, agreed to finance and distribute them. The movie *Jaws* was nearly canceled midway in production because of heavy cost overruns, and the script for *Back to the Future* was initially rejected by every studio. Vogel, *Entertainment Industry Economics*, 2011, 115.

[264] Economists such as Richard Caves (2000) found that only a few basic features typified the organizational structure of all creative industries, be they movies, art, music, books, or live performances. Prominent among the features was the large sunk-cost nature of these activities and the resulting need to use options contracts among the many coordinating parties involved in the financing, production, and distribution of creative goods and services. For example, music recording contracts generally took all factors into account (including issues of creative control, ownership of masters, publishing-rights ownership, etc.), and were typically structured as funds in which a fixed amount was set aside to accommodate the estimated cost of recording and the artist's advance (the "recoupment fund"). Advances may have been, in turn, further governed by formulas such as floor and ceiling payments contingent on performance. Funds ranged from as little as a few thousand dollars for beginners to well into the millions for superstars. In some instances funds served as de facto loans. For example, given that probably fewer than 10 percent of musicians initially recoup their royalty advances, a recording contract is essentially a loan from the label to the artist, who is expected to pay the loan back out of the royalties that are earned over time. Vogel, *Entertainment Industry Economics*, 2011, 145, 265–66.

[265] Masnick, "Nice to See How Content Creators Have More Power," February 14, 2011.

(consumers) rather than relying on large company contracts and advances. Kickstarter, one of the most widely used platforms, recently reported that since its inception in 2008, over $200 million had been pledged to independent films pitched on its site, over $100 million for music, and $50 million for publishing.[266]

As the name suggests, crowdfunding is collaborative funding online, where small contributions from many individuals can finance a particular project. Kickstarter, IndieGoGo, and Rockethub are widely used for all kinds of creative projects, while other sites devote themselves exclusively to authors (Pubslush, Unbound), musicians (Artistshare, Pledge Music), or filmmakers (Seed & Spark). Models vary by crowdfunding website, but most involve pledges toward a stated goal in exchange for copies of the eventual completed work, signed memorabilia, or access to the creative process.[267] Box 5.1 describes crowdfunding models and their utility for SMEs across industries. This model of relying on fans to support the artist leverages the Internet's ability to communicate on a large scale, making it possible to pool many small donations.[268] Artists seeking donations are encouraged to actively promote their crowdfunding campaigns—for example, by reaching out to established fans through email and social media.[269] In addition to serving as a way to raise money, crowdfunding can be an effective marketing tool, enabling artists to build and strengthen relationships with fans and generate enthusiasm and publicity for their projects.

Crowdfunding sites are viewed by industry participants as a "democratizing" force in the creative industries. First, they allow individual consumers and creators to decide which works will be produced;[270] moreover, they give artists an opportunity to present their work directly to consumers, rather than work under contract with an industry intermediary.[271] An aspiring artist is more likely to achieve successful financing on a crowdfunding site than to sign a deal with a major record label, film studio, or publishing house. Forty-four percent of projects on Kickstarter, for example, reach their financing goal.[272] Projects vary widely in terms of ambition, artistic sophistication, and budget.[273] Some lower-budget projects may never have been on the radar of major content intermediaries, or were never intended by the artist to be marketed to a

[266] Kickstarter website, "Kickstarter Stats," https://www.kickstarter.com/help/stats (accessed April 6, 2014).

[267] Barnett, "Top 10 Crowdfunding Sites for Fundraising," May 8, 2013; Kickstarter website https://www.kickstarter.com/; IndieGoGo website https://www.indiegogo.com/; Artistshare website http://www.artistshare.com/v4/.

[268] Knowledge@Wharton, "Can You Spare a Quarter?" December 8, 2010.

[269] NPR notes that for crowdfunding to work, a fan base that can be easily engaged online is key. Kelley, "Crowdfunding for Musicians Isn't the Future," September 25, 2012.

[270] For example, Unbound, a crowdfunding site specifically for books, says it "democratizes the book commissioning process by enabling authors and readers to make decisions about what does or doesn't get published." Solon, "Kickstarter for Books Launches," May 29, 2011; Guardian, "Why Crowdfunding Is the World's Incubation Platform," April 10, 2013.

[271] Kelley, "Crowdfunding for Musicians Isn't the Future," September 25, 2012.

[272] "Kickstarter Stats," Kickstarter Website (accessed March 29, 2014).

[273] For example, musician Amanda Palmer raised over $1 million on Kickstarter, while lesser-known artist Libber Schrader raised $8,000 on Pledge Music, enough to record her album. Kickstarter Website, https://www.kickstarter.com/projects/amandapalmer/amanda-palmer-the-new-record-art-book-and-tour (accessed March 29, 2014); Knowledge@Wharton, "Can You Spare a Quarter?" December 8, 2010.

Box 5.1 Crowdfunding enables entrepreneurs across industries

Crowdfunding is emerging as an alternative to public and private financing for small companies across a wide range of industries, democratizing the investment process. According to a report by Massolution, crowdfunding platforms globally raised $2.7 billion in 2012, up from $1.5 billion in 2011, and were expected to reach $5.1 billion in 2013. The majority of crowdfunded revenues in 2012 were raised by platforms based in North America ($1.6 billion) and Europe ($0.9 billion).

There are two primary models for crowdfunding: donation-based and investment-based. Donation-based crowdfunding is the original model and currently the most prevalent. This is the model typically used for creative projects such as those described in this case study. Funders donate toward a stated goal in exchange for a "reward"—a copy of the product or work once it is developed, access to the creative process, or other types of perks. By contrast, investment crowdfunding involves the sale of ownership or shares in the project, and has the potential for financial return if successful. The viability of this model in the United States will likely be affected by SEC implementation of the Jumpstart Our Business Startups (JOBS) Act of 2012, which allows equity crowdfunding but creates special regulations for it.

Crowdfunding can be used to fund businesses, inventions, artistic works, and social causes. While Kickstarter and Indiegogo are the most well-known for creative projects, other platforms include Crowdfunder (businesses), Crowdrise (charity and social causes), Appbackr (mobile apps), AngelList (tech startups), and Quirky (inventions).

Crowdfunding removes the obstacle of needing to prove a project's merit to traditional investors and venture capitalists. Instead, the decision whether a project is worthy of funding is left to the global community of customers or supporters. A successful crowdfunding campaign can also demonstrate a market for a particular product or idea, reducing the risk for traditional investors, such as angels and venture capitalists, down the line. Such early investors may even be among the crowd, investing in equity crowdfunding projects and providing valuable expertise.

Sources: Massolution, *2013CF: The Crowdfunding Industry Report*, 2013; Ringlemann, "Why Crowdfunding Is the World's Incubation Platform," April 10, 2013; Barnett, "Top 10 Crowdfunding Sites for Fundraising," May 8, 2013; Thorpe, "Where Does Crowdfunding Go From Here?" February 1, 2014; Caldbeck, "Crowdfunding," August 7, 2013.

mass audience. Crowdfunding provides such projects with a financing option commensurate with the project's ambitions. However, while some commentators suggest that crowdfunding is best suited for niche artists and is unlikely to "discover" the next big talent, crowdfunded artists have nonetheless won Grammies, Oscar nominations, and acceptance into major film festivals.[274] Even so, successful crowdfunding requires outreach and hard work on the part of the artist, and may not be a sustainable model for artists after they have reached a certain level of success.[275]

---

[274] Jazz artist Maria Schneider (funded through ArtistShare) won multiple Grammys; film *Innocente* (partially funded through Kickstarter) won an Oscar; film *Blue Ruin* (Kickstarter) won an award at the Cannes Film Festival. Over 100 Kickstarter-funded films have been released theatrically, and more than a dozen have been picked up for national television broadcast. Kickstarter-funded films have represented 10 percent of films at the Sundance Film Festival in each of the last three years. Knowledge@Wharton, "Can You Spare a Quarter?" December 8, 2010; Strickler, Dvorkin, and Holm, "$100 Million Pledged to Independent Film," January 3, 2013; Kelly, "Sundance 2014 Embraces 20 Kickstarter Funded Films," January 30, 2014.

[275] Kelley, "Crowdfunding for Musicians Isn't the Future," September 25, 2012.

Crowdfunding may also be used to supplement the traditional model. For example, Artistshare, a crowdfunding platform designed specifically for musicians, has partnered with jazz record label Blue Note in an arrangement in which fans shoulder recording costs, the record label helps with promotion, and musicians retain ownership of their recordings.[276] Additionally, a successful crowdfunding campaign may prove the existence of a particular artist's market, making a deal with an intermediary, such as a record label, more likely and less risky.[277] Industry participants seem to agree that major labels are less able to subsidize up-and-coming artists than they once were, so the deals they do sign are more likely to be with artists that have demonstrated a following, through crowdfunding or other means.[278]

In addition to crowdfunding as a financing option, online distribution platforms occasionally make grants to independent content producers to help develop higher-quality content or to market that content more effectively. This in turn drives ad revenues for the distribution platform. For example, in 2012, YouTube gave a total of $1 million in grants to 100 content producers to improve the quality of their videos. YouTube has also built production facilities that are available to content producers for free.[279] Vimeo, another video sharing platform, recently created a $500,000 fund to help crowdfunded films develop their audience and market their products, in exchange for hosting the content on Vimeo.[280]

Production

Internet technologies have also affected the way ideas are developed, recorded, and replicated. Most fundamentally, transmission of digital content over the Internet has made high-quality replication of creative works virtually costless. While this development has made copyright infringement a pervasive concern among rights holders, it has also enabled new digital distribution models.[281] The content industries' shift from physical to digital products is effectively eliminating the once-costly replication/manufacturing stage of the supply chain.

Additionally, technological advances in computer hardware, software, and recording equipment have reduced the cost to record creative works, though these advances are not necessarily Internet-based.[282] Increasingly sophisticated software is available both on- and offline to make it easier to record and edit music and video. Moreover, as illustrated by the "blog to book" trend, in which popular blogs are turned into digitally or physically published books, the

[276] Chinen, "Blue Note to Partner with ArtistShare," May 8, 2013.

[277] *Guardian*, "Why Crowdfunding Is the World's Incubation Platform," April 10, 2013.

[278] Kelley, "Crowdfunding for Musicians Isn't the Future," September 25, 2012.

[279] The production facilities are in Los Angeles, London, and Tokyo; a New York studio will open in 2014. Kaufman, "Chasing Their Star, on YouTube," February 1, 2014.

[280] Kelly, "Vimeo Launches Marketing Program," January 18, 2014.

[281] International Intellectual Property Alliance, written testimony to the USITC, March 21, 2014, 4-7; industry representatives, interviews by Commission staff, Los Angeles, CA, June 4, 2014.

[282] Wunsch-Vincent, *Economics of Copyright and the Internet*, 2013. For smaller filmmakers, musicians, and book authors, the advent of low-cost, high-quality digital recording devices, editing software, and inexpensive network capabilities have reduced the cost of production and replication in some instances almost to zero. Vogel, *Entertainment Industry Economics*, 2011, 47–49.

creative production platform may literally be an Internet website.[283] While this case study focuses on commercial content products—books, video, and music, whether digital or physical—it is important to note that there is a vast amount of noncommercial user-created content on the Internet, in the form of blogs, tweets, posts, and social media profiles. All of these were created directly on Internet platforms, and at least some of them may later become part of a commercial product or service.

The Internet also affects the development of original creative ideas themselves by providing the means for consumers, either directly or indirectly, to dictate the creative works they would like to see produced. Indirectly, this may happen as artists use data on the consumption and sales of their works to see what appeals to their audience, and tailor future works accordingly. This kind of data collection and analysis may be easier for large distribution platforms, as opposed to individual artists, but some platforms give artists the ability to track consumption.[284] Indirect fan influence may also result from creators knowing their donor demographic in a crowdfunding campaign. The screenwriter of the *Veronica Mars* movie, which raised $5.7 million from fans on Kickstarter, reportedly made creative choices according to what he felt fans of the television series wanted to see, approaching his writing "as a love letter to fans."[285] More directly, consumer influence on the creative process may increase as artists develop specific works in exchange for crowdfunding donations. For example, a New York musician reportedly agreed to compose a song for a particularly avid fan who donated $1,000 towards her crowdfunding goal of $8,000.[286] Some industry commentators have suggested that reader-commissioned books via crowdfunding-like platforms could be the next evolution in the book economy.[287]

Distribution

Choice, flexibility, and direct access to audiences through new digital platforms have empowered content creators to take greater control over their own products and services, both creatively and commercially.[288] Not all creative content is designed to appeal to a mass audience. While this is a potentially fatal characteristic in the traditional industry value chain, which is constrained by physical distribution and inventory costs, digital distribution has removed this barrier to entry for the most part. Additionally, the growing acceptance and popularity of independent or self-created material on major digital retail platforms (e.g., Apple, Amazon) as well as through specialized distributors—e.g., Deezer (music) and Smashwords (books)—has further expanded smaller content creators' distribution reach. For instance, both

---

[283] *Mashable*, "From Blog to Book Deal," December 17, 2009.

[284] Netflix, for example, did this when deciding to fund production of *House of Cards*—rather than guessing at what its users might like, it used subscriber viewing data to establish that an audience existed. Ernst & Young, *Sustaining Digital Leadership!* 2014.

[285] Faye, "Life after Mars," March 14, 2014.

[286] Knowledge@Wharton, "Can You Spare a Quarter?" December 8, 2010.

[287] Gartland, "Will Crowdfunding Books Replace Author Advances?" (accessed March 27, 2014).

[288] Cameron and Bazelon, "The Impact of Digitization on Business Models," June 2011, 6–7, 21, 47; Bruns, "Digital Distribution of Independent Music Artists," 2012, 31, 45; industry representatives, interviews with Commission staff, Los Angeles, CA, June 4, 2014.

Amazon and Barnes & Noble have established their own digital publishing arms—Kindle Direct Publishing and Nook Press, respectively—where independent authors can self-publish e-books within hours. In 2012, 27 of the top 100 e-books sold (by unit) on Kindle devices were from Kindle Direct Publishing authors; in 2013, 25 percent of monthly e-books sales (by unit) through Barnes & Noble's Nook Book Store were attributed to self-published authors from all sources.[289]

In the content industries, the Internet helps to match consumers to appropriate suppliers, thereby promoting digital trade. Through the "long tail effect," consumers can readily access thousands of niche content products.[290] Because inventory constraints are absent with Internet distribution, the relative importance to industry revenues and profits of the blockbuster hits is likely to decline as consumers purchase a much wider range of content products, albeit in low volumes. The constraint in the new Internet-distribution model is consumers' ability to search for content efficiently, and here the role of the search/aggregator services becomes central.[291]

Given the importance of search costs to content consumers, digital distributors may need to offer more robust and diverse content catalogues to attract users. In the movie industry, this creates opportunities for low-budget, quick-turnaround projects that need not necessarily appeal to a broad audience.[292] To illustrate, the increase in capacity for digital video distribution has meant that mainstream Hollywood studios cannot or will not occupy the entire available digital inventory. Hence, micro-movie studios have stepped in to provide niche content for some of the largest media outlets. One example is The Asylum, a U.S. studio with an output of about 28 films in 2012, compared to an average of 15 films for the largest movie studios, on a significantly lower budget. The company secured several digital distribution deals with Amazon, Netflix, and Xbox (Microsoft), among others, to create direct-to-video movies that parody major box office titles—e.g., *King of the Lost World* (based on the popular *King Kong*). The studio's business model is to simply ask their customers (digital distribution

---

[289] It is important to note that market quantification by number of units sold can provide inconsistent revenue data, since most digital authors are allowed to price their own works. Most digital authors generally keep their prices on the lower end of the range. (In the case of Nook, prices run from $0.99 to $199.99 per unit, with royalties based on the given price; other retailers can base royalties on a flat rate, with 25 percent being common.) The number of units sold may be a more relevant metric to independent e-book authors, as opposed to publishing houses, since many write for a diverse array of reasons (discussed below). Sutter, "Self-published e-book author: 'Most of my months,'" September 7, 2012; Barnes & Noble, "NOOK Introduces NOOK Press," April 9, 2013; *Economist,* "Digital Media: Counting the Change," August 17, 2013.

[290] The "Long Tail effect" is a concept first made popular by Chris Anderson, former editor-in-chief of *Wired* magazine and author of *The Long Tail* (2006). It refers to the phenomenon of a long, rightwards extension of the industry demand curve, as the Internet and digital distribution allow online services to carry unlimited inventory, leading to theoretically infinite consumer choice and an optimal matching of supply and demand. The availability of a nearly infinite range of products over the Internet creates demand for previously unavailable products—and therefore sales and profits—where there was not demand before; and the combined industry volumes from Internet distribution could come to outweigh the volumes for the "hits" produced under the old model. Anderson, "The Long Tail," October 2004; Vogel, *Entertainment Industry Economics*, 2011, 49–50; USITC hearing transcript, September 25, 2013, 34–35 (testimony of Jim Cook, Mozilla).

[291] Vogel, *Entertainment Industry Economics*, 2011, 49–50; USITC hearing transcript, September 25, 2013, 34–35 (testimony of Jim Cook, Mozilla).

[292] *Economist,* "Digital Media: Counting the Change," August 17, 2013.

platforms), "exactly what they want in a film, how much they'll pay for it, and when they'll need it—and The Asylum delivers."[293] The average turnaround time for an Asylum movie is six months, compared with at least a year for a major studio film. Furthermore, the average Asylum film budget is $250,000, far less than the millions budgeted for a film from one of the major studios—and the Asylum movie is entirely financed by cash flow. In the 12-month period before October 2012, The Asylum earned $12 million, which is about as much as a big-studio box office "flop" would earn in its opening weekend.[294]

Marketing and Promotion

SME content creators were largely shut out of marketing and promotion in the past. Through the development of digital technologies, however, information costs have fallen and new value chains for marketing and promotion have emerged.[295] In theory, creative content products are "experience goods" whose yield remains uncertain until they are actually bought and watched, listened to, or read. As with any line of goods and services, prospective consumers devote time and money to gather any input that will raise their chances, for instance, of spending the evening at a good movie rather than a bad one.[296] Before the Internet, this information was primarily available through the sellers of the creative goods and services themselves (movie studios, record labels, and publishing houses) via radio and television ads placed in expensive prime-time viewing and listening hours, premium retail venues, or carefully chosen print space. Although the sellers were providing information relevant to the consumer's choice, consumers also knew that these sellers had an incentive to "puff" or overstate quality at times. While other sources of information may have lacked this bias, they were more costly to seek out or simply unavailable to many consumers.[297] The Internet has empowered niche artists by providing more opportunities to engage with audiences that now demand more control over what type of creative content they are willing to consume, share, and promote through social media.[298]

Social media can be seen as a hybrid element in the marketing and promotion mix. It combines characteristics of traditional tools (companies talking to customers) with a highly magnified form of word of mouth (customers talking to one another), in which corporate marketing managers' power to control the content and frequency of information transmission is severely eroded. Social media is also a hybrid in that it springs from mixed technology and media origins

---

[293] Pomerantz, "Schlock and Awe," October 22, 2012, 50–52.

[294] With their growing success as a niche content producer, The Asylum noted that 2012 would be the last year they would produce 28 movies. Instead of producing 2 or 3 titles per month, they planned to focus on making fewer movies, with some of their upcoming films already slated for theatrical and digital release. Pomerantz, "Schlock and Awe," October 22, 2012, 50–52.

[295] However, greater access to digital distribution platforms has meant that more creative works are accessible than ever before, increasing search costs for consumers and pitting more SMEs against one another for recognition. Therefore, the implementation of effective and efficient digital search and recommendation tools (aggregators) are fundamental to the long tail theory. Vogel, *Entertainment Industry Economics*, 2011, 49–51.

[296] Caves, Creative Industries: Contracts between Art and Commerce, 2000, 189.

[297] Caves, Creative Industries: Contracts between Art and Commerce, 2000, 189.

[298] Amobi, "Movies and Entertainment," December 2013, 8; Mangold and Faulds, "Social Media: The New Hybrid Element," 2009, 360–62; Borghi et al., "Determinants in the Online Distribution of Digital Content," 2012, 6–7; PwC, "Global Entertainment and Media Outlook: 2013–2017," 2014.

that enable instantaneous, real-time communication, using multimedia formats and numerous digital platforms (Facebook, YouTube, blogs, etc.) with global reach. The emergence of a highly educated, affluent, and increasingly skeptical and demanding consumer population has contributed to the acceptance of social media as an information tool facilitating market transactions.[299]

The rise of more sophisticated digital distribution platforms has allowed independent and/or smaller content creators to be discovered by their audiences.[300] A survey by Bain & Company reports that "sharing playlists with friends, 'liking' a film on Facebook, or reviewing a book on Amazon have now become mainstream ways to influence consumer choice."[301] Moreover, it has opened the door to new business models allowing new types of interaction between niche creative content producers and potential consumers. For instance, smaller artists or artist teams do not always have the time, funds, or expertise to make a new product in one go. Using various crowdfunding models, such artists could release one track from an album or one chapter from a book at a time instead of waiting for all the components to be completed. They could gain both a cash boost to help continue the project and a way to build a direct and interactive relationship with their fans through their Facebook, Twitter, or other social media accounts.[302]

However, although the Internet's low market entry barriers make room for more content creators, they also tend to create a cluttered environment—one where effective and efficient discovery grows more difficult as more SMEs enter the market.[303] Hence, technologies that can be used to aid the discovery process have become even more important today, particularly for smaller content creators.[304] Social media networks and distribution platforms are becoming increasingly integrated in order to provide better-targeted advertising and marketing capabilities[305] and more refined recommendation engines.[306] To illustrate, popular Internet

---

[299] Mangold and Faulds, "Social Media: The New Hybrid Element," 2009, 360–62.

[300] Cameron and Bazelon, "The Impact of Digitization on Business Models," June 2011, 5; *Economist*, "Discovering Musical Talent," October 22, 2011.

[301] Colombani and Videlaine, "The Age of Curation," November 2013, 8.

[302] Rich Bengloff (President, A2IM), telephone interview by USITC staff, March 25, 2014; DiMA, "Digital Media," 2013, 6, 10.

[303] Vogel, *Entertainment Industry Economics*, 2011, 50–51; Nielsen, "Global Trust in Advertising and Brand Messages," September 2013, 3.

[304] Vogel, *Entertainment Industry Economics*, 2011, 50–51; Cameron and Bazelon, "The Impact of Digitization on Business Models," June 2011, 6–7.

[305] Facebook, in an effort to enhance its Internet advertising platform, is reshaping its targeted advertising strategy. Instead of solely relying on what Facebook users reveal about themselves on their own network, the company is also accessing outside sources of data to learn more about their users' preferences in order to sell advertising that is "more finely targeted to them." Sengupta, "What You Didn't Post, Facebook May Still Know," March 25, 2013.

[306] Colombani and Videlaine, "The Age of Curation," November 2013, 6–8.

radio platforms such as iHeartRadio, Pandora,[307] and Slacker, among others, broadcast streaming playlists using algorithms based on the users' listening habits and preferences. These platforms allow listeners to create a "seed" station using a favorite artist or tag for a specific genre, emotion, or instrument. From there, the recommendation algorithm creates an ongoing stream of music using a playlist consisting of well-known songs and artists, along with similar ones that are less known.[308] These online streaming platforms have also allowed independent labels to reach audiences beyond national borders, generating revenue in markets where the artist has had no previous physical presence (e.g., CD distribution, live performances).[309]

Another example of how the Internet helps small, independent creators reach consumers is Maker Studios (U.S.), one of the largest "multichannel" networks on YouTube.[310] Maker distributes content produced by independent filmmakers—in this case, short-form videos catering to the "millennial" generation.[311] Maker is unique in that it supplies its content only through YouTube. This relationship is particularly important to smaller content creators seeking to become discovered by a wider audience, because once a viewer subscribes to one of these channels, they're automatically notified when new content becomes available. The notifications, in turn, help networks generate regular views on multiple devices, enabling YouTube to deliver even more content—and more video advertisements. Since Maker Studio's footprint in YouTube is so large,[312] subscribing to one of their channels enables new viewers to sift through the sea of countless video uploads and better connect with the content creators of their choice.[313]

Bottom Line for Content Creators and Consumers

It is important to note that while the new Internet environment may be creating more opportunities for creators, it does not necessarily mean that more will meet with traditional commercial success.[314] The same democratization that lowers the barriers to entry to

---

[307] Pandora's analytical process includes the "Music Genome Project," in which Pandora music analysts analyze the characteristics of individual songs, adding the information to a "huge" database. The service matches song characteristics to user preferences to determine which songs are included in each user's playlists. Pandora then continually refines the song selection based on user feedback. "We have more than 30 billion pieces of feedback from listeners—songs they like and don't like." Ernst & Young (EY), "Sustaining Digital Leadership!" 2014, 23.

[308] Trumbull et al., "Using Personalized Radio," 2014.

[309] *Economist*, "The Music Industry: Beliebing in Streaming," March 22, 2014.

[310] Multichannel networks are companies that work with multiple YouTube channels to assist creators in producing and funding content, provide management, and advise in audience development. Acuna, "3 Reasons Hollywood Is Investing Heavily," April 2, 2014; AP, "Disney's Big-Money Move for Maker," March 26, 2014.

[311] "Millennials," born between the early 1980s and 2000, are estimated to account for about $990 billion in annual spending power worldwide. Steel, "Entertainment: Generation Next," September 19, 2013; Grover, "Disney to Buy YouTube Network Maker Studios," March 24, 2014.

[312] Maker Studios maintains 55,000 channels that generate 5.5 billion views a month. AP, "Disney's Big-Money Move for Maker," March 26, 2014.

[313] AP, "Disney's Big-Money Move for Maker," March 26, 2014.

[314] As pointed out at a USITC hearing, the question of whether artists are better off has no clear answers. Artists have greater opportunity for their music to reach the public and greater control over their product, but the effect on compensation—whether they are "breaking big" or making a living—is less clear. USITC hearing transcript, September 25, 2013, 131–34 (testimony of Markham Erickson, representing the Internet Association).

distributing content on the Internet also presents a challenge in terms of earning revenue, due to both piracy and the compensation structure for licensed activities.[315] For example, the sheer volume of content uploaded to sites such as YouTube presents consumers and advertisers with ever more difficult choices about where to spend their minutes—and their dollars. As a result, the prices advertisers are willing to pay are reportedly dropping.[316] Some content creators have concluded that while YouTube is a good place to attract an audience and build a brand, it is not a sustainable model for generating revenue.[317] Similarly, many musicians report struggling to derive meaningful revenues from online streaming services, even without sharing a portion of royalties with an industry middleman.[318]

The upside is that artists have the opportunity to retain greater creative control and to connect with an audience that might otherwise be completely unreachable.[319] The founder and CEO of Smashwords has pointed out that writers are motivated by a variety of things, including the joy of creative expression.[320] From a commercial standpoint, they also have the unprecedented ability to build a brand and develop an audience via social media that may then allow them to generate revenues through other mechanisms, such as selling collateral physical goods, or even by signing a deal with traditional industry middlemen.[321] Many artists have been discovered on social media and offered lucrative contracts, including Colbie Caillat on MySpace and Justin Bieber on YouTube.[322] The existence of a proven audience takes some of the guesswork out of the traditional gatekeepers' role, and the publisher, record label, or film studio will be more willing to take a risk on the content with a developed brand. The question of whether creators are better off in the Internet era is yet to be decided.

Consumers are also major beneficiaries in a world where small and independent creators have more opportunity to distribute their works online outside the traditional model. First, because there are fewer middlemen, creators get a greater share of per unit revenue when they retain their own copyrights; as a result, prices can be lower and still enable the creator to earn the

---

[315] The ubiquity of unlicensed content puts pressure on licensed distributors to compete with "free content." For a discussion of digital distribution mechanisms for monetizing content, see USITC, *Digital Trade 1,* 2-9 to 2-12.

[316] Kaufman, "Chasing Their Star, on YouTube," February 1, 2014.

[317] Kaufman, "Chasing Their Star, on YouTube," February 1, 2014. YouTube itself generated $5.6 billion in ad revenue in 2013.

[318] Sydell, "How Musicians Make Money," September 26, 2012.

[319] Kelley, "Crowdfunding for Musicians Isn't the Future," September 25, 2012.

[320] Mark Coker, Smashwords, telephone interview by USITC staff, March 7, 2014; Coker, "10 Reasons Indie Authors Will Capture 50%," March 5, 2014.

[321] For example, the Smashwords website candidly suggests that it is possible an author may never sell a book, but that authors should view self-publishing as a long-term investment in their writing careers, enabling them to develop a global readership and leverage viral marketing. Smashwords Website, "About Smashwords," updated November 2013 (accessed March 12, 2014). Similarly, a YouTube representative reportedly suggested that what the online video sharing platform offers is the "chance to build a worldwide viewership that can lead to income from sources other than direct ads." Kaufman, "Chasing Their Star," February 1, 2014.

[322] When Caillat topped 200,000 friends and 22 million song plays on MySpace, she signed a deal with a major record label. Justin Bieber began posting home videos of himself singing on YouTube, leading to tens of thousands of views, putting him on the radar of Justin Timberlake and Usher and ultimately resulting in a record deal. Mansfield, "22 Million Clicks Later," October 7, 2007; Adib, "Justin Bieber Is on the Brink of Superstardom," November 14, 2009.

same per-unit profit on a work.[323] Some online distribution platforms allow creators to set their own prices, or even offer their work for free.[324]

Second, consumers have greater choice of creative content. Most would consider this to be a benefit, though it is possible that too many options may obscure the best works, forcing consumers to spend more time searching for quality content, as mentioned above. But reducing search costs and organizing information are hallmarks of many Internet technologies.[325] Search engines present and organize relevant content, digital distribution platforms may make recommendations based on a consumer's past use and profile, and user reviews and social media lend word-of-mouth support, all of which is designed to make it easier for consumers to find content suited to their taste.[326]

Because consumers are presented with this relatively unedited array of content, they influence more directly which books gain notoriety and success, as opposed to publishers, record labels, and movie studios, which curate content based on their predictions of consumer taste. Commentators have suggested that the balance is shifting towards consumers, who are the new gatekeepers of artist attention, respect, and success.[327]

Case Study 2: Facilitating Greater Capacity Utilization in the Travel and Lodging Industry

Over the past 15 years, the Internet has had a profound impact on the travel and lodging industry, reshaping how business is conducted and enabling the emergence of entirely new business models. Starting in the late 1990s, many travel and lodging companies—particularly those in the airline, hotel, and car rental segments—began building websites allowing consumers to search for travel information and buy tickets or make reservations online. Although these websites allowed companies to reduce costs, the popularity of such sites with consumers, who could now self-provide travel agent services, led to large-scale disruption in the travel agency industry. While traditional travel agents either went out of business or morphed into corporate travel services, online travel agents (OTAs) like Expedia, Orbitz, and Priceline thrived, ultimately becoming the primary sales channel in the travel agency industry. Internet distribution of travel and lodging services also allowed airlines, hotels, and other service providers in the industry to increase capacity utilization, typically by offering discounted fares/reservations on brand-specific and OTA websites. The Internet has also enabled the

---

[323] For example, 60 to 80 percent of the list price of an e-book goes to authors who self-publish on Smashwords, as compared to 13 to 18 percent for traditionally published authors. This means that Indie authors can price their products lower than traditional publishers, potentially attracting more consumers, while still earning a higher margin on each unit sold. Coker, "Indie Ebook Author Community to Earn More," March 5, 2014.

[324] Some distribution platforms, such as YouTube, provide content free to the consumer and generate revenues through advertising. Even distribution models that don't rely on advertising may encourage that some works be offered free in order to build awareness of the authors and drive future sales. For example, see Smashwords website, https://www.smashwords.com/about/supportfaq#pricing (accessed April 16, 2014).

[325] OECD, The Economic and Social Role of Internet Intermediaries, April 2010, 43.

[326] See, generally, Vogel, *Entertainment Industry Economics*, 2011, 50.

[327] Gartland, "The New Era of Book Publishing" (accessed February, 2014).

emergence of so-called peer-to-peer sharing. Using websites and smartphone apps, peer-to-peer sharing companies facilitate short-term rental transactions between consumers and the owners of unused private capacity, mainly idle automobiles and spare rooms in private homes.

Background

Before the Internet era, consumers made reservations and bought tickets for travel services using two main methods: direct purchases and purchases through an intermediary. Perhaps the most common method of buying travel services was by calling (or visiting the office of) a travel agent. Travel agents had access to global distribution systems (GDSs)—specialized networks that link directly to the internal databases of travel service companies. Playing an intermediary role between the buyers and sellers of travel services, travel agents used GDSs to provide consumers with an unbiased, cross-sectional view of availability and prices for a range of travel service providers.[328] For example, if a customer wanted to fly from New York to Chicago, a travel agent would use the GDS to provide departure dates/times and pricing for all competing airlines that offered services between those two cities. In return for their services, rather than ask travelers for a fee, travel agents charged travel service providers a commission.

Although travel agents accounted for the lion's share of travel sales in the pre-Internet era, a small but meaningful amount of travel sales were conducted directly between customers and travel providers. In such transactions, travelers would engage in a type of self-service, calling travel providers directly, inquiring about availability and prices, and making reservations/buying tickets over the telephone. In some travel segments, particularly the airline segment, travel providers also sold tickets directly to travelers in sales offices located in major cities.[329]

The Internet's Impact on the Direct Sales Channels

Following the broad-based adoption of the Internet in the late 1990s and early 2000s, the distribution and sales of travel services began to evolve. Travel service providers quickly realized that developing company-specific websites and selling tickets/reservations directly to consumers let them significantly lower costs. In the airline industry, for example, the move to sell tickets on specially designed airline websites reduced costs for call-center operators and real estate leases (for city ticket offices), as well as commissions and fees paid to travel agents and companies offering GDS services.[330] Travel providers' development of sales websites also benefited consumers by enhancing their ability to provide self-service.[331] Travelers—freed from the need to contact individual establishments or busy call centers—liked the convenience of being able to peruse services offerings, schedules, and pricing and, ultimately, purchase travel services using personal computers in their homes or offices. Over the next few years, travel provider websites became even more appealing and easy to use. Airline websites, for example,

---

[328] *Airline Weekly,* "Changing Channels: Airline Distribution," June 2010, 3.

[329] Ibid.

[330] Ibid.

[331] For more information on the self-service economy, see Castro Atkinson, and Ezell, *Embracing the Self-Service Economy,* April 14, 2010.

began to offer flight status updates, loyalty program redemptions, and online check-in and seat selection, as well as the ability to print boarding passes at home. Some airline websites also began to offer a broader array of travel services,[332] such as hotels and car rental services.[333]

The Internet's Impact on Intermediary Sales Channels

The arrival of the Internet threatened the travel agency industry with redundancy. By 2012, for example, 63 percent of travelers consulted online reviews before booking a hotel, while 92 percent booked hotels over the Internet.[334] Some travel agencies—often smaller agencies that were unable to adapt to the increasing use of the Internet to distribute travel services—simply went out of business. Other agencies—particularly larger ones like Carlson Wagonlit, American Express, and BCD Travel—shifted their focus away from individual consumers to corporate clients. These firms offer customized booking services for the often complex itineraries of corporate travelers, and provide travel consulting services to corporate human resources departments.[335]

While some travel agents suffered during this period of upheaval, others prospered. Since the late 1990s, OTAs like Expedia, Priceline.com, Travelocity, and Orbitz,[336] which predominantly interact with customers through dedicated travel websites, have taken substantial market share from traditional travel agents.[337] OTAs have largely prospered by putting the core intermediation services offered by travel agents online, creating functional, easy-to-use websites that allow consumers to browse and/or purchase travel services at any time of the day or night.

OTAs provide the core intermediation services of aggregating information and facilitating searches by connecting individual consumers directly to GDS networks. When a consumer uses Expedia, for example, to search for a hotel room, the parameters pertaining to city location, price point, and calendar date entered on the Expedia website are relayed over the Internet to a GDS service, which then executes a search across virtually all hotels in the destination city. By providing information on a large number of pricing and availability options, OTA websites reduce the information asymmetries that once arose between consumers and travel providers. Where possible, OTAs also offer extensive information on the services profiled on their websites. In the hotel segment, for example, OTAs typically feature not only basic information

---

[332] Corridore, *Industry Surveys: Airlines*, December 2013; *Economist*, "Flying from the Computer," October 1, 2005; *Airline Weekly*, "Changing Channels: Airline Distribution," June 2010, 3.

[333] For examples see the United Airlines company website, https://www.united.com (accessed April 8, 2014) and the British Airways company website, http://www.britishairways.com (accessed April 8, 2014).

[334] Galloway, *L2 Digital Index: Hotels*, January 31, 2013, 2.

[335] *Economist*, "The Click and the Dead," July 3, 2010; *Airline Weekly*, "Changing Channels: Airline Distribution," June 2010, 3. Examples of services offered to human resources departments include travel policy development, data management, and cost reduction advisory.

[336] Expedia and Travelocity were founded in 1996, Priceline in 1997, and Orbitz in 2001.

[337] Corridore, Industry Surveys: Airlines, December 2013.

like hotel addresses and telephone numbers, but also property photos, lists of hotel services, and descriptions of room amenities. [338]

OTAs also facilitate transactions between consumers and travel service providers by fulfilling another key role of intermediaries: enhancing trust. Most OTAs allow previous customers to write reviews of the travel services that they've booked through the site, particularly for hotels and cruises. [339] To further strengthen trust, some OTAs also verify their reviews. Expedia, for example, offers "Expedia Verified Reviews," in which it vets and verifies reviewers, including confirming that reviewers actually paid for a room in the reviewed hotel. [340]

The Internet's Impact on Capacity Utilization

Many travel services are characterized by "perishable" inventory. For example, airline seats for a particular flight cannot be sold after the plane departs, meaning that any empty seats are wasted. To minimize the losses associated with unused travel capacity, many travel service providers have developed sophisticated inventory management systems that attempt to estimate demand on different days, weeks, months, and even seasons. Airlines, for example, use such systems to calculate the share of seats that should be sold on a flight on any given date, a practice known as "yield management." [341] The goal of these systems is to alert airline managers to abnormal booking patterns, allowing them to raise or lower fares on scheduled flights before any given flight's departure in an attempt to maximize capacity utilization and profits. As the departure date approaches, airlines typically try to fill unsold seats by offering deeply discounted fares via both proprietary and OTA websites. Many hotels, car rental agencies, and cruise lines also use yield management techniques to fill unused capacity.

In the airline industry, one academic study has found that travelers' use of OTA and airline company websites to research and buy airline tickets has allowed airlines to increase domestic passenger load factors, or capacity utilization, from 62 percent in 1993 to 80 percent in 2007, after ranging between 57 percent and 63 percent in the years since deregulation. [342] The study also found that decreases in airline costs due to higher load factors have in large part been passed on to consumers through lower prices. [343]

---

[338] For examples, see the websites of Expedia (http://www.expedia.com/), Orbitz (http://www.orbitz.com/), and Priceline.com (http://www.priceline.com/).

[339] Ibid.

[340] Expedia website, http://mediaroom.expedia.com/travel-news/expedia-overhauls-hotel-reviews-consumers-can-now-sort-verified-reviews-shared-interest- (accessed March 21, 2014).

[341] Corridore, *Industry Surveys: Airlines*, December 2013, 28. Many hotels, cruise lines, and car rental agencies also use yield management techniques.

[342] Dana, "Internet Penetration and Capacity Utilization," May 6, 2013, 2. The authors of the paper argue that the use of the Internet as the primary method of investigation and booking airline reservations is the responsible for most, if not all, of this increase in airlines' load factors. U.S. civil air travel was deregulated in 1978 with the passage of the Airline Deregulation Act of 1978.

[343] Dana, "Internet Penetration and Capacity Utilization," May 6, 2013, 36.

The Internet and Private Capacity Utilization

Internet intermediaries are not only helping travel companies achieve higher capacity utilization rates, but are also supporting the better utilization of private capacity, largely in the form of peer-to-peer rental companies. Peer-to-peer renting refers to rental transactions between individual consumers that are primarily enabled by intermediary companies using Internet and mobile technologies. Over the past several years, more than 200 intermediary rental companies have been established, mostly in the United States, funded by more than $2 billion in venture capital.[344] Collectively, the activities of these companies are popularly dubbed "the sharing economy," although a wide range of monikers have been applied—"the collaborative economy," "the peer economy," "the access economy," "collaborative consumption," and "asset-light lifestyle."[345] To date, the most popular and fastest-growing peer-rental services are those based around lodging and car rentals, with perhaps the best-known examples of intermediary companies being Airbnb and Uber.

Founded in 2008, Airbnb, a San Francisco-based startup backed by more than $300 million in venture capital funding,[346] offers an online platform for individuals to list unoccupied accommodations—mostly private apartments and rooms in private homes—for short-term rental.[347] Using either Airbnb's website or its app, potential guests can browse listings, contact hosts, peruse reviews, and make reservations. Peer-to-peer companies offering similar services include Roomorama, BedyCasa, and FlipKey, along with several others.

Uber, founded in San Francisco in 2009, provides taxi-like services by matching available chauffeur-driven cars with prospective passengers using an app.[348] Users, who must pre-register, request car service by using the Uber app to select their preferred vehicle type, which can range from low-cost cars to high-luxury sedans.[349] After a car is selected, the Uber app then uses global positioning system (GPS) technologies to detect the user's location and dispatch the closest car. The app can also be used to view rates, get route quotes, view the driver's name and car details, call or message the driver, and monitor the driver's progress on a map. Companies competing with Uber include Lyft and SideCar.[350] The automobile segment also includes peer-to-peer car rental services (as opposed to the taxi-like services described above),

---

[344] Dembosky, "Start-ups: Shareholder Societies," August 7, 2013.

[345] *Economist*, "All Eyes on the Sharing Economy," March 9, 2013.

[346] Wilhelm, "After Raising $200M More, Airbnb Built a Replica," December 3, 2013.

[347] Airbnb company website, https://www.airbnb.com/wishlists/airbnb_picks (accessed February 10, 2014). In addition to apartments and rooms, the Airbnb website also features more exotic accommodations, including castles, boats, train cars, lighthouses, and even geodesic domes.

[348] USITC, hearing transcript, March 7, 2013, 334; Uber company website, https://www.uber.com (accessed February 11, 2014). Users can also book rides using the Uber website or by sending a text message to Uber.

[349] Uber company website, https://www.uber.com (accessed February 11, 2014). Uber's car services, which vary by city market, offer cars in five vehicle classes: uberX (low-cost cars), uberTaxi (traditional taxi cabs), UberBlack or UberExec (high-end sedans), UberSUV (sport utility vehicles), and UberLux (high-luxury vehicles).

[350] *Economist*, "Remove the Roadblocks," April 26, 2014.

in which intermediary companies, mainly BuzzCar, GetAround, RelayRides, and Tamyca, facilitate the temporary rental of privately owned cars.[351]

Although peer rental companies in the auto and lodging segments face a growing number of legal and regulatory issues (box 5.2), the peer-rental business model has also been applied to a variety of other business segments. DogVacay and Rover, for example, help match dog sitters and dog owners, while BoatBound facilitates short-term boat rentals. Peer rental sites also exist for tools (Zilok), parking spaces (ParkingPanda), bicycles (Spinlister), and errands (TaskRabbitt), among others.[352]

Box 5.2 Peer-to-peer rental companies: Growing pains

As peer-to-peer rental companies become more common, several have begun to encounter various legal, insurance, and regulatory issues. For example, although most car-sharing companies require drivers to carry personal insurance, and most carry $1 million policies themselves, insurance issues are becoming increasingly problematic. Many standard insurance policies do not cover accidents "arising out of the ownership of a vehicle while it is being used as a public or livery conveyance." As a result, some amateur drivers who were unaware of their legal exposure have decided to stop working with car-sharing agencies. In addition, many insurance companies have cancelled the policies of customers that use their vehicles for car sharing. Although amateur drivers have the option of obtaining commercial insurance, such policies are often difficult to obtain and quite expensive.[353]

Many peer-to-peer sharing companies also face growing regulatory scrutiny, particularly in the accommodation- and car-sharing segments. In 2012, an Uber driver's car was impounded in Washington, DC, as part of a sting operation conducted by the city taxicab commission, on the grounds that Uber was operating an unlicensed taxicab service.[354] Also in 2012, the California Public Utilities Commission levied $20,000 fines against Lyft, SideCar, and Uber for "operating as passenger carriers without evidence of public liability and property damage insurance coverage" and "engaging employee-drivers without evidence of workers' compensation insurance." Although social media campaigns and appeals by Uber resulted in the rollback of regulatory actions in the case of Washington, DC, pushback from city and state regulators remains an ongoing problem in the car-sharing segment.[355]

Accommodation-sharing companies have also run into legal problems, particularly related to zoning regulations and rules for temporary rentals. In many U.S. cities, for example, regulations prohibit rentals of less than 30 days in properties that are not inspected and licensed. In Amsterdam, Netherlands, individuals renting a room or apartment are required to have a permit and to comply with other rules,

---

[351] BuzzCar website, http://www.buzzcar.com/ (accessed April 29, 2014); Getaround website, http://www.getaround.com/ (accessed April 29, 2014); RelayRides website, https://relayrides.com/ (April 29, 2014); Tamyca website, http://www.tamyca.de/ (accessed April 29, 2014).

[352] DogVacay website, http://dogvacay.com/ (accessed April 29, 2014); Rover website, http://www.rover.com/ (accessed April 29, 2014); Boatbound website, https://boatbound.co/ (accessed April 29, 2014); Zilok website, http://us.zilok.com/ (accessed April 29, 2014); ParkingPanda website, https://www.parkingpanda.com/ (accessed April 29, 2014); Spinlister website, https://www.spinlister.com/ (accessed April 29, 2014); TaskRabbit website, https://www.taskrabbit.com/ (accessed April 29, 2014).

[353] Huet, "Drivers for Uber, Lyft Stuck in Insurance Limbo," February 2, 2014.

[354] Greene, "Upstart Car Service Butts Heads with D.C.'s Taxis," National Public Radio, January 31, 2012.

[355] *Economist*, "All Eyes on the Sharing Economy," March 9, 2013.

with city officials actually using Airbnb's website to track down illegal renters.[356] San Francisco is considering a similar regime: it would allow rentals of less than 30 days provided the owner lives there the majority of the time, registers with the city, and pays the city's 14 percent hotel tax.[357] In New York City, a 2010 law prohibits the renting of rooms or homes for less than a month unless the owner is present. Perhaps as a result of these and other municipal regulations, some landlords have evicted tenants for renting their apartments on Airbnb.[358]

Tax issues are also becoming a concern for peer-to-peer sharing companies, particularly those in the lodging sector. In April 2012, for example, San Francisco's treasurer ruled that Airbnb and similar sites were not exempt from the city's hotel tax, and the company announced in April 2014 that it will begin collecting hotel taxes in San Francisco later in the year.[359] The possibility of collecting hotel taxes on shared accommodations has been raised in a number of other cities around the world, including New York City.[360]

In response to growing regulatory scrutiny, some peer-to-peer sharing companies have started to lobby local governments to change what they see as outdated rules and regulations. Airbnb, for example, recently hired Yahoo's former head of public affairs to help it clarify, and even try to amend, the laws that it faces in dozens of jurisdictions around the world. Some cities are responsive to such lobbying. San Francisco, as noted above, is rewriting its city laws to allow accommodation sharing, with certain restrictions. Airbnb has also won victories in Hamburg, Germany, and Amsterdam, Netherlands, convincing local authorities to relax laws preventing owners from renting their homes.[361]

Much like OTAs, peer rental companies act as intermediaries in facilitating transactions between the lessors and lessees of lodging, travel, and other amenities, almost all of which would remain unused in the absence of peer-sharing websites. Perhaps the most important role that peer rental companies fulfill is facilitating searches by aggregating enormous amounts of information. Airbnb, for example, allows users to search more than 500,000 short-term rental listings in 192 countries using either its website or its smartphone app.[362] Similarly, BuzzCar, a car-sharing website, catalogs and facilitates the search for more than 7,000 unused automobiles in France.[363]

Peer sharing companies also facilitate transactions between lessees and lessors by building trust. Nearly all peer-to-peer rental sites, for example, use ratings and reviews—which tend to create social norms that encourage good behavior—to overcome safety concerns on the part of both owners and users. Uber, for example, reports that its review system has the effect of weeding out both bad drivers and bad passengers.[364] Many sites, particularly ones dealing with

---

[356] *Economist*, "All Eyes on the Sharing Economy," March 9, 2013; *Economist*, "Remove the Roadblocks," April 26, 2014.

[357] *Economist*, "Remove the Roadblocks," April 26, 2014.

[358] *Economist*, "All Eyes on the Sharing Economy," March 9, 2013.

[359] *Economist*, "All Eyes on the Sharing Economy," March 9, 2013; Said, "Airbnb to Collect Hotel Taxes for San Francisco Rentals," *SFGate.com*, April 1, 2014.

[360] Carr, "Inside Airbnb's Grand Hotel Plans," April 2014.

[361] Dembosky, "Start-ups: Shareholder Societies," August 7, 2013.

[362] Airbnb company website, https://www.airbnb.com/about/about-us (accessed February 10, 2014).

[363] Buzzcar website, http://www.buzzcar.com/fr/ (accessed March 24, 2014).

[364] *Economist*, "All Eyes on the Sharing Economy," March 9, 2013. The ratings and review system also tends to create a "social proof" effect, in which users or listings with the most reviews are assumed to be highly popular, whereas those with few reviews appear less attractive.

lodging and car rentals, also reportedly perform background checks, looking into credit histories, driving records, and criminal records for both owners and users. Several peer-to-peer rental companies also integrate with Facebook to allow owners and users to see if they have common network friends.

Peer sharing sites also facilitate transactions by helping to reduce the risks—faced by both lessees and lessors—associated with doing business with an unknown private party. Airbnb, for example, does not provide immediate reservation confirmation of rental accommodations, allowing both parties to the transaction to back out based on ratings, reviews, or other factors.[365] To protect lessors, some peer-sharing companies, particularly those involved with lodging and automobile sharing, provide insurance. For example, in 2011, after a lessor reported that one of their Airbnb guests had vandalized (and stolen articles from) their accommodation,[366] Airbnb added a "property protection program" covering property loss of up to $50,000 due to vandalism and theft.[367] In 2012, Airbnb increased its property insurance program to $1 million via a partnership with Lloyd's of London.[368] Similarly, to protect automobile owners, Uber automatically charges users' credit cards,[369] reducing the risk of nonpayment.

Case Study 3: How the Internet Reduces Job Search Frictions and Lowers Unemployment

The use of the Internet for job searches has increased dramatically in recent years, reducing search costs and other job market frictions and transforming a marketplace once dominated by newspaper classifieds and recruitment firms. According to one study, nearly 75 percent of young unemployed workers used the Internet to look for work in 2009, up from 25 percent in 2000.[370] As job search has moved online, recruitment firms are increasingly challenged by a profusion of online employment search engines and social media sites, which have "changed the balance" between jobseekers and recruiters. The variety and number of online resources often enable jobseekers to bypass recruiters and access firms directly.[371]

Recruitment data illustrate how the Internet has become an indispensable tool for jobseekers, prospective employers and recruiters; online networks and social media are now the primary means by which the job market operates. The wide range of job information available online,

[365] *Economist*, "All Eyes on the Sharing Economy," March 9, 2013.

[366] Bly, "Plot Thickens in Airbnb Vacation Rental Horror Story," August 3, 2011. Several similar incidents involving vandalism, theft, and other illegal activities by Airbnb guests were also reported in 2011 and 2012.

[367] Arrington, "Airbnb Offers Unconditional Apology, and $50,000," August 1, 2011.

[368] Ngak, "Airbnb Will Insure Up to $1 Million," CBSNews, May 23, 2012; Airbnb company website, https://www.airbnb.com/terms/host_guarantee (accessed February 18, 2014). Insurance through Airbnb is subject to a large number of exclusions (e.g. cash, jewelry, motor vehicles, and artwork) and is in excess of the property owner's property insurance coverage.

[369] Uber website, https://www.uber.com/ (accessed March 25, 2014).

[370] Kuhn and Mansour, "Is the Internet Job Search Still Ineffective?" July 29, 2013.

[371] Sundheim, "The Internet's Profound Impact on the Recruiting Industry," April 2, 2013.

such as company websites, social media, chat rooms, message boards, and blogs,[372] enables jobseekers to gather information quickly about occupations and firms. A variety of websites such as Vault.com offer salary data by industry, company, organization, and industry rankings, ratings, and reviews.[373] When the information-gathering phase is completed, job seekers are then able to connect and apply to organizations easily and at low cost through online job search engines and employer or recruiter websites.[374] Internet technologies also enable human resources staff and recruiters to substantially broaden their search scope and reduce search costs, as they can filter and process large volumes of applications and other data to find the best candidates.[375] Moreover, hiring managers are increasingly using social media to investigate job applicants, which can significantly impact hiring decisions.[376] Recruiters are also using social media websites to reach potential candidates who are not necessarily currently looking for employment.[377] In addition, Internet technologies facilitate communications between candidates and potential employers through the use of email and social media, which speeds and eases the application process.[378]

The sheer volume of searchable employment data is enormous, and many job search sites have evolved from mere job boards to a source for a variety of career services. Monster.com, the web's largest job search engine, among scores of such sites,[379] has more than 25 million biographies and 800,000 job postings. According to the company, the site is visited by 1.6 million job seekers daily, with 20,000 resumes added every day.[380] While Monster.com serves all sectors, sites oriented to a particular industry, such as Dice.com (computer and tech jobs), AllRetailJobs.com, and HealthJobsUSA.com, provide sector-specific postings and job information.[381] LinkedIn, another leading career website, combines social networking with employment services and has a network of over 250 million members in 200 countries.[382] The LinkedIn site enables jobseekers to maintain personnel files including resumes, work products, and writing samples for recruiters and companies to search in real time. Facebook also has created an employment board where users can search and apply directly for jobs by industry, skill, and location, as well as share job information with their social networks.[383]

---

[372] Ibid.

[373] Vault.com, "About Us," http://www.vault.com/about-us/company-overview (accessed January 24, 2014).

[374] Stevenson, "The Internet and Job Search," March 2008.

[375] Hogenson, "The Internet Comes of Age" (accessed May 6, 2014).

[376] Crosstab, "Online Reputation in a Connected World," January 2010; Hogenson, "The Internet Comes of Age," Hudson, 4.

[377] Hogenson, "The Internet Comes of Age" (accessed May 6, 2014).

[378] Stevenson, "The Internet and Job Search," March 2008.

[379] Hogenson, "The Internet Comes of Age" (accessed May 6, 2014).

[380] Ibid.

[381] Caloa, "The Facebook Job Board Is Here," November 14, 2012.

[382] LinkedIn, "About Us," http://www.linkedin.com/about-us (accessed January 4, 2014). Unlike many other social media companies, LinkedIn relies less on advertising (just over 25 percent of revenues) and more on fees from recruiters (about 60 percent of revenues). As a result of this focus on employers, LinkedIn has recently announced plans to expand its services by listing internal job opportunities at as well as external ones. Albergotti, "LinkedIn Wants to Help You Stay," April 10, 2014.

[383] Caloa, "The Facebook Job Board Is Here," November 14, 2012.

Widespread use of Internet tools has improved the efficiency of the labor market, and the consequent reduction in job search costs likely represents a significant benefit to the U.S. economy. Frictional unemployment occurs at all times during the economic cycle, because workers who are displaced by firms changing their staffing requirements typically search for a period of time before finding a new job in which they are productively employed and adequately compensated.[384] By reducing search costs and, therefore, the personal investment in time and money it takes for a worker to find a new job, the Internet can reduce frictional unemployment and therefore help to reduce overall unemployment.

The effect of the Internet on unemployment in a given economy can be estimated using econometric modeling. For 69 countries during the period 2004–12, the Commission has estimated how each country's total unemployment rate in a given year is related to its rate of Internet usage, while controlling for other country and year effects. For the United States, for example, the actual 2012 unemployment rate is estimated to have been 0.29 percentage points lower than it would have been if Internet usage rates in 2012 were at the lower 2006 rates. The expansion in the use of Internet tools for job search in the United States is likely to have taken place earlier than in some other countries, however, implying a relatively small estimated impact in the United States during that time. Estimates for the impact of changed Internet usage on the unemployment rates of Canada, Germany, Japan, Korea, and the United Kingdom were similarly low (ranging between a 0.13 percentage point reduction for Korea and a 0.43 percentage point reduction for the United Kingdom). In countries where the use of Internet tools for job search is likely to have expanded more recently, estimated reductions in unemployment rates are much larger. Brazil's 2012 unemployment rate is estimated to have been 1.03 percentage points lower than it would have been at 2006 Internet usage rates. Russia's is estimated at 1.97 percentage points lower; China's, at 2.51 percentage points lower. The details of these econometric analyses are provided in appendix H.

Case Study 4: Increasing Collaboration and Integration in Online Services—The Economic Contributions of Application Programming Interfaces

Application programming interfaces (APIs)—links that allow one software program to interact with another software program[385]—have become a widely used tool for increasing online collaboration and integration. APIs exemplify how new online software tools facilitate communication both among businesses and between businesses and their customers. This API-driven collaboration, reflects the surge in use of Internet-enabled mobile devices, social media, and mobile apps, all of which use APIs extensively.[386] For example, APIs are central to the operations behind smartphone apps, and thus are an important technology enabling digital

---

[384] Frictional unemployment is a component of the overall rate of unemployment, which also includes cyclical factors and other structural elements.

[385] Specifically, an API is a toolset of protocols and routines that direct how one software application can interact with another. Stafford, "What CIOs, Developers Should Know," October 15, 2013.

[386] Gat and Succi, "A Survey of the API Economy" (accessed May 13, 2014).

trade.[387] This case study examines the benefits of APIs for the businesses that use them to improve their product offerings and operational efficiency, for the developers who use them to create new software applications, and for consumers generally.

Current APIs are characterized by their simplicity, accessibility, and ability to build off existing Internet architecture.[388] APIs make it easier for software developers to combine data from various sources to create or enhance features and add functionality to applications. For example, location-based services, one important type of application, rely upon APIs such as the Google Maps API for functions such as finding a location, displaying information in a map, and estimating the time and distance of a trip.[389] A familiar example would be Yelp!, a crowd-sourced review service, which uses Google Maps to show the locations of service providers such as restaurants in a given area on their website and mobile application. The Google Maps API, used by over 800,000 sites, enables users to overlay data on a customized map with features such as satellite imagery, street views, driving directions, and an extensive places database.[390] Google offers the Google Maps API for free, but higher-demand users, or those that will charge a fee for their product, use the Google Maps API for Business, which offers more features but also requires a fee.[391]

APIs are important to businesses across a wide range of industries. According to one industry analyst, 75 percent of Fortune 1000 firms will be using APIs in their website and mobile applications by the end of 2014, and by 2017 50 percent of business-to-business collaboration is expected to take place through Internet communications applications that rely on APIs.[392]

Benefits to Businesses from Using APIs

APIs present important opportunities for digital trade for many industries because they allow companies to use existing hardware and software in a wide range of new ways.[393] Software programs that draw on multiple APIs from various websites can benefit from advanced

---

[387] Brecht, "M-Commerce on the Rise" (accessed April 21, 2014). Mobile devices carry people's interests, calendars, contacts, history, preferences, and location. As natural aggregators, they provide valuable context, which can be used to drive better decisions and more effective actions. IBM Corporation, "Global Technology Outlook 2013," 2013, 4.

[388] Industry participants, telephone interview by USITC staff, April 7, 2014. While APIs existed well before the Internet era, they have been used most recently to connect smartphones, computers, tablets, etc. (so-called Web APIs), and these are the focus of this case study. Representational state transfer (RESTful) APIs are a fairly new type of API and have come to dominate Internet communications; 89 percent of all API calls are to a RESTful API. SearchSOA.com, "API, Mobile Top List," October 7, 2013.

[389] BlackBerry Limited website, "Using BlackBerry WebWorks APIs," http://developer.blackberry.com/bbos/html5/documentation/using_webworks_apis.html (accessed April 21, 2014).

[390] Google website, "Google Maps API for Business," http://www.google.com/enterprise/mapsearth/products/mapsapi.html (accessed April 21, 2014).

[391] Duncan, "Why Are Companies Defecting from Google Maps?" March 8, 2012.

[392] Stafford, "What CIOs, Developers Should Know," October 15, 2013.

[393] Software increasingly permeates almost every industry and product. Retail, video, telephony, and music are examples of industries that are becoming software-driven. Willmott and Balas, "Winning in the API Economy," 2013, 28.

functionalities that would be almost impossible to create from scratch.[394] These new functionalities allow businesses to offer an expanding array of innovative products and services.

Businesses' use of APIs often focuses on improving revenue growth and customer engagement with their brands.[395] Companies that deploy APIs benefit from using this technology in several ways, including by improving internal efficiency, harnessing innovation from new sources, and expanding their customer base through new business partnerships.[396] For example, a company seeking to broaden customer engagement might tap into Twitter to create an application with a customized search bar which visitors could use to look for recent inquiries and requests on its site. The company could then publish this API to encourage third-party developers to use it in other applications.[397] As a result, the company is able to expand its user base without having to spend money to develop niche industry code, while keeping its own source code proprietary.

APIs allow companies to access and process data a large number of sources in real or near-real time, as demonstrated by software-driven companies like Amazon Web Services (AWS), Salesforce.com, and Expedia.[398] AWS, for example, uses more than 35 APIs to provide Internet services such as global computing, networking, storage, analytics, application, and deployment for other websites or client-side applications.[399] These APIs are essential to AWS's operations and are the gateway for customer requests for computing resources and services.[400] AWS has handled all Amazon.com retail Web services since 2010.[401] At Salesforce.com, APIs are central to integrating and extending its enterprise customer relationship management product offerings.[402] Expedia, Inc., one of the world's largest online travel services, states that 90 percent of its business comes via Internet applications that use APIs to enable the exchange of data between users and its reservation systems. The Expedia affiliate network of developers has more than 7,500 partners in 33 countries.[403]

---

[394] A mashup is an application which combines at least two different services from disparate, and even competing, websites. A mashup could overlay traffic data from one source on the Internet over maps from Yahoo, Microsoft, Google, or any content provider; PC.Net Glossary, http://pc.net/glossary/ (accessed April 25, 2014).

[395] Medrano, "Welcome to the API Economy," August 29, 2012, 21. In 2003, much of the content on a Web page likely came from a database source; in 2014, a single webpage will likely show content, advertising, links, and widgets that could be pulling the information from multiple API-driven sources. Lane, "A Field Guide to Web APIs," October 23, 2013, 16.

[396] Wilmott and Balas, "Winning in the API Economy," 2013, 22.

[397] Moore, "Twitter Files for IPO," September 12, 2013.

[398] Industry participants, telephone interview by USITC staff, April 7, 2014.

[399] Amazon Web Services, "What Is Amazon Web Services?" April 2, 2014.

[400] Golden, "Amazon Web Services for Dummies," September 2013, 26.

[401] In 2012, AWS commissioned a study of the long-term economic implications of moving workloads onto Amazon cloud infrastructure services. The study determined that the five-year total cost of ownership of developing, deploying, and managing critical applications in AWS delivered a 72 percent savings compared with deploying the same resources on-premise or in hosted environments. The findings also showed a 626 percent return on investment over five years. According to the study, scale economies have enabled AWS to reduce its prices 40 times since 2006. Rand and Hendrik, "The Business Value of Amazon Web Services," December 2013, 2, 22.

[402] Salesforce.com website, https://developer.salesforce.com/docs/atlas.en-us.salesforce1api.meta/salesforce1api/salesforce1_api_preface.htm (accessed April 21, 2014).

[403] McKinsey & Company, "APIs: Three Steps," January 2014, 1; Expedia Affiliate Network website, http://www.expediaaffiliate.com/index.php (accessed April 4, 2104).

Many companies allow outside parties access to their APIs to build new functionalities into applications.[404] Companies may charge for the use of their APIs or make them available to developers for free. One such collection, the Mozilla Developer Network, provides documentation, education, and a community for developers of all types.[405] Another, Microsoft DirectX, enables developers to create games, multimedia features, and applications for the Windows operating system.[406]

APIs Enable Innovation from New Sources

Established companies use APIs to open their systems to wider use—for example, by allowing developers to access and benefit from the established customer base.[407] In so doing, they seek to draw on the innovation capabilities of third-party developers, improve the customer experience, increase demand for complementary goods and services, and open new markets.[408] AT&T, for example, has transformed its network into a digital platform by allowing third-party developers to tap into its network capabilities; the AT&T Customer Profile API is software code that allows users to take advantage of AT&T's user data to create mobile applications that securely autopopulate a purchase form with a subscriber's address and personal information.[409]

The automobile industry is beginning to use APIs to connect vehicles with mobile devices. General Motors has an API that enables smartphone applications to control multiple vehicle operations. By publishing its APIs, the company has opened up its software development to allow both internal teams and external partners to add new functions, such as suggesting low-priced fueling locations based on the current gas tank level.[410] Ford Motor Co. grants external developers access its communications system, *Sync*, through a collection of APIs called *AppLink*. *AppLink* gives developers access to Ford's voice- and human-machine interfaces, which can be integrated into the applications they are building. As a consequence of this collaboration, customers see improved functionality; drivers can, for example, access their Pandora music app through voice command.[411]

---

[404] PwC, "Consumerization of APIs: Scaling integrations," 2012.

[405] Mozilla Developer Network website https://developer.mozilla.org/en-US (accessed April 25, 2014).

[406] Microsoft Windows website, Windows/Development Center/Desktop, http://msdn.microsoft.com/en-us/library/windows/desktop/ee663279 (accessed May 5, 2014).

[407] Industry representative, telephone interview by USITC staff, March 10, 2014; Gat and Succi, "A Survey of the API Economy," (accessed May 13, 2014), 4.

[408] Crawford, "Talkin' Bout an App Store Revolution," January 28, 2014.

[409] AT&T, "AT&T Announces New Call Management API," January 7, 2013.

[410] General Motors website, "Developer APIs, GM Development Tools," https://developer.gm.com/apis (accessed April 28, 2014).

[411] As a final production step, the app is tested by Ford; Laskowski, "Ford's Connected Car Revs Up with APIs," March 2014.

APIs Expand Business Networks

The speed as well as the extent of API-driven change is encouraging businesses to adopt new business models that rely on network effects.[412] Companies are increasingly forming ecosystems of enterprises, that include partners and value-adding firms, where business functions are delivered collaboratively through Internet applications powered by APIs.[413] These ecosystems are altering the production and delivery of goods and services in the previously cited telecommunications and automotive industries, as well as many others, including retail, transportation, and banking.[414]

Companies with successful ecosystems have deployed APIs that benefit all parties involved.[415] Amazon states that it employs the technology to drive its own sales and enhance partners' revenue, while eBay says it uses APIs to add millions of listings and to assist eBay sellers by automating the effort of maintaining an eBay presence.[416] On its website, Skype explains that it uses its API to enable delivery of Skype's Voice over Internet Protocol (VOIP) services on as many devices and platforms as possible, yielding benefits for its partners as well.[417] According to industry experts, such ecosystems "enable an enterprise to broaden the reach of its digital assets, increase revenue, accelerate and expand partnerships, and create innovation."[418] These ecosystems also greatly enrich digital trade in the global economy.[419]

End-User (Consumer) Benefits

APIs and other related Internet technologies widely used in digital trade provide significant gains and efficiencies to consumers as well as businesses. APIs give consumers unprecedented opportunities to make connections and to access vast amounts of information. As a result, they are an important part of the way the Internet is changing how consumers communicate and

---

[412] With network effects, each side attracts more of the other (e.g., eBay buyers and sellers); networks of communicating agents (whether human or machine) acquire value from the many connections available between online resources. In accordance with what is known as Metcalfe's law, the value of a telecommunications network such as the Internet is proportional to the square of the number of connected users of the system. In social media networks, for example, this means that the greater the number of users, the more valuable the service is to the community. APIs bring these benefits to software components.

[413] IBM Corporation, "Global Technology Outlook 2013," 2013, 5.

[414] There are numerous challenges to building and maintaining a software application ecosystem with multiple industries and many types of users, including the need to build networks of people, processes, and software very rapidly. APIs are likely to form an important part of a complex and evolving product offering. Enhanced mobile capabilities, for example, drive richer data collection that can be used to give customers increasingly personalized experiences. Industry experts note that important interactions go beyond business transactions, and include communications on social media and other non-commercial collaboration. IBM, "API Management Is the SOA Renaissance," 2013, 7.

[415] 3scale, "Taking the Long View on API Ecosystems," July 13, 2012.

[416] Amazon Services, "Amazon Marketplace Web Service," https://developer.amazonservices.com/index.html/186-8365499-9516726 (accessed May 5, 2014); 3scale, "Taking the Long View on API Ecosystems," July 13, 2012.

[417] VOIP services allow the delivery of communications services, including voice and video phone calls, via the Internet. Skype website, "Skype URIs," https://developer.skype.com/skype-uris (accessed April 2, 2014).

[418] Jinghran, "Data as Currency and Catalyst in the App Economy," 2013, 2.

[419] World Economic Forum, "Digital Ecosystem Convergence," 2007, 2.

shop.[420] Many social media networks that consumers use every day rely on APIs.[421] APIs are the software links that enable users to share content, such as opinions, photos, and videos, across different platforms, often using the same login and sharing subscriber information.[422] Increasingly, consumers are taking control of how and where they connect—expecting "anywhere, anytime, any device" accessibility and engagement[423]—and this is leading companies to use APIs to provide customer-specific services such as reward programs and location-based marketing.[424]

Consumers and citizens are also benefiting from the recent increase in the use of APIs in government websites and applications. In the United States, governments at the city, state, and federal levels use APIs to allow citizens online to access public sector information ranging from census data to U.S. postal service zip codes.[425] With the help of this technology, people are now able to find information, communicate with government agencies, and obtain government services more quickly and easily.

Challenges and Concerns

While APIs have become a pervasive technology, their use and the increased connectedness that they enable can raise concerns. For software developers, there is the risk that software applications may stop working because they rely on APIs that have been subsequently changed or withdrawn by their providers. For example, an API provider might upgrade the software an API connects to, change how APIs connect to its services, or no longer wish to make its data available to be integrated into new or existing software applications. These changes can reduce the functionality of existing applications, and discourage the development of new applications, which could result in a lower degree of reliability for software applications calling upon APIs over a long period.

As with other aspects of digital trade, issues of data consistency and security are also likely to be important. Because APIs make it possible for many data providers and users to link together, data management becomes more complex. It becomes more difficult to track the location of specific data at a given time, and each use of the data is likely to require additional authentication. As businesses seek to comply with privacy regulations, and the relationships between businesses become more complex, ensuring safe handling of customer data is likely to become more challenging.[426]

---

[420] Willmott and Balas, "Winning in the API Economy," 2013, 41; Digitalgov, "The API Briefing," Digitalgov.gov blog, http://www.digitalgov.gov/category/code/api/page/2/ (accessed July 22, 2014).

[421] Gunelius, "What Is an API?" October 31, 2011.

[422] Smith, "This Is How the Top Social Networks Think," April 15, 2014.

[423] PwC, "Exploiting the Value from Growing Information," 2012; Gupta, "Work Anywhere, Anytime" (accessed May 8, 2014).

[424] Accenture, "Winning and Retaining the Digital Consumer," April 2013, 3, 13.

[425] Programmable Web, "ProgrammableWeb API Category: Government" (accessed May 5, 2014).

[426] Industry representatives, telephone interview by USITC staff, April 7, 2014.

Bibliography

3scale. "The API Economy." http://www.3scale.net/api-economy (accessed January 28, 2014).

Accenture. "Winning and Retaining the Digital Consumer," April 2013.
    http://www.accenture.com/SiteCollectionDocuments/PDF/Accenture-Winning-and-
    Retaining-the-Digital-Consumer.pdf.

Acuna, Kristen. "3 Reasons Hollywood Is Investing Heavily in YouTube Content Producers."
    Business Insider, April 2, 2014.
    http://www.businessinsider.com/why-hollywood-is-buying-multi-channel-networks-
    2014-4.

Adib, Desiree. "Justin Bieber Is on the Brink of Superstardom." ABC News, November 14, 2009.

Airline Weekly. "Changing Channels: Airline Distribution." Special Report. *Airline Weekly*,
    June 2010.

Albergotti, Reed. "LinkedIn Wants to Help You Stay at Your Company." *Wall Street Journal Blog*,
    April 10, 2014.
    http://blogs.wsj.com/digits/2014/04/10/linkedin-wants-to-help-you-stay-at-your-
    company/.

Amobi, Tuna N. "Industry Surveys: Movies and Entertainment." *Standard & Poor's Industry
    Survey*, December 2013.

Anderson, Chris. "The Long Tail." *Wired*, October 2004.
    http://archive.wired.com/wired/archive/12.10/tail.html.

Arrington, Michael. "Airbnb Offers Unconditional Apology, and $50,000 Insurance Guarantee."
    TechCrunch, August 1, 2011.
    http://techcrunch.com/2011/08/01/airbnb-offers-unconditional-apology-and-50000-
    insurance-guarantee/.

Associated Press (AP). "Disney's Big-Money Move for Maker Signals Promising Times for Tech
    Entrepreneurs." *Billboard*, March 26, 2014.
    http://www.billboard.com/biz/articles/news/tv-film/5944963/disneys-big-money-
    move-for-maker-signals-promising-times-for-tech.

AT&T. "AT&T Announces New Call Management API and Alpha API Program." News release,
    January 7, 2013.
    http://www.att.com/gen/pressroom?pid=23651&cdvn=news&newsarticleid=35916.

Barnes & Noble Booksellers. "NOOK Introduces NOOK Press: Innovative New Publishing Platform for Authors." News release, April 9, 2013. http://www.barnesandnobleinc.com/press_releases/04_09_13_nook_press_release.html.

Barnett, Chance. "Top 10 Crowdfunding Sites for Fundraising." *Forbes*, May 8, 2013. http://www.forbes.com/sites/chancebarnett/2013/05/08/top-10-crowdfunding-sites-for-fundraising/.

BCD Travel. *Global Travel Distribution Trends*. White paper, 2007. http://www.bcdtravel.us/global/show_document.asp?id=aaaaaaaaaaasefo.

Blackberry Limited. "Using BlackBerry WebWorks APIs." http://developer.blackberry.com/bbos/html5/documentation/using_webworks_apis.html (accessed April 21, 2014).

Bly, Laura. "Plot Thickens in Airbnb Vacation Rental Horror Story." *USAToday*, August 3, 2011. http://travel.usatoday.com/destinations/dispatches/post/2011/07/plot-thickens-airbnb-renter-horror-story/179250/1 (accessed February 18, 2014).

Borghi, M., M. Maggiolino, M.L. Montagnani, and M. Nuccio. "Determinants in the Online Distribution of Digital Content: An Exploratory Analysis." *European Journal of Law and Technology* 3, no. 2 (2012): 1–29. http://eprints.bournemouth.ac.uk/20844/1/BorghiMaggiolino-Montagnani-Nuccio_Determinants.pdf.

Boyd, Mark. "6 Business Benefits of Private APIs." *Nordic APIs Blog,* February 13, 2014. http://nordicapis.com/business-benefits-of-private-apis.

Brecht, Daniel. "M-Commerce on the Rise." *Mobile Commerce Insider*, April 16, 2014. http://www.mobilecommerceinsider.com/topics/mobilecommerceinsider/articles/376351-m-commerce-the-rise-constitutes-fifth-all-cash.htm.

Bruns, Christoph. "Digital Distribution of Independent Music Artists: An Economic Analysis of Rights, Costs, and Market Potential." Diploma thesis, University of Cologne (Germany), 2012.

Caldbeck, Ryan. "Crowdfunding – Why Angels, Venture Capitalists and Private Equity Investors All May Benefit." *Forbes*, August 7, 2013.

Caloa, J.J. "The Facebook Job Board Is Here." *Forbes*, November 14, 2012. http://www.forbes.com/sites/jjcolao/2012/11/14/the-facebook-job-board-is-here-recruiting-will-never-look-the-same/.

Cameron, Lisa, and Coleman Bazelon. "The Impact of Digitization on Business Models in Copyright-Driven Industries: A Review of the Economic Issues." Prepared for The National Academies (The Committee on the Impact of Copyright Policy on Innovation in the Digital Era), June 2011.

Carr, Austin. "Inside Airbnb's Grand Hotel Plans." *Fast Company*, April 2014. http://www.fastcompany.com/3027107/punk-meet-rock-airbnb-brian-chesky-chip-conley.

Castro, Daniel, Robert D. Atkinson, and Stephen Ezell. *Embracing the Self-Service Economy*. The Information Technology and Innovation Foundation, April 14, 2010. http://www.itif.org/publications/embracing-self-service-economy.

Caves, Richard E. *Creative Industries: Contracts between Art and Commerce*. Cambridge, MA: Harvard University Press, 2000.

Chinen, Nate. "Blue Note to Partner with ArtistShare." *New York Times*, May 8, 2013.

Christopherson, Susan. "Hollywood in Decline? U.S. Film and Television Producers beyond the Era of Fiscal Crisis." *Cambridge Journal of Regions, Economy and Society* 6, no. 1 (2013): 141–57.

Coker, Mark, "10 Reasons Indie Authors Will Capture 50% of the Ebook Market by 2020," Smashwords Blog, March 5, 2014. http://blog.smashwords.com/.

———. "Indie Ebook Author Community to Earn More than Traditional Ebook Authors." *Smashwords Blog,* March 5, 2014. http://blog.smashwords.com/.

Colombani, Laurent, and François Videlaine. "The Age of Curation: From Abundance to Discovery." Bain & Company, November 19, 2013. http://www.bain.com/publications/articles/the-age-of-curation-from-abundance-to-discovery.aspx.

Corridore, Jim. "Industry Surveys: Airlines." *S&P Capital IQ*, December 2013.

Crawford, Steve. "Talkin' Bout an App Store Revolution: Enabling and Monetizing the API Economy." Wired.com, January 28, 2014. http://www.wired.com/2014/01/talkinboutapp-store-revolution-enabling-monetizing-api-economy.

Crosstab. "Online Reputation in a Connected World." Microsoft-sponsored study, January 2010. http://www.microsoft.com/security/resources/research.aspx#reputation.

Dana, James D. Jr., and Eugene Orlov. "Internet Penetration and Capacity Utilization in the U.S. Airline Industry," May 6, 2013. Forthcoming in *American Economic Journal: Microeconomics.*
http://www.economics.neu.edu/dana/Dana/Professor_James_Dana_Research_files/Dana%20Orlov%2005%2007%202013.pdf.

Dembosky, April, and Tim Bradshaw. "Start-ups: Shareholder Societies." *Financial Times*, August 7, 2013.
http://www.ft.com/intl/cms/s/2/4dd675fe-eae8-11e2bfdb00144feabdc0.html#-axzz2tyFXT8YU.

Digital Media Association (DiMA). "Digital Media: Growth, Innovations, and Challenges," 2013.
http://www.digmedia.org/component/content/article/82-resources/539-digital-media-growth-innovation-and-challenges-2013.

Duncan, Geoff. "Why Are Companies Defecting from Google Maps?" *Digital Trends,* March 8, 2012.
http://www.digitaltrends.com/mobile/why-are-companies-defecting-from-google-maps/#!bad8vJ.

Economist. "All Eyes On the Sharing Economy," March 9, 2013.
http://www.economist.com/news/technology-quarterly/21572914-collaborative-consumption-technology-makes-it-easier-people-rent-items.

———. "Digital Media: Counting the Change," August 17, 2013.
http://www.economist.com/news/business/21583687-media-companies-took-battering-internet-cash-digital-sources-last.

———. "Discovering Musical Talent: A New Improved Hit Machine," October 22, 2011.
http://www.economist.com/node/21533423.

———. "Flying From the Computer," October 1, 2005.
http://www.economist.com/node/4455692.

———. "Remove the Roadblocks," April 26, 2014.
http://www.economist.com/news/leaders/21601257-too-many-obstacles-are-being-placed-path-people-renting-things-each-other-remove.

———. "The Click and the Dead," July 3, 2010. http://www.economist.com/node/16478931.

———. "The Music Industry: Beliebing in Streaming," March 22, 2014.
http://www.economist.com/node/21599350.

Ernst & Young (EY). "Sustaining Digital Leadership!" 2014.
http://www.ey.com/Publication/vwLUAssets/EY-Sustaining-digital-leadership/$FILE/EY-Sustaining-digital-leadership.pdf.

European Commission. "Internationalisation of European SMEs," 2010.
.http://ec.europa.eu/enterprise/policies/sme/market-access/files/internationalisation_of_european_smes_final_en.pdf.

Expedia, Inc. "Expedia Overhauls Hotel Reviews: Consumers Can Now Sort Verified Reviews by Shared Interest." News release, March 8, 2012.
http://mediaroom.expedia.com/travelnews/expedia-overhauls-hotel-reviews-consumers-can-now-sort-verified-reviews-shared-interest.

Farquharson, Alistair. "APIs: A Soup to Nuts Analysis." *Cloud Computing Journal*, March 31, 2014. http://cloudcomputing.sys-con.com/node/3032241.

Faye, Denis. "Life after Mars." Writers Guild of America, March 14, 2014.
http://www.wga.org/content/default.aspx?id=5474.

Galloway, Scott. *L2 Digital Index: Hotels*. L2DigitalThinkTank.com, January 31, 2013.
http://www.l2thinktank.com/research/hotels-2013.

Gartland, Matt. "The New Era of Book Publishing: For the People, By the People." Winning Edits, n.d. http://winningedits.com/book-publishing-for-the-people/ (accessed February, 2014).

———. "Will Crowdfunding Books Replace Author Advances and Further Empower Readers?" Winning Edits, n.d. (accessed March 27, 2014).

Gat, Israel, and Giancarlo Succi. "A Survey of the API Economy." Cutter Consortium. Executive Update 14, no. 6 (2013). http://www.cutter.com/content-and-analysis/resource-centers/agile-project-management/sample-our-research/apmu1306.html.

Gilpin, Mike. "Want to Join the API Economy? Here's How." *Mike Gilpin's Blog*, Forrester Research, August 22, 2013. http://blogs.forrester.com/blog/95.

Golden, Bernard. *Amazon Web Services for Dummies*. John Wiley & Sons, September 2013.

Google Inc. "Form 10-K for Fiscal Year Ended December 31, 2012." Annual report for the Securities and Exchange Commission, January 29, 2013.
http://www.sec.gov/Archives/edgar/data/1288776/000119312513028362/d452134d10k.htm or https://investor.google.com/pdf/20121231_google_10K.pdf.

Greene, David. "Upstart Car Service Butts Heads with D.C.'s Taxis." National Public Radio, January 31, 2012. http://www.npr.org/2012/01/31/146123433/upstart-car-service-butts-heads-with-d-c-s-taxis.

Grover, Ronald. "Disney to Buy YouTube Network Maker Studios for $500 million." Reuters, March 24, 2014. http://www.reuters.com/article/2014/03/24/us-disney-maker-idUSBREA2N1PV20140324.

Guardian. "Why Crowdfunding Is the World's Incubation Platform," April 10, 2013. http://www.theguardian.com/media-network/media-network-blog/2013/apr/10/crowdfunding-businesses-social-projects.

Gunelius, Susan. "What Is an API and Why Does it Matter?" *SproutSocial*, October 31, 2011. http://sproutsocial.com/insights/api-definition.

Hogenson, George. "The Internet Comes of Age for the Recruitment Industry." Hudson Highland Center for Global Performance Thought Leadership Series, n.d. http://us.hudson.com/Portals/US/documents/White%20Papers/Hudson-internet-value-in-recruitment-industry.pdf (accessed May 6, 2014).

Huet, Ellen. "Drivers for Uber, Lyft Stuck in Insurance Limbo." *SFGate,* February 2, 2014. www.sfgate.com. http://www.sfgate.com/bayarea/article/Drivers-for-Uber-Lyft-stuck-in-insurance-limbo-5183379.php.

IBM Corporation. "API Management Is the SOA Renaissance: Converging SOA and API Management as a Catalyst for Business Innovation and Growth." IBM Software Thought Leadership White Paper, November 2013. http://public.dhe.ibm.com/common/ssi/ecm/en/wsw14217usen/WSW14217USEN.PDF.

———. "Global Technology Outlook 2013." IBM research report, April 2013. http://www.zurich.ibm.com/pdf/isl/infoportal/Global_Technology_Outlook_2013.pdf.

Jinghran, Anant. "Data as Currency and Catalyst in the App Economy." Apigee Insights e-book, February 2013. http://pages.apigee.com/apigee-insights-ebooks-sr.html (available with registration).

Kaufman, Leslie. "Chasing Their Star, on YouTube." *New York Times*, February 1, 2014. http://www.nytimes.com/2014/02/02/business/chasing-their-star-on-youtube.html?_r=0.

Kelley, Frannie. "Crowdfunding for Musicians Isn't the Future; It's the Present." NPR, September 25, 2012. http://turnstylenews.com/2012/09/25/crowdfunding-for-musicians-isnt-the-future-its-the-present/.

Kelly, Samantha Murphy. "Vimeo Launches Marketing Program to Help Crowdfunded Filmmakers." Mashable, January 18, 2014. http://mashable.com/2014/01/18/vimeocrowdfunding-program/.

Kelly, Liz. "Sundance 2014 Embraces 20 Kickstarter Funded Films." *Examiner*, January 30, 2014. http://www.examiner.com/article/sundance-2014-embraces-20-kickstarter-funded-films.

Kuhn, Peter, and Hani Mansour. "Is the Internet Job Search Still Ineffective?" July 29, 2013.

Lane, Kin. "A Field Guide to Web APIs." GigaOm Research report, sponsored by Restlet, October 23, 2013. http://research.gigaom.com/report/a-field-guide-to-web-apis/.

Laskowski, Nicole. "Ford's Connected Car Revs Up with APIs and External App Developers." SearchCIO.com. http://searchcio.techtarget.com/opinion/Fords-connected-car-revs-up-with-APIs-and-external-app-developers (accessed March 24, 2014).

Mangold, Glynn W., and David J. Faulds. "Social Media: The New Hybrid Element of the Promotion Mix." *Business Horizons* 52 (2009): 357–365. http://www.researchgate.net/publication/222415599_Social_media_The_new_hybrid_element_of_the_promotion_mix.

Mansfield, Brian. "22 Million Clicks Later, MySpace Launches Colbie Caillat's Career." *USA Today*, October 7, 2007. http://usatoday30.usatoday.com/life/music/news/2007-10-07-colbie-caillat_N.htm?csp=34.

Mashable. "From Blog to Book Deal: How 6 Authors Did It," December 17, 2009. http://mashable.com/2009/12/17/blog-to-book/.

Masnick, Mike. "Nice to See How Content Creators Have More Power over Middlemen." *TechDirt*, February 14, 2011. https://www.techdirt.com/articles/20110210/15534113046/nice-to-see-how-content-creators-have-more-power-over-middlemen.shtml.

Massolution. 2013CF: The Crowdfunding Industry Report, 2013.

McKinsey & Company. "APIs: Three Steps to Unlock the Data Economy's Most Promising New Go-to-Market Channel," January 2014. http://mckinseyonmarketingandsales.com/apis-three-steps-to-unlock-the-data-economys-most-promising-new-go-to-market-channel.

McKinsey Global Institute. "Disruptive Entrepreneurs: An Interview with Eric Ries," April 2014. http://www.mckinsey.com/Insights/High_Tech_Telecoms_Internet/Disruptive_entrepreneurs_An_interview_with_Eric_Ries?cid=other-eml-alt-mgi-mck-oth-1404.

Medrano, Roberto. "Welcome to the API Economy." *Forbes*, August 29, 2012. http://www.forbes.com/sites/ciocentral/2012/08/29/welcome-to-the-api-economy/3/.

Moore, Heidi. "Twitter Files for IPO in First Stage of Stock Market Launch." *Guardian*, September 12, 2013. http://www.theguardian.com/technology/2013/sep/12/twitter-ipo-stock-market-launch.

Ngak, Chenda. "Airbnb Will Insure Up to $1 Million in Property Damage." *CBSNews*, May 23, 2012. http://www.cbsnews.com/news/airbnb-will-insure-up-to-1-million-in-property-damage/.

Nielsen. "Global Trust in Advertising and Brand Messages," September 2013. http://www.nielsen.com/us/en/reports/2013/global-trust-in-advertising-and-brand-messages.html.

Organisation for Economic Co-operation and Development (OECD). *The Economic and Social Role of Internet Intermediaries*, April 2010. http://172.16.3.34:9090/progress?pages&id=1614022236&fileName=NDQ5NDkwMjMucGRm&url=aHR0cDovL3d3dy5vZWNkLm9yZy9pbnRlcm5ldC9pZWNvbm9teS80NDk0OTAyMy5wZGY=&serv=1&foo=22.

Pomerantz, Dorothy. "Schlock and Awe." *Forbes,* October 22, 2012.

PricewaterhouseCoopers (PwC). "The Business Value of APIs." *Technology Forecast*, Issue 2, 2012. http://www.pwc.com/us/en/technology-forecast/2012/issue2/download.jhtml (accessed March 4, 2014).

———. "Demystifying the Online Shopper: 10 Myths of Multichannel Retailing," 2013. http://www.pwc.com/gx/en/retail-consumer/retail-consumer-publications/global-multi-channel-consumer-survey/2012-multi-channel-survey.jhtml.

———. "Global Entertainment and Media Outlook: 2013–2017; Key Industry Themes," 2014. http://www.pwc.com/gx/en/global-entertainment-media-outlook/insights-and-analysis.jhtml.

ProgrammableWeb. "ProgrammableWeb API Category: Government." http://www.programmableweb.com/featured/government-mashups-and-apis (accessed May 5, 2014).

Ringlemann, Danae, "Why Crowdfunding Is the World's Incubation Platform," *Guardian*, April 10, 2013.

Rochette, Westcott. "Industry Surveys: Publishing and Advertising." *Standard & Poor's*, December 2013.

Said, Carolyn. "Airbnb to Collect Hotel Taxes for San Francisco Rentals." *SFGate.com*, April 1, 2014. http://www.sfgate.com/news/article/Airbnb-to-collect-hotel-taxes-for-San-Francisco-5365352.php.

Solon, Olivia. "Kickstarter for Books Launches." *Wired*, May 29, 2011. http://www.wired.co.uk/news/archive/2011-05/29/unbound-publishing-platform.

Sengupta, Somini. "What You Didn't Post, Facebook May Still Know." *New York Times*, March 25, 2013. http://www.nytimes.com/2013/03/26/technology/facebook-expands-targeted-advertising-through-outside-data-sources.html?pagewanted=all&_r=0.

Smith, Cooper. "This Is How the Top Social Networks Think about Their Users—and Why It Matters." *Business Insider,* April 15, 2014. http://www.businessinsider.com/this-is-how-the-top-social-networks-think-about-their-users-2014-4#ixzz2zYKzkxcx.

Stafford, Jan. "What CIOs, Developers Should Know about the 'API economy.'" *SearchSOA*, October 15, 2013. http://searchsoa.techtarget.com/feature/What-CIOs-developers-should-know-about-the-API-economy.

Steel, Emily. "Entertainment: Generation Next." *Financial Times*, September 19, 2013. http://www.ft.com/cms/s/2/68707e76-204b-11e3-b8c6-00144feab7de.html#axzz2yz21SXcb.

Stevenson, Betsey. "The Internet and Job Search." NBER Working Paper No. 13886, March 2008. http://www.nber.org/papers/w13886.

Strickler, Nancy, Eli Dvorkin, and Elisabeth Holm. "$100 Million Pledged to Independent Film." *Kickstarter Blog*, January 3, 2013. https://www.kickstarter.com/blog/100-million-pledged-to-independent-film.

Sundheim, Ken. "The Internet's Profound Impact on the Recruiting Industry." *Forbes*, April 2, 2013.

Sutter, John D. "Self-published E-book Author: 'Most of My Months Are Six-figure Months.'" *CNN.com*, September 7, 2012. http://www.cnn.com/2012/09/07/tech/mobile/kindle-direct-publish/.

Sydell, Laura. "How Musicians Make Money (by the Fraction of a Cent) on Spotify." NPR, September 26, 2012. http://www.npr.org/blogs/therecord/2012/09/26/161758720/how-musicians-make-money-by-the-fraction-of-a-cent-on-spotify.

Thorpe, Devin. "Where Does Crowdfunding Go From Here? Experts Explain." *Forbes*, February 1, 2014.

Trumbull, Douglas R., Alexander J. Wolf, Justin A. Zupnick, Alexander E. Spirgel, Kristofer B. Stensland, Stephen P. Meyerhofer, Andrew R. Horwitz, and Thorsten Joachims. "Using Personalized Radio to Enhance Local Music Discovery," 2014. http://www.cs.cornell.edu/People/tj/publications/turnbull_etal_14a.pdf.

U.S. International Trade Commission (USITC). Hearing transcript in connection with inv. no. 332-531 and 332-540, *Digital Trade in the U.S. and Global Economies: Part 1 and Part* 2, March 7, 2013.

———. Hearing transcript in connection with inv. No. 332-540, *Digital Trade in the U.S. and Global Economies: Part 2*, September 25, 2013.

———. *Digital Trade in the U.S. and Global Economies: Part 1 (Digital Trade 1)*. USITC Publication 4415. Washington, DC: USITC, 2013. http://usitc.gov/publications/332/pub4415.pdf.

Vogel, Harold L. Entertainment Industry Economics: A Guide for Financial Analysis. New York: Cambridge, 2011.

Vukovic, Darko. "APIs, Connectors and Integration Applications." Republished by Ross Mason in *Enterprise Integration Zone* (blog), DZone, May 5, 2014. http://java.dzone.com/articles/apis-connectors-and.

Wharton School of Business. "Can You Spare a Quarter? Crowdfunding Sites Turn Fans into Patrons of the Arts." *Knowledge@Wharton,* December 8, 2010. http://knowledge.wharton.upenn.edu/article/can-you-spare-a-quarter-crowdfunding-sites-turn-fans-into-patrons-of-the-arts/#.

Wilhelm, Alex. "After Raising $200M More, Airbnb Built a Replica of the Dr. Strangelove War Room in Its Office." *TechCrunch*, December 3, 2013. http://techcrunch.com/2013/12/03/with-a-fresh-200m-in-the-bank-airbnb-built-a-replica-of-the-dr-strangelove-war-room-in-its-office/.

Willmot, Steven. "Taking the Long View on API Ecosystems." *3scale Blog,* July 13, 2012. http://www.3scale.net/2012/07/taking-the-long-view-on-api-ecosystems.

———. "The API Economy: API Provider Perspective." Presentation to European Identity Summit 2012, Munich, Germany, April 19, 2012. http://www.slideshare.net/3scale/the-api-economy-api-provider-perspective-european-identity-summit-2012.

Willmott, Steven, and Guillaume Balas. *Winning in the API Economy.* 3scale e-book, November 1, 2013. http://www.scribd.com/doc/180797060/Winning-in-the-API-Economy.

World Economic Forum (WEF) with McKinsey & Company. *Risk and Responsibility in a Hyperconnected World: Implications for Enterprises*, January 2014. http://www.mckinsey.com/insights/business_technology/risk_and_responsibility_in_a_hyperconnected_world_implications_for_enterprises.

Wunsch-Vincent, Sacha. "Economics of Copyright and the Internet: Moving to an Empirical Assessment Relevant in the Digital Age." World Intellectual Property Organization. Economic Research Working Paper no. 9, 2013. http://www.wipo.int/export/sites/www/econ_stat/en/economics/pdf/wp9.pdf.

Yap, Jamie. "Opening Up APIs Brings In Benefits." *ZDNet*, December 7, 2011. http://www.zdnet.com/opening-up-apis-brings-in-benefits-2062303135.

Chapter 6
Case Studies: The Rise of Big Data

This second group of case studies describes one of the most important ways industries are increasing their digital trade—they are leveraging the Internet by harnessing "big data" to derive insights that improve products, services, and production processes across industries. As business activity has moved to the Internet, a new generation of technologies has emerged that enables businesses to extract economic benefits from the collection and analysis of very large volumes of a wide variety of data. "Big data" is the industry term for very large, high-volume datasets composed of structured and unstructured data from a wide variety of sources, often collected at high velocity in "real time." Examples include click streams from search engines, financial transaction data from electronic markets, or environmental or location data from machine sensors and telematics—the so-called "Internet of Things."[427] Recent developments in data communications, storage, and management, as well as more sophisticated algorithms for analysis—all enabled by growth in cloud computing capability—are opening up opportunities for innovation and higher productivity across the economy.[428]

Big data analytics help companies improve revenues and lower costs throughout their business. Using advanced statistical and visualization techniques, companies are able to gain insights into their customers' preferences and requirements, optimize pricing and the efficiency of marketing spending, and design new products and services that can be tailored to specific customers or types of customer. On the cost side, firms can make efficiency savings from using data analysis and predictive modeling to monitor and optimize processes throughout the value chain: procurement, production, inventory management, distribution, and customer service.[429] These new capabilities bring with them issues of implementation, however, including concerns about data privacy and the ownership of intellectual property.[430]

The application of data analysis in all areas of commerce is one of the most profound effects of the Internet. An innovative example of data collection and analysis over the Internet in an unusual setting—Japan after the Fukushima nuclear crisis—is described in box 6.1.

---

[427] Unstructured data are data that do not reside in fixed fields—for example, free-form text from books, articles, emails, etc., and untagged audio and video streams. In contrast, structured data are data that reside in fixed fields, such as data in databases and spreadsheets. Manyika et al., "Big Data: The Next Frontier," May 2011, 33; Russom, "Big Data Analytics," Q4 2011.

[428] Manyika et al., "Big Data: The Next Frontier," May 2011, 15.

[429] Predictive modeling is a commonly used statistical technique to predict future behavior. Brown, Court, and McGuire, "Views from the Front Lines," March 10, 2014; Schönberger and Cukier, *Big Data: A Revolution*, 2013, 145.

[430] A recent report from a number of senior administration officials to the President highlighted the wide-ranging impact of "Big Data" innovations. The report recommended ways for citizens and industry to take advantage of these innovations while still safeguarding privacy, fairness, and self-determination. Executive Office of the President, "Big Data: Seizing Opportunities, Preserving Values," May 1, 2014.

Box 6.1 Data collection inspired by Fukushima: An example of crowdsourcing and big data analytics in the nonprofit sector

The crowdsourcing of radiation data collection related to the 2011 nuclear accident in Japan is an example of an innovative use of Internet technologies. It involves the electronic collection of large data sets that are then analyzed and disseminated digitally for public use by a non-profit organization formed for this purpose, Safecast.

In March 2011, an earthquake measuring almost 9.0 on the Richter scale, and the massive tsunami that resulted, caused an accident at the Fukushima Daiichi nuclear facility. The Japanese government began monitoring the radioactivity emitted by the plant immediately after the accident, but citizens in the area and throughout Japan wanted to learn more about local levels of radiation. Within a week of the accident, Safecast was founded to coordinate the collection and mapping of radiation measurements from locations across Japan (currently numbering about 800).

The volunteer organization was initially funded by donations crowdfunded on Kickstarter, as well as direct donations from individuals. (Kickstarter is discussed in chapter 5 of this report.) In cooperation with other groups, including Tokyo Hacker Space, Keio University, and MIT Media Lab, Safecast coordinated a crowdsourcing effort to collect radiation measurements throughout Japan, including within danger zones. Individuals in various locations around Japan measured radiation levels with Geiger counters and uploaded the data to the Internet using WiFi.

As of December 2013, over 14 million data points had been collected. These data have been used to create real time maps and other data visualizations depicting local Japanese radiation levels which can be accessed freely online, including through social media. A variety of sensors and vehicles are currently being used because of the difficult conditions; for example, unmanned aerial vehicles are being deployed in areas that are hard to reach or considered unsafe. A similar effort is underway in 2014 on the U.S. west coast, measuring radiation levels to determine if emissions from Fukushima are reaching the United States.

Sources: Cruz, "After Fukushima," March 4, 2014; Ilet, "Counting the Human Value," December 6, 2013; Johnson, "Crowdsourced Radiation Monitoring Website," January 14, 2014; Kinney, "Fukushima Radiation near Half Moon Bay?" March 23, 2014; Mack, "From Tokyo to California," March 15, 2011; Perlman, "Fukushima Radiation Could Reach Pacific Coast," February 26, 2014; various pages on Safecast website (see bibliography); Strickland, "Measuring Radiation in Fukushima with Pocket Geigers," September 4, 2013.

The following four case studies highlight the impact on costs, output, and innovation of incorporating data analytics into the business processes of industries in all three major sectors of the economy—services, manufacturing, and agriculture:

Case study 5: *Data analytics innovations in the insurance industry.* The Internet enables insurers to collect large sets of data from various sources that were previously unavailable, and to analyze them using new, more sophisticated techniques. This case study describes the application of data analytics by insurers to risk selection and pricing, the introduction of usage-based insurance (UBI), combating claims fraud, and improving operational efficiency.

Case study 6: *Machine-to-machine (M2M) communications in manufacturing.* Internet technologies allow manufacturers to embed sensors in a variety of machinery and equipment to share environmental and performance information—such as temperature and humidity or production error rates— wirelessly between machines on the factory floor and machines in remote locations. This case study examines the importance of M2M communications in the production process and the role of Internet-connected things (also known as the "Internet of Things" [431]) in the manufacturing sector.

Case study 7: *Digital innovations in agriculture.* M2M communications technologies are also being applied in novel ways to make farms more productive. This case study describes how digital innovations in agriculture can be used to help improve crop yields and farm efficiency.

Case study 8: *Online customer data collection.* The collection of data about Internet users offers valuable opportunities to companies and benefits to Internet users, but also presents significant risks to both parties. This case study describes various methods of online customer data collection, examines the approaches business are taking to derive data from consumers, and discusses the attendant consumer privacy concerns.

Case Study 5: Data Analytics Innovations in the Insurance Industry

Insurance companies' business processes are being transformed as they move to adopt three important digital technologies—cloud computing, mobile apps, and advanced data analytics. Insurers offer products through online channels (both their own websites and aggregator sites) as well as traditional agent networks. They manage customer relationships and claims processing via website portals, email, and mobile apps, as well as direct telephone and postal communications. Even more fundamentally, they are changing their approach to pricing, underwriting, and managing risk with the advent of complex data analytics.[432] The insurance sector has not been the fastest to undertake digital transformation; rather, it has been the communications-dependent information sector and the transaction-intense sectors such as banking and retail distribution that have led the way. But now that the process has begun, the potential for changes in the basic insurance business model is significant.[433]

While the insurance industry has a long history of employing sophisticated data analysis, it has largely been actuarial analysis of risk probabilities for certain risk classes, using historical insurance claims data. With the advent of Internet communications and cloud computing technologies, insurers can now collect large datasets of various types, including real-time behavioral data from current policyholders, drawing on a very broad range of sources. Examples include information about customer enquiries from click streams on company websites and social media; machine sensor outputs giving location and environmental data of vehicles or goods in transit; unstructured text data generated by the insurance claims process

---

[431] The Internet of Things refers to the embedding of Internet-networked sensors and controls in physical products, such as aircraft engines, production equipment, or smart electricity meters, which communicate with users and provide real-time data measurements. Chui, Löffler, and Roberts, "The Internet of Things," March 2010.

[432] Accenture, "The Digital Insurer: A New Era in Insurance," December 6, 2012, 4.

[433] Ernst & Young, "Insurance in a Digital World," October 1, 2013, 4–5; Massey, "Advanced Business Analytics Enable Better Decisions," November 2010, 4.

and other communications with customers; and publicly available statistical data from governments and other sources.[434] Alongside the expansion of data sources resulting from Internet communications, scale economies gained by using cloud computing have enabled the development of more sophisticated data analysis and predictive modeling techniques. For insurers, this can be a "game-changer." Better information about risk factors and customer behavior allows insurers to offer better-tailored products, to price risks more exactly, and to lower their loss ratio (payouts for losses on policies/premiums written) for all types of insurance.[435] Many industry participants indicate that the use of data analytics and predictive modeling can give early adopters a significant competitive advantage.[436]

Competitive Drivers for Adopting Advanced Data Analytics in Insurance

Insurance firms' investments in information technology (IT), including Internet technologies, are guided by their two key business priorities: to improve the customer experience and to increase operational efficiency. As a result, leading insurance firms are using data analytics in many different ways throughout their business—in product development, marketing and sales, policy administration, claims management, risk assessment, and asset management. Their objectives include targeting low-risk customers; developing more customized, granular pricing schemes; and improving underwriting risk calculations.[437] IT investments are being made most urgently in (1) expanding online documentation; (2) introducing so-called "quote-and-bind" technology; (3) improving underwriting software; and (4) detecting fraudulent claims.[438] Data analytics are an obvious component of the underwriting process and efforts to detect fraud, but analytics applications also enable "instant" customer checks and individualized pricing as customers seek to sign up for policies online. Using analytics in these ways has the potential to lower an insurer's loss-ratio through better estimations of risk and appropriate product pricing.[439]

As insurance companies apply data analytics techniques more widely, they are seeing benefits. According to a senior executive with one global insurer, "The area of data and analytics is where value has been most visible, pushing us to become a digital insurer."[440] In a recent survey of U.S. and Canadian property and casualty insurers conducted by Towers Watson, nearly 80 percent of firms reported that predictive modeling—typically used to test the

---

[434] Russom, "Managing Big Data," Q4 2013, 6.

[435] Brat et al., "Big Data: The Next Big Thing?" March 25, 2013, 2–3.

[436] Hoying et al., "Improve P&C Profitability and Premium Growth," January 9, 2014.

[437] Brat et al., "Big Data: the Next Big Thing?" March 25, 2013, 2. In order to price insurance products correctly, insurers must assess the potential size and likelihood of the risk event being insured. By selling an insurance policy to a customer, the insurer is "underwriting" the risk—in other words, transferring the risk from the customer to the insurer.

[438] "Quote-and-bind" technology refers to websites designed to lead a prospective customer through the policy specification and sign-up process in one sitting. MSM Software, "IT and Operational Functions in General Insurance Strategy," April 4, 2013, 4.

[439] Hoying et al., "Improve P&C Profitability and Premium Growth," January 9, 2014.

[440] BCG, "Becoming a 'Digital Insurer': An Interview with Cathryn Riley," 26–27.

effectiveness of product design, marketing, and pricing—has improved their profitability, and between 35 and 40 percent of firms said that it had a positive impact on market share.[441] Another survey, conducted by the Aberdeen Group in mid-2013, found that insurance companies that used predictive modeling saw a significantly greater increase in the number of policies sold than companies that did not use it, and they achieved a 50 percent higher policy renewal ratio.[442]

Applying Data Analytics to Risk Selection and Pricing

Risk selection and pricing are the primary areas where insurers apply data analytics. For example, access to real-time data supplied by loss adjusters working at claims sites helps underwriters to price new policies more accurately.[443] According to the Towers Watson survey, 85 percent of U.S. property and casualty insurers reported that sophisticated underwriting and risk selection techniques using predictive modeling improved rate accuracy, and at least 74 percent reported a positive impact on loss ratios.[444] As a result, nearly half of the insurance carriers surveyed reported that predictive modeling increased their willingness to underwrite new business, because they were able to price risks more accurately. These included 45 percent of personal line carriers (those offering property and casualty insurance, such as auto insurance, house insurance, and travel insurance, to individuals) and 48 percent of commercial line carriers (those offering all types of property and casualty insurance to businesses).[445] Although few U.S. property and casualty insurers do so at the moment, many firms have plans to use the advanced data analysis techniques of price integration and price optimization. Price integration uses models of customer behavior, competitors' costs, and underwriting losses to estimate profit and sales volume under various pricing scenarios, while price optimization adds a mathematical search algorithm to price integration modeling in order to arrive at the pricing level that maximizes profit and sales.[446]

Several types of data are used by insurance providers to estimate policy risks more precisely, and therefore to price policies more accurately. AXA Global Direct, for example, uses information from social networks, Web cookies, and police reports to help assess potential customers and to offer attractive pricing for a variety of types of insurance.[447] "Geocoding," the identification of the location of an object using radar, mobile, or Internet-connected devices, allows insurance providers to consider the specific geographic location of an object in their

---

[441] Stoll and Southwood, "Predictive Modeling Usage," March 2014, 4.

[442] Of the companies surveyed, those using predictive modeling averaged an 8 percent year-on-year increase in the number of policies sold, compared to a 6 percent increase for companies not using predictive modeling; and those using predictive modeling registered a 9 percent policy renewal ratio compared to 6 percent for those who did not. Aberdeen Group, "Analytics in Insurance: Expect the Unexpected," November 2013, 4.

[443] Stoll and Southwood, "Predictive Modeling Usage," March 2014, 5; Ordnance Survey, "The Big Data Rush," April 25, 2013.

[444] Stoll and Southwood, "Predictive Modeling Usage," March 2014, 3.

[445] Ibid., 4.

[446] Ibid., 5.

[447] Gentrup, "Courage Can Eliminate Fears about 'Big Data,'" March 4, 2014. A Web cookie is software embedded in a website that sends a message to the server each time a user opens the website.

calculation of underwriting risk. This helps insurers assess property risks on an individual basis, such as when insuring a home located in a floodplain, and it also allows insurers to group existing customers' risks according to location. The use of social media data, geocoding data, and other types of data derived from interactions with individual customers can raise privacy issues, however, introducing the need for insurance providers to address the concerns of policyholders and regulators about how personal customer data is gathered, stored and used.[448]

In another example, providers of life insurance are moving to improve their mortality risk selection by using predictive modeling on prescription drug databases and aggregated medical test data. To this end, some medical lab companies are undertaking underwriting analysis on behalf of life insurers. For example, they can calculate a mortality risk score associated with specific levels of certain health indicators, such as blood pressure and the ratio of high-density to low-density lipoproteins (the proteins that transport cholesterol in the bloodstream), using information from their aggregated lab history data and government data detailing the wider population's death profile. However, outsourcing data analysis is sometimes problematic; life insurers may have difficulty laying off risks with reinsurers if they rely on an external provider that uses proprietary, "black box" algorithms for their underwriting assessment.[449]

Telematics and Usage-based Insurance

Predictive modeling has also become widely adopted by auto insurers, with 80 percent of North American firms using it in 2013. In fact, many insurance companies have taken the next step and have introduced usage-based insurance (UBI) plans based on information collected via telematics. Telematics are in-car IT devices that typically have an interface with the car's electronic systems, some form of wireless communication via a wide area network, and GPS location tracking capability. The use of telematics gives insurers real-time information about how, when, and where an auto-insurance policyholder drives his/her car; as a result, the insurer can better assess the risk of an accident, and the insured driver may be able to pay lower premiums. Applying predictive analytics to the data generated by telematics devices can represent a competitive advantage for providers because it allows risk to be priced directly rather than on the basis of actuarial analysis by gender or age. Insurers can also target underwriting to a specific risk class of customers—for example, the low-risk driver market—to gain market share. Consumers participate because of the possibility of lowering their premiums by as much as 30–40 percent.[450]

Although more than 70 insurers worldwide currently offer telematics-based UBI products, these types of policies represent no more than 1 percent of total policies written in most markets. Italy has the highest penetration of UBI policies in its auto insurance market—about

---

[448] Johnson, "Is Geocoding Right for You?" August 7, 2013; *Reactions*, "Social Media's Role in Fighting Insurance Fraud," April 26, 2013.

[449] Hughes, "Preferred Risk in Life Insurance," November 2012, 10.

[450] Accenture, "A New Era in Insurance," December 6, 2012; Berg Insight, "Car Telematics and Wireless M2M," report summary, 2014; Brat et al., "Telematics: The Test for Insurers," December 4, 2013, 1.

3.5 percent—and 19 out of the top 20 Italian insurers offer UBI products.[451] In 2013, 18 percent of U.S. personal auto insurers and 12 percent of commercial carriers had UBI programs in place, while nearly half of personal auto insurers had formal plans to introduce UBI—up from around a third the previous year.[452] Industry forecasts suggest that UBI products could increase to as much as 10 percent of the auto insurance policies written in the next three to five years.[453] Progressive Insurance, a leading provider of telematics-based auto insurance in the U. S. market, reports that consumer adoption is growing quickly; one-third of Progressive's direct customers are signing up for a telematics plan, and the company now has 1.5 million UBI customers, up from 1 million at the start of 2013.[454] Progressive wrote over $2 billion in UBI premiums in 2013.[455] According to many industry observers, within a few years it will likely be necessary for insurers to offer a UBI program to remain competitive in the sector.[456]

Industry observers also expect that insurance companies will take advantage of the Internet of Things in other contexts in coming years. Health and activity data (such as pulse rate, blood pressure and level of activity) collected by wearable bio-sensors, for example, offer the possibility of individual health risk monitoring and assessment, and customized health and life insurance.[457]

Combating Claims Fraud

Predictive and advanced analytics—of text drawn from customer communications, policyholder details, policy terms, and previous claims; of postings on social media; and of location data from smartphones and sensors, for example—have proved particularly powerful tools for combating claims fraud. Using regression models and advanced techniques such as natural language processing (NLP), insurers can more quickly and accurately identify claims that need further investigation.[458] As a result, legitimate claims can be processed more quickly, improving customer satisfaction while reducing payouts on fraudulent claims.[459] The cost to insurers of claims fraud is significant; the Insurance Information Institute estimates, for example, that about half of U.S. property and casualty insurers lose between 11 and 30 cents per premium dollar earned to opportunistic fraud (when individuals inflate damages or repairs, or provide false information to reduce the premium they are charged).[460] One industry observer estimates that better fraud detection as the result of big data analytics could lead to savings of around 2 percent on written premiums.[461] In specific cases, the results have been more impressive: one

[451] Brat et al., "Telematics: The Test for Insurers," December 4, 2013, 2.

[452] Stoll and Southwood, "Predictive Modeling Usage," March 2014, 1–2.

[453] Brat et al., "Telematics: The Test for Insurers," December 4, 2013, 2.

[454] McMahon, "Progressive's Dave Pratt on the Evolution of UBI," February 12, 2014.

[455] McMahon, "Progressive's Snapshot Passes 10 Billion Mile Marker," March 21, 2014.

[456] Accenture, "A New Era in Insurance," 2012; Brat et al., "Telematics: The Test for Insurers," December 4, 2013, 2.

[457] Leigh, "Life Insurers Must Now Prepare," September 25, 2013.

[458] Russom, "Managing Big Data," Q4 2013, 6.

[459] Reactions, "Social Media's Role in Fighting Insurance Fraud," April 26, 2013; Cognizant, "Using Advanced Analytics to Combat P&C Claims Fraud," December 2012, 4.

[460] Cognizant, "Using Advanced Analytics to Combat P&C Claims Fraud," December 2012, 2.

[461] Brat et al., "Big Data: the Next Big Thing for Insurers?" March 25, 2013, 2.

U.S. property and casualty insurer identified $20 million of fraudulent claims within three months of starting to use advanced analytics.[462]

Insurers acknowledge that using predictive analytics is the most efficient and effective way to detect fraud, and as a consequence they are directing their IT spending towards this effort.[463] To meet demand from insurance companies and other institutions seeking to address fraud and financial crime, IT services providers are moving into this market, offering innovative, targeted software, cloud services, and data analysis capabilities.[464] Implementing data analytics technologies can be complex and time-consuming for insurers, however, and concerns about data privacy also need to be addressed.[465] As a result, large insurance companies have adopted big data analytics more often than small companies. According to the Towers Watson survey, 48 percent of large carriers are either using or are nearly ready to roll out predictive analytics for fraud detection, compared with 26 percent of midsize carriers. No small carriers have or are in the process of implementing fraud applications, and only 23 percent of small carriers are beginning to explore such applications.[466]

Use of Data Analytics to Improve Operational Efficiency

While introducing data analytics to customer analysis, pricing, and underwriting is where companies are likely to see the biggest impacts on revenues and profitability, insurance firms are also using data analytics to improve their internal processes and lower their operating costs. Business planning and forecasting models which use real-time data feeds from across the corporate group give senior managers, and potentially regulators, a detailed picture of current business conditions and projected probabilities under various macroeconomic and risk scenarios. For example, Aviva, a large U.K.-based insurer, uses a cloud-based, business modeling and planning platform from an outside provider for forecasting and scenario analysis, and the company reports that the time it needs to generate new planning numbers has been significantly cut.[467] Using electronically captured data from the business, insurers can also better assess the effectiveness of a particular insurance program with statistical studies of actual-vs.-expected losses and claims.[468] Analytical software that calculates risk profiles and optimizes capital allocation is also increasingly being used by insurance firms as they work to show they are complying with the new risk-based capital requirements being imposed by

---

[462] Cognizant, "Using Advanced Analytics to Combat P&C Claims Fraud," December 2012, 6.

[463] Ibid., 7.

[464] IBM's recently introduced "Infinity" system has a record of increasing the success rate in pursuing fraudulent claims from 50 percent to 88 percent. IBM, "IBM Launches New Software and Consulting Services," March 20, 2014; Hamm, "Big Data: How Infinity Sniffs Out Insurance Fraud," March 20, 2014.

[465] Cognizant, "Using Advanced Analytics to Combat P&C Claims Fraud," December 2012, 7.

[466] Stoll and Southwood, "Predictive Modeling Usage," March 2014, 5.

[467] Anaplan, "Aviva Case Study: Aviva Brings Agility" (accessed April 14, 2014). Cloud-based provision of data analytics platforms is one example of how cloud computing is enabling firms in many sectors to access a wide range of sophisticated services that blend data storage, management and analytics. According to a recent KPMG survey, the most significant benefits of cloud computing are expected by business leaders to be improved business efficiencies/improved productivity and lower costs. KPMG, "Technology Innovation Survey 2013," 2013, 14.

[468] Hughes, "Preferred Risk in Life Insurance," November 2012, 10.

regulators. Such software is connected to company databases, which are often stored in a "private cloud."[469]

Claims management is another area where insurance companies are starting to use predictive modeling.[470] As mentioned above, modeling techniques can greatly enhance fraud detection. In addition, a capability for real-time data processing allows quicker claims transaction processing and lowers costs. One South African insurer notes that by using predictive analytics it can handle its legitimate insurance claims within an hour—an astonishing 70 times faster than previously—and it can reduce expenses associated with sending claims adjusters to visit clients by identifying low-risk claims.[471] Applying predictive modeling to claims management is not yet widespread in the industry, but is expected to be adopted by many leading firms in the next few years.[472]

Case Study 6: Machine-to-Machine (M2M) Communication Is Improving Production Processes

As the Internet of Things has become increasingly pervasive in consumer products like smart appliances, cars, and cell phones, it has also become an important part of the manufacturing environment for many firms. M2M communication is the industrial subset of the Internet of Things, and it encompasses the production and transmission of big data[473] by everything from testing tools to heavy machinery in production environments.[474] M2M capabilities (also described as the "industrial Internet" or "industrial Internet of Things") allow manufacturers to use a web of embedded sensors to share environmental and performance information wirelessly between machines on the factory floor and machines in remote locations. This information flow and network access enables manufacturers to make a variety of improvements to their production processes. They have the ability to analyze performance data to optimize manufacturing processes; to monitor equipment for weaknesses and failures in order to provide maintenance and lessen equipment downtimes; to find issues in production and fix them to improve product quality; to identify needs across multiple production sites

---

[469] Solvency II in Europe and the National Association of Insurance Commissioners' newly adopted Risk Management and Own Risk and Solvency Assessment (RMORSA) Model Act in the United States are the primary examples of the move to risk-based capital requirements for the international insurance industry. Sullivan, "What Does NAIC's Adoption of RMORSA Model Act Mean?" September 14, 2012; IBM Algorithmics, "Internal Models for Insurance Companies," July 2012, 2–5; IBM Algorithmics, "Solvency II—Setting Higher Goals," June 2013, 3–4.

[470] Hoying et al., "Improve P&C Profitability," January 09, 2014.

[471] Jacobs, "'Big Data Comes to Africa," March 3, 2014.

[472] Gartner forecasts that by 2015, approximately 10 percent of insurers in mature markets will be using analytics for real-time processing. Weiss, "2013 Industry Predicts: Digitalization," January 30, 2012.

[473] In the manufacturing context, big data are large sets of metadata that describe behavior, surroundings, and interactions of the device with other objects. According to a recent survey by research firm Gartner, 28 percent of manufacturing firms have made investments in big data technologies and 31 percent plan to do so within the next two years. Kart, "Big Data Industry Insights," March 18, 2014.

[474] Hamblen, "AT&T and GE Join Up," October 9, 2013.

rapidly in order to allocate resources and inventory efficiently;[475] and to increase predictability in manufacturing cycles. [476]

M2M communication increases productivity by giving workers more information about their equipment and outputs, and allowing them to make decisions accordingly. However, this does not come without risks: a single vulnerability in a company network can create security problems. Also, connecting devices to each other and having direct network access to machinery could open manufacturers to previously minimal risks, such as the risk of unauthorized persons gaining remote access to manufacturing processes or proprietary data.[477] Manufacturers currently work to balance the risks and returns, and as connected machines become more widely used in production facilities, more work can be done to research and mitigate risks. Although firms connected to the industrial Internet of Things may find that the data generated by their systems are more complex and numerous than they can process, many manufacturers are already seeing benefits from having M2M systems in place.[478] The overall impact of this technology is significant; producers are able to optimize yield and quality, while improving energy and production efficiency and reducing costs.[479]

Benefits of M2M Communication

Above all, it is the potential for increased process efficiency that drives manufacturing firms to adopt M2M technologies.[480] On the factory floor, connected machines allow operators to monitor real-time performance data, change production patterns remotely, identify failures, and receive instant notification when disruptions and failures occur. In the long-term, these abilities can translate to infrastructure and process improvements, as big data from machinery provide insights into which functions improve product quality and yields and point to ways to minimize machine downtime. Manufacturers use M2M systems to varying degrees, but almost any factory can potentially use M2M systems. To do so, they need communications infrastructure, connected devices, and the software and resources necessary to store and analyze big data. An SME may only have one connected machine that monitors one variable of production, but the data provided by that tool can still help the SME to improve efficiency in

---

[475] Annunziata and Evans, "The Industrial Internet@Work," 2013. These improvements can help manufacturers to lower costs, improve time to market, better manage environmental concerns, increase process transparency, better manage resources like staffing and machine uptime, improve safety, introduce and test production changes more rapidly, produce more varied and customizable products with fewer manual changes to manufacturing processes, increase abilities to diagnose problems or identify needed upgrades, perform remote maintenance, and improve product yield and quality. Prouty and Paquin, "Three Steps to Make Your Manufacturing Systems Intelligent," January 30, 2014; Jacobson, "Getting Business Value from Manufacturing Execution Systems," December 12, 2013.

[476] Hessman, "The Dawn of the Smart Factory," February 14, 2013; Löffler and Tschiesner, "The Internet of Things," June 2013.

[477] Perlroth, "Hackers Lurking in Vents and Soda Machines," April 7, 2014.

[478] Economist, "Data, Data Everywhere," February 25, 2010.

[479] Brynjolfsson and McAfee, The Second Machine Age, 2014; industry representative, interview by USITC staff, San Jose, CA, April 30, 2014.

[480] Kart, "Big Data Industry Insights," March 18, 2014.

that one area. However, SMEs may be less likely to implement M2M technology in existing factories due to upfront technology costs.[481]

Many industry observers have an optimistic view of the role of the Internet of Things in advancing manufacturing's economic future. McKinsey estimates that the entire Internet of Things—including factory M2M communication, but also systems for tracking inventory movement, individual "smart" devices for health monitoring, and systems for remote monitoring of infrastructure and utilities—may add between $2.7 and $6.2 trillion in economic value each year between now and 2025. In particular, they predict that $0.9–2.3 trillion in annual growth will come from the manufacturing sector, 80–100 percent of which will be directly impacted by the Internet of Things by 2025. By that year, McKinsey estimates that the Internet of Things, including M2M communication, will be improving manufacturing productivity by 2.5–5.0 percent through savings in maintenance costs, efficient resource allocation, and operating savings.[482]

Similarly, a Cisco Systems forecast finds that the Internet of Things may have a global economic impact of $14.4 trillion (or a 21 percent boost to aggregate corporate profits) between 2013 and 2022, with the United States accounting for 32 percent of those economic gains. The prediction includes gains from more than 20 different Internet of Things benefits, including $2.0 trillion from smart factories; $0.3 trillion from connected buildings; $1.03 trillion from decreases in product time to market; and $0.7 billion from savings in firms' supply chains. Cisco estimates that 27 percent of the global economic benefits from Internet of Things will come from the manufacturing sector.[483]

For its part, General Electric (GE) has estimated that 46 percent of industries can take direct advantage of M2M communication in factories and in the field. GE anticipates that over the next 20 years, productivity gains from the implementation and use of M2M systems alone may add as much as $10–$15 trillion to global gross domestic product (GDP).[484] GE has also suggested that using M2M technology in its own production facilities could improve GE employee productivity by up to 1.5 percent annually.[485]

Examples of How Firms Use M2M Communication to Increase Efficiency

As noted above, an especially important use for M2M systems is in helping firms increase production efficiency. With machines generating constant data on outputs and quality, manufacturers can make process changes on the spot without losing valuable testing time or

---

[481] Industry representative, interview by USITC staff, San Jose, CA, April 30, 2014.

[482] Manyika et al., "Disruptive Technologies," May 2013.

[483] Bradley, Barbier, and Handler, "Embracing the Internet of Everything," 2013.

[484] Annunziata and Evans, "The Industrial Internet@Work," 2013.

[485] Fitzgerald, "An Internet for Manufacturing," January 28, 2013.

making manual equipment changes. They can also optimize their use of energy and inputs, analyze product yields, and reduce production equipment downtime.[486]

Many large manufacturers, particularly in the high technology sphere, are finding M2M communication invaluable in their production processes. One such firm is Intel. In 2013, Intel used 2012 big data from its production equipment to optimize production processes and reduce the time it takes to validate chip designs by 25 percent, significantly shortening time to market. In 2012, Intel also used M2M capabilities to connect its machines into a networked failure-protection system for its data centers that links multiple factories. This system reduced Intel's average recovery time for site failures from more than an hour to less than two minutes. As a result, Intel saved $800,000 by reducing the amount of server and database storage needed over three factory automation databases.[487]

Siemens, a global electronics firm, has found the Internet of Things helpful in increasing transparency and improving manufacturing patterns through better monitoring of its machinery. Siemens uses M2M systems to link up resource scheduling systems and factory machines in areas where production is too complex and difficult to manage manually. This helped the machines in its Electronic Works factory in Germany to reach a 99 percent reliability rate.[488] Machinery monitoring can include robotics monitoring, and firms that use robotic machinery to perform complex or dangerous tasks can use M2M systems to oversee and modify robotic processes.[489]

GE, a strong advocate for the Internet of Things in manufacturing as well as many other contexts, uses M2M communication in its factories to monitor and improve manufacturing processes. As part of its "Brilliant Factory" system, GE manufacturing workers can remotely pull up real-time process data on tablets to monitor specific activities.[490] GE also monitors and collects sensor data from products deployed in the field (such as aircraft engines) about their behavior in use and their wear-and-tear to gain insights into how to improve the way these products are manufactured. Process optimization from these insights has led to a 1 percent improvement in GE jet engine and gas turbine efficiency, which has the potential to save the company billions of dollars.[491] In another example, one GE battery production plant has more than 10,000 sensors on its machines to monitor parts and materials used, temperatures and air pressure, and even the progress of the manufacturing process. All components of these batteries are tracked with a bar code and serial number, and GE has used the big data generated to pinpoint exactly where in the manufacturing process factors that lead to battery failure are most likely to occur. This has led to process improvements to decrease battery

---

[486] USITC, *Digital Trade 1*, 2013; Russom, *Big Data Analytics*, Fourth Quarter 2011; industry representative, interview by USITC staff, San Jose, CA, April 30, 2014.
[487] Intel, Accelerating Business Growth through IT, 2013.
[488] Hessman, "The Dawn of the Smart Factory," February 14, 2013.
[489] Nerseth, "Rise of the Automatons," January 2014.
[490] GE Reports, "Meet Your Maker," February 25, 2014.
[491] Kart, "Big Data Industry Insights," March 18, 2014.

failure rates, a key measure of product quality. The overall goal is to achieve continuous improvement in the production process.[492]

General Motors (GM) uses a network of plant floor controls that connects more than 150 factories globally to design uniform manufacturing processes, perform real-time updates to processes, and allow maintenance and monitoring to be initiated from one hub rather than being coordinated separately out of each site. Through this network of plant floor controls, GM has reduced downtime and inventory carrying costs by approximately 70 percent. Using connected machines has also allowed GM to reduce dramatically the time it takes to install and manage plant floor software on its networks because software and configurations are now standardized and can be deployed remotely. Over five years, Cisco estimates that GM's use of M2M communication in its factories resulted in large benefits through cost savings and increased profits, including $53 million saved through more efficient allocation of labor, $5 million in savings from increased knowledge of inventory needs, and $76 million in increased profit from improved system uptime.[493]

M2M communication is not just important to very large manufacturers or to firms producing high-technology products. Mohawk Fine Papers, a New York-based paper manufacturer, monitors its machinery's energy use and is also starting to use M2M systems to determine when machines need maintenance; for example, one system monitors calcium buildup on a vacuum pump, calling for maintenance only when the buildup reaches a certain level. This reduces resource costs and could reduce downtime because employees do not need to perform periodic machine maintenance checks.[494]

Risks and Vulnerabilities of the Internet of Things

Although connected machines can offer valuable efficiency and quality improvements, collecting big data from communicating devices and using the data to make changes to manufacturing processes is accompanied by certain risks. These risks include cybersecurity breaches and potential disruptions from technology failures.

Cybersecurity breaches can be damaging to manufacturing firms.[495] IT system vulnerabilities might allow outsiders to access proprietary big data on manufacturing processes or machine functions, to steal trade secrets, or even to change or shut down machine functions. Security breaches not only create costs from loss of production time and the need to increase security infrastructure after the incident, but can also trigger negative media attention and distrust from customers. When comparing concerns across different business sectors, the World Economic Forum finds that cybersecurity-related breakdowns of digital infrastructure in the cloud and the

---

[492] Fitzgerald, "An Internet for Manufacturing," January 28, 2013; GE Reports, "Meet Your Maker," February 25, 2014.
[493] Cisco Systems, "General Motors," 2010.
[494] Fitzgerald, "An Internet for Manufacturing," January 28, 2013.
[495] Further discussion on the effects of cyber incidents on firms can be found in chapter 2. Chapter 4 also discusses privacy issues and other barriers to international trade.

Internet of Things would cause the most production delays and have the largest adverse effects on companies.[496] Cisco estimates that there are currently 10 billion devices connected to the Internet, and they expect that number to grow to 50 billion by 2020.[497] With so many devices available to connect to manufacturing firm networks, managing security vulnerabilities across the network and on individual devices is a significant challenge for M2M communications users.[498] Typically, many areas of firm activity are connected to secure company networks, and a single vulnerability can open the entire system to harm.[499]

M2M-related service disruptions arising from technological failures may also become a serious risk for manufacturers. With multiple machines connected and, in some cases, linked specifically to provide backup for each other in the case of a failure, a malfunction can create unanticipated disruptions or headaches. In addition, for many companies, it is likely that the machines connected to the production network are of various ages and technical specifications, and this added system complexity increases the chance that a technical failure will create production problems. To counter this possibility, companies plan for system failures by programming machines with set production patterns that will prevail even if connectivity is disrupted. While a connection failure may temporarily interrupt access to sensor-sourced data, it should not halt production.[500]

Case Study 7: Digital Innovations in Agriculture

Novel Internet-based M2M communication technologies are part of the fast-growing U.S. precision farming market (with sales reaching $3.7 billion by 2018, according to one industry observer).[501] Farmers have traditionally walked their fields or used aerial and satellite photography to improve crop yield and farm efficiency. Such efforts, however, can be time consuming and costly, and may not identify problems in a timely way. Missing early signs of disease or infestation can result in crop damage, lower yields, and substantial monetary losses.[502] The introduction of M2M technologies can help improve crop yields and reduce crop damage through quicker, more precise diagnosis, enhancing investment returns as a result.[503]

---

[496] WEF with McKinsey & Company, Risk and Responsibility in a Hyperconnected World, January 2014.

[497] Bradley, Barbier, and Handler, "Embracing the Internet of Everything," 2013.

[498] IHS Technology, "Rise of Wireless Technology Poses Security Risks," February 3, 2014.

[499] Perlroth, "Hackers Lurking in Vents and Soda Machines," April 7, 2014.

[500] Moor, "Connecting with the Industrial Internet of Things (IIoT)," October 29, 2013.

[501] Forbes, "DuPont's Encirca Farm Services," March 11, 2014. While the range of activities and technologies included under the heading "precision farming" varies, new ways of using the capability of connected machines is central to recent innovations in agriculture.

[502] Huting, "Do You Really Know Your Fields?" August 2013, 22; Anderson, "Agricultural Drones," n.d. (accessed April 24, 2014); U.S. farmer, telephone interviews by USITC staff, December 11, 2013, and February 3, 2014. Although farmers ideally should inspect their crops weekly, the high cost of each inspection (often exceeding $800 for an average-sized farm of about 400 acres) can result in less frequent inspections. Commercial farms can have upwards of 1,400 acres. Canadian agronomist, telephone interview by USITC staff, May 20, 2014.

[503] Huting, "Do You Really Know Your Fields?" August 2013, 22; Anderson, "Agricultural Drones," n.d. (accessed April 24, 2014); U.S. farmer, telephone interviews by USITC staff, December 11, 2013, and February 3, 2014; Canadian farmer, interview by USITC staff, May 13, 2014; Canadian agronomist, telephone interview by USITC staff, May 20, 2014.

With Internet-connected sensors on farm equipment and unmanned aerial vehicles (UAVs), and new techniques for data mapping and analysis delivered through cloud computing providers, farmers are able to collect, process, and interpret large amounts of real-time, location-specific data about the status of crops, soil nutrients, and water. Action can then be taken earlier, more quickly, and with greater accuracy.[504] Better information about the health of their crops is likely to be all the more valuable to farmers given that they already face great economic uncertainty from changing weather conditions and volatile market prices.[505]

M2M Communications-based Packages Delivering Agricultural Solutions

Many large agricultural companies have introduced products and services based on digital M2M communications to meet strong customer demand. John Deere, for example, offers a service processing very large datasets that combine data from multiple external sources (e.g., location-specific weather forecasts and crop-planting histories) with information collected from sensors installed on its farm equipment (e.g., data on soil conditions and water levels). The service uses these data to generate real-time, farm-specific guidance for planting, harvesting, and plowing, as well as projections of crop yields. Farmers can access these data services instantaneously via computer or mobile applications. Bayer CropScience and DuPont (both individually and in separate collaborations with John Deere), as well as Monsanto (leveraging several recent acquisitions), are developing similar comprehensive packages. These technology packages integrate time-sensitive information derived from farm-equipment sensors with data analytics and other cloud computing services to deliver agricultural solutions to farmers.[506]

Typically, these subscription-based packages allow interactive cycles of data collection and dissemination between farmers, their equipment (e.g., tractors and planters), farm product companies, local services providers such as seed dealers and agronomists, and others in the agricultural community, via wireless connections and mobile applications.[507] For example, crop and soil data collected by sensors as a tractor traverses a field can be wirelessly transmitted to

---

[504] *Forbes*, "DuPont's Encirca Farm Services," March 11, 2014. The sensors and UAVs are typically equipped with GPS capability as well as wireless communications, so that observed information can be mapped precisely.

[505] U.S. farmer, telephone interview by USITC staff, April 18, 2014. It was noted during the interview that a key benefit of the additional technology is to reduce some of the uncertainties farmers face. An international example of the value of organized data collection in agriculture is a rural initiative implemented in India called "e-Choupal." ITC Limited, a private-sector Indian agricultural export company, has established an Internet-based database for Indian farmers containing data about a wide variety of supply chain variables. Farmers can also seek interactive information via e-mail from sector experts about best practices. This information portal assists in enhancing the efficiency and competitiveness of the Indian agricultural sector and individual farmers. ITC Limited, "E-Choupal," n.d. (accessed April 25, 2014).

[506] Bayer CropScience, "Bayer, John Deere Join Forces on Agronomic Data," March 14, 2014; Kaskey, "DuPont Joins Deere in Big Data Challenge," November 8, 2013; Monsanto, "FieldScripts: FieldScripts Will Be the First," n.d. (accessed March 15, 2014).

[507] One agronomist, who provides "prescriptions" to farmers based on such data, notes that these services mesh agronomic knowledge with "data crunching," allowing farmers to better manage the collected data. Canadian agronomist, telephone interview by USITC staff, May 20, 2014.

an agricultural company. The company can, in turn, create maps of the terrain and analyze the data to identify the best crops or treatments. Numerous current and historical factors are woven into the analysis, including "grain moisture, historical yields and nutrient deficiencies."[508] The company then sends the data analysis and instructions over the Internet back to the farmer, who can wirelessly transmit it to equipment such as a planter to automatically program the desired seeding and/or crop treatment (figure 6.1).

Figure 6.1 Interactive digital data transfer chain between the agricultural community and equipment

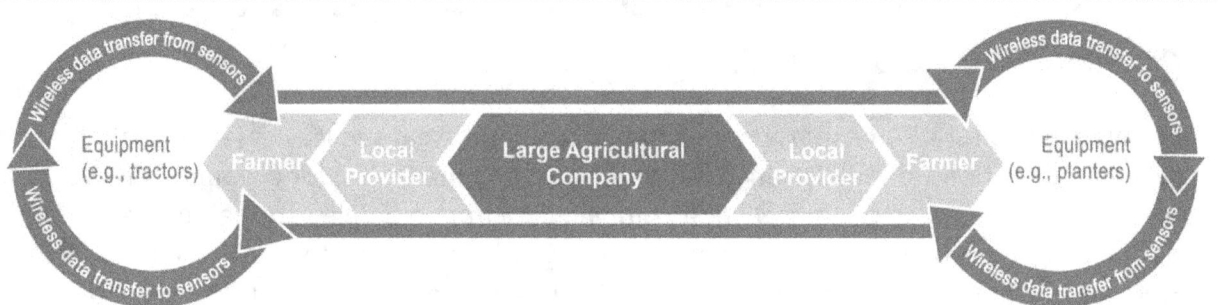

Source: USITC staff.

Although sources say it is too early to quantify the costs and benefits to all parties, some preliminary industry estimates exist. DuPont and Monsanto estimate that the benefits to farmers in terms of additional revenue from increased yields (on the order of $25–$50 per acre) could be more than twice the cost of their M2M data services ($10–$20 per acre in 2014). For example, Monsanto reports that trials in 2013 of its service with corn farmers in Illinois, Indiana, Iowa, and Minnesota increased farmers' yields by 5–10 bushels of corn per acre on average, equivalent to an increase of $25–$50 gross revenue per acre, assuming a price of $5 per bushel of corn. [509] While this brief cost-benefit comparison suggests that such services may be economically feasible for farmers, the comparison does not take into account other costs that would influence farmers' decisions, such as any required initial investment in computers, smartphones, or other devices, as well as training costs.[510] Service providers, on the other hand, see significant revenue growth potential from offering these innovative services. For example, DuPont has stated that it expects to accrue an additional $500 million annually from providing such services (equal to about 4 percent of its 2013 revenue from agricultural products).[511]

---

[508] Kaskey, "DuPont Joins Deere in Big Data Challenge," November 8, 2013.

[509] Kaskey, "Monsanto Buying Climate Corp.," October 2, 2013; *Forbes*, "DuPont's Encirca Farm Services," March 11, 2014.

[510] For example, according to one source, adding a computer to tractors to monitor planting can cost about $4,000; retrofitting older equipment with the necessary hardware and software can amount to about $8,000; and retrofitting with GPS equipment can cost about $15,000. Dreibus, "A Speedier Way to Sow," May 23, 2014, B1.

[511] *Forbes*, "DuPont's Encirca Farm Services," March 11, 2014; Kaskey, "DuPont Joins Deere in Big Data Challenge," November 8, 2013.

Growing Use of Unmanned Aerial Vehicles (UAVs)

Taking advantage of recent innovations in several technologies—GPS, machine automation and robotics, and M2M communications—farmers are also starting to fly UAVs to conduct crop inspections more efficiently, when airspace regulations allow them to do so. These "agricultural drones" are equipped with remote sensors and cameras that can stream information back to the farmer's own device or to a cloud-based data analytics services provider. UAVs can be programmed to fly specific, scheduled circuits over particular areas and to transfer the information wirelessly to the farmer's tablet or smart phone, giving farmers accurate and comparable real-time data.[512] Using UAVs in this way can significantly lower inspection costs—estimates suggest that the cost of inspections falls significantly from about $2 per acre to $0.50 per acre—possibly prompting more frequent inspections and potentially increasing farm productivity as a result of both lower input costs and better crop yields. The ability to make more frequent and precise inspections helps farmers to identify problems in crop development early enough to treat (or even prevent) them.[513]

It is expected that UAVs will be integrated into U.S. airspace in 2015, and a report published by the Association for Unmanned Vehicle Systems International (AUVSI) estimates that U.S. agriculture will account for about 80–90 percent of the "known potential markets" for UAVs by 2025.[514] The estimated value of such markets for commercial UAVs in the United States is expected to grow in the first three years after UAVs are integrated into U.S. airspace, from $1.1 billion of added value in the first year to $3.5 billion in the third year. AUVSI predicts that value-added will continue to grow in later years, rising to over $5.1 billion per annum in 2025 (the 10th year in the AUVSI's forecast).[515] In the first three years, the introduction of UAVs is expected to lead to the creation of about 70,000 jobs (for UAV production and development, as well as the application of UAVs in agriculture and elsewhere). By 2025, cumulative job creation is expected to total more than 100,000 jobs.[516]

UAVs are already being used for farming and other commercial applications in other countries: for example, unmanned helicopters have been used in Japan for spraying crops for over 20

---

[512] U.S. farmer, telephone interviews by USITC staff, December 11, 2013, and February 3, 2014. Remote sensors on UAVs increase efficiency by providing specialized images (e.g., aerial, topographical, and multispectral, including infrared).

[513] Although some UAVs with professional remote sensor systems can cost as much as $40,000–$50,000, those characterized as being in the "hobbyist" range (including ones that farmers might buy) could cost $1,000–$10,000. Farmers reportedly see this latter price band as a relatively low-cost approach, given the much higher cost of other farm equipment and the substantial benefits the UAVs will likely generate (e.g., lowered costs paired with increased productivity). Industry representative and U.S. farmer, telephone interviews by USITC staff, December 11, 2013, and February 5, 2014; Anderson, "Agricultural Drones," n.d. (accessed April 24, 2014); Precision Drones, "Drones for Agricultural Crop Surveillance." n.d., http://precisiondrone.com/drones-for-agriculture.html (accessed January 31, 2014).

[514] AUVSI, *The Economic Impact of Unmanned Aircraft Systems Integration,* March 2013, 2; Warwick, "AUVSI—Precision Agriculture Will Lead Civil UAS," March 12, 2013.

[515] AUVSI, The Economic Impact of Unmanned Aircraft Systems Integration, March 2013, 19.

[516] AUVSI, *The Economic Impact of Unmanned Aircraft Systems Integration,"* March 2013, 2; Toscano, "AUVSI Encourages FAA," January 27, 2014.

years.[517] Canada has also begun to introduce regulations for the use of UAVs within and beyond visual range for numerous applications, including agriculture, requiring UAV operators to obtain a Special Flight Operation Certificate.[518] In 2012, France announced regulations opening up its airspace to civilian UAVs, the first country to do so. By the end of 2013, over 200 operators had licenses to fly UAVs in France, and some of these operators are using UAVs to collect agricultural data.[519]

However, widespread adoption of wirelessly connected UAVs in the United States and many other markets has been delayed by regulatory hurdles. U.S. national regulators are only just starting the process of integrating civilian UAVs into the national airspace. As indicated earlier, the Federal Aviation Administration (FAA) is not expected to open U.S. airspace to commercial UAVs until September 2015.[520] AUVSI has requested that the FAA consider allowing limited use of UAVs in areas such as rural farms until the FAA's rules are finalized.[521] In addition, there may be other regulatory issues related to allocation of wireless airwave spectrum, given that UAVs will likely require access in order to navigate and communicate.[522]

Online Privacy Considerations to Be Addressed

The adoption of Internet technologies in many other industry contexts has raised widespread security concerns, regardless of the data collection method used. U.S. farmers, too, have expressed disquiet about the potential security of their data once collected. It is likely that measures to protect farmers' competitive information and individual data privacy will need to be introduced as the use of these services becomes more widespread.[523] Monsanto has already said it will enter into confidentiality agreements with farmers to protect data.[524] As noted by one industry participant, continued two-way data collaboration and cooperation between the

---

[517] In 1991, the Japanese Ministry of Agriculture, Forestry, and Fishery introduced a policy of promoting the use of unmanned helicopters in crop-dusting for rice farming. Koebler, "Drones Will Revolutionize Farming First, Not Delivery," December 16, 2013; Nicas, "From Farms to Films," March 11, 2014, B1; Yamaha Motor Australia, "History." http://rmax.yamaha-motor.com.au/history (accessed June 16, 2014).

[518] Transport Canada, "Unmanned Air Vehicle (UAV)," May 3, 2010.

[519] Under France's rules, drones are specifically authorized to engage in agricultural activities, package delivery, advertising (e.g., towing a banner), firefighting, and aerial observation, among other activities. Elzas, "Over 200 Operators Licensed to Fly," December 31, 2013; Hogan Lovells, "Preparing for the Swarm," Winter 2013, 4.

[520] The FAA Modernization and Reform Act of 2012 mandated that the FAA integrate civil UAVs into U.S. airspace by September 30, 2015. In November 2013, the FAA published a five-year roadmap for doing this, and has since selected test site operators, as part of its process to determine how to integrate UAVs into the national airspace. FAA, *Integration of Civil Unmanned Aircraft Systems*, November 2013; Hogan Lovells, "Preparing for the Swarm," Winter 2013, 3–4.

[521] Toscano, "AUVSI Encourages FAA," January 27, 2014.

[522] Hogan Lovells, "Preparing for the Swarm," Winter 2013, 5–6.

[523] U.S. farmer, telephone interview by USITC staff, February 3, 2014; Bunge, "Big Data Comes to the Farm," February 25, 2014, 1.

[524] Rye, "There's an App for 300-Bushel Corn," August 23, 2013.

farmers and others in the agricultural community, including the large agricultural companies, would ideally create a viable value chain beneficial to all parties.[525]

Case Study 8: Internet User Data Collection—Balancing Benefits with Privacy Concerns

The previous case studies in this report have each focused on a particular type of business activity—farming, manufacturing, content creation, and so on. The following case study, by contrast, looks at an activity that crosses sectors—one that, in fact, now permeates many areas of digital trade: the collection of data about Internet users. This activity offers valuable opportunities to business and other organizations, and can benefit Internet users as well. But it also presents significant risks to both parties. This case study describes how companies gather data about individual Internet users; the value to consumers of the services enabled by the information collected, as well as to the companies that collect it; and consumers' concerns about how companies use the data, along with the companies' responses. Findings from the Commission's survey on firms' concerns about data privacy and collection are presented in chapter 4.

Companies Use Many Tools to Collect and Aggregate Information about Internet Users' Activities Online

Companies and other organizations online often collect information about Internet users that visit their websites. Collectively, the tools described in box 6.2 allow companies to collect information about users' searches, other websites visited, time spent on the site, pages and other links opened, physical location, previous visits to the website, log-in information, and custom settings specified by the user.

Box 6.2 How websites collect information from users

Websites collect information from people accessing the website from a computer or mobile device Web browser or application through various evolving methods, including the following.

Cookies are text files that a website server sends to a Web browser and that the browser uses to transmit information about the computer to the website server.[526] The operator of the website sends first-party cookies. The website operator can also allow a partner, such as an advertising network, to send and place a cookie. Since this is done by a third party, it is called a third-party cookie. For example, the website http://www.news.com sends two cookies, one from news.com, the first-party cookie, and another cookie from advertisinginfo.com, the third-party cookie.[527]

---

[525] Canadian agronomist, telephone interview by USITC staff, May 20, 2014.
[526] Barth, "HTTP State Management Mechanism," April 2011.
[527] IAB, "Cookies on Mobile 101," November 2013, 3.

Web beacons, also called clear gifs, or 1x1 pixels, transmit information about which specific pages or sections of pages the browser viewed.

Device identifiers or statistical IDs are used by websites accessed from mobile phones or wireless devices to collect information.[528]

The information that websites can collect is limited to information on the computer's Internet browser and information transmitted between the website server and the browser. This allows companies to collect both personally identifiable information (PII) and non-personally identifiable information (non-PII). PII is information such as a name, email address, mailing address, or phone number.[529] Many companies state that they only collect PII that is provided on the site, and use it to respond to requests and queries.[530] Non-PII includes demographic information (such as city or state), website activity information, Internet Protocol (IP) address, browser type, language, and time of visit.[531]

Internet User Data Collection Helps Digital Services Evolve and Become More Efficient

Companies use consumer data collected online to derive value through two broad approaches.[532] The first approach uses personal data to create new or more efficient services, and generates revenues on a subscription basis or through advertising to users. These companies market directly to Internet users. The second approach uses personal data to construct profiles of consumer preferences and buying patterns, and generates revenue by selling access to those profiles or consumer lists. [533]

There is substantial overlap between these two approaches, and it is important to note that many companies take both approaches to earn revenue from services enabled by consumer data. Many companies attract users with an efficient service, and then collect data about the users that can be monetized. For example, Google, one of the largest companies by revenue in data-driven services and marketing, collects information about *how* people use its Web services and also collects information *about* the people that use its services. Google develops its own digital services to attract and keep users and collects information from that user pool; 71 percent of Google's advertising revenue comes from Google's own websites,[534] which include search, e-mail, calendar, documents handling, online storage, and map services.[535] Many of these services only charge for use above certain thresholds, and only a small

---

[528] Ibid., 6.

[529] IAB, "Self-Regulatory Program for Online Behavioral Advertising," 25–26 (accessed March 20, 2014).

[530] Google website, "Information We Share: Privacy Policy," https://www.google.com/policies/privacy/#infouse (accessed April 11, 2014).

[531] Yahoo website, "Right Media Exchange Privacy Policy," https://info.yahoo.com/privacy/us/biz/rightmedia/details.html (accessed April 11, 2014).

[532] David, Kalapesi, and Rose, "Unleashing the Value of Consumer Data," January 2, 2013, 2.

[533] Whitney, "Poll: Most Won't Pay to Read Newspapers Online," January 13, 2010.

[534] $31.2 billion of Google's $43.7 billion in advertising revenues came from advertising placed on its own websites. Google Inc. "Form 10-K 2012," 59.

[535] Google AdWords website, "About the Google Display Network," https://support.google.com/adwords/answer/2404190 (accessed February 6, 2014).

percentage of users pay for the service.[536] The users who do not pay for online services are assumed to be willing to exchange information about their online activity in return for the free service.[537]

Internet User Data Enables Incremental Product Evolution

The first approach operates with user data to create new or more efficient services. Companies and organizations use aggregated data about thousands of individuals to improve their service. The goal is to use large amounts of information collected from large numbers of individuals, as discussed in case study 5 above, to optimize a service or solution.[538]

Some of the companies that do this do not in fact earn any revenue from this activity, but do so to strengthen their work in the second approach, data-driven marketing, which is described below. Other companies or organizations that take this approach simply aim to develop a new or better service, with no profit motive, as described below. Many of the services offer an intangible benefit, so measuring its value proves difficult.

Companies and organizations collect and use consumer data gathered online to offer a multitude of services, which are highly diverse and therefore difficult to categorize. Three examples are cited below to demonstrate the breadth of valuable activities enabled by the collection of user data:

- Collecting users' locations makes it far easier for map services to give directions; for services that review and recommend restaurants to locate nearby eating places; and for transportation services to dispatch vehicles. These types of apps use their own data in robust ways to improve services and to gain paying customers using the services.

- Data about how people read online books or e-books, such as the pages read, chapters skipped, or footnotes opened, allow companies to identify the most effective format to publish content. For example, a service called Aptara uses data from users to optimize the layout and presentation of books for reading comprehension, especially educational literature and textbooks, with the aim of enhancing learning.[539]

- Data submitted by users about their health or lifestyle allows companies to study public health issues. Lumos Labs, which designs online exercises to train cognitive functions,[540] collects data from its users, with their consent, that the company's science

---

[536] For example, only 3 million of 71 million users paid to listen to Pandora online radio in 2013. Voglin, "Not Enough People in the U.S.," October 2, 2014.

[537] Quelch, "How to Value the Advertising-Supported Internet," June 29, 2009; Deighton and Kornfeld, "Economic Value of the Advertising-Supported Internet," September 2012.

[538] Dean, Kalapesi, and Rose, "Unleashing the Value of Consumer Data," January 2, 2013, 24.

[539] USITC, hearing transcript, Moffett Field, CA, September 25, 2013, 214 (testimony of Pavan Arora, vice president, Aptara).

[540] Day, "Online Brain-training: Does It Really Work?" April 20, 2013.

team and academic institutions investigate through the Human Cognition Project.[541] These groups can use the large datasets and anonymous information about the users to study neuroscience topics, such as age-related cognitive decline.[542]

Internet User Data Helps Reduce Search Frictions

The second approach that companies take to derive value from consumer information collected online is to offer marketing services to producers or sellers of goods and services. The producers and sellers pay the companies that have collected or manage the data for the opportunity to market to interested consumers, identified based on the data about their Web browsing history. Access to detailed data about Internet users reduces the cost to companies of searching for people who are likely to be sales prospects.[543] This type of service is also called online behavioral advertising (OBA).[544]

By one simple measure, the value of personal data is what companies are willing to pay to access it. Unfortunately, this figure is not easy to come by. The Interactive Advertising Bureau (IAB), which produces quarterly surveys on Internet advertising revenues, reported that Internet advertising revenues in 2013 totaled $42.78 billion. This sum, however, accounts for only a small share of the total value created for companies that use Internet user data, and also includes revenues that do not depend on user data.[545] Another measure, from the Data-Driven Marketing Institute (DDMI), estimates that data-driven marketing contributed $156 billion in value-added revenues to the U.S. economy in 2012.[546] Still another method used to estimate the value of Internet marketing is the surplus[547] that consumers derive from advertising-supported websites, which is the difference between the value of Internet services to consumers and the actual price (i.e., nothing) that they paid for those services. The Boston Consulting Group has estimated the consumer surplus of the Internet to be at least $2,528 per person in the United States.[548]

A major part of data-driven Internet marketing is targeted advertising. Companies, known as ad delivery platforms or data managers, collect, aggregate, and anonymize information sourced from multiple websites to complete a list of attributes that is linked to a specific Web browser, which the companies assume represents an individual.[549] They collect this data from thousands

---

[541] Lumos Labs, interview by USITC staff, San Francisco, CA, April 16, 2013.

[542] Lumos Labs, "Human Cognition Project," Lumos Labs website, http://www.lumosity.com/hcp/get_involved/researcher (accessed February 6, 2014).

[543] Deighton and Johnson, "The Value of Data: Consequences," 19, October 18, 2013.

[544] TRUSTe, "What is Online Behavioral Advertising," http://www.truste.com/consumer-privacy/about-oba/ (accessed April 15, 2014).

[545] PricewaterhouseCoopers, "IAB internet advertising revenue report, 2013 full year results," April 2014, 2.

[546] Deighton and Johnson, "The Value of Data: Consequences," 14, October 18, 2013.

[547] Consumer surplus is the difference between the price that a consumer would be willing to pay for a good or service, and the price that the consumer did pay for that good or service.

[548] Dean, Kalapesi, and Rose, "Unleashing the Value of Consumer Data," January 2, 2013, 24.

[549] Experian website, "Mosaic USA Consumer Lifestyle Segmentation," http://www.experian.com/marketing-services/consumer-segmentation.html (accessed March 20, 2014).

of websites, using third-party cookies to build a large list of interests associated with an individual or unique Web browser.[550] The companies anonymize the information by removing any PII, but they link the data with a unique identifier, such as an IP address or an assigned string of numbers.[551] Finally, the ad platforms or data managers can detect when a person visits a certain website—for example, for dress shoes—and then sell the right to shoe companies to show advertisements for dress shoes on that same browser on different websites that are part of the same ad network.[552]

This marketing sector has vague borders and includes many companies that escape simple categorization. Many traditional advertising and marketing firms have expanded their services to offer marketing that uses anonymized data about Internet users. For example, WPP, a holding group for communications and advertising firms, lists 34 companies among its holdings that are "digital partners."[553] These include Internet companies that identify themselves as technology leaders, digital media platforms, Web publishing services, social networks, or platforms for real-time public self-expression. Ultimately, the common characteristic is that the firms each earn a large share of their revenues, often more than 80 percent, from Internet advertising.[554]

Internet Users' Concerns about Data Collected Online

An industry representative stated, "mainstream users do not always understand the consequences of their online actions. Many are unaware of the tradeoffs that are implicit in getting these services for free and what happens behind the scenes to the services and their data."[555] Nonetheless, Internet users are reportedly increasingly concerned about the information available about them online and how companies use it. According to a Pew study, "55% of Internet users have taken steps to avoid observation by specific people, organizations, or the government."[556] TRUSTe found that 92 percent of U.S. Internet users were concerned

---

[550] Ibid.

[551] Yahoo website, "Right Media Exchange Privacy Policy," https://info.yahoo.com/privacy/us/biz/rightmedia/details.html (accessed April 11, 2014); Facebook website, "Information We Receive and How It Is Used," https://www.facebook.com/about/privacy/your-info (accessed April 25, 2014).

[552] Google AdWords website, "Using Remarketing to Reach People," https://support.google.com/adwords/answer/2453998?hl=en (accessed February 6, 2014); Digital Advertising Alliance of Canada, http://youradchoices.ca/faq (accessed April 15, 2014).

[553] WPP Group website, "Digital Offerings Delivered through WPP Digital," http://www.wpp.com/wpp/about/whatwedo/wppdigital/#all (accessed March 20, 2014).

[554] Google earned 95 percent of its $50.2 billion 2012 revenues from ad sales (reported in its 2012 Form 10-K). Yahoo "generate[s] revenue principally from display advertising on Yahoo! Properties and from search advertising on Yahoo! Properties and Affiliate sites" (reported in its 2012 Form 10-K). Facebook earned 84 percent of worldwide revenue in 2012 from advertising (reported in its 2012 annual report).

[555] USITC, hearing transcript, Moffett Field, CA, September 25, 2013, 35 (testimony of Jim Cook, chief financial officer, Mozilla).

[556] Rainie et al., "Anonymity, Privacy, and Security Online," September 5, 2013.

about their online privacy, and that the percentage of the respondents "avoiding" companies they believe fail to protect their privacy has grown.[557] The most commonly cited reason for concern about online privacy was "businesses sharing my personal information with other companies." [558] Even services that do not sell or reveal user data face privacy concerns;[559] across all online activities, the surveys and polls cited above reveal that people believe companies lack the proper mechanisms to keep their personal information safe.[560]

Internet architects and engineers have also taken note of user concerns and responded by creating programs that allow users to control what information is collected—for instance, by preventing servers from sending third-party cookies.[561] A 2011 conference of the Worldwide Web Consortium (W3C)—an international community focused on developing web standards—discussed this issue and commented on increasing consumer interest in Web browsers that allowed Internet users to determine what information was collected.[562]

Consumers have taken action to defend their privacy on the Internet. Thousands of users have filed complaints with the U.S. Federal Trade Commission (FTC) about what they assert are violations of their privacy online. The FTC catalog of consumer protection complaints does not have a specific category for online data abuse, but the number of complaints about related areas where violations of digital privacy are likely to occur has risen. These include identity theft, the subject of 290,056 consumer complaints in 2013, and impostor scams, the subject of 121,720 complaints. (Complaints about identity theft made up 14 percent of all complaints filed that year, while those about impostor scams made up 6 percent of all complaints).[563] Due to the increase in complaints in this area, an FTC staff report in 2010 recommended that "commercial entities that collect or use consumer data that can be reasonably linked to a specific consumer, computer, or other device" create a "Do Not Track" feature. The report recognized, however, that there are "'commonly accepted data practices" for the collection of certain types of data for which consent should not be required.[564] The FTC has taken enforcement action when companies have deceptively gathered information on consumers. For example, the FTC found that a company named Epic "sniffed" the browsing history of Internet

[557] TRUSTe, "TRUSTe 2014 US Consumer Confidence Privacy Report," March 20, 2014, 3.

[558] Ibid.

[559] USITC, hearing transcript, Moffett Field, CA, September 25, 2013, 219 (testimony of Pavan Arora, vice president, Aptara).

[560] Urban, Hoofnagle, and Li, *Mobile Phones and Privacy*, July 11, 2012.

[561] IAB, "FAQ on Mozilla's Intention" (accessed April 18, 2014).

[562] W3C, W3C Workshop on Web Tracking and User Privacy, April 28–29, 2011, http://www.w3.org/2011/track-privacy/agenda.html (accessed April 18, 2014).

[563] FTC, "Consumer Sentinel Network Data Book," 2014, 6.

[564] FTC, "Protecting Consumer Privacy," 2010.

users to identify users that had visited any of more than 54,000 domains, including pages relating to financial and medical concerns.[565]

Internet Companies Are Working to Maintain Their Users' Trust

Several sources report that the online data marketing industry recognizes the risk that consumer concerns pose to their business. As stated by a leading non-profit Web browser designer, "The loss of user trust is far more dangerous than the loss of any potential revenues. Trust is the true currency that needs to be protected in the future of digital online lives."[566] If all Internet users blocked cookies, Web beacons, and other scripts that collect information about how they use the Internet and mobile applications, then many online services would fail to provide the benefits that they promise, and companies like Google, Yahoo, WordPress, and other data-driven marketing firms would lose large shares of their revenue streams.[567]

The United States does not have an omnibus legal environment that requires companies to provide data access and remediation to consumers. However, the companies that offer marketing services based on Internet user data or OBA have created overlapping service rules, guidelines, and codes of conduct to build and maintain user trust.[568] A few actions taken by companies to increase consumer trust of data usage include:

- Self-regulatory principles: The Self-Regulatory Program for Online Behavioral Advertising, developed by the American Association of Advertising Agencies, the Association of National Advertisers, the Direct Marketing Association and the IAB in conjunction with the Council of Better Business Bureaus, was created to help protect consumers' privacy rights.[569] This program applies to mobile advertising as well.

---

[565] FTC, "FTC Settlement Puts an End to 'History Sniffing,'" December 5, 2012. "History sniffing" is the practice of determining whether a consumer has previously visited a webpage by checking how a user's browser styles the display of a hyperlink. For example, if a consumer has previously visited a webpage, the hyperlink to that webpage may appear in purple, and if the consumer has not previously visited a webpage, the hyperlink may appear in blue. History-sniffing code would sniff whether the consumer's hyperlinks to specific webpages appeared in blue or purple. See FTC website, http://www.ftc.gov/sites/default/files/documents/cases/2013/03/130315 epicmarketplacecmpt.pdf (accessed June 10, 2014).

[566] USITC, hearing transcript, Moffett Field, CA, September 25, 2013, 36 (testimony of Jim Cook, chief financial officer, Mozilla).

[567] Yahoo! Inc., "Form 10-K," 2013, 25; Google Inc. "Form 10-K," 2013, 59.

[568] According to one industry expert, U.S. companies approach privacy using common-law principles, which focus on the use of the data. This differs from the European approach, which treats privacy as a human right, "so that the data itself has a tangible value to the user." USITC, hearing transcript, Moffett Field, CA, September 25, 2013, 84 (testimony of Markham Erickson, general counsel of the Internet Association and partner, Steptoe & Johnson). The USITC's *Digital Trade 1*, 2013, includes a full discussion of global approaches to personal privacy, discussing the sectoral approach to U.S. privacy law and the characteristic of targeted enforcement actions. USITC, *Digital Trade 1*, 2013, 5-09 to 5-10.

[569] IAB, "Self-Regulatory Program for Online Behavioral Advertising" (accessed March 20, 2014).

- Corporate codes of conduct: For example, WPP, a holding company which owns many agencies and firms that provide data management platforms and targeted advertising services, created a Data Code of Conduct in early 2013 that, among other topics, commits "to protecting consumer, client and employee data in accordance with national laws and industry codes."[570]

- Limits on advertising clients' marketing: Most companies that provide targeted advertising services control the use or disclosure of knowledge about medical, financial and other concerns in advertising by their customers.[571]

- Online blocking tools: Mozilla, which makes the Firefox Web browser, announced in 2011 that it would block all third-party cookies on the browser. Microsoft Internet Explorer, Apple Safari, and Google Chrome today also offer tools that block cookies.

Companies and Consumers Working Toward a Balance

As noted above, consumers have generally implicitly accepted free services in return for allowing the service provider to collect data from the user, some of which can be anonymized and sold as a marketing product. Increasingly, consumers are more concerned about how that data is aggregated to build unique profiles; the marketing pools into which the service provider places the customer, and for which they would receive targeted advertisements; and the extent to which other companies or people may gain access to these data.[572]

The search engine and Internet marketing industries recognize the risks of collecting data, but they do so because of the value it offers. It must, therefore, keep the trust of users if it is to continue its business operations.[573] On the one hand, privacy and consumer advocates say that even anonymized information can be so comprehensive and provide marketers with so much information that it constitutes a privacy violation. On the other hand, digital marketers argue that the rich level of detail about individual consumers, anonymized and aggregated, efficiently

---

[570] WPP PLC, *Annual Report 2012*, n.d. (accessed March 20, 2014), 146.

[571] For example, Google restricts any advertiser from "creating a remarketing list or creating ad content that specifically seeks to reach people in ways that are prohibited; creating ad content which implies knowledge of personally identifiable or sensitive information about the site or app visitor, even when the remarketing list has been created without using such information; including products which fall into these sensitive categories, such as pharmaceutical products, in any data feeds." The sensitive products enumerated by Google are "interest or participation in adult activities (including alcohol, gambling, adult dating, pornography, etc.); sexual behavior or orientation; racial or ethnic information; political affiliation; trade union membership or affiliation; religion or religious belief; negative financial status or situation; health or medical information; status as a child under 13; the commission or alleged commission of any crime." Google, Policy for advertising based on interests and location, https://support.google.com/adwordspolicy/answer/143465 (accessed January 29, 2014).

[572] *Forbes*, "In Brands We Trust," March 4, 2012.

[573] USITC hearing transcript, Washington, DC, March 7, 2013, 48–50 (testimony of Christopher Wolf, Future of Privacy Forum).

connects marketers with consumers likely to buy their products and removes search frictions.[574]

---

[574] *Forbes*, "In Brands We Trust," March 4, 2012; "Trust on the Internet," August 30, 2012.

Bibliography

Aberdeen Group. "Analytics in Insurance: Expect the Unexpected." Sector Insight Report, November 2013.

Accenture. "The Digital Insurer: A New Era in Insurance—Cloud Computing Changes the Game," December 6, 2012. http://www.accenture.com/us-en/Pages/insight-digital-insurer-new-era-insurance-cloud-computing-changes-game.aspx.

Anaplan. "Aviva Case Study: Aviva Brings Agility to Group Planning and Forecasting with Anaplan." Anaplan website. https://www.anaplan.com/customers/aviva-casestudy/ (accessed April 14, 2014).

Anderson, Chris. "Agricultural Drones." *MIT Technology Review*, n.d. http://www.technologyreview.com/featuredstory/526491/agricultural-drones/ (accessed April 24, 2014).

Annunziata, Marco, and Peter C. Evans. "The Industrial Internet@Work." General Electric, 2013. https://www.ge.com/sites/default/files/GE_IndustrialInternetatWork_WhitePaper_20131028.pdf.

Association for Unmanned Vehicle Systems International (AUVSI). *The Economic Impact of Unmanned Aircraft Systems Integration in the United States.* Arlington, VA: AUVSI, March 2013. http://higherlogicdownload.s3.amazonaws.com/AUVSI/958c920a-7f9b-4ad2-9807f9a4e95d1ef1/UploadedImages/New_Economic%20Report%202013%20Full.pdf.

Barth, A. "HTTP State Management Mechanism," RFC 6265, Internet Engineering Task Force (IETF), U.C. Berkeley, April 1, 2011. http://tools.ietf.org/html/rfc6265.

Bayer CropScience. "Bayer, John Deere Join Forces on Agronomic Data." News release. In *CropLife*, March 14, 2014. http://www.croplife.com/crop-inputs/bayer-john-deere-join-forces-on-agronomic-data/.

Berg Insight. "Car Telematics and Wireless M2M." Report brochure, 2014. http://www.berginsight.com/ReportPDF/ProductSheet/bi-car5-ps.pdf.

BigData-Startups. "John Deere Is Revolutionizing Farming with Big Data," n.d. http://www.bigdata-startups.com/BigData-startup/john-deere-revolutionizing-farming-big-data/ (accessed March 12, 2014).

Boston Consulting Group. "Becoming a 'Digital Insurer'—an Interview with Cathryn Riley, Aviva's COO." *IT Advantage*, September 26, 2013. https://www.bcgperspectives.com/content/interviews/information_technology_strateg y_insurance_cathryn_riley_becoming_digital_insurer/.

Bradley, Joseph, Joel Barbier, and Doug Handler. "Embracing the Internet of Everything to Capture Your Share of $14.4 Trillion." Cisco Systems, 2013. http://www.cisco.com/web/about/ac79/docs/innov/IoE_Economy.pdf.

Brat, Eric, Stephen Heydorn, Matthew Stover, and Martin Ziegler. "Big Data: the Next Big Thing for Insurers?" *BCG Perspectives*, March 25, 2013. https://www.bcgperspectives.com/content/articles/insurance_it_performance_big_dat a_next_big_thing_for_insurers/.

Brat, Eric, Davide Corradi, Ofir Eyal, Tim Hoying, and Yasushi Sasaki. "Telematics: The Test for Insurers." *BCG Perspectives*, December 4, 2013. https://www.bcgperspectives.com/content/articles/insurance_telematics_test_insurers /.

Brown, Brad, David Court, and Tim McGuire. "Views from the Front Lines of the Data-Analytics Revolution." *INN Breaking News*, March 10, 2014. http://www.insurancenetworking.com/news/views-front-lines-data-analytics-revolution-mckinsey-33985-1.html. *This article was originally published in McKinsey Quarterly.*

Brynjolfsson, Erik, and Andrew McAfee. The Second Machine Age: Work, Progress, and Prosperity in a Time of Brilliant Technologies. New York, NY: W.W. Norton & Company, 2014.

Bunge, Jacob. "Big Data Comes to the Farm, Sowing Mistrust." *Wall Street Journal*, February 25, 2014.

Chui, Michael, Markus Löffler, and Roger Roberts. "The Internet of Things." McKinsey, March 2010. http://www.mckinsey.com/insights/high_tech_telecoms_internet/the_internet_of_thin gs.

Cisco Systems. "General Motors Prepares for Future with Next-Generation Information Networks for Global Manufacturing Operations; On Track to Achieve 166% ROI over Five Years," 2010. http://www.cisco.com/web/strategy/docs/manufacturing/Cisco-AutoCaseStudy-GM.pdf.

Cognizant. "Using Advanced Analytics to Combat P&C Claims Fraud." Cognizant Reports, December 2012. http://www.cognizant.com/InsightsWhitepapers/Using-Advanced-Analytics-to-Combat-PandC-Claims-Fraud.pdf.

Columbia School of International and Public Affairs (SIPA). "e-Choupal – Empowering Indian Farmers via the Internet." Website of a 2007 SIPA course ("New Media and Development Communication"), n.d. http://www.columbia.edu/itc/sipa/nelson/newmediadev/Empowering%20Farmers%20-%20India.html (accessed April 25, 2014).

Crovitz, Gordon. "Liberate the Drones of Commerce." *Wall Street Journal*, January 12, 2014.

Cruz, Laurence. "After Fukushima: Crowd-Sourcing Initiative Sets Radiation Data Free." The Network: Cisco's Technology News Site, March 4, 2014. http://newsroom.cisco.com/press-release-content?articleId=1360403.

Day, Elizabeth. "Online Brain-Training: Does It Really Work?" *Observer*, April 20, 2013. http://www.theguardian.com/science/2013/apr/21/brain-training-online-neuroscience-elizabeth-day.

De La Merced, Michael J. "Alibaba Confirms It Will Begin I.P.O. Process in U.S." Dealbook, *New York Times,* March 16, 2014. http://dealbook.nytimes.com/2014/03/16/alibaba-confirms-it-will-begin-i-p-o-process-in-u-s/.

Dean, David, Carl Kalapesi, and John Rose. "Unleashing the Value of Consumer Data." *Boston Consulting Group IT Advantage—Outlook*, January 2, 2013. https://www.bcgperspectives.com/content/articles/digital_economy_consumer_insight_unleashing_value_of_consumer_data/.

Deere & Co. "Automated Crop Reporting: Question and Answer," n.d. http://www.deere.com/en_US/docs/agriculture/crop_insurance/pdfs/acr/acr_qa_customer.pdf (accessed March 12, 2014).

———. "New John Deere Strategy Takes Intelligent Farming to the Next Level." News release, November 13, 2011. https://www.deere.com/wps/dcom/en_INT/our_company/news_and_media/press_releases/2011/nov/farm_sight.page.

Deighton, John, and Peter A. Johnson. *The Value of Data: Consequences for Insight, Innovation and Efficiency in the U.S. Economy.* Data-Driven Marketing Institute, Washington, DC, October 18, 2013. http://ddminstitute.thedma.org/.

Deighton, John, and Leora D. Kornfeld. *Economic Value of the Advertising-Supported Internet Ecosystem.* Interactive Advertising Bureau. New York: IAB, September 2012. http://www.iab.net/media/file/iab_Report_September-24-2012_4clr_v1.pdf.

Deloitte Touche Tohmatsu, Ltd. "The Digital Transformation of Customer Services," 2013. http://issuu.com/deloittenl/docs/digital_transformation_customer_services.

Dreibus, Tony C. "A Speedier Way to Sow Is Changing Farm Work." *Wall Street Journal*, May 23, 2014. http://online.wsj.com/news/articles/SB20001424052702304908304579566043904022508 (subscription required).

Elzas, Sarah. "Over 200 Operators Licensed to Fly Civilian Drones in France." Radio France Internationale, December 31, 2013. http://www.english.rfi.fr/france/20131231-over-200-operators-licenced-fly-civilian-drones-france.

Ernst & Young (EY). "Insurance in a Digital World: the Time Is Now. EY Global Insurance Digital Survey 2013," October 1, 2013. http://www.ey.com/GL/en/Industries/Financial-Services/Insurance/Insurance-in-a-digital-world--The-time-is-now.

Executive Office of the President. *Big Data: Seizing Opportunities, Preserving Values,* May 1, 2014. http://www.whitehouse.gov/sites/default/files/docs/big_data_privacy_report_may_1_2014.pdf .

Farm Industry News. "John Deere Adds Several Environmental Sensors to Field Connect Soil Monitoring System," March 1, 2013. http://farmindustrynews.com/tools/john-deere-adds-several-environmental-sensors-field-connect-soil-monitoring-system.

Federal Trade Commission (FTC). "Consumer Sentinel Network Data Book for January–December 2013." Washington, DC: FTC, 2014. http://www.ftc.gov/system/files/documents/reports/consumer-sentinel-network-data-book-january-december-2013/sentinel-cy2013.pdf.

———. "FTC Settlement Puts an End to 'History Sniffing' by Online Advertising Network Charged with Deceptively Gathering Data on Consumers." Press release, December 5, 2012. http://www.ftc.gov/news-events/press-releases/2012/12/ftc-settlement-puts-end-history-snpiffing-online-advertising.

———. "Protecting Consumer Privacy in an Era of Rapid Change: A Proposed Framework for Businesses and Policymakers." Preliminary FTC Staff Report. Washington, DC: FTC, 2010. http://www.ftc.gov/sites/default/files/documents/reports/federal-trade-commission-bureau-consumer-protection-preliminary-ftc-staff-report-protecting-consumer/101201privacyreport.pdf.

Felix, Samantha. "How to Stop Facebook from Tracking You." *Business Insider*, September 12, 2014. http://www.businessinsider.com/heres-how-to-stop-facebook-from-tracking-you-2012-9?op=1.

Fitzgerald, Michael. "An Internet for Manufacturing." *MIT Technology Review*, January 28, 2013. http://www.technologyreview.com/news/509331/an-internet-for-manufacturing.

Forbes. "DuPont's Encirca Farm Services to Bolster Agricultural Revenues." March 11, 2014. http://www.forbes.com/sites/greatspeculations/2014/03/11/duponts-encirca-farm-services-to-bolster-agricultural-revenues/.

———. "In Brands We Trust—Why Brands Must Treat Trust Like Gold." March 4, 2012. http://www.forbes.com/sites/steveolenski/2014/03/04/in-brands-we-trust-why-brands-must-treat-trust-like-gold/2/.

———. "Trust on the Internet: The Solution Is Ahead." August 30, 2012. http://www.forbes.com/sites/kostaperic/2012/08/30/the-internet-the-digital-economy-and-trust-where-are-we/.

General Electric. "Meet Your Maker: The Third Industrial Revolution Will Be Crowdsourced and Digitized." *GE Reports*, February 25, 2014. http://www.gereports.com/post/77834521966/meet-your-maker.

Gentrup, Anna. "Courage Can Eliminate Fears about 'Big Data,' German IT specialists say." *Insurance Day*, March 4, 2014. https://www.insuranceday.com/generic_listing/it/courage-can-eliminate-fears-about-big-data-german-it-specialists-say.htm?origin=internalSearch.

Google Inc. "Form 10-K for Fiscal Year Ended December 31, 2012." Annual report for the Securities and Exchange Commission, January 29, 2013. http://www.sec.gov/Archives/edgar/data/1288776/000119312513028362/d452134d10k.htm or https://investor.google.com/pdf/20121231_google_10K.pdf.

Hamblen, Matt. "AT&T and GE Join Up on Wireless Global Controls for Industrial Machines." *Computerworld*, October 9, 2013. http://www.computerworld.com/s/article/9243091/AT_T_and_GE_join_up_on_wireless_global_controls_for_industrial_machines.

Hamm, Steve. "Big Data: How Infinity Sniffs Out Insurance Fraud." IBM Smarter Planet blog, March 20, 2014. http://asmarterplanet.com/blog/2012/03/big-data-how-infinity-sniffs-out-insurance-fraud.html (accessed March 27, 2014).

Hessman, Travis. "The Dawn of the Smart Factory." *IndustryWeek*, February 14, 2013. http://www.industryweek.com/print/technology/dawn-smart-factory.

Hogan Lovells. "Preparing for the Swarm: Ensuring our Airwaves and Airspace Can Accommodate Transformational Drone Technology." *Global Media and Communications Quarterly*, Winter 2013.

Hoying, Tim, James Platt, Michael Bongartz, and Yasushi Sasaki. "Improve P&C Profitability and Premium Growth: Six Steps." *BCG Perspectives*, January 09, 2014. https://www.bcgperspectives.com/content/articles/insurance_financial_institutions_improve_p_c_profitability_premium_growth/.

Hughes, Matthew. "Preferred Risk in Life Insurance." SCOR inFORM whitepaper, November 2012. http://www.scor.com/images/stories/pdf/library/scor-inform/Preferred%20Risk%20in%20Life%20Insurance.pdf.

Huting, Kathy. "Do You Really Know Your Fields?" *Farm Industry News*, August 2013. http://farmindustrynews.com/sitefiles/farmindustrynews.com/files/uploads/2013/07/FIN_22-25_UAVs.pdf.

IBM Algorithmics. "Internal models for insurance companies: Components, considerations and benefits." IBM White Paper, July 2012. http://www-01.ibm.com/common/ssi/cgi-bin/ssialias?infotype=SA&subtype=WH&htmlfid=YTW03268USEN#loaded.

———. "Solvency II—Setting Higher Goals for Comparative Advantage." IBM White Paper, June 2013. http://public.dhe.ibm.com/common/ssi/ecm/en/ytw03295usen/YTW03295USEN.PDF.

IBM Corporation. "IBM Launches New Software and Consulting Services to Help Organizations Tackle $3.5 Trillion Lost Annually to Fraud and Financial Crime." news release, March 20, 2014. http://www-03.ibm.com/press/us/en/pressrelease/43459.wss.

IHS Technology. "Rise of Wireless Technology Poses Security Risks for Manufacturers." Press release, February 3, 2014. http://press.ihs.com/press-release/design-supply-chain/rise-wireless-technology-poses-security-risks-manufacturers.

Ilett, Dan. "Counting the Human Value in the Internet of Things." *Greenbang: The Newsletter*, December 6, 2013. http://www.greenbang.com/counting-the-human-value-of-the-internet-of-things_25723.html.

Intel. "Accelerating Business Growth through IT: 2012-2013 Intel IT Performance Report," 2013. http://www.intel.com/content/dam/www/public/us/en/documents/reports/2012-2013-intel-it-performance-report.pdf.

Interactive Advertising Bureau (IAB). "Cookies on Mobile 101: Understanding the Limitations of Cookie-Based Tracking for Mobile Advertising," November 2013. http://www.iab.net/media/file/CookiesOnMobile101Final.pdf.

———. "FAQ on Mozilla's Intention to Block Third-Party Cookies." http://www.iab.net/mozilla (accessed April 18, 2014).

———. "Self-Regulatory Program for Online Behavioral Advertising," October 4, 2010. http://www.iab.net/public_policy/self-reg.

———. "IAB Display Advertising Guidelines," February 26, 2012. http://www.iab.net/displayguidelines.

ITC Limited. "E-Choupal," n.d. http://www.itcportal.com/businesses/agri-business/e-choupal.aspx (accessed April 25, 2014).

Jacobs, Sherelle. "'Big Data Comes to Africa." *ThisIsAfricaOnline.com*, March 3, 2014. http://www.thisisafricaonline.com/News/Big-Data-comes-to-Africa?ct=true.

Jacobson, Simon. "Getting Business Value from Manufacturing Execution Systems." Gartner webinar presentation, December 12, 2013.

Johnson, Carolyn Y. "Crowdsourced Radiation Monitoring Website to Measure Fukushima's Footprint." *Science in Mind* (blog), *Boston Globe,* January 14, 2014. http://www.boston.com/news/science/blogs/science-in-mind/2014/01/14/-crowdsourced-radiation-monitoring-website-measure-fukushima-footprint/U1B4mLiqWbpkwfcS1YGaJM/blog.html.

Johnson, Johnell. "Is Geocoding Right for You?" *Acord Weekly*, Vol 4, Issue 32 (August 7, 2013). https://www.acord.org/media/newsletters/Newsletters/20130807_v-04_i-32_version_2.pdf.

Kachroo, Vinod, and Arunashish Majumdar. "Data in the Digital Era—Driving New Business Models and Results for Insurers." Tata Consultancy Services White Paper, April 2014.

Kart, Lisa. "Big Data Industry Insights." Gartner webinar presentation 49361, March 18, 2014.

Kaskey, Jack. "DuPont Joins Deere in Big Data Challenge to Monsanto." *Bloomberg Businessweek*, November 8, 2013. http://www.businessweek.com/news/2013-11-08/dupont-joins-deere-on-software-in-big-data-challenge-to-monsanto.

———. "Monsanto Buying Climate Corp. to Add Big Data for Farmers." *Bloomberg Businessweek*, October 2, 2013. http://www.bloomberg.com/news/2013-10-02/monsanto-to-buy-climate-corp-profit-forecast-trails-estimates.html.

Kinney, Aaron. "Fukushima Radiation near Half Moon Bay? State Health Officials Offer Final Verdict." *San Jose Mercury News*, March 23, 2014. http://www.mercurynews.com/san-mateo-county-times/ci_25404983/fukushima-radiation-near-half-moon-bay-state-health.

Koebler, Jason. "Drones Will Revolutionize Farming First, Not Delivery," December 16, 2013. http://motherboard.vice.com/blog/drones-will-revolutionize-farming-first-not-delivery.

KPMG. *Technology Innovation Survey 2013*, 2013. http://www.kpmg.com/SK/en/IssuesAndInsights/ArticlesPublications/Documents/Technology%20Innovation%20Survey%202013.pdf (accessed April 14, 2014).

Leigh, Stephen. "Life Insurers Must Now Prepare for the Internet of Things." Gartner Research, September 25, 2013. https://www.gartner.com/doc/2596520/life-insurers-prepare-internet-things (subscription required).

Löffler, Markus, and Andreas Tschiesner. "The Internet of Things and the Future of Manufacturing." McKinsey, June 2013. http://www.mckinsey.com/Insights/Business_Technology/The_Internet_of_Things_and_the_future_of_manufacturing.

Luccio, Matteo. "Precision Agriculture: Sensors Drive Agricultural Efficiency." *Sensors and Systems*, January 22, 2013. http://www.sensorsandsystems.com/article/features/29160-precision-agriculture-sensors-drive-agricultural-efficiency.html.

Mack, Eric. "From Tokyo to California, Radiation Tracking Gets Crowdsourced." *CNET*, March 15, 2011. http://www.cnet.com/news/from-tokyo-to-california-radiation-tracking-gets-crowdsourced/.

Manyika, James, Michael Chui, Brad Brown, Jacques Bughin, Richard Dobbs, Charles Roxburgh, and Angela Hung Byers. "Big Data: The Next Frontier for Innovation, Competition, and Productivity." McKinsey Global Institute, May 2011. http://www.mckinsey.com/insights/business_technology/big_data_the_next_frontier_for_innovation.

Manyika, James, Michael Chui, Jacques Bughin, Richard Dobbs, Peter Bisson, and Alex Marrs. "Disruptive Technologies: Advances that Will Transform Life, Business, and the Global Economy." McKinsey Global Institute, May 2013. http://www.mckinsey.com/insights/business_technology/disruptive_technologies.

Massey, Karen . "Advanced Business Analytics Enable Better Decisions in Banking." IDC Financial Insights White Paper, November 2010.

McMahon, Chris. "Progressive's Dave Pratt on the Evolution of UBI." Insurance Experts' Forum blog on *Insurance Networking News*, February 12, 2014. http://www.insurancenetworking.com/blogs/progressives-dave-pratt-on-the-evolution-of-ubi-33842-1.html.

———. "Progressive's Snapshot Passes 10 Billion Mile Marker." *INN Breaking News*, March 21, 2014. http://www.insurancenetworking.com/news/progressives-snapshot-passes-10-billion-mile-marker-34065-1.html.

Monsanto. "FieldScripts: FieldScripts℠ Will be the First Commercial Product from Monsanto's IFS Platform." http://www.monsanto.com/products/pages/fieldscripts.aspx (accessed March 15, 2014).

———. "Monsanto Company to Purchase Planting Technology Developer Precision Planting, a Leader in Delivering Yield through Technology." News release, May 23, 2012. http://news.monsanto.com/press-release/monsanto-company-purchase-planting-technology-developer-precision-planting-leader-deli.

Moor Insights & Strategy. "Connecting with the Industrial Internet of Things (IIoT)," October 29, 2013. http://www.moorinsightsstrategy.com/wp-content/uploads/2013/10/Connecting-with-the-Industrial-Internet-of-Things-IIoT-by-Moor-Insights-Strategy.pdf.

MSM Software. "IT and Operational Functions in General Insurance Strategy: Allies or Opponents?" MSM Whitepaper, April 4, 2013. http://www.msmsoftware.com/resources/strategic-decisions/it-operational-functions-in-general-insurance-strategy-allies-or-opponents.aspx.

Nerseth, Per-Vegard. "Rise of the Automatons: ABB and the Evolution of Robotics." CapGemini Consulting. *Digital Transformation Review* No. 5, January 2014. http://ebooks.capgemini-consulting.com/Digital-Transformation-Review-5/#/1/zoomed.

Nicas, Jack. "From Farms to Films, Drones Find Commercial Uses." *Wall Street Journal*, March 11, 2014. http://online.wsj.com/news/articles/SB20001424052702304732804579425342990070808 (fee required).

Ordnance Survey. "The Big Data Rush: How Data Analytics Can Yield Underwriting Gold." Ordnance Survey Report, co-sponsored by Chartered Insurance Institute and Chartered Institute of Loss Adjusters, April 25, 2013. http://www.ordnancesurvey.co.uk/about/news/2013/the-big-data-rush.html.

Perlman, David. "Fukushima Radiation Could Reach Pacific Coast by April." *SFGate*, February 26, 2014. http://www.sfgate.com/science/article/Fukushima-radiation-could-reach-Pacific-coast-by-5264277.php.

Perlroth, Nicole. "Hackers Lurking in Vents and Soda Machines." *New York Times*, April 7, 2014. http://www.nytimes.com/2014/04/08/technology/the-spy-in-the-soda-machine.html.

Precision Farming Dealer Newsletter. "Deere Adds Array of Environmental Sensors to Field Connect," March 14, 2013. 2013 https://farm-equipment.com/pages/Spre/PFD-Precision-News-John-Deere-adds-array-of-environmental-sensors-to-Field-Connect-March-14,-2013.php.

PricewaterhouseCoopers (PwC). *IAB Internet Advertising Revenue Report: 2013 Full Year Results.* PricewaterhouseCoopers for the Interactive Advertising Bureau (IAB), April 2014. http://www.iab.net/media/file/IAB_Internet_Advertising_Revenue_Report_FY_2013.pdf.

Prouty, Kevin, and Reid Paquin. "Three Steps to Make Your Manufacturing Systems Intelligent and to Distribute That Knowledge with Greatest Efficiency." Aberdeen Group, January 30, 2014. http://www.aberdeen.com/Aberdeen-Library/8823/AI-intelligent-manufacturing-systems.aspx.

Quelch, John. "How to Value the Advertising-Supported Internet." *HBR Blog Network, Harvard Business Review,* June 29, 2009. http://blogs.hbr.org/2009/06/how-to-value-the-advertisingsu/.

Rainie, Lee, Sara Kiesler, Ruogu Kang, and Mary Madden. "Anonymity, Privacy, and Security Online." *Pew Internet and American Life Project*, September 5, 2013. http://pewinternet.org/Reports/2013/Anonymity-online/Summary-of-Findings.aspx.

Reactions, "Social Media's Role in Fighting Insurance Fraud." April 26, 2013.

Russom, Philip. *Big Data Analytics.* TDWI Best Practices Report, Q4 2011. http://tdwi.org/research/list/tdwi-best-practices-reports.aspx.

———. "Managing Big Data." TDWI Best Practices Report, Q4 2013. http://www.pentaho.com/sites/default/files/uploads/resources/tdwi_best_practices_report-_managing_big_data.pdf.

Rye, Clayton. "There's an App for 300-Bushel Corn: Monsanto Program Can Write Prescriptions for Each Field." *Farm-News.com*, August 23, 2013. http://www.farm-news.com/page/content.detail/id/509361/There-s-an-app-for-300-bushel-corn.html?nav=5005.

Safecast. "About Safecast." *Safecast Blog*, n.d. http://blog.safecast.org/about/ (accessed April 24, 2014).

———. "Safecast Flyer." n.d. http://blog.safecast.org/wpcontent/uploads/2011/05/SAFECASTflyer.pdf (accessed April 24, 2014).

———. "Safecast Air Force (Drone Program)." *Safecast Blog*, May 6, 2013. http://blog.safecast.org/2013/05/safecast-air-force-drone-program.

Mayer-Schönberger, Viktor, and Kenneth Cukier. *Big Data: A Revolution That Will Transform How We Live, Work, and Think*. Boston: Houghton Mifflin Harcourt. 2013.

Stoll, Brian, and Klayton Southwood. "Predictive Modeling Usage for Property and Casualty Insurers Grows: 2013 Predictive Modeling Benchmarking Survey." Towers Watson report, March 2014. http://www.towerswatson.com/en/Insights/Newsletters/Americas/americas-insights/2014/predictive-modeling-usage-for-property-casualty-insurers-grows.

Strickland, Eliza. "Measuring Radiation in Fukushima with Pocket Geigers and bGeigies." *TechTalk* (blog), *IEEE Spectrum*, September 4, 2013. http://spectrum.ieee.org/tech-talk/energy/nuclear/measuring-radiation-in-fukushima-with-pocket-geigers-and-bgeigies.

Sullivan, Tom. "What Does NAIC's Adoption of RMORSA Model Act Mean?" September 14, 2012. *Property Casualty 360o*. http://www.propertycasualty360.com/2012/09/14/what-does-naics-adoption-of-rmorsa-model-act-mean.

Toscano, Michael. "AUVSI Encourages FAA to Allow Limited Small UAS Operations." Letter to Administrator Huerta, FAA, January 27, 2014. http://higherlogicdownload.s3.amazonaws.com/AUVSI/958c920a-7f9b-4ad2-9807-f9a4e95d1ef1/UploadedFiles/1%2027%2014%20Letter%20on%20sUAS%20NPRM%20Delay.pdf.

Transport Canada. "Unmanned Air Vehicle (UAV)." May 3, 2010. http://www.tc.gc.ca/eng/civilaviation/standards/general-recavi-brochures-uav-2270.htm.

TRUSTe. "TRUSTe 2014 US Consumer Confidence Privacy Report," March 20, 2014. http://www.truste.com/us-consumer-confidence-index-2014/.

U.S. Department of Transportation (USDOT). Federal Aviation Administration (FAA). *Integration of Civil Unmanned Aircraft Systems (UAS) in the National Airspace System (NAS) Roadmap*, November 2013. http://www.faa.gov/about/initiatives/uas/media/uas_roadmap_2013.pdf.

U.S. International Trade Commission (USITC). Hearing transcript in connection with inv. no. 332-531 and 332-540, *Digital Trade in the U.S. and Global Economies: Part 1 and Part* 2, March 7, 2013.

———. Hearing transcript in connection with inv. No. 332-540, *Digital Trade in the U.S. and Global Economies: Part 2*, September 25, 2013.

———. *Digital Trade in the U.S. and Global Economies: Part 1 (Digital Trade 1)*. USITC Publication 4415. Washington, DC: USITC, 2013. http://usitc.gov/publications/332/pub4415.pdf.

———. "The Role of Services in Manufacturing." Chapter 3 in *Economic Effects of Significant U.S. Import Restraints (Eighth Update),* December 2013. http://usitc.gov/publications/332/pub4440.pdf.

Urban, Jennifer M., Chris Jay Hoofnagle, and Su Li. *Mobile Phones and Privacy.* Berkeley, California: Berkeley Center for Law and Technology, July 11, 2012.

Verizon RISK Team. *2013 Data Breach Investigations Report.* Verizon, 2013. http://www.verizonenterprise.com/resources/reports/rp_data-breach-investigations-report-2013_en_xg.pdf.

Voglin, Andrei. "Not Enough People in the U.S. to Justify Pandora Valuation." *Seeking Alpha*, October 2, 2014. http://seekingalpha.com/article/1725402-not-enough-people-in-the-u-s-to-justify-pandora-valuation.

Warwick, Graham. "AUVSI—Precision Agriculture Will Lead Civil UAS." *Things with Wings: The Civil Aviation Blog, AviationWeek.com*, January 1, 2014. http://aviationweek.com/blog/auvsi-precision-agriculture-will-lead-civil-uas.

Weiss, Juergen. "2013 Industry Predicts: Digitalization Will Make Insurers More Agile," Gartner webinar presentation, January 30, 2013. http://my.gartner.com/portal/server.pt?open=512&objID=202&mode=2&PageID=5553&ref=webinar-rss&resId=2272220 (subscription required).

Whitney, Lance. "Poll: Most Won't Pay to Read Newspapers Online." *CNET News*, January 13, 2010. http://www.cnet.com/news/poll-most-wont-pay-to-read-newspapers-online/.

Wichita Eagle. "DuPont, Deere Launch Precision Farming to Challenge Monsanto," November 10, 2013. http://www.kansas.com/2013/11/10/3107890/dupont-deere-launch-precision.html.

World Economic Forum (WEF) with McKinsey & Company. *Risk and Responsibility in a Hyperconnected World: Implications for Enterprises*, January 2014. http://www.mckinsey.com/insights/business_technology/risk_and_responsibility_in_a_hyperconnected_world_implications_for_enterprises.

Yamaha Motor Australia, "History." n.d. http://rmax.yamaha-motor.com.au/history (accessed June 16, 2014).

Chapter 7
Case Studies: How the Internet Is Facilitating International Trade

In this chapter, the international component of digital trade is considered, with two case studies illustrating how the Internet is facilitating foreign direct investment and cross-border trade. The Internet assists companies operating in foreign markets to communicate with suppliers and customers. At the same time, the smooth functioning of the Internet also relies heavily on the free flow of data across borders. The two case studies in this chapter examine the international issues related to digital trade:

- Case study 9: *The global competitiveness of U.S. Internet companies.* U.S. Internet companies have increasingly engaged in international trade as the global Internet user base has expanded. This case study examines the global market share and competitiveness of U.S. Internet companies. It also describes the various challenges U.S Internet companies encounter in expanding abroad as well as the global competitiveness of foreign Internet companies.

- Case study 10: *Facilitating SME exports.* The Internet is revolutionizing international commerce by enabling businesses of every size to participate and benefit from global trade. This case study explains how the Internet makes it easier for SMEs to export by enhancing their ability to connect with customers and suppliers globally.

Case Study 9: The Global Competitiveness of U.S. Internet Companies

U.S. Internet companies have increasingly engaged in international digital trade as the global Internet audience has expanded. Americans made up 66 percent of worldwide Internet users in 1996, but only 13 percent in 2012.[575] As U.S. Internet companies have grown their user base outside the United States, they have built leading positions in the global markets for search engines, video streaming, social media, and online auctions and retail.[576] Foreign revenues have generally made up an increasing share of these companies' overall revenues, but the companies continue to create significantly higher revenue per user in the United States than abroad. Despite the global success of U.S. Internet companies, foreign Internet companies have

---

[575] comScore, "UK Digital Future in Focus," February 2013, 6.

[576] Public data about the global market for Internet services have notable limitations. There are no standardized methods for estimating Internet market share, unique visitors, and active users. Companies that collect data across the industry have differing and often unclear methodologies, so their results may be difficult to analyze and compare. Internet companies collecting data on their own visitors may also have different methods of measurement.

succeeded—and now even lead—in certain markets like China and Russia. This case study describes the global reach of leading U.S.-headquartered Internet companies by reviewing their global market share and overseas revenues, as well as broader factors including global competition and trade barriers.

Global Market Share and Competitiveness

To build a strong presence in global markets, Internet companies need to create a user base by offering attractive services that appeal to an international audience; maintain and expand that user base by offering new features; and develop a reliable source of revenues and medium-term profitability. Several U.S. Internet companies have done precisely this, and now are leading providers in the global market for certain Internet services. One estimate of the most popular websites in the world in July 2013 (in terms of unique visitors) put sites from U.S. organizations—Google, Microsoft,[577] Facebook, Yahoo, Wikimedia Foundation,[578] and Amazon—in the top six spots.[579] Another ranking in January 2014 based on page views and unique visitors placed U.S.-run websites as 15 of the top 25 global sites.[580] Within most of the world's largest economies, U.S. websites are at the top in attracting visitors (table 7.1).

In Japan, Germany, France, the United Kingdom, Brazil, and India, U.S. sites receive more daily and monthly visitors than their local competitors do. Only in China and Russia do domestic sites receive more visitors and page views than U.S. sites. Alexa's[581] ranking of top sites by country yields similar results in major markets around the globe: sites from U.S. companies sit at the top in all countries except China and Russia.[582]

---

[577] Microsoft does not release country-by-country or regional revenue numbers for its Online Services Division, which includes Bing and other search-related products. Given this lack of data, Microsoft websites are not discussed in detail in this case study. For more information, see Microsoft, "Form 10-K," July 30, 2013, 6.

[578] Wikimedia Foundation is the nonprofit organization that runs Wikipedia. As Wikimedia Foundation is a nonprofit, its websites will not be discussed in detail in this case study.

[579] comScore, "The Digital World in Focus," 2013, 14.

[580] The U.S. sites include Google, Facebook, YouTube, Yahoo, Wikipedia, Amazon, Live.com (a Microsoft search engine), LinkedIn, Twitter, Blogspot, and Bing. For details, see Alexa, "Top Sites," n.d. (accessed January 31, 2014).

[581] Alexa, a subsidiary of Amazon, provides data analytics services for commercial Web traffic data. Alexa, "About Us," http://www.alexa.com/about (accessed July 24, 2014).

[582] The 30 countries with the highest nominal GDPs (excluding the United States and China) had an average of 7.5 U.S.-owned sites in their top 10 sites on Alexa, "Top Sites," n.d. (accessed March 11, 2014). A discussion of why Chinese firms have succeeded in their home market is located in the section "Competition, Barriers, and Challenges in Foreign Markets" below.

Table 7.1 Top Web properties in leading economies

Country	Top two Web properties	Number of U.S. companies in top 10	Non-U.S. companies among the top 10	2013 Networked Readiness Index (rank)
China	Tencent Sohu	0	Tencent, Sohu, Baidu, Alibaba, SINA, Xunlei, Youku, Netease, Qihoo, Phoenix Television	4.03 (58)
Japan	Yahoo Google	5	FC2, NHN Corporation, CyberAgent, Rakuten, NTT Group	5.24 (18)
Germany	Google Facebook	6	Deutsche Telekom, Axel Springer, United Internet, Hubert Burda Media	5.43 (13)
France	Google Microsoft	6	Orange, CCM Benchmark, Iliad/Free.fr, Axel Springer	5.06 (21)
United Kingdom	Google Microsoft	9	BBC	5.64 (7)
Brazil	Google Terra-Telefonica	4	Terra-Telefonica, UOL, Globo, R7 Portal, IG Portal, Grupo Abril	3.97 (60)
Russia	Mail.Ru Yandex	3	Mail.Ru, Yandex, VK, Ucoz, RosBusiness Consulting, Rambler Media, Avito.Ru	4.13 (54)
India	Google Facebook	6	Times Internet Limited, BitTorent, Network 18, Rediff	3.88 (69)

Sources: Compiled by USITC from ComScore, "China/Taiwan Hong Kong Digital Future in Focus," October 2013, 17; ComScore, "Japan Digital Future in Focus," October 15, 2013, 23; ComScore, "Germany Digital Future in Focus," March 2013, 28; ComScore, "France Digital Future in Focus," March 2013, 28; ComScore, "UK Digital Future in Focus," March 2013, 28; ComScore, "Brazil Digital Future in Focus," March 2013, 21; ComScore, "Europe Digital Future in Focus," October 2013, 43; ComScore, "India Digital Future in Focus," August 22, 2013, 22; World Economic Forum, "The Global Information Technology Report, 2014," 2014.

Note: ComScore calculates top web properties by unique visitors in a given month. The month was December 2012 for all countries except China (March 2013), Japan (May 2013), and India (March 2013). The World Economic Forum's Networked Readiness Index is composed of a mixture of quantitative and survey data designed to assess a country's ability to benefit from the information and communications technologies that drive Internet-based economic activity.

Overseas Expansion, Users, and Revenues

U.S. Internet companies have opened foreign offices in key markets to grow their user base and maintain competitiveness. Local data centers allow companies to give users faster and more reliable access to their sites.[583] Foreign research and development (R&D) offices attract local tech talent, develop new products, and target services to local or regional markets.[584] U.S. companies have also expanded abroad through acquisitions of foreign Internet companies.[585]

As they have expanded into foreign markets, leading U.S. Internet companies have increased the size of their audience abroad. They have grown their foreign user base as U.S. user growth has leveled off, and they have seen foreign revenues account for an increasing share of overall

---

[583] USITC hearing transcript, March 7, 2013, 44–45, (testimony of Michael Mandel, Progressive Policy Institute).

[584] For example, Google has large offices in France and Ireland along with major data centers in Finland, Belgium, Ireland, Taiwan, and Singapore while Microsoft has R&D offices across the world, including major offices in India, China, Ireland, and the United Kingdom. For more information, see Microsoft, "Form 10-K," July 30, 2013, 9 and Google, "Data Center Locations," n.d. (accessed March 19, 2014), http://www.google.com/about/datacenters/inside/locations/index.html.

[585] For more information on foreign direct investment (FDI) by leading Internet companies, see USITC, *Digital Trade 1*, July 2013, 4-11 to 4-19.

revenues (figure 7.1). For leading U.S. Internet companies, foreign users greatly outnumber U.S. users as of 2013 (table 7.2).

Figure 7.1 Foreign revenues of selected U.S. Internet companies, 2002–13

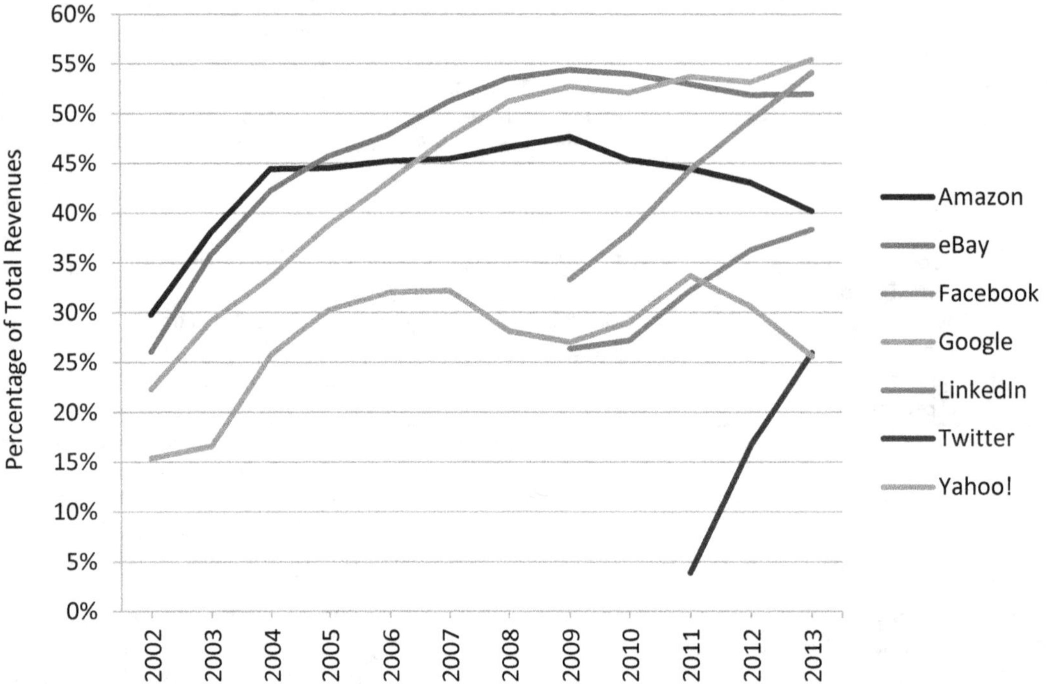

Sources: Compiled by USITC from annual reports to the Securities and Exchange Commission (SEC): Amazon, "Form 10-K," 2002–14; eBay, "Form 10-K", 2002–14; Facebook, "Form 10-K," 2011–14; Google, "Form 10-K," 2004–14; LinkedIn, "Form 10-K," 2012–14; Twitter, "Form 10-K," March 6, 2014; and Yahoo "Form-10K," 2002–14.
Notes: Location for revenues is generally based on the billing addresses of customers and advertisers. For Facebook and Amazon, foreign revenues are underrepresented because the companies provide only combined revenue data for the United States and Canada. For Yahoo, foreign revenues from 2002–09 exclude all revenues from the Americas.

Table 7.2 Users, revenues, and average revenue per user (ARPU) for leading U.S. Internet companies

Company	Period	Monthly active users (millions)	Percent foreign users	Revenues (millions)	Percent foreign revenue	ARPU— U.S. users	ARPU— foreign users
Facebook	7/1/2013 to 9/30/2013	1,172	83%	$2,016	52%	$4.85	$1.08
Google	7/1/2013 to 9/30/2013	1,200	84%	$14,893	55%	$34.64	$8.17
LinkedIn	7/1/2013 to 9/30/2013	259	66%	$393	38%	$2.74	$0.87
Twitter	1/1/2013 to 6/30/2013	218	77%	$254	25%	$3.88	$0.37
Yahoo!	7/1/2013 to 9/30/2013	800	75%	$1,139	29%	$4.11	$0.54

Sources: Original calculations by USITC based on data compiled from comScore, "comScore Media Metrix Ranks Top 50 U.S. Web Properties," August 21, 2013; Facebook, "Form 10-Q," November 1, 2013; Gallagher, "Yahoo Monthly Active Users Are Up 20% to 800M," September 11, 2013; "Yahoo Is Bigger than Google," August 27, 2013; Google, "Form 10-Q," November 1, 2013; Twitter, "Form S-1," October 3, 2013; Yahoo, "Form 10-Q," November 12, 2013.

Notes: Data for companies cover the period July 1, 2013 to September 30, 2013, except for Twitter, whose data cover January 1, 2013, to June 30, 2013. These quarterly or semiannual revenues data are not comparable with annual data in figure 7.1. Facebook combines the United States and Canada in its data on revenues and users. Facebook calculates ARPU based on the average of users at the beginning and the end of the quarter. Google revenues include Motorola Mobile revenues. LinkedIn's number for monthly active users represents for total LinkedIn members; LinkedIn does not provide data on monthly users by geography. Twitter ARPU differs from Twitter's number for revenue per 1,000 timeline views. Data for ARPU are not comparable across firms but are illustrative of the difference between U.S. and foreign ARPU.

Even with the growth in foreign user base and foreign revenues, U.S. Internet companies' revenue per user is much higher in the United States than in the rest of the world. Internet companies find it harder to generate advertising revenue abroad due to differences in markets and regulations. Table 7.2 shows the huge disparity between average revenue per user (ARPU) for U.S. users and foreign users.

Advertisers pay more to reach consumers online in the United States than they do in most other countries. According to eMarketer, North America is the largest regional market for online ad spending, with 38.6 percent of global spending.[586] Online ad spending per Internet user for 2013 was $174 in the United States; only in Australia, the United Kingdom, and Norway did advertisers spend more per user.[587] In contrast, spending per user was $97 in Germany, $67 in France, $53 in Korea, $26 in Russia, $25 in Brazil, and $23 in China.[588] The maturity of online advertising markets likely determines some of the differences in ad spending, as do different business cultures' willingness to market online.[589] Many advertisers particularly value U.S. Internet users because their disposable income is higher than that of Internet users in many other countries.[590]

Regulations and restrictions on Internet usage, data usage, or advertising practices may also explain lower revenues per user abroad. For example, stricter data privacy regulations in Europe may explain in part the disparity in digital ad spending between the United States and most European countries. Internet companies may be less effective in acquiring or using user-specific data to target their ads in Europe: one study shows that online advertising in the EU

---

[586] eMarketer, "U.S. Stays Atop Global Ad Market," September 26, 2013.
[587] Ibid.
[588] Ibid.
[589] For a detailed discussion, see Liu-Thompkins, "Online Advertising: A Cross-Cultural Synthesis," 2012, 307–10.
[590] Depillis, "Facebook's New Users Are Overseas," October 30, 2013.

was 65 percent less effective (as measured by "intent to purchase") after the EU changed its data privacy regulations in 2002.[591]

Competition, Barriers, and Challenges in Foreign Markets

Despite success in many foreign markets, leading U.S. Internet companies encounter a variety of challenges in expanding abroad. These include overcoming linguistic and cultural differences; dealing with unclear legal liability; protecting intellectual property; maintaining user trust; meeting requirements for data protection; and combating other barriers to trade.[592] These challenges leave space for foreign Internet companies to succeed in their home markets.

Foreign Internet companies appear most competitive when they effectively target their domestic services to match local cultural preferences. One example of a highly competitive foreign Internet company operating in its domestic market is TaoBao, as discussed in box 7.1. Foreign Internet companies may differentiate their products by offering access to creative content—original or pirated—that their U.S. competitors cannot offer due to licensing challenges.

Box 7.1 How TaoBao overcame eBay in China

U.S. Internet companies are not always successful in their efforts to expand in key foreign markets. In the consumer-to-consumer auction market, eBay acquired EachNet, a Chinese auction website, in early 2003 and formally launched eBay China in 2004 with the goal of securing a long-term, dominant position.[593] eBay set up the same approach in China that it had used elsewhere in the world: fees for sellers, organization by categories of products, and email communication between buyers and sellers.[594]

To counter eBay, the China-based Alibaba Group started TaoBao, its own consumer-to-consumer auction website, in 2003. TaoBao sought an advantage by providing free services (eBay charged fees to sellers) and by better adapting online auctions to Chinese culture. For example, the site was organized like a Chinese department store. TaoBao also gave buyers and sellers real-time, back-and-forth messaging to develop "swift guanxi," an approximation of the close relationships that fuel Chinese business culture.[595]

TaoBao's adaptations led to success. From 2003 to 2005, eBay's market share in China fell from 79 percent to 36 percent, while TaoBao's grew from 8 percent to 59 percent.[596] eBay exited the market in December 2006. By 2013, TaoBao held a 96 percent market share in online consumer-to-consumer auctions in China.[597]

---

[591] Goldfarb and Tucker, "Privacy Regulation and Online Advertising," 2011, 68.
[592] Google, "Form 10-K," February 12, 2014, 11–17 and Microsoft, "Form 10-K," July 30, 2013, 16. For a detailed discussion of barriers, see USITC, *Digital Trade 1*, July 2013, chapter 5, and chapter 4 of this report.
[593] *BusinessWeek*, "Online Extra: eBay's Patient Bid on China," March 14, 2004.
[594] Stanford Graduate School of Business, "TaoBao vs. eBay China", January 4, 2010, 10.
[595] LaFevre, "Why eBay Failed in China," June 14, 2013.
[596] *Economist,* "China's Pied Piper," September 21, 2006.
[597] LaFevre, "Why eBay Failed in China," June 14, 2013.

Sometimes they also benefit from trade barriers or content licensing issues that restrict the ability of U.S. companies to participate in the market, as described further in this section. In Alexa's ranking of the top 25 global sites, non-U.S. companies feature prominently: two (VK and Yandex) are Russian, and the rest are Chinese (Baidu, Tencent, Alibaba Group, SINA Corporation, NetEase, and Qihoo 360).[598] U.S. sites reportedly held the top six global spots in July 2013, while sites from Chinese companies held the remaining four.[599] In addition, Alexa's rankings from individual countries show that foreign consumers often turn to local sites for shopping, news and entertainment, Web portals, and classified listings.[600] Box 7.2 provides a discussion of U.S. consumers using foreign websites and Web content providers.

Box 7.2 Foreign Internet companies in the United States

Foreign Internet companies routinely seek users, revenues, and funding in the United States, but have not generally achieved wide audiences. To attract users they may need to offer services, features, or content that existing U.S. companies do not offer.[601]

Online retail: Alibaba Group (China) operates international wholesaler supplier websites that reach U.S. buyers, but has not entered the wider consumer market. In 2013, Alibaba invested in several small U.S. Internet companies, which may be a prelude to further expansion in the online retail market.[602] Alibaba announced in March 2014 that it plans to pursue an initial public offering (IPO) in the United States.[603]

Music and video streaming: European companies Rdio and Spotify launched music streaming services in the United States in 2010 and 2011. They have built small user bases in competition with the established U.S. company Pandora—as well as with Apple and Google, both of which launched U.S. music streaming services in 2013.[604] In video, the French company DailyMotion has a strong presence in France but has achieved limited market penetration in the United States.[605] DailyMotion is seeking to draw more U.S. users by offering original shows in 2014.[606]

Media: Media sites from the United Kingdom, including the British Broadcasting Corporation (BBC) and the Daily Mail, have attracted a growing user base in the United States—but they generally seem to

---

[598] Alexa, "Top Sites," n.d. (accessed January 31, 2014). The listed companies are all privately owned.

[599] comScore, "The Digital Future in Focus," 2013, 14.

[600] For the 30 countries with the highest nominal GDPs (excluding the United States and China), 25 percent of top sites were local. Of these local sites, 36 percent were for news and entertainment; 21 percent were for shopping or classifieds; 20 percent were for social networking or gaming; 18 percent were search or Web portals; and 5 percent were other sites. Drawn from Alexa, "Top Sites," n.d. (accessed March 11, 2014).

[601] Keating, "Can WeChat?" December 11, 2013.

[602] Kan, "China's Alibaba Expands U.S. Reach," October 24, 2013.

[603] De La Merced, "Alibaba Confirms It Will Begin I.P.O. Process," March 16, 2014.

[604] In a survey asking Americans if they had listened to particular streaming music services in the preceding month, Pandora was ranked first (31 percent), while Spotify was ranked fourth (6 percent). See Thompson, "Why Would Anybody Ever Buy Another Song?" March 14, 2014.

[605] DailyMotion had 2,778 million videos viewed in 2012 in the United States, compared to 188,758 million videos viewed for Google sites. For more information, see ComScore, "U.S. Digital Future in Focus," February 2013, 24; ComScore, "France Digital Future in Focus," March 2013, 36.

[606] Schwartzel and Schechner, "DailyMotion Tries Original Shows," February 27, 2014.

reach a niche audience.[607] The BBC largely distributes online content in the United States through U.S. partners like Netflix, Apple, Google, and Hulu.[608]

Social Media and Search: SINA Corporation (China), Naver (Korea), Yandex (Russia), VK (Russia), and other top global sites attract a small number of U.S. visitors seeking language-specific or culture-specific material. Although VK and Yandex offer English-language versions, they have not built a broader U.S. audience.[609] Baidu (China), Weibo (China), and other companies have made IPOs on U.S. stock markets to seek capital, but have not planned to otherwise expand their U.S. presence.[610] Tencent (China) recently opened an office in San Francisco to help promote its social messaging app WeChat.[611]

Retail and News

For online retail, local sites have been able to prosper in many countries due to existing "brand recognition and customer loyalty."[612] In Australia, for example, local online retailers accounted for around 73 percent of total online sales in January 2013.[613] Local news sites in many countries offer local or regional reporting targeted to cultural and linguistic norms, and benefit from brand loyalty when linked with well-known local television stations, radio stations, or newspapers.[614]

Search Engines

In the search engine market, home-grown sites lead the domestic markets in three countries: Korea (Naver), Russia (Yandex), and China (Baidu).[615] Naver built its market position at a time when the Internet did not feature much Korean-language content by cultivating user-generated material and by building its own database of Korean-language results.[616] Naver's search results are more locally oriented than those of U.S. competitors and de-emphasize the search results derived from web-crawling (e.g., search results from Google, Bing, and Yahoo) in favor of suggested content (i.e., content selected based on data collected about the user).[617] In Russia, Yandex—which had 61.7 percent of the Russian search market in July 2013—was specifically designed for searching in the Russian language, and seeks to emphasize local or regional

---

[607] Haughney, "British Tabloid's Web Site Makes Foray," May 9, 2013.

[608] BBC Worldwide, *Annual Review 2012/13,* 2013, 14.

[609] Pavelek, "VKontakte Demographics," February 2013.

[610] Weibo Corporation, "Amendment No. 3 to Form F-1," April 14, 2014, 60.

[611] Keating, "Can WeChat?" December 11, 2013.

[612] PwC, "Demystifying the Online Shopper," 2013, 26.

[613] Doyle, "Australian Buyers Prefer Domestic Online Retailers," April 16, 2013.

[614] European newspapers make up 10 percent of the 100 top print newspapers (by circulation) but make up 40 percent of the top 100 daily newspaper websites (by unique visitors per month). For more information, see Leurdijk, Slot, and Nieuwenhuis, "Statistical, Ecosystems and Competitiveness Analysis," 2012, 69–74.

[615] For more information about search engines and their business models, see USITC, *Digital Trade 1*, 2013, 2-26 to 2-27.

[616] Larson, "Why Google Must Succeed in Korea," August 8, 2008.

[617] Kaji, "New Trend Emerging," May 15, 2013. For more information about how companies collect and use consumer data, see case study 7 below.

content.[618] In China, Baidu's growth into the leading search engine has taken place during pervasive Internet censorship by the Chinese government that disadvantages foreign competitors.[619] Baidu also formerly offered users easy access to "allegedly infringing materials" such as unlicensed music content.[620]

Social Media

In social media, local sites have struggled to succeed amid the rise of Facebook—except in Russia and China. VK, formerly known as vKontakte, is the leading social network in Russia.[621] VK replicates Facebook's look, feel, and features and has attracted Russian users by offering free access to unlicensed music, film, and television content.[622] In China, QZone, Renren, and other local social networks have battled for users in absence of competition from Facebook, whose activities in China are restricted; examples of specific restrictions in the Chinese market are described in box 7.3. A strong user base at home, however, is no guarantee of strong revenues: Weibo, a Twitter-like micro-blogging site that is majority-owned by SINA Corporation, had 143.8 million monthly active users in March 2014, but also incurred a $38 million net loss (20 percent of revenues) in 2013.[623]

Box 7.3 Specific limitations in China

Censorship barriers can sometimes explain the success of foreign Internet companies, particularly in China, where U.S. firms report facing the most censorship-related obstacles.[624] Due to government laws and regulations on the Internet in China,[625] U.S. companies such as Facebook, Twitter, and Google are banned, blocked, or unwilling to provide their services directly in the country.[626] In their absence,

---

[618] Lunden, "Yandex Posts Q2 2013 Sales Of $281M," July 25, 2013; East-West Digital News, "Yandex vs. Google: Why the US Giant Failed," May 19, 2011.

[619] USITC, *Digital Trade 1*, July 2013, 5-22.

[620] Baidu began to offer licensed copies of many songs after reaching a licensing agreement with several major record companies in 2011. Although Baidu was subsequently removed from the U.S. Trade Representative's list of "notorious markets" for intellectual property piracy, it "remains a problematic marketplace," according to USTR. For more detail, see USTR, *2013 Out-of-Cycle Review of Notorious Markets*, February 12, 2014, 4–5; USTR, *Out-of-Cycle Review of Notorious Markets,* February 28, 2011, 1; Martin, "Baidu Removed From U.S. 'Notorious Markets' Piracy List," December 20, 2011.

[621] For more information about social media companies and their business models, see USITC, *Digital Trade 1*, 2013, 2-21 to 2-24.

[622] For more information, see Buley, "Facebook's Russian Frenemy," July 13, 2009; USTR, *2013 Out-of-Cycle Review of Notorious Markets*, February 12, 2014, 10–11; Edwards, "Facebook Is Failing in Europe," October 15, 2012.

[623] Weibo, "Amendment No. 3 to Form F-1," Annual report for the Securities and Exchange Commission, April 14, 2014.

[624] USITC questionnaire, weighted responses to question 5.1. For further discussion of censorship-related barriers, including those in China, see chapter 4.

[625] For a longer discussion of China's laws and regulations on the Internet, see USITC, *Digital Trade 1,* 2013, 5-20 to 5-22.

[626] U.S. Internet companies often provide services in written Chinese in Hong Kong and Taiwan. Internet users in China can access these sites through Virtual Private Networks (VPNs) or other methods, but these face frequent disruptions, interventions by censors, and slow access speeds. For more information, see Chander, "How Censorship Hurts Chinese Internet Companies," August 12, 2013.

Chinese companies have captured the majority of users and revenues in social networking, micro-blogging, and search: in March 2013, all of the top ten websites in China were run by Chinese companies.[627] In contrast, the top four websites in March 2013 in Taiwan and Hong Kong—markets that have similar cultural characteristics but less Internet censorship—were run by Yahoo, Google, Facebook, and Microsoft.[628] Youku and Tencent garnered the most video viewers in China in June 2013, while Google (which owns YouTube) and Yahoo topped the charts in Taiwan and Hong Kong—with Youku the sixth-most popular site in each market.[629] The pattern is similar for social networks and news sources.[630]

Streaming Video and Music

U.S. sites that provide access to licensed content face challenges in engaging in international digital trade.[631] Licensing creative content such as music, television shows, and films abroad requires a large up-front investment and can be difficult in markets without clear statutory regimes.[632] In markets with weaker copyright enforcement, companies may struggle to attract users who can get unlicensed content elsewhere.[633] Netflix, which introduced streaming content services in the United States in 2007, entered foreign markets with a 2010 launch in Canada and subsequent launches in selected Latin American and European countries.[634] Through September 30, 2013, however, Netflix's up-front investments in international content licensing and marketing have outweighed international revenues.[635] Pandora, a U.S.-based music streaming company, has a long-term plan to expand into foreign markets but has expressed concerns that the necessary investments would create substantial risks with no guarantee of returns.[636]

Foreign Companies Outside Their Home Countries

Even with success at home, foreign Internet companies have generally struggled to attract users in markets in which U.S. Internet companies have achieved leading market positions. For example, China-based Baidu launched services in Japan in January 2008 but had not achieved profitability as of early 2013; the company stated that it was not sure whether it would ever do so.[637] Overall, Baidu's foreign revenues in 2012 were $17.2 million, which constituted less than 1 percent of its total revenues.[638] Russian companies VK and Yandex have attracted foreign

---

[627] Sites are ranked by unique visitors. For more information, see comScore, "China/Taiwan Hong Kong Digital Future in Focus 2013," October 2013, 17.

[628] comScore, "China/Taiwan Hong Kong Digital Future in Focus 2013," October 2013, 19–21.

[629] Ibid., 24.

[630] Ibid., 27, 47.

[631] For more information on video and music streaming services, see USITC, *Digital Trade 1*, 2013, 2-15 to 2-16 and 2-18 to 2-20.

[632] Pandora, "Form 10-K," March 19, 2013, 28.

[633] International Intellectual Property Alliance, written submission to the USITC, March 21, 2014, 3–5; Pandora, "Form 10-K," March 19, 2013, 28.

[634] Netflix, "Form 10-Q," October 25, 2013, 23.

[635] Ibid., 25.

[636] Pandora, "Form 10-K," March 19, 2013, 28.

[637] Baidu, "Form 20-F," March 27, 2013, 16.

[638] Ibid., 53.

users only in countries near Russia. VK holds a leading position in the social media markets in Ukraine and Belarus and a strong position in several other central and eastern European countries, but has not built a large user base elsewhere.[639] Although many foreign Internet companies are seeking to expand in the United States, they have achieved only limited success in penetrating the already crowded U.S. market, as discussed in box 7.2 above.

Nevertheless, foreign companies continue to seek to grow their global user bases, and some are succeeding. For example, China-based company Tencent is making a global push for its social messaging app WeChat. WeChat has garnered 100 million users outside of China and has become the fifth most downloaded smartphone app in the world.[640]

Case Study 10: Facilitating SME Exports

The Internet is enabling businesses of every size to participate in and benefit from global trade.[641] Through the Internet, SMEs can overcome many impediments associated with exporting that traditionally only larger firms could manage.[642] At the same time, advances in digital technology and logistics are providing ever more efficient channels for connections and delivery between SMEs and consumers worldwide.[643] According to one analysis, growth in U.S. SME exports of products and services via the Internet far exceeds total export growth.[644] Factors driving worldwide consumer demand for SMEs' products and services include not only consumers' ability to shop in many outlets for price, but also their interest in the "global hunt" for unique products and "brand authenticity."[645] SMEs use the Internet to connect with customers and suppliers, to provide product information to prospective buyers, and to take or place orders. Many sales are transacted on company websites, but the emergence of large online retail platforms (like eBay), mobile payment services, and other Web-based transaction services is also fueling SME trade. At the same time, the ability to use the Internet to gather product information and to purchase inputs from a wide range of suppliers is reducing SMEs' costs and enhancing their export competitiveness.[646] SMEs in both developed and developing economies increasingly recognize that adopting Internet technologies is imperative; in one

---

[639] Yandex has built a broad audience in Cyrillic-alphabet market, but only 5 percent of its revenues in 2012 came from advertisers outside of Russia (Yandex, "Form 20-F," March 11, 2013, 13.) For more information, see Dillow, "Yandex Searches past Its Language Barrier," November 13, 2013; Hopkins, "VK.com Russia's #1 Social Network," December 26, 2013; Pavelek, "VKontakte Demographics," February 2013.

[640] Keating, "Can WeChat?" December 11, 2013.

[641] USITC, hearing transcript, September 25, 2013, 232 (testimony of David London, eBay Inc.).

[642] These impediments include marketing costs (finding foreign customers), shipping costs, preparation of customs documentation, and other technical and regulatory matters related to exporting. The Internet is also an important tool for SMEs in developing countries to gain access to international markets. See eBay, "Enabling Traders to Enter and Grow," March, 2012; Dalberg, "Impact of the Internet on Africa," April 2013.

[643] eBay, "Enabling Traders to Enter and Grow," October, 2012; Meltzer, "Supporting the Internet As a Platform," Brookings, February 2014, 3.

[644] Gresser, "Lines of Light," May 8, 2012, 6.

[645] PayPal, "Modern Spice Routes," 2013, 1.

[646] Meltzer, "Supporting the Internet as a Platform," February 2014, 1.

recent survey of SMEs in Africa, over 80 percent of business owners viewed the Internet as critical to their businesses' growth.[647]

Digital Intensity Is Tied to SME Growth and Export Performance

Data from the Commission's survey show that the Internet is a critical marketing and sales channel for U.S. SMEs.[648] According to the USITC questionnaire, 81 percent of U.S. SMEs in digitally intensive industries surveyed use the Internet for advertising and marketing, and nearly the same percentage conduct market research online. The Commission's questionnaire also found that a substantial majority of U.S. SMEs (between 70 and 86 percent) rely on the Internet to buy products and services.[649] Moreover, the questionnaire data show that the Internet is a critical sales channel for U.S. SMEs. According to USITC estimates, one-third of SMEs reported that they sell and deliver products and services online, while 46 percent sell products and services online that are delivered physically—nearly the same percentage share as large U.S. firms.[650]

Other questionnaire data also provide evidence of the Internet's importance to SME exporters. According to McKinsey Global Institute, which surveyed 4,800 SMEs in 13 major economies, firms with a strong Web presence grew twice as fast as firms with little or no Web presence.[651] Similarly, digitally intensive SMEs had export revenues more than double the rate of predominately offline SMEs.[652] Another recent study found that SMEs that were heavy users of the Internet grew faster than medium-to-light users and were 50 percent more likely to sell products and services outside their region than SMEs with less Web intensity.[653] An analysis comparing eBay sellers and traditional offline exporters found that online exporters (eBay sellers) are substantially smaller, face lower entry and fixed costs to exporting, and reach more foreign markets than traditional offline exporters.[654] A study by the European Commission found that SMEs engaged in e-commerce were more active in international markets and that the Internet has enabled firms of all sizes to overcome many barriers to trade.[655]

---

[647] Dalberg survey of nearly 1,000 SMEs across Ghana, Kenya, Nigeria, and Senegal. Dalberg, "Impact of the Internet on Africa," April 2013, 7.

[648] For a discussion of digitally intensive firms included in the Commission questionnaire, see chapter 2.

[649] Including products and services delivered online and physically delivered.

[650] USITC calculations of weighted responses to the Commission questionnaire.

[651] McKinsey's estimate of a SME's Internet-usage intensity is based on the penetration of Internet technology used by the SME, including Web technology usage by employees, clients, and suppliers. McKinsey, "Internet Matters," May 2011, 18, 22.

[652] McKinsey, "Internet Matters," May 2011, 3.

[653] Boston Consulting Group, "The Connected World," January 2014, 19–20.

[654] Lendle, "An Anatomy of Online Trade," September 2013, 35.

[655] European Commission, "Internationalisation of European SMEs," 2010, 7, 9, 42.

Although there are no specific official U.S. data on SME exports[656] enabled by the Internet, industry observers assert that the scope of total online trade is large and expanding rapidly.[657] Data from the Commission's questionnaire show that U.S. SMEs in digitally intensive industries exported 1.9 percent of their total online sales in 2012; the value of these exports was over $4.4 billion.[658] Exports of products and services ordered online and physically delivered accounted for more than twice as much revenue as those delivered digitally. By sector, U.S. SMEs in the digital communications, wholesale, and retail sectors had the largest export shares of online sales among digitally intensive SMEs, ranging from 3 to 8 percent of total online sales. Of note, although SMEs increasingly use digital channels to market products and services internationally, the Commission's questionnaire found that large U.S. firms in digitally intensive industries exported a much larger share (6 percent) of their total online sales of products and services than SMEs in 2012, for a far greater value ($35 billion) of total online sales.[659]

A number of other studies show that Internet enabled SME exports are significant and growing. A survey examining online purchasing in six large markets (United States, Germany, Brazil, United Kingdom, China, and Australia) suggests that cross-border shopping via the Internet accounted for 16 percent of total online sales in these countries in 2013, with online international transactions expected to grow by 300 percent by 2018.[660] These key markets had 94 million online shoppers who spent $105 billion in foreign markets in 2013. By 2018, the number is expected to increase to 130 million customers spending an estimated $307 billion.[661] Another study commissioned by eBay and focusing on Australian SMEs found that 78 percent of eBay's sellers export, compared to just 2 percent for all Australian businesses. On average,

---

[656] SMEs (digitally intensive and non-digitally intensive) accounted for 98 percent of the total number of U.S. exporters (297,995) and for $449 billion, or one-third, of the total value of U.S. goods exports in 2012 (latest available data). Most U.S. SME exports are business-to-business transactions, led by wholesale industries (43 percent share by value), manufacturing (34 percent), and other (24 percent). Statistics calculated from USDOC, U.S. Census Bureau, "2012 Exports by Company Type and Employment Size," April 3, 2014, 11. SMEs also contribute to U.S. exports indirectly, as providers of productive inputs to U.S. exporters both large and small. For analysis of SME indirect exports, see USITC, *Small and Medium-Sized Enterprises: Characteristics*, 2010, 5-1 to 5-19.

[657] Industry research suggests that a substantial share of total products and services trade (SMEs and large firms) is being facilitated by the Internet. E-commerce (Internet-based commercial transactions) expanded dramatically in recent years, coinciding with the expansion of digital networks, and is the fastest-growing segment of global sales. At 14 percent, growth in U.S. retail e-commerce outpaced growth in brick-and-mortar retail sales fourfold in 2013. Comscore, "U.S. Digital Future in Focus 2014," 36.

[658] These SMEs sold an estimated $227.1 billion online, accounting for 6.2 percent of their total sales in 2012. This includes products and services ordered online and either delivered online or delivered physically or in person.

[659] An analysis of EU firm data by UNCTAD also notes that large firms are more active in e-commerce (19 percent of sales) compared to smaller firms (4 percent of sales) in 2010. Fredriksson, "Workshop on E-Commerce, Development and SMEs," 8–9 April 2013. UNCTAD also has a database with statistics on the share of firm's online transactions for certain countries. Although there is no category directly relating to SMEs (defined as less than 500 employees), the data for certain developed countries (excluding the United States), such as France, the United Kingdom, and Germany, show that a substantial proportion of businesses in these countries with 50–249 employees had online sales and made online purchases during 2003–2011. UNCTAD, UNCTADSTAT database (accessed January 10, 2014).

[660] PayPal, "Spice Routes," 2013, 5.

[661] Ibid., 2.

Australian SMEs using eBay shipped to 28 different export destinations, while traditional exporters shipped to just 3 foreign markets.[662]

The Internet has also led to a substantial increase in international trade in professional services. Many professional services, such as those providing architectural plans or legal documents, are particularly suited for electronic delivery, as they can be easily digitized. Although there are no official data specifically focused on U.S. digital exports of professional services, the U.S. Department of Commerce estimates that the upper bound for such exports was $135.8 billion in 2011 (latest available data).[663] As over 99 percent of all professional services firms are SMEs,[664] SMEs likely supply a substantial share of such exports. In fact, a 2010 Commission report concluded that SMEs accounted for half of professional services export revenues. The Commission also found that 21 percent of professional services SMEs' total revenues were from exports in 2007, a higher percentage than the export revenues realized by large firms.[665]

The Internet Lowers Marketing and Export Transaction Costs for SMEs

The Internet has fundamentally transformed how many SMEs connect with customers. Small retail merchants are no longer subject to the proximity burden of supply, requiring customers to visit and purchase from brick-and-mortar stores; now that they have a "limitless universe of customers," locally or around the world.[666] According to a study commissioned by eBay, the Internet reduces the costly trade frictions that had been significant impediments to SME exports in the past. Examples of such frictions include geographical distance and differences in national income, languages, and legal systems. For SMEs that use the eBay platform, regression analysis indicates that such factors matter 60 percent less in online transactions than in offline ones, primarily because of a reduction in frictions relating to information and trust in online transactions.[667] As a result, trade is no longer the province of large firms; the smallest firms operating on eBay export at nearly the same rate (94 percent) as the largest sellers (97 percent).[668]

---

[662] eBay, "Commerce 3.0: Enabling Australian Export Opportunities," July 2013, 3.

[663] U.S. exports of all digitally delivered services are estimated at $357.4 billion in 2011, which accounts for over half of all U.S. services exports. This figure represents the upper bound of digitally exported services because there is no direct measure of services that are digitally traded. Nicholson and Noonan, "Digital Economy and Cross-Border Trade," January 27, 2014, 2.

[664] U.S. Census, "Number of Firms, Number of Establishments," October 2012.

[665] USITC, *Small and Medium-Sized Enterprises: Characteristics*, 2010, 3-12.

[666] For a description of the estimated economy-wide effects of reduced international trade costs due to the use of digital technologies, see chapter 3. Boston Consulting Group, "The Connected World," January 2014, 19.

[667] The study focused on users of the eBay platform versus offline firms and used the gravity model regression analysis described in Lendle et al., "There Goes Gravity," August 2012. Factors in the regression analysis are summarized in eBay, "Enabling Traders to Enter," October 2012.

[668] eBay, "Enabling Traders to Enter," October 2012, 4.

A Variety of Online Platforms and Services Make It Much Easier and Less Costly for SMEs to Export

Small businesses can reach customers (both businesses and individual consumers) through their own websites, and also on a variety of other digital platforms, including both general and specialized sites. The availability of sales platforms such as Amazon, eBay, Etsy, and others that connect SMEs with foreign markets has been critical to the rapid growth of SME exports. For example, on eBay, one of the world's largest platform sites, SMEs are the overwhelming majority of sellers, and nearly all of the site's commercial sellers export.[669] On Etsy, a website composed mainly of SMEs selling crafts and other "unique goods," a third of all transactions cross international borders.[670] These platforms facilitate trade by providing services that promote confidence and trust between international sellers and buyers. Such services include tracing and tracking international shipments and helping with customs procedures, which fosters transparency and allows both parties to understand the full cost of their cross-border transaction.[671]

Many of these platforms also partner with other technology and logistics companies to facilitate exports for SMEs. For example, eBay has a global shipping program with logistic partner Pitney Bowes. The program allows U.S. SMEs to ship products to a U.S. processing facility where logistics functions are coordinated by Pitney Bowes, including parcel processing (preparing parcels for international delivery), shipping, tracking, and customs documentation. All of these services can be accessed and priced on the eBay website.[672] Other logistics and express delivery firms, including UPS and Federal Express, also provide trade facilitation and logistics services that are geared to SMEs navigating international markets.[673] Falling costs and the increasing ease of transporting products to most locations around the world is an important factor spurring SME exports. Moreover, many of these firms are strong supporters of trade-liberalizing measures that would specifically benefit SMEs; they advocate increasing *de minimis*

---

[669] Commercial sellers are those with annual sales of at least $10,000. Lendle et al., "There Goes Gravity," August 2012, 2.

[670] Etsy "About," https://www.etsy.com/about (accessed February 12, 2014).

[671] USITC, hearing transcript, September 25, 2013, 67–68.

[672] USITC, hearing transcript, September 25, 2013, 336. For a complete description of the program, see eBay, "Global Shipping Program." http://pages.ebay.com/shipping/globalshipping/buyer-tnc.html (accessed February 20, 2014); eBay, "eBay Presents Ideas," February 26, 2013. http://www.ebaymainstreet.com/news-events/ebay-presents-ideas-pilot-custom-solutions-small-traders (accessed April 1, 2013).

[673] The costs and expense of logistics paperwork is also declining with the increased use of digital technology allowing paperless invoices. These invoices integrate order, invoice, and shipment data to expedite global customs procedures. UPS website, http://www.ups.com/content/us/en/bussol/browse/intl_trade_tools_tech.html (accessed April 1, 2013).

customs values[674] and replacing paper customs forms with digitized documentation, thereby lowering delivery time and costs. According to industry observers, these are the two reforms that would have the most positive effect on U.S. and global SME export growth.[675]

SME exporters also benefit from a wide array of other Internet-based services that assist with back-end operations and systems, such as payroll, supply and stock management, billing, and other supply chain management functions.[676] Many such business services are available as "cloud services," which can significantly reduce labor, equipment, and software costs. [677] Cloud computing allows SMEs to benefit from cutting-edge technology without IT infrastructure and maintenance costs.[678] In one survey, SME business owners commented that the availability of these services is a significant factor driving their growth.[679]

Secure and Convenient Payment Systems Promote SME Trade

Consumers are concerned that credit and other data could be stolen and are particularly wary of cross-border transactions.[680] Security is the leading concern for online cross-border shoppers, and security issues are considered a key impediment to future growth. Therefore, secure and easy online payment systems are major catalysts for SME transactions between relatively small sellers and buyers.[681] Internet-based payment services such as eBay's PayPal are designed to eliminate the risk for both parties. PayPal serves as a financial intermediary for convenient, fast, and secure transactions between online buyers and sellers in 26 currencies and 193 countries.[682] Etsy also provides a payment service, "Direct Checkout," that allows buyers and sellers to transact sales in over nine currencies.[683] The evolution of fast and secure online payment systems, including digital wallets that can be accessed anywhere with mobile

---

[674] Imported items priced below the *de minimis* value are not subject to customs duties or taxes and require minimal clearance procedures and paperwork. The United States currently has a *de minimis* value of $200 for goods entering the country. Many industry observers believe higher *de minimis* values globally would facilitate international trade by SMEs. eBay, "Being a Global Small Business: Opportunities and Barriers," January 18, 2014; McNerney, President's Export Council, letter to President Obama, September 19, 2013; USITC, hearing transcript, September 25, 2013, 238.

[675] eBay, "Roundtable Discussion," January 18, 2014.

[676] Dahlberg, "Impact of the Internet on Africa," April 2013, 8.

[677] According to one study, cloud-assisted technologies have reduced IT costs in India by one-third. Dahlberg, "Impact of the Internet on Africa," April 2013. 41.

[678] OECD, "Internet Economy Outlook," October 2012, 80.

[679] Dahlberg, "Impact of the Internet on Africa," April 2013, 8.

[680] PayPal, "Spice Routes," 2013, 7.

[681] Electronic payments were 75 percent by number and 50 percent by value of noncash payments in 2009 and are increasingly facilitating cross-border transactions. PayPal, "21st Century Regulation," n.d. (accessed January 21, 2014), 4.

[682] PayPal has 143 million active accounts and accepts payment in 26 currencies in 193 markets. PayPal, "About PayPal," https://www.paypal-media.com/about (accessed March 11, 2014).

[683] Etsy, "Direct Checkout Is Now Global!" http://www.etsy.com/blog/news/2013/direct-checkout-is-now-global/ (accessed January 21, 2014).

devices, has provided easier, more efficient, and more secure transactions for consumers, facilitating international sales and promoting SME trade.[684]

The Growth of Mobile Devices Benefits SME Trade

Mobile devices that can wirelessly connect to the Internet, including smartphones and tablets, are another key technology providing SMEs with export potential. Purchases made with these devices are the fastest-growing segment in global retail, accommodating 10.5 percent of e-commerce retail sales in 2013.[685] SMEs seeking to expand their export presence are increasingly designing websites functionally enabled for smartphones.[686] In 2013, the cross-border mobile markets in the United States, the United Kingdom, Germany, Australia, and Brazil totaled $36 billion, representing one-third of all cross-border shopping in these key markets; this figure is forecast to triple in five years.[687] In many developing countries, the critical Internet link between U.S. SMEs and foreign customers is through smartphones. For example, one study found that in China, cross-border shopping with smartphones and tablets accounted for 75 percent of all foreign online purchases. The same study found that 80 percent of all cross-border shoppers highly valued mobile-friendly websites, particularly in China and Brazil.[688] The rapid growth of smartphones and tablets also provides export opportunities for app developers, which are primarily SMEs.[689] Given the proliferation of smartphone technology globally, app technology exports are substantial. One industry observer predicted that the value of app development will grow to $46 billion by 2016.[690]

Social Media Also Have an Important Role in Promoting SME Trade

Social networking and consumer review sites are vital low-cost channels by which SMEs interface with customers and are important information resources for domestic and foreign consumers. Many SMEs reach customers through Facebook, Twitter, and other social network websites, which promote both social and commercial connections.[691] YouTube is another critical resource for SMEs, allowing them to promote and demonstrate their products and services at low cost anywhere around the globe and allowing customers to browse products virtually without in-person contact. For example, a U.S. student developed a device that connects smartphones with gaming consoles; the SME he founded, with half of its sales outside the United States, relies on a YouTube video linked to his website to demonstrate the

---

[684] PayPal, "21st Century Regulation," n.d. (accessed January 21, 2014).

[685] Comscore, "U.S. Digital Future in Focus 2014," 36.

[686] Zurich Insurance Group, "SME Business Risk in a Web-Based Economy," September 2012.

[687] eBay, "Spice Routes," 2013, 10.

[688] Ibid.

[689] For example, Apple's iOS platform had over 100,000 active app developers in 2012, mostly SMEs, many producing no more than four apps per firm. OECD, "Internet Economy Outlook, 2012," 2012, 163–64.

[690] USITC hearing transcript, March 7, 2013, 68 (testimony of Jake Colvin, National Foreign Trade Council, Inc.).

[691] Meltzer, "Supporting the Internet as a Platform," February 2014, 1; Boston Consulting Group, "The Internet Economy in the G-20," March 2012, 16.

product.[692] Online review sites, such as Yelp and Angie's List, and customer reviews of sellers' products and services posted on eBay, Amazon, and other platforms are critical tools for online consumers, including foreign customers. Such sites lower information-gathering costs for consumers and businesses, leading to greater confidence in and security for online transactions, including foreign sales.

Digital Communications and Cloud Computing Present Tremendous Export Opportunities for SMEs, but Also Risks

The heavy reliance on Internet-based technologies for key business functions, such as sales, marketing, and human resources functions, exposes SMEs to substantial digital risks, including hacking, viruses, and server downtime.

According to one study, 40 percent of cyber-attacks were directed towards SMEs in 2011.[693] In a survey of UK firms, 87 percent of small businesses reported an online security breach in 2012.[694] According to this survey, the implementation of basic digital security measures by small businesses was generally weak compared to larger firms. There are also multiple risks associated with SMEs' increasing dependence on cloud services that need to be set against the cost savings from the pay-as-you-go model. Key SME business functions such as data management, storage, and processing are now often handled by outside servers and networks, which are beyond the control of SMEs; the interruption of such services could be devastating to a small Internet-based business.[695] Other Internet-related risks arise from the increasing use of foreign materials and components sourced through Internet suppliers. When a problem arises requiring a product recall, it may be difficult for SMEs to get these online suppliers to take responsibility.[696] Despite these and other online risks, the expansion of digital technology is expected to lead to continued growth in SME exports.

---

[692] GameKlip website, "About GameKip" http://buy.thegameklip.com/ (accessed January 13, 2014). The company ships worldwide using the U.S. Postal Service and accepts payments through PayPal and major credit cards. The website also provides estimated shipping times.

[693] Zurich Insurance Group, "SME Business Risk in a Web-Based Economy," September 2012, 8.

[694] Government of the UK, Department for Business, Innovation and Skills, "2013 Information Security Breaches Survey," 2013, 3.

[695] Fredriksson, "Workshop on E-Commerce, Development and SMEs," April 8–9, 2013.

[696] Zurich Insurance Group, "SME Business Risk in a Web-Based Economy," September 2012, 7.

Bibliography

Alexa. "Top Sites." http://www.alexa.com/topsites/global (accessed various dates).

———. "Top Sites in China." http://www.alexa.com/topsites/countries/CN (accessed December 11, 2013).

———. "Top Sites in Russia." http://www.alexa.com/topsites/countries/RU (accessed December 11, 2013).

———. "Top Sites in Saudi Arabia." http://www.alexa.com/topsites/countries/SA (accessed December 16, 2013).

Amazon. "Form 10-K." Annual report for Securities and Exchange Commission, January 30, 2013.

———. "Form 10-K." Annual report for Securities and Exchange Commission, March 11, 2005.

Amazon Marketplace Web Service. "What Is Amazon Web Services?" April 2, 2014. https://developer.amazonservices.com/index.html/186-8365499-9516726.

Baidu. "Form 20-F." Annual report for Securities and Exchange Commission, March 27, 2013.

BBC Worldwide. *Annual Review 2012/13.* BBC Worldwide, 2013. http://www.bbcworldwide.com/annual-review/annual-review-2013.aspx (accessed February 3, 2014).

Boston Consulting Group. *The Connected World: Greasing the Wheels of the Internet Economy.* Independent report prepared for the Internet Corporation for Assigned Names and Numbers, January 2014. https://www.icann.org/en/news/presentations/bcg-internet-economy-27jan14-en.pdf.

———. "The Internet Economy in the G-20." March 2012.

Buley, Taylor. "Facebook's Russian Frenemy with Benefits." *Forbes*, July 13, 2009. http://www.forbes.com/2009/07/13/facebook-vkontakte-russia-technology-internet-facebook.html.

BusinessWeek. "Online Extra: eBay's Patient Bid on China," March 14, 2004. http://www.businessweek.com/stories/2004-03-14/online-extra-ebays-patient-bid-on-china.

Chander, Anupam. "How Censorship Hurts Chinese Internet Companies." *Atlantic*, August 12, 2013. http://www.theatlantic.com/china/archive/2013/08/how-censorship-hurts-chinese-internet-companies/278587/.

comScore. "China/Taiwan Hong Kong Digital Future in Focus 2013," October 2013.
http://www.comscore.com/Insights/Presentations_and_Whitepapers/2013/2013_China_Digital_Future_in_Focus_Webinar.

———. "comScore Media Metrix Ranks Top 50 U.S. Web Properties for July 2013," August 21, 2013.
http://www.comscore.com/Insights/Press_Releases/2013/8/comScore_Media_Metrix_Ranks_Top_50_US_Web_Properties_for_July_2013.

———. "France Digital Future in Focus 2013," March 2013.
http://www.comscore.com/Insights/Presentations_and_Whitepapers/2013/2013_France_Digital_Future_in_Focus.

———. "The Digital World in Focus," 2013.
http://www.comscore.com/Insights/Presentations_and_Whitepapers/2013/The_Digital_World_in_Focus.

———. "U.S. Digital Future in Focus 2013," February 2013.
http://www.comscore.com/Insights/Presentations_and_Whitepapers/2013/2013_US_Digital_Future_in_Focus.

———. "U.S. Digital Future in Focus 2014," April 2, 2014. http://www.comscore.com/Insights/Presentations_and_Whitepapers/2014/2014_US_Digital_Future_in_Focus.

———. "UK Digital Future in Focus 2013," February 2013.
http://www.comscore.com/Insights/Presentations_and_Whitepapers/2013/2013_UK_Digital_Future_in_Focus.

Dahlberg. *Impact of the Internet in Africa,* April 2013.
http://www.impactoftheinternet.com/pdf/Dalberg_Impact_of_Internet_Africa_Full_Report_April2013_vENG_Final.pdf.

De La Merced, Michael J. "Alibaba Confirms It Will Begin I.P.O. Process in U.S." Dealbook, *New York Times,* March 16, 2014. http://dealbook.nytimes.com/2014/03/16/alibaba-confirms-it-will-begin-i-p-o-process-in-u-s/.

Depillis, Lydia. "Facebook's New Users Are Overseas, Where It Can't Make Much Money Off Them." *Washington Post Wonkblog*, October 30, 2013.
http://www.washingtonpost.com/blogs/wonkblog/wp/2013/10/30/facebooks-new-users-are-overseas-where-it-cant-make-much-money-off-them/.

Dillow, Clay. "Yandex Searches past Its Language Barrier." CNNMoney, November 13, 2013. http://tech.fortune.cnn.com/2013/11/13/yandex-searches-language-barrier/.

Doyle, Michael. "Australian Buyers Prefer Domestic Online Retailers Rather Than International Ones." The Website Marketing Group, April 16, 2013. http://blog.twmg.com.au/australian-buyers-prefer-domestic-online-retailers-rather-than-international-ones/.

East-West Digital News. "Yandex vs. Google: Why the US Giant Failed to Conquer Russia," May 19, 2011. http://www.ewdn.com/2011/05/19/yandex-vs-google-why-the-us-giant-failed-to-conquer-russia/.

eBay. "Being a Global Small Business: Opportunities and Barriers." conference presentation, Washington DC, January 18, 2014.

———. "Commerce 3.0: Enabling Australian Export Opportunities," July 2013. http://www.ebaymainstreet.com/sites/default/files/eBay_Commerce-3.0_Enabling-Australian-Export-Opportunities.pdf.

———. "Enabling Traders to Enter and Grow on the Global Stage." October 2012. http://www.ebaymainstreet.com/sites/default/files/EBAY_US-Marketplace_FINAL.pdf.

———. "Form 10-K." Annual report for Securities and Exchange Commission, February 17, 2010.

———. "Form 10-K." Annual report for Securities and Exchange Commission, February 1, 2013.

eBay Enterprise. "Multi-Device Ownership: Implications for Retailers and Consumers," November 2013. http://www.ebayenterprise.com/commersations/publications/multi_device_ownership_implications_for_retailers_and_consumers/.

Edwards, Jim. "Facebook Is Failing in Europe—And It's All Russia's Fault." *Business Insider*, October 25, 2012. http://www.businessinsider.com/facebook-is-failing-in-europe--and-its-all-russias-fault-2012-10.

eMarketer. "U.S. Stays Atop Global Ad Market, but Others Rank Higher per Capita," September 26, 2013. http://www.emarketer.com/Article/US-Stays-Atop-Global-Ad-Market-Others-Rank-Higher-per-Capita/1010248.

European Commission. "Internationalisation of European SMEs," 2010. http://ec.europa.eu/enterprise/policies/sme/market-access/files/internationalisation_of_european_smes_final_en.pdf.

Facebook. "Form 10-K." Annual report for Securities and Exchange Commission, February 1, 2013.

———. "Form 10-Q." Quarterly report for Securities and Exchange Commission, July 1, 2012.

———. Quarterly report for Securities and Exchange Commission, July 25, 2013.

———. Quarterly report for Securities and Exchange Commission, November 1, 2013.

Fernandes, Ivan. "Vkontakte Is Facebook's Formidable Rival in Russia." *AdAge*, June 23, 2012.
http://adage.com/article/global-news/vkontakte-facebook-s-formidable-rival-russia/235331/.

Fredriksson, Torbjörn. "E-commerce and Development: Key Trends and Issues." Presentation for WTO Workshop on E-Commerce, Development and SMEs, Geneva, Switzerland, April 8–9, 2013.

Gallagher, Billy. "Yahoo Monthly Active Users Are Up 20% to 800M, Including 350M on Mobile, Says Marissa Mayer." TechCrunch, September 11, 2013.
http://techcrunch.com/2013/09/11/marissa-mayer-yahoo-monthly-active-users-are-up-20-to-800m-including-350m-on-mobile/.

Goldfarb, Avi, and Catherine E. Tucker. "Privacy Regulation and Online Advertising."
Management Science 68, no. 57 (2011): 57–71.

Google Inc. "Form 10-K for Fiscal Year Ended December 31, 2012." Annual report for the Securities and Exchange Commission, January 29, 2013.
http://www.sec.gov/Archives/edgar/data/1288776/000119312513028362/d452134d10k.htm or https://investor.google.com/pdf/20121231_google_10K.pdf.

Google. "Form 10-K." Annual report for Securities and Exchange Commission, February 12, 2010.

———. Annual report for Securities and Exchange Commission, March 30, 2005.

Google. "Form 10-Q." Quarterly report for Securities and Exchange Commission, October 24, 2013.

Gresser, Edward. *Lines of Light: Data Flows as a Trade Policy Concept*. Progressive Economy, May 8, 2012.

Haughney, Christine. "British Tabloid's Web Site Makes Foray Into America." *New York Times*, May 9, 2013. http://www.nytimes.com/2013/05/10/business/media/britains-daily-mail-web-site-makes-foray-into-america.html.

Hopkins, Ben. "VK.com Russia's #1 Social Network, Yandex #1 Site." *Rusbase*, December 26, 2013. http://rusbase.com/news/author/benhopkins/vkcom-russias-1-social-network-yandex-1-site/.

Kaji, Taro. "New Trend Emerging in South Korea's Search Engine Market." Covario, May 15, 2013. http://www.covario.com/2013/05/new-trend-in-south-korea-search-engine-market-is-naver-still-dominant/.

Kan, Michael. "China's Alibaba Expands U.S. Reach with New Investment Group." *InfoWorld*, October 24, 2013. http://www.infoworld.com/d/the-industry-standard/chinas-alibaba-expands-us-reach-new-investment-group-229452.

Keating, Joshua. "Can WeChat?" *Slate*, December 11, 2013. http://www.slate.com/articles/technology/the_next_silicon_valley/2013/12/wechat_going_international_tencent_aims_for_china_s_first_globally_known.html.

LaFevre, Rosella Eleanor. "Why eBay Failed in China," June 14, 2013. http://www.psmag.com/business-economics/why-ebay-failed-in-china-taobao-swift-guanxi-60072/.

Larson, James F. "Why Google Must Succeed in Korea, for Korea's Benefit." *Korea's Information Society* (blog), August 8, 2008. http://www.koreainformationsociety.com/2008/08/why-google-must-succeed-in-korea-for.html.

Lendle, Andreas. "An Anatomy of Online Trade: Evidence from eBay Exporters," September 2013. http://www10.iadb.org/intal/intalcdi/PE/2013/12982a06.pdf.

Lendle, Andreas, Marcelo Olarreaga, Simon Schropp, and Pierre-Louis Vézina. "There Goes Gravity: How eBay Reduces Trade Costs." Centre for Economic Policy Research Discussion Paper No. 9094, August 2012. https://www.ebaymainstreet.com/sites/default/files/How-eBay-Reduces-Trade-Costs.pdf.

Leurdijk, Andra, Mijke Slot, and Ottilie Nieuwenhuis. "Statistical, Ecosystems and Competitiveness Analysis of the Media and Content Industries: The Newspaper Publishing Industry." Technical Report. Seville: European Commission Joint Research Centre, 2012. http://ipts.jrc.ec.europa.eu/publications/pub.cfm?id=5380.

LinkedIn. "Form 10-Q." Quarterly report for Securities and Exchange Commission, October 29, 2013.

Liu-Thompkins, Yuping. "Online Advertising: A Cross-Cultural Synthesis." In *Handbook of Research on International Advertising,* edited by Shintaro Okazaki, 303–24. Cheltenham, UK: Edward Elgar, 2012.

Lunden, Ingrid. "Yandex Posts Q2 2013 Sales of $281M, Ad Revenue Up 35%, Profit Up 48%." *TechCrunch*, July 25, 2013. http://techcrunch.com/2013/07/25/yandex-posts-q2-2013-sales-of-281m-ad-revenue-up-35-profit-up-48/.

Martin, Eric. "Baidu Removed From U.S. 'Notorious Markets' Piracy List after Music Pact." Bloomberg, December 20, 2011. http://www.bloomberg.com/news/2011-12-20/china-s-baidu-dropped-from-u-s-notorious-markets-piracy-list.html.

McKinsey Center for Business Technology. *Perspectives on Digital Business,* January 2012. http://www.google.com/url?sa=t&rct=j&q=&esrc=s&source=web&cd=1&ved=0CCIQFjA A&url=http%3A%2F%2Fwww.mckinsey.com%2F~%2Fmedia%2Fmckinsey%2Fdotcom%2 Fclient_service%2FBTO%2FPDF%2FMCBT_Compendium_Perspectives_on_Digital_Busin ess.ashx&ei=yqGQUi_DMrLsASAoIBI&usg=AFQjCNHit5WVqrOYRrwEhHUGStMgEAJNqg& bvm=bv.68235269,d.cWc.

McKinsey Global Institute, *Internet Matters: The Net's Sweeping Impact on Growth, Jobs, and Prosperity,* May 2011. http://www.mckinsey.com/insights/high_tech_telecoms_internet/internet_matters.

McNerney, James. President's Export Council. Letter to President Obama, September 19, 2013. http://trade.gov/pec/ (accessed July 15, 2014).

Meltzer, Joshua. "Supporting the Internet as a Platform for International Trade: Opportunities for Small and Medium-Sized Enterprises and Developing Countries." Brookings Global Economy and Development Working Paper 69, February 2014. http://www.brookings.edu/~/media/research/files/papers/2014/02/internet%20intern ational%20trade%20meltzer/02%20international%20trade%20version%202.pdf.

Microsoft. "Form 10-K." Annual report for Security and Exchange Commission, July 30, 2013.

Netflix. "Form 10-Q." Quarterly report for Securities and Exchange Commission, October 25, 2013.

Nicholson, Jessica R., and Ryan Noonan. *Digital Economy and Cross-Border Trade: The Value of Digitally-Deliverable Services.* U.S. Department of Commerce. Economics and Statistics Administration, January 27, 2014. http://www.esa.doc.gov/sites/default/files/reports/documents/digitaleconomyandtrad e2014-1-27final.pdf.

Organisation for Economic Co-operation and Development (OECD). *OECD Internet Economy Outlook 2012*, October 2012. http://www.oecd.org/sti/ieconomy/ieoutlook.htm.

Pandora. "Form 10-K." Annual report for Securities and Exchange Commission, March 19, 2013.

Pavelek, Ondrej. "VKontakte Demographics," February 2013. http://www.slideshare.net/andrewik1/v-kontakte-demographics.

PayPal. "21st Century Regulation: Putting Innovation at the Heart of Payment Regulation." eBay Inc., n.d. (accessed March 15, 2014). http://172.16.3.34:9090/progress?pages&id=1102133492&fileName=UGF5UGFsLVBheW1lbnQtUmVndWxhdGlvbnMtQm9va2xldC1VUy5wZGY=&url=aHR0cDovL3d3d3l5lYmF5bWFpbnN0cmVldC5jb20vc2l0ZXMvZGVmYXVsdC9maWxlcy9QYXlQYWwtUGF5bWVudC1SZWd1bGF0aW9ucy1Cb29rbGV0LVVTLnBkZg==&serv=2&foo=2.

———. "Modern Spice Routes," 2013.

PricewaterhouseCoopers (PwC). "Demystifying the Online Shopper: 10 Myths of Multichannel Retailing," 2013. http://www.pwc.com/gx/en/retail-consumer/retail-consumer-publications/global-multi-channel-consumer-survey/2012-multi-channel-survey.jhtml.

Schwartzel, Erich, and Sam Schechner. "Dailymotion Tries Original Shows in Bid for U.S. Viewers." *Digits Blog*, *Wall Street Journal,* February 27, 2014. http://blogs.wsj.com/digits/2014/02/27/dailymotion-tries-original-shows-in-bid-for-u-s-viewers/.

Stanford Graduate School of Business. "TaoBao vs. eBay China." Case IB-88, January 4, 2010. https://gsbapps.stanford.edu/cases/documents/ib88.pdf.

Thompson, Derek. "Why Would Anybody Ever Buy Another Song?" *Atlantic,* March 14, 2014. http://www.theatlantic.com/business/archive/2014/03/why-would-anybody-ever-buy-another-song/284420/.

Twitter. "Form S-1." Registration statement for Securities and Exchange Commission, October 3, 2013.

United Nations Conference on Trade and Development (UNCTAD). UNCTADSTAT database. http://unctadstat.unctad.org (accessed various dates).

United States Department of Commerce (USDOC). U.S. Census Bureau. "A Profile of U.S. Importing and Exporting Companies, 2011–2012." Exhibit 1a, "2012 Exports by Company Type and Employment Size." News release, April 3, 2014. http://www.census.gov/foreign-trade/Press-Release/edb/2012/edbrel.pdf.

U.S. International Trade Commission (USITC). Hearing transcript in connection with inv. no. 332-531 and 332-540, *Digital Trade in the U.S. and Global Economies: Part 1 and Part* 2, March 7, 2013.

———. Hearing transcript in connection with inv. No. 332-540, *Digital Trade in the U.S. and Global Economies: Part 2*, September 25, 2013.

———. *Digital Trade in the U.S. and Global Economies: Part 1 (Digital Trade 1)*. USITC Publication 4415. Washington, DC: USITC, 2013. http://usitc.gov/publications/332/pub4415.pdf.

———. Small and Medium-Sized Enterprises: Characteristics and Performance, USITC Publication 4189. Washington, DC: USITC, 2010.

U.S. Trade Representative (USTR). *2013 Out-of-Cycle Review of Notorious Markets,* February 12, 2014. http://www.ustr.gov/about-us/press-office/reports-and-publications/2014.

———. *Out-of-Cycle Review of Notorious Markets,* December 20, 2011. http://www.ustr.gov/webfm_send/2595.

———. *Out-of-Cycle Review of Notorious Markets,* February 28, 2011. http://www.ustr.gov/webfm_send/2595.

Weibo Corporation. "Amendment No. 3 to Form F-1." Annual report for the Securities and Exchange Commission, April 14, 2014.

World Economic Forum. "The Global Information Technology Report 2014: Rewards and Risks of Big Data," 2014. http://www3.weforum.org/docs/WEF_GlobalInformationTechnology_Report_2014.pdf.

Yahoo Inc. "Form 10-K." Annual report for the Securities and Exchange Commission, March 1, 2013. http://investor.yahoo.net/secfiling.cfm?filingID=1193125-13-85111&CIK=1011006.

———. "Form 10-Q." Quarterly report for Securities and Exchange Commission, November 12, 2013.

Yandex. "Form 20-F." Annual Report for Securities and Exchange Commission, March 11, 2013.

Appendix A
Request Letter

RON WYDEN, OREGON, CHAIRMAN

JOHN D. ROCKEFELLER IV, WEST VIRGINIA
CHARLES E. SCHUMER, NEW YORK
DEBBIE STABENOW, MICHIGAN
MARIA CANTWELL, WASHINGTON
BILL NELSON, FLORIDA
ROBERT MENENDEZ, NEW JERSEY
THOMAS R. CARPER, DELAWARE
BENJAMIN L. CARDIN, MARYLAND
SHERROD BROWN, OHIO
MICHAEL F. BENNET, COLORADO
ROBERT P. CASEY, JR., PENNSYLVANIA
MARK R. WARNER, VIRGINIA

ORRIN G. HATCH, UTAH
CHUCK GRASSLEY, IOWA
MIKE CRAPO, IDAHO
PAT ROBERTS, KANSAS
MICHAEL B. ENZI, WYOMING
JOHN CORNYN, TEXAS
JOHN THUNE, SOUTH DAKOTA
RICHARD BURR, NORTH CAROLINA
JOHNNY ISAKSON, GEORGIA
ROB PORTMAN, OHIO
PATRICK J. TOOMEY, PENNSYLVANIA

JOSHUA SHEINKMAN, STAFF DIRECTOR
CHRIS CAMPBELL, REPUBLICAN STAFF DIRECTOR

United States Senate

COMMITTEE ON FINANCE

WASHINGTON, DC 20510-6200

July 28, 2014

The Honorable Meredith Broadbent
Chairman
U.S. International Trade Commission
500 E Street, SW
Washington, DC 20436

332-540

Dear Chairman Broadbent:

In a letter dated December 13, 2012, the Committee requested, pursuant to section 332(g) of the Tariff Act of 1930, that the Commission institute an investigation and provide two reports on the role of digital trade in the U.S. and global economies. The Commission delivered its first report on July 14, 2013. The delivery date for the second report, originally requested for July 14, 2014, was subsequently changed to July 29, 2014. I am now amending the Committee's request to ask that the Commission provide its completed report no later than August 11, 2014.

Sincerely,

Ron Wyden
Chairman

MAX BAUCUS, MONTANA, CHAIRMAN

JOHN D. ROCKEFELLER IV, WEST VIRGINIA   ORRIN G. HATCH, UTAH
KENT CONRAD, NORTH DAKOTA   CHUCK GRASSLEY, IOWA
JEFF BINGAMAN, NEW MEXICO   OLYMPIA J. SNOWE, MAINE
JOHN F. KERRY, MASSACHUSETTS   JON KYL, ARIZONA
RON WYDEN, OREGON   MIKE CRAPO, IDAHO
CHARLES E. SCHUMER, NEW YORK   PAT ROBERTS, KANSAS
DEBBIE STABENOW, MICHIGAN   JOHN ENSIGN, NEVADA
MARIA CANTWELL, WASHINGTON   MICHAEL B. ENZI, WYOMING
BILL NELSON, FLORIDA   JOHN CORNYN, TEXAS
ROBERT MENENDEZ, NEW JERSEY   TOM COBURN, OKLAHOMA
THOMAS R. CARPER, DELAWARE   JOHN THUNE, SOUTH DAKOTA
BENJAMIN L. CARDIN, MARYLAND

RUSSELL SULLIVAN, STAFF DIRECTOR
CHRIS CAMPBELL, REPUBLICAN STAFF DIRECTOR

United States Senate

COMMITTEE ON FINANCE

WASHINGTON, DC 20510–6200

December 13, 2012

DOCKET NUMBER

2922

Office of the Secretary
Int'l Trade Commission

The Honorable Irving A. Williamson
Chairman
U.S. International Trade Commission
500 E Street, SW
Washington, DC 20436

Dear Chairman Williamson,

I am writing to request that the U.S. International Trade Commission (Commission) conduct two investigations under section 332(g) of the Tariff Act of 1930 (19 U.S.C. §1332(g)) regarding the role of digital trade in the U.S. and global economies.

Digital trade has increased rapidly in recent years, and is an increasingly important activity within the global economy. The emergence of digital trade is part of the broader transformation in global economic activity associated with the Internet. According to researchers, the Internet has fostered GDP growth, improved productivity for large and small firms, acted as a catalyst for job creation, and provided substantial value to individual users. At the same time, policymakers are facing unprecedented challenges as they seek to ensure that digital trade remains open while producers' and consumers' data remain secure.

To assist in better understanding the role of digital trade in the U.S. economy as well as the aforementioned challenges, I request that the Commission conduct two investigations and provide the reports, as described below.

Investigation 1: Based on a review of literature and other available information, I request that the Commission provide a report that, to the extent practicable:

- Describes U.S. digital trade in the context of the broader economy.
- Examines U.S. and global digital trade, the relationship to other cross-border transactions (e.g., foreign direct investment), and the extent to which digital trade facilitates and enables trade in other sectors.
- Describes notable barriers and impediments to digital trade.
- Outlines potential approaches for assessing the linkages and contributions of digital trade to the U.S. economy, noting any challenges associated with data gaps and limitations. Such contributions and linkages may include effects on consumer welfare, output, productivity, innovation, business practices, and job creation.

The report should be delivered seven months from the date of this letter.

1

Investigation 2: Based on available information—including a survey of U.S. firms in selected industries particularly involved in digital trade and the application of approaches outlined in the first report—I request that the Commission provide a second report that, to the extent practicable:

- Estimates the value of U.S. digital trade and the potential growth of this trade. Potential growth estimates should highlight any key trends and discuss their implications for U.S. businesses and employment.
- Provides insight into the broader linkages and contributions of digital trade to the U.S. economy. Such linkages and contributions may include effects on consumer welfare, output, productivity, innovation, business practices, and job creation.
- Presents case studies that examine the importance of digital trade to selected U.S. industries that use or produce such goods and services. If possible, some of the case studies should highlight the impact of digital trade on small and medium-sized enterprises (SMEs).
- Examines the effect of notable barriers and impediments to digital trade on selected industries and the broader U.S. economy.

The Commission's approach to fulfilling these objectives should be shaped by the extent to which it can develop appropriate analytical frameworks and collect the requisite data.

This second report should be delivered nineteen months from the date of this letter.

I intend to release both of the reports to the public in their entirety. Therefore, neither report should contain any confidential business or national security information.

Sincerely,

Max Baucus
Chairman

2

Appendix B
Federal Register Notice

INTERNATIONAL TRADE COMMISSION

[Investigation No. 332–540]

Digital Trade in the U.S. and Global Economies, Part 2; Institution of Investigation and Scheduling of Hearing

AGENCY: United States International Trade Commission.

ACTION: Institution of investigation, opportunity to appear at public hearing and provide written submissions, and extension of deadlines for filing requests to appear at hearing and pre-hearing briefs and statements.

SUMMARY: In response to a request from the Senate Committee on Finance (Committee) dated December 13, 2012 (received on December 14, 2012) under section 332(g) of the Tariff Act of 1930 (19 U.S.C. 1332(g)), the U.S. International Trade Commission has instituted the second of two investigations, investigation No. 332–540, *Digital Trade in the U.S. and Global Economies, Part 2.* The Commission's report in this investigation will build upon the approaches outlined in the Commission's report in the first investigation, No. 332–531, *Digital Trade in the U.S. and Global Economies, Part 1,* which is scheduled to be transmitted to the Committee by July 14, 2013. The Commission has previously announced that it will hold a public hearing in the two investigations on March 7, 2013.

DATES:

February 28, 2013: New deadline for filing requests to appear at the public hearing.

February 28, 2013: New deadline for filing pre-hearing briefs and statements.

March 7, 2013: Public hearing.

March 14, 2013: Deadline for filing post-hearing briefs and statements.

March 21, 2014: Deadline for filing all other written submissions.

July 14, 2014: Transmittal of Commission report to the Committee.

ADDRESSES: All Commission offices, including the Commission's hearing rooms, are located in the United States International Trade Commission Building, 500 E Street SW., Washington, DC. All written submissions should be addressed to the Secretary, United States International Trade Commission, 500 E Street SW., Washington, DC 20436. The public record for this investigation may be viewed on the Commission's electronic docket (EDIS) at *https://edis.usitc.gov/edis3-internal/app.*

FOR FURTHER INFORMATION CONTACT: Project Leader James Stamps (202–205–3227 or *james.stamps@usitc.gov*) or Deputy Project Leader David Coffin (202–205–2232 or *david.coffin@usitc.gov*) for information specific to this investigation. For information on the legal aspects of these investigations, contact William Gearhart of the Commission's Office of the General Counsel (202–205–3091 or *william.gearhart@usitc.gov*). The media should contact Margaret O'Laughlin, Office of External Relations (202–205–1819 or *margaret.olaughlin@usitc.gov*). Hearing-impaired individuals may obtain information on this matter by contacting the Commission's TDD terminal at 202–205–1810. General information concerning the Commission may also be obtained by accessing its Web site (*http://www.usitc.gov*). Persons with mobility impairments who will need special assistance in gaining access to the Commission should contact the Office of the Secretary at 202–205–2000.

Background: As requested by the Committee, the Commission will base its report in this second investigation on available information, including a survey of U.S. firms in selected industries particularly involved in digital trade and the application of approaches outlined in the first report. To the extent practicable, this second report will:

• Estimate the value of U.S. digital trade and the potential growth of this trade (with the potential growth estimates to highlight any key trends and discuss their implications for U.S. businesses and employment);

• Provide insight into the broader linkages and contributions of digital trade to the U.S. economy (such linkages and contributions may include effects on consumer welfare, output, productivity, innovation, business practices, and job creation);

• Present case studies that examine the importance of digital trade to selected U.S. industries that use or produce such goods and services, with some of the case studies to highlight, if possible, the impact of digital trade on small and medium-sized enterprises; and

• Examine the effect of notable barriers and impediments to digital trade on selected industries and the broader U.S. economy.

The Commission expects to transmit this second report to the Committee by July 14, 2014.

The Commission published notice of institution of the first investigation, investigation No. 332–531, *Digital Trade in the U.S. and Global Economies, Part 1,* and the scheduling of a public

hearing for both investigations, in the **Federal Register** of January 14, 2013 (78 FR 2690). The Commission will transmit its report to the Committee in this first investigation by July 14, 2013. As requested by the Committee, in its first report the Commission will:

• Describe U.S. digital trade in the context of the broader economy;

• Examine U.S. and global digital trade, the relationship to other cross-border transactions (e.g., foreign direct investment), and the extent to which digital trade facilitates and enables trade in other sectors;

• Describe notable barriers and impediments to digital trade; and

• Outline potential approaches for assessing the linkages and contributions of digital trade to the U.S economy, noting any challenges associated with data gaps and limitations; such contributions and linkages may include effects on consumer welfare, output, productivity, innovation, business practices, and job creation.

For the purposes of these reports, the Commission is defining "digital trade" to encompass commerce in products and services delivered over digital networks. Examples include software, digital media files (e.g., e-books and digital audio files), and services such as data processing and hosting. The report will also examine how other industries, such as financial services and retailing, make use of digital products and services for production and trade.

Public Hearing: A public hearing in connection with these investigations will be held at the U.S. International Trade Commission Building, 500 E Street SW., Washington, DC, beginning at 9:30 a.m. on March 7, 2013. Requests to appear at the public hearing should be filed with the Secretary, no later than 5:15 p.m., February 28, 2013, in accordance with the requirements in the "Submissions" section below. All pre-hearing briefs and statements should be filed not later than 5:15 p.m., February 28, 2013; and all post-hearing briefs and statements responding to matters raised at the hearing should be filed not later than 5:15 p.m., March 14, 2013. In the event that, as of the close of business on February 28, 2013, no witnesses are scheduled to appear at the hearing, the hearing will be canceled. Any person interested in attending the hearing as an observer or nonparticipant should contact the Office of the Secretary at 202–205–2000 after February 28, 2013, for information concerning whether the hearing will be held.

Written Submissions: In lieu of or in addition to participating in the hearing, interested parties are invited to submit written statements concerning these investigations. All written submissions should be addressed to the Secretary, and should be received not later than 5:15 p.m., March 21, 2014. All written submissions must conform with the provisions of section 201.8 of the Commission's *Rules of Practice and Procedure* (19 CFR 201.8). Section 201.8 and the Commission's Handbook on Filing Procedures require that interested parties file documents electronically on or before the filing deadline and submit eight (8) true paper copies by 12:00 p.m. eastern time on the next business day. In the event that confidential treatment of a document is requested, interested parties must file, at the same time as the eight paper copies, at least four (4) additional true paper copies in which the confidential information must be deleted (see the following paragraph for further information regarding confidential business information). Persons with questions regarding electronic filing should contact the Secretary (202–205–2000).

Any submissions that contain confidential business information (CBI) must also conform to the requirements of section 201.6 of the *Commission's Rules of Practice and Procedure* (19 CFR 201.6). Section 201.6 of the rules requires that the cover of the document and the individual pages be clearly marked as to whether they are the "confidential" or "non-confidential" version, and that the confidential business information is clearly identified by means of brackets. All written submissions, except for confidential business information, will be made available for inspection by interested parties.

In its request letter, the Committee stated that it intends to make the Commission's reports available to the public in their entirety, and asked that the Commission not include any confidential business information or national security classified information in the reports that the Commission sends to the Committee. Any confidential business information received by the Commission in this investigation and used in preparing this report will not be published in a manner that would reveal the operations of the firm supplying the information.

By order of the Commission.
Issued: February 19, 2013.

Lisa Barton,
Acting Secretary to the Commission.

[FR Doc. 2013–04161 Filed 2–22–13; 8:45 am]

BILLING CODE 7020–02–P

INTERNATIONAL TRADE COMMISSION

[Investigation No. 337–TA–870]

Certain Electronic Bark Control Collars; Notice of Institution of Investigation; Institution of Investigation Pursuant to 19 U.S.C. 1337

AGENCY: U.S. International Trade Commission.

ACTION: Notice.

SUMMARY: Notice is hereby given that a complaint and a motion for temporary relief were filed with the U.S. International Trade Commission on January 14, 2013, under section 337 of the Tariff Act of 1930, as amended, 19 U.S.C. 1337, on behalf of Radio Systems Corporation of Knoxville, Tennessee. Supplements to the complaint were filed on February 6, 2013. The complaint alleges violations of section 337 based upon the importation into the United States, the sale for importation, and the sale within the United States after importation of certain electronic bark control collars by reason of infringement of certain claims of U.S. Patent No. 5,927,233 ("the '233 patent"). The complaint further alleges that an industry in the United States exists as required by subsection (a)(2) of section 337.

The complainant requests that the Commission institute an investigation and, after the investigation, issue an exclusion order and a cease and desist order.

The motion for temporary relief requests that the Commission issue a temporary limited exclusion order and temporary cease and desist order prohibiting the importation into and the sale within the United States after importation of certain electronic bark control collars that infringe claims 1, 3, 6, 8, 9, and 15 of the '233 patent during the course of the Commission's investigation.

ADDRESSES: The complaint, except for any confidential information contained therein, is available for inspection during official business hours (8:45 a.m. to 5:15 p.m.) in the Office of the Secretary, U.S. International Trade Commission, 500 E Street SW., Room 112, Washington, DC 20436, telephone (202) 205–2000. Hearing impaired individuals are advised that information on this matter can be obtained by contacting the Commission's TDD terminal on (202) 205–1810. Persons with mobility impairments who will need special assistance in gaining access to the Commission should contact the

Office of the Secretary at (202) 205–2000. General information concerning the Commission may also be obtained by accessing its Internet server at *http://www.usitc.gov*. The public record for this investigation may be viewed on the Commission's electronic docket (EDIS) at *http://edis.usitc.gov*.

FOR FURTHER INFORMATION CONTACT: The Office of Unfair Import Investigations, U.S. International Trade Commission, telephone (202) 205–2560.

Authority: The authority for institution of this investigation is contained in section 337 of the Tariff Act of 1930, as amended, and in section 210.10 of the Commission's Rules of Practice and Procedure, 19 CFR 210.10 (2012).

Scope of Investigation: Having considered the complaint, the U.S. International Trade Commission, on February 14, 2013, *ordered that*—

(1) Pursuant to subsection (b) of section 337 of the Tariff Act of 1930, as amended, an investigation be instituted to determine whether there is a violation of subsection (a)(1)(B) of section 337 in the importation into the United States, the sale for importation, or the sale within the United States after importation of certain electronic bark control collars by reason of infringement of one or more of claims 1, 3, 6, 8, 9, and 15 of the '233 patent, and whether an industry in the United States exists as required by subsection (a)(2) of section 337;

(2) Pursuant to section 210.58 of the Commission's Rules of Practice and Procedure, 19 CFR 210.58, the motion for temporary relief under subsection (e) of section 337 of the Tariff Act of 1930, which was filed with the complaint, is provisionally accepted and referred to the presiding administrative law judge for investigation;

(3) For the purpose of the investigation so instituted, the following are hereby named as parties upon which this notice of investigation shall be served:

(a) The complainant is: Radio Systems Corporation, 10427 Petsafe Way, Knoxville, TN 37932.

(b) The respondent is the following entity alleged to be in violation of section 337, and is the party upon which the complaint is to be served: Sunbeam Products, Inc., d/b/a Jarden Consumer Solutions, 2381 NW Executive Center Drive, Boca Raton, FL 33431.

(c) The Office of Unfair Import Investigations, U.S. International Trade Commission, 500 E Street SW., Suite 401, Washington, DC 20436; and

(4) For the investigation so instituted, the Chief Administrative Law Judge, U.S. International Trade Commission,

Dated: July 26, 2013.

David Newman,

Federal Register Liaison.

[FR Doc. 2013–18637 Filed 8–1–13; 8:45 am]

BILLING CODE 4311–AM–P

DEPARTMENT OF THE INTERIOR

Bureau of Land Management

[13X LLWYR02000 L14300000.ER0000 242A.00]

Change in Dates of Seasonal Closure of Public Land in the Bald Ridge Area, Park County, WY

AGENCY: Bureau of Land Management, Interior.

ACTION: Notice.

SUMMARY: Notice is hereby given to change the dates of the seasonal closure of public land in the Bald Ridge Area that was published in the **Federal Register** on Thursday, August 5, 1999 (64 FR 42711). The previous closure was in effect from December 15 through April 30 each winter and spring season to all use, except for specifically authorized vehicles. Pursuant to this Notice, the Bald Ridge area located south of the Clarks Fork of the Yellowstone River and west and north of Hogan Reservoir of Park County, Wyoming on public land administered by the Bureau of Land Management (BLM) Cody Field Office, is now closed from January 1 through April 30 of each winter and spring season to all use (such as human presence, hiking, horseback riding, mountain bike riding, cross-country skiing, and all motorized use), except for specifically authorized activities. The total acreage of this closure is 6,036 acres. This action is being taken for resource protection of essential wintering habitat for elk and mule deer. No access into this area will be allowed unless permitted by the Authorized Officer (BLM, Cody Field Manager).

DATES: This change of seasonal closure dates is effective March 7, 2013, and will remain in effect until modified or rescinded by the Authorized Officer.

FOR FURTHER INFORMATION CONTACT:
Michael Stewart, Field Manager, BLM, Cody Field Office at:
- *Telephone:* 307–578–5900;
- *Email:* m75stewa@blm.gov
- *Address:* 1002 Blackburn Street, Cody, WY 82414

Persons who use a telecommunications device for the deaf (TDD) may call the Federal Information Relay Service (FIRS) at 1–800–877–8339 to contact the above individual during normal business hours. The FIRS is available 24 hours a day, 7 days a week, to leave a message or question with the above individual. You will receive a reply during normal business hours.

SUPPLEMENTARY INFORMATION: The Cody Field Office is responsible for the management of essential wildlife habitat in the Bald Ridge area of the Absaroka Front and other crucial habitat areas located throughout the Bighorn Basin. These essential habitat areas and management thereof are covered under the Cody Resource Management Plan (RMP), which was signed on November 9, 1990. "Seasonal restrictions will be applied as appropriate to surface-disturbing and disruptive activities and land uses on big game crucial habitat, including wintering ranges and elk calving areas." (Cody RMP, p. 40).

The Bald Ridge area is crucial wintering habitat for big game. Increasing visitor activity such as horseback riding, hiking and antler hunting has caused impacts to the wintering herds. These activities are stressing game animals during a period when the animals are most susceptible to stress-related health effects that could cause death. These activities also force the herds to be displaced from their winter habitat. The Cody Field Office published a Notice in the **Federal Register** on Friday, March 29, 1996 (61 FR 14159), that closed the Bald Ridge area from December 15 through April 30 each winter and spring season. The Cody Field Office subsequently extended the seasonal closure in a second Notice in the **Federal Register** on Thursday, August 5, 1999 (64 FR 42711).

The December 15 closure date was largely based on the ending date of an elk hunting season as established by the Wyoming Game and Fish Department. In recent years the Wyoming Game and Fish Department determined it was necessary to harvest additional elk in the Bald Ridge area and extended the end of the elk hunting season to December 31. At the request of the Wyoming Game and Fish Department, members of the public, and an adjoining private landowner, the Cody Field Office determined it was necessary for the seasonal closure of the Bald Ridge area to coincide with the December 31 end of the elk hunting season. The BLM Cody Field Office analyzed the date change in Environmental Assessment WY–020–EA13–20. A Finding of No Significant Impact (FONSI) was signed on March 7, 2013. Subsequently, a Decision Record was signed on March 7, 2013.

The following described BLM-administered lands south of the Clarks Fork of the Yellowstone River and west of Hogan Reservoir are included in this seasonal closure:

Sixth Principle Meridian, Wyoming

T. 56 N., R. 103 W.,
  Tracts 81 and 82, tracts 88 to 97, inclusive, tracts 107 to 109, inclusive, tracts 113 to 116, inclusive, and tracts 119 to 122, inclusive;
  Sec. 7, SE¼SE¼;
  Sec. 8, SW¼SW¼;
  Sec. 16, lots 5 and 11;
  Sec. 17, lots 1 to 6, inclusive, and W½W½;
  Sec. 18;
  Sec. 19;
  Sec. 20;
  Sec. 21, lots 1 to 4, inclusive, W½NW¼, SW¼, and SW¼SE¼;
  Sec. 22, lot 7;
  Sec. 27, lots 1, 2, and 8;
  Sec. 28, lots 1 to 6, inclusive, N½, and NW¼SE¼;
  Sec. 29, lots 1 to 3, inclusive, N½, and W½SW¼;
  Sec. 30;
  Sec. 31, lots 5 to 7, inclusive, N½NE¼, E½NW¼, and NE¼SW¼;
  Sec. 32, lots 4, 5, 7, and 8, and NW¼NW¼;
  Sec. 33, lots 1 to 8, inclusive, W½SW¼, and E/12SE¼.

Authority for closure and restriction orders is provided under 43 CFR subpart 8341.2 (a and b), 8364.1. Violations of this closure are punishable by a fine not to exceed $1500 and (or) imprisonment not to exceed 12 months.

Larry Claypool,

Acting State Director.

[FR Doc. 2013–18565 Filed 8–1–13; 8:45 am]

BILLING CODE 4310–22–P

INTERNATIONAL TRADE COMMISSION

[Investigation No. 332–540]

Digital Trade in the U.S. and Global Economies, Part 2; Proposed Information Collection; Comment Request; Digital Trade 2 Questionnaire

AGENCY: United States International Trade Commission

ACTION: In accordance with the provisions of the Paperwork Reduction Act of 1995 (44 U.S.C. Chapter 35), the U.S. International Trade Commission (Commission) hereby gives notice that it plans to submit a request for approval of a questionnaire to the Office of Management and Budget for review and requests public comment on its draft collection.

DATES: To ensure consideration, written comments on the questionnaire must be submitted on or before October 1, 2013.

ADDRESSES: Direct all written comments to James Stamps, Project Leader, U.S. International Trade Commission, 500 E Street SW., Washington, DC 20436 (or via email at *james.stamps@usitc.gov*).

ADDITIONAL INFORMATION: Copies of the questionnaire and supporting investigation documents may be obtained from project leader James Stamps (*james.stamps@usitc.gov* or 202–205–3227) or deputy project leader David Coffin (*david.coffin@usitc.gov* or 202–205–2232). Supporting documents may also be downloaded from the Commission Web site at *http://www.usitc.gov/ research_and_analysis/ What_We_Are_Working_On.htm.* Hearing-impaired individuals may obtain information on this matter by contacting the Commission's TDD terminal at 202–205–1810. General information concerning the Commission may also be obtained by accessing its Web site (http://www.usitc.gov). Persons with mobility impairments who will need special assistance in gaining access to the Commission should contact the Office of the Secretary at 202–205–2000.

Purpose of Information Collection: The information requested by the questionnaire is for use by the Commission in connection with Investigation No. 332–540, *Digital Trade in the U.S. and Global Economies, Part 2,* instituted under the authority of section 332(g) of the Tariff Act of 1930 (19 U.S.C. 1332(g)). This investigation was requested by the Senate Committee on Finance (Committee). The Committee requested that this investigation include a survey of U.S. firms in selected industries particularly involved in digital trade. The Commission expects to deliver its report to the Committee by July 14, 2014.

Summary of Proposal

(1) *Number of forms submitted:* 1.

(2) *Title of form:* Digital Trade in the U.S. and Global Economies, Part 2 Questionnaire.

(3) *Type of request:* New.

(4) *Frequency of use:* Industry questionnaire, single data gathering, scheduled for 2013.

(5) *Description of respondents:* Companies in industries particularly involved in digital trade.

(6) *Estimated number of respondents:* 15,000.

(7) *Estimated total number of hours to complete the questionnaire per respondent:* 3 hours.

(8) Information obtained from the questionnaire that qualifies as confidential business information will be so treated by the Commission and not disclosed in a manner that would reveal the individual operations of a firm.

SUPPLEMENTARY INFORMATION:

I. Abstract

The U.S. Senate Committee on Finance has directed the Commission to produce a report that: (1) Estimates the value of U.S. digital trade, and the potential growth of this trade; (2) provides insight into the broader linkages and contributions of digital trade to the U.S. economy; (3) presents case studies that examine the importance of digital trade to selected U.S. industries that use or produce such goods and services; and (4) examines the effect of notable barriers and impediments to digital trade on selected industries and the broader U.S. economy. The Commission will base its report on a review of available data and other information, including the collection of primary data through a survey of U.S. firms in industries particularly involved in digital trade.

II. Method of Collection

Respondents will be mailed a letter directing them to download and fill out a form-fillable PDF questionnaire. Once complete, respondents may submit it by uploading it to a secure webserver, emailing it to the study team, faxing it, or mailing a hard copy to the Commission.

III. Request for Comments

Comments are invited on: (1) Whether the proposed collection of information is necessary; (2) the accuracy of the agency's estimate of the burden (including hours and cost) of the proposed collection of information; (3) ways to enhance the quality, utility, and clarity of the information to be collected; and (4) ways to minimize the burden of the collection of information on respondents, including through the use of automated collection techniques or other forms of information technology.

The draft questionnaire and other supplementary documents may be downloaded from the USITC Web site at *http://www.usitc.gov/332540comments.*

Comments submitted in response to this notice will be summarized and/or included in the request for OMB approval of this information collection; they will also become a matter of public record.

By order of the Commission

Issued: July 30, 2013.

Lisa R. Barton,
Acting Secretary to the Commission.
[FR Doc. 2013–18685 Filed 8–1–13; 8:45 am]
BILLING CODE 7020–02–P

INTERNATIONAL TRADE COMMISSION

Certain Welded Large Diameter Line Pipe From Japan; Investigation No. 731–TA–919 (Second Review); Notice of Commission Determination To Conduct a Portion of the Hearing In Camera

AGENCY: U.S. International Trade Commission.

ACTION: Closure of a portion of a Commission hearing.

SUMMARY: Upon the timely request of respondents, the Commission has determined to conduct a portion of its hearing in the above-captioned investigation scheduled for August 1, 2013, in camera. See Commission rules 207.24(d), 201.13(m) and 201.36(b)(4) (19 CFR 207.24(d), 201.13(m) and 201.36(b)(4)). The remainder of the hearing will be open to the public.

FOR FURTHER INFORMATION CONTACT: Michael K. Haldenstein, Office of the General Counsel, U.S. International Trade Commission, telephone 202–205–3041. Hearing-impaired individuals are advised that information on this matter may be obtained by contacting the Commission's TDD terminal on 202–205–3105.

SUPPLEMENTARY INFORMATION: The Commission believes that respondents JFE Steel Corporation and Nippon Steel & Sumitomo Metal Corporation have justified the need for a closed session. In making this decision, the Commission nevertheless reaffirms its belief that whenever possible its business should be conducted in public.

The hearing will include the usual public presentations by domestic producers and by respondents, with questions from the Commission. In addition, the hearing will include a 10-minute in camera session for a confidential presentation by respondents. Each session will be followed by an in camera rebuttal presentation by domestic producers and questions from the Commission relating to the BPI. During the in camera session the room will be cleared of all persons except those who have been granted access to BPI under a Commission administrative protective order (APO) and are included on the Commission's APO service list in this investigation and the respondent witnesses (Atsuhito

FOR FURTHER INFORMATION CONTACT: To request additional information about this ICR, contact Ben Erichsen, Chief, Commercial Services Program, at (202) 513–7156 (telephone) or ben_erichsen@nps.gov (email). You may review the ICR online at *http://www.reginfo.gov.* Follow the instructions to review Department of the Interior collections under review by OMB.

SUPPLEMENTARY INFORMATION:
OMB Control Number: 1024–0029.
Title: National Park Service Concessions.
Service Form Number(s): 10–356 and 10–356A.
Type of Request: Revision of a currently approved collection.

Description of Respondents: Individuals, businesses, and nonprofit organizations.

Respondent's Obligation: Required to obtain or retain a benefit.

Frequency of Collection: Annually for financial reports, ongoing for recordkeeping, and on occasion for the remaining requirements.

Activity	Number of respondents	Number of annual responses	Completion time per response	Total annual burden hours
Proposal—Large Concession	30	30	240 hours	7,200
Proposal—Small Concession	60	60	80 hours	4,800
Amendments	1	1	1 hour	1
Appeals	1	1	30 minutes	1
Request To Construct a Capital Improvement—Large Projects.	31	31	16 hours	496
Request To Construct a Capital Improvement—Small Projects.	89	89	8 hours	712
Construction Report—Large Project	31	31	56 hours	1,736
Construction Report—Small Project	89	89	24 hours	2,136
Application to Sell or Transfer a Concession Operation.	20	20	80 hours	1,600
Form 10–356	150	150	16 hours	2,400
Form 10–356A	350	350	4 hours	1,400
Recordkeeping—Large Concessions	150	150	800 hours	120,000
Recordkeeping—Small Concessions	350	350	50 hours	17,500
Totals	1.352	1.352		159,982

Estimated Annual Nonhour Burden Cost: $425,000.

Abstract: Private businesses under contract to the National Park Service manage food, lodging, tours, whitewater rafting, boating, and many other recreational activities and amenities in more than 100 national parks. These services gross more than $1 billion every year and provide jobs for more than 25,000 people during peak season.

The regulations at 36 CFR Part 51 primarily implement Title IV of the National Parks Omnibus Management Act of 1998 (Pub. L. 105–391), which provides legislative authority, policies, and requirements for the solicitation, award, and administration of NPS concession contracts. The information collection requirements associated with NPS concessions are currently approved under four OMB control numbers. During our review for this renewal, we discovered some additional requirements that need OMB approval. In this revision of 1024–0029, we are including all of the information collection requirements associated with applying for and operating NPS concessions. If OMB approves this revision, we will discontinue OMB Control Numbers 1024–0125, 1024–0126, and 1024–0231.

Comments: On March 7, 2013, we published in the **Federal Register** (78 FR 14822) a notice of our intent to request that OMB approve this information collection. In that notice, we solicited comments for 60 days, ending on May 6, 2013. We did not receive any comments.

We again invite comments concerning this information collection on:

• Whether or not the collection of information is necessary, including whether or not the information will have practical utility;

• The accuracy of our estimate of the burden for this collection of information;

• Ways to enhance the quality, utility, and clarity of the information to be collected; and

• Ways to minimize the burden of the collection of information on respondents.

Comments that you submit in response to this notice are a matter of public record. Before including your address, phone number, email address, or other personal identifying information in your comment, you should be aware that your entire comment, including your personal identifying information, may be made publicly available at any time. While you can ask OMB in your comment to withhold your personal identifying information from public review, we cannot guarantee that it will be done.

Dated: August 16, 2013.

Leonard E. Stowe,
Acting Information Collection Clearance Officer, National Park Service.

[FR Doc. 2013–20395 Filed 8–20–13; 8:45 am]

BILLING CODE 4310–EH–P

INTERNATIONAL TRADE COMMISSION

[Investigation No. 332–540]

Digital Trade in the U.S. and Global Economies, Part 2; Scheduling of an Additional Public Hearing

AGENCY: United States International Trade Commission.

ACTION: Scheduling of additional public hearing in Moffett Field, CA.

SUMMARY: The Commission has scheduled a public hearing in investigation No. 332–540, *Digital Trade in the U.S. and Global Economies, Part 2* at the NASA Ames Research Center in Moffett Field, California beginning at 9:30 a.m. on Wednesday, September 25, 2013.

DATES: September 12, 2013: Deadline for filing requests to appear at the public hearing.

September 18, 2013: Deadline for filing pre-hearing briefs and statements.

September 25, 2013: Public hearing.

October 3, 2013: Deadline for filing post-hearing briefs and statements.

March 21, 2014: Deadline for filing all other written submissions.

July 14, 2014: Transmittal of Commission report to the Senate Committee on Finance.

ADDRESSES: All written submissions should be addressed to the Secretary, United States International Trade Commission, 500 E Street SW., Washington, DC 20436. The public record for this investigation may be viewed on the Commission's electronic docket (EDIS) at *https://edis.usitc.gov/ edis3-internal/app.*

FOR FURTHER INFORMATION CONTACT: Project Leader James Stamps (202–205– 3227 or *james.stamps@usitc.gov*) or Deputy Project Leader David Coffin (202–205–2232 or *david.coffin@ usitc.gov*) for information specific to this investigation. For information on the legal aspects of these investigations, contact William Gearhart of the Commission's Office of the General Counsel (202–205–3091 or *william.gearhart@usitc.gov*). The media should contact Margaret O'Laughlin, Office of External Relations (202–205– 1819 or *margaret.olaughlin@usitc.gov*). Hearing-impaired individuals may obtain information on this matter by contacting the Commission's TDD terminal at 202–205–1810. General information concerning the Commission may also be obtained by accessing its Web site (*http://www.usitc.gov*). Persons with mobility impairments who will need special assistance in gaining access to the Commission should contact the Office of the Secretary at 202–205–2000.

Background: The additional hearing relates to the second of two reports that the Commission is preparing on the role of digital trade in the U.S. and global economies at the request of the U.S. Senate Committee on Finance. The Commission held a public hearing in connection with both reports in Washington, DC, on March 7, 2013. The first report, *Digital Trade in the U.S. and Global Economies, Part 1,* Investigation No. 332–531, will be available to the public on August 15, 2013, on the Commission's Web site (*http:// www.usitc.gov*). As requested by the Committee, the Commission will base its report in this second investigation on available information, including a survey of U.S. firms in selected industries particularly involved in digital trade and the application of approaches outlined in the first report. To the extent practicable, this second report will:

• estimate the value of U.S. digital trade and the potential growth of this trade (with the potential growth estimates to highlight any key trends and discuss their implications for U.S. businesses and employment);

• provide insight into the broader linkages and contributions of digital trade to the U.S. economy (such linkages and contributions may include effects on consumer welfare, output, productivity, innovation, business practices, and job creation);

• present case studies that examine the importance of digital trade to selected U.S. industries that use or produce such goods and services, with some of the case studies to highlight, if possible, the impact of digital trade on small and medium-sized enterprises; and

• examine the effect of notable barriers and impediments to digital trade on selected industries and the broader U.S. economy.

The Commission expects to transmit this second report to the Committee by July 14, 2014. For the purposes of this investigation, the Commission is defining "digital trade" to encompass commerce in products and services delivered via the Internet as well as commerce in products and services that is facilitated by the use of the Internet and Internet-based technologies. Commerce includes both U.S. domestic economic activity as well as international trade.

Public Hearing: The additional hearing will be held at the NASA Ames Conference Center/NASA Research Park, Building 152, Room 171, 200 Dailey Road, Moffett Field, CA, beginning at 9:30 a.m. on Wednesday, September 25, 2013. Requests to appear at the public hearing should be filed with the Secretary, no later than 5:15 p.m., September 12, 2013, in accordance with the requirements in the "Requests to Appear" section below. All pre-hearing briefs and statements should be filed not later than 5:15 p.m., September 18, 2013; and all post-hearing briefs and statements responding to matters raised at the hearing should be filed not later than 5:15 p.m., October 3, 2013. In the event that, as of the close of business on September 12, 2013, no witnesses are scheduled to appear at the hearing, the hearing will be canceled. Any person interested in attending the hearing as an observer or nonparticipant should contact the Office of the Secretary at 202–205–2000 after September 12, 2013, for information concerning whether the hearing will be held.

This field hearing is being planned in conjunction with a field hearing to be held on September 26, 2013 for Inv. No. 332–541, *Trade Barriers that U.S. Small and Medium-sized Enterprises Perceive as Affecting Exports to the European Union.* Interested persons who wish to present consolidated statements and testimony relevant to both investigations are invited to do so on Wednesday, September 25, 2013.

Requests To Appear: Requests to appear at the Moffett Field, CA hearing may be in the form of a letter, which should be on company or other appropriate stationery. Requests should identify the name, title, and company or other organizational affiliation (if any), address, telephone number, email address, and industry or main line of business of the company, if any, of the person signing the request letter and of the persons who plan to appear at one or both hearings. Requests to appear may be made by mail or delivered in person to the Commission's Office of the Secretary (see **ADDRESSES**), or may be filed by email sent to *digitaltrade@ usitc.gov.* The Commission does not accept requests filed by fax.

Written Submissions: In lieu of or in addition to participating in the hearing, interested parties are invited to submit written statements concerning this investigation. Such submissions should be addressed to the Secretary, and should be received not later than 5:15 p.m., March 21, 2014. All written submissions must conform to the provisions of section 201.8 of the Commission's *Rules of Practice and Procedure* (19 CFR 201.8). Section 201.8 and the Commission's Handbook on Filing Procedures require that interested parties file documents electronically on or before the filing deadline and submit eight (8) true paper copies by 12:00 p.m. eastern time on the next business day. In the event that confidential treatment of a document is requested, interested parties must file, at the same time as the eight paper copies, at least four (4) additional true paper copies in which the confidential information must be deleted (see the following paragraph for further information regarding confidential business information). Persons with questions regarding electronic filing should contact the Secretary (202–205–2000).

Any submissions that contain confidential business information (CBI) must also conform to the requirements of section 201.6 of the *Commission's Rules of Practice and Procedure* (19 CFR 201.6). Section 201.6 of the rules requires that the cover of the document and the individual pages be clearly marked as to whether they are the "confidential" or "non-confidential" version, and that the confidential business information is clearly identified by means of brackets. All written submissions, except for confidential business information, will be made available for inspection by interested parties.

In its request letter, the Committee stated that it intends to make the Commission's reports available to the public in their entirety, and asked that the Commission not include any confidential business information or national security classified information in the reports that the Commission sends to the Committee. Any confidential business information received by the Commission in this investigation and used in preparing this report will not be published in a manner that would reveal the operations of the firm supplying the information.

By order of the Commission.

Issued: August 15, 2013

Lisa R. Barton,

Acting Secretary to the Commission.

[FR Doc. 2013–20387 Filed 8–20–13; 8:45 am]

BILLING CODE 7020–02–P

INTERNATIONAL TRADE COMMISSION

[Investigation No. 332–541]

Trade Barriers That U.S. Small and Medium-sized Enterprises Perceive as Affecting Exports to the European Union; Scheduling of an Additional Public Hearing With Simplified Filing Procedures

AGENCY: United States International Trade Commission.

ACTION: Scheduling of additional public hearing in Moffett Field, CA.

SUMMARY: The Commission has scheduled an additional public hearing in Inv. No. 332–541, *Trade Barriers that U.S. Small and Medium-sized Enterprises Perceive as Affecting Exports to the European Union,* to be held beginning at 9:30 a.m., September 26, 2013, at the NASA Ames Research Center at Moffett Field, CA. This hearing is in addition to a previously announced public hearing in this investigation to be held at the U.S. International Trade Commission Building, 500 E Street SW., Washington, DC, beginning at 9:30 a.m. on October 8, 2013. Procedures for filing requests to appear have been changed for both hearings to encourage the appearance of small businesses.

This field hearing is being scheduled in conjunction with a field hearing to be held on September 25, 2013, also at the NASA Center in Moffett Field, CA in a second Commission investigation, No. 332–540, *Digital Trade in the U.S. and Global Economies, Part 2,* requested by

the Senate Committee on Finance. Interested persons who wish to present consolidated statements and testimony relevant to both investigations are invited to do so on Wednesday September 25, 2013.

DATES: September 12, 2013: Deadline for filing requests to appear at the Moffett Field, CA hearing.

September 18, 2013: Deadline for filing pre-hearing briefs and statements.

September 26, 2013: Public hearing in Moffett Field, CA.

October 3, 2013: Deadline for filing post-hearing briefs.

October 15, 2013: Deadline for filing all other written submissions.

January 31, 2014: Transmittal of Commission report to the USTR.

ADDRESSES: All written submissions should be addressed to the Secretary, United States International Trade Commission, 500 E Street SW., Washington, DC 20436. The public record for this investigation may be viewed on the Commission's electronic docket (EDIS) at *https://edis.usitc.gov/edis3-internal/app.*

FOR FURTHER INFORMATION CONTACT: Project Leader William Deese (202–205–2626 or *william.deese@usitc.gov*) or Deputy Project Leader Tamar Khachaturian (202–205–3299 or *tamar.khachaturian@usitc.gov*) for information specific to this investigation. For information on the legal aspects of these investigations, contact William Gearhart of the Commission's Office of the General Counsel (202–205–3091 or *william.gearhart@usitc.gov*). The media should contact Margaret O'Laughlin, Office of External Relations (202–205–1819 or *margaret.olaughlin@usitc.gov*). Hearing-impaired individuals may obtain information on this matter by contacting the Commission's TDD terminal at 202–205–1810. General information concerning the Commission may also be obtained by accessing its Internet server (*http://www.usitc.gov*). Persons with mobility impairments who will need special assistance in gaining access to the Commission should contact the Office of the Secretary at 202–205–2000.

Background: The hearing relates to a report that the Commission is preparing at the request of the United States Trade Representative (USTR) under section 332(g) of the Tariff Act of 1930 (19 U.S.C. 1332(g)). The USTR requested that the Commission prepare a report that catalogs trade barriers that U.S. small and medium-sized enterprises (SMEs) perceive as disproportionately affecting their exports to the EU, compared to those of larger U.S.

exporters to the EU. In the request letter, the USTR stated that the United States, in the Transatlantic Trade and Investment Partnership (TTIP) negotiations with the European Union (EU), is seeking to strengthen the participation of SMEs in transatlantic trade and to address trade barriers that may disproportionately impact small businesses. The notice announcing the institution of this investigation and the Washington, DC, hearing on October 8, 2013, was published in the **Federal Register** of July 30, 2013 (78 FR 45969); the notice is also posted on the Commission's Web site at *www.usitc.gov.*

The Commission is particularly interested in receiving information and views from SMEs and related organizations about trade-related barriers faced by U.S. SMEs in exporting goods or services to the EU and about EU trade barriers by economic sector or by special issue. (For purposes of this report, an SME is defined as a firm with fewer than 500 U.S.-based employees.) The Commission is also interested in receiving information and views about specific trade barriers in individual EU countries; the relative effect on exports of different EU trade barriers; and ways in which SME participation in transatlantic trade might be strengthened.

Public Hearing: The additional hearing will be held at the NASA Ames Conference Center/NASA Research Park, Building 152, Room 171, 200 Dailey Road, Moffett Field, CA, beginning at 9:30 a.m. on September 26, 2013. Requests to appear at the public hearing should be filed with the Secretary, no later than 5:15 p.m. (eastern daylight time), September 18, 2013, in accordance with the requirements in the "Requests to Appear" section below. All pre-hearing briefs and statements should be filed no later than 5:15 p.m. (eastern daylight time), September 18, 2013; and all post-hearing briefs and statements should be filed not later than 5:15 p.m., October 3, 2013. In the event that, as of the close of business on September 12, 2013, no witnesses are scheduled to appear at the hearing, the hearing will be canceled. Any person interested in attending the hearing as an observer or nonparticipant should contact the Office of the Secretary at 202–205–2000 after September 12, 2013, for information concerning whether the hearing will be held.

Requests To Appear: Requests to appear at the Moffett Field, CA, and Washington, DC, hearings may be in the form of a letter, which should be on company or other appropriate

Land Policy and Management Act of 1976, as amended, the BLM, as lead agency, and Reclamation and Western, as cooperating agencies, prepared the Draft Environmental Impact Statement (EIS) that was published in the **Federal Register** on April 27, 2012, (77 FR 25165). Subsequently, the agencies held public meetings on the document in the communities of Kingman, Peach Springs, White Hills, and Dolan Springs, Arizona. The Final EIS was published on May 17, 2013, (78 FR 29131). The National Park Service, the Arizona Game and Fish Department, Mohave County, and the Hualapai Tribe were also cooperating agencies.

The No Action Alternative and four action alternatives were analyzed in the Final EIS. The proposed action, Alternative A, called for the use of approximately 38,099 acres of BLM-managed land and 8,960 acres of Reclamation-administered land. Alternative B would require approximately 30,872 acres of BLM-managed land and 3,848 acres of Reclamation-administered land. Alternative C called for the use of 30,178 acres of BLM-managed land and approximately 5,124 acres of Reclamation-administered land. Alternative E would require approximately 35,329 acres of BLM-managed land and 2,781 acres of Reclamation-administered land. Alternative E is BLM's and Reclamation's preferred alternative and represents a combination of Alternatives A and B.

It is the decision of the BLM and Reclamation to approve Alternative E, including associated infrastructure and a switching station, and issue ROW grant and ROU contract, respectively, across Federal lands for the construction, operation, maintenance, and decommissioning of the Project to BP Wind Energy; and for the BLM to issue a ROW grant to Western for the construction, operation, and maintenance of a switching station, subject to terms and conditions of the ROW grants and ROU contract, plan of development, and mitigation measures. Full implementation of this decision is contingent upon BP Wind Energy and Western obtaining all applicable permits and approvals. This decision is based on the information contained in the Draft and Final EIS.

Because this decision is approved by the Acting Assistant Secretary for Land and Minerals Management, it is not subject to administrative appeal (43 CFR 4.5 and 4.410(a)(3)).

Authority: 40 CFR 1506.6.

Jamie Connell,
Acting Deputy Director of Operations, Bureau of Land Management.
[FR Doc. 2013–22575 Filed 9–16–13; 8:45 am]
BILLING CODE 4310–32–P

INTERNATIONAL TRADE COMMISSION

[Investigation No. 332–540]

Digital Trade in the U.S. and Global Economies, Part 2; Submission of Questionnaire for OMB Review

AGENCY: United States International Trade Commission.

ACTION: Notice of submission of request for approval of a questionnaire to the Office of Management and Budget. This notice is being given pursuant to the Paperwork Reduction Act of 1995 (44 U.S.C. Chapter 35).

Purpose of Information Collection: The information requested by the questionnaire is for use by the Commission in connection with investigation No. 332–540, *Digital Trade in the U.S. and Global Economies, Part 2.* The investigation was instituted under section 332(g) of the Tariff Act of 1930 (19 U.S.C. 1332(g)) at the request of the U.S. Senate Committee on Finance. The Commission expects to deliver its report to the Committee by July 14, 2014.

Summary of Proposal

(1) Number of forms submitted: 1.
(2) Title of form: Digital Trade Questionnaire.
(3) Type of request: New.
(4) Frequency of use: Industry questionnaire, single data gathering, scheduled for 2013.
(5) Description of respondents: Companies in the United States in industries that the USITC considers particularly digitally-intensive (i.e. firms that make particularly intensive use of the Internet and Internet technology in their business activities).
(6) Estimated number of questionnaires to be mailed: 10,000.
(7) Estimated total number of hours to complete the questionnaire per respondent: 30 hours.
(8) Information obtained from the questionnaire that qualifies as confidential business information will be so treated by the Commission and not disclosed in a manner that would reveal the individual operations of a firm.

Additional Information or Comment: Copies of the questionnaire and supporting documents may be obtained from project leader James Stamps (*james.stamps@usitc.gov* or 202–205–3227) or deputy project leader David Coffin (david.coffin@usitc.gov or 202–205–2232). Comments about the proposal should be directed to the Office of Management and Budget, Office of Information and Regulatory Affairs, Room 10102 (Docket Library), Washington, DC 20503, Attention: Docket Librarian. All comments should be specific, indicating which part of the questionnaire is objectionable, describing the concern in detail, and including specific suggested revision or language changes. Copies of any comments should be provided to Andrew Martin, Chief Information Officer, U.S. International Trade Commission, 500 E Street SW., Washington, DC 20436, who is the Commission's designated Senior Official under the Paperwork Reduction Act.

General information concerning the Commission may also be obtained by accessing its Internet address (*http://www.usitc.gov*). Hearing impaired individuals are advised that information on this matter can be obtained by contacting the TDD terminal on 202–205–1810. Persons with mobility impairments who will need special assistance in gaining access to the Commission should contact the Secretary at 202–205–2000.

By order of the Commission.
Issued: September 12, 2013.

Lisa R. Barton,
Acting Secretary to the Commission.
[FR Doc. 2013–22545 Filed 9–16–13; 8:45 am]
BILLING CODE 7020–02–P

JOINT BOARD FOR THE ENROLLMENT OF ACTUARIES

Advisory Committee Meeting

AGENCY: Joint Board for the Enrollment of Actuaries.

ACTION: Notice of Federal Advisory Committee meeting.

SUMMARY: The Executive Director of the Joint Board for the Enrollment of Actuaries gives notice of a closed meeting of the Advisory Committee on Actuarial Examinations.

DATES: The meeting will be held on October 18, 2013, from 8:30 a.m. to 5:00 p.m.

ADDRESSES: The meeting will be held at Crowne Plaza San Antonio Riverwalk, 111 East Pecan Street, San Antonio, TX 78205.

FOR FURTHER INFORMATION CONTACT: Patrick W. McDonough, Executive

Appendix C
Calendar of Hearing

CALENDAR OF PUBLIC HEARING

Those listed below appeared as witnesses at the United States International Trade Commission's hearing:

Subject:	Digital Trade in the U.S. and Global Economies, Part 2
Inv. No.:	332-540
Date and Time:	September 25, 2013 - 9:30 am (PST)

Sessions were held in connection with this investigation at the NASA Ames Research Center in Moffett Field, CA.

ORGANIZATION AND WITNESS:

PANEL 1

The Internet Association
Washington, DC

> **Markham Erickson**, General Counsel and Partner,
> Steptoe & Johnson

Application Developers Alliance
Washington, DC

> **Jon Potter**, President

Mozilla
Mountain View, CA

> **Jim Cook**, Chief Financial Officer

IBM Corporation
Armonk, NY

> **Anick Fortin-Cousens**, Privacy Officer, Growth Markets Program
> & Director, Corporate Privacy

1

ORGANIZATION AND WITNESS:

PANEL 2

Newegg Inc.
City of Industry, CA

        Lee Cheng, Chief Legal Office and Corporate Secretary

Motion Picture Association of America, Inc.
Washington, DC

        John McCoskey, Executive Vice President *and* Chief
            Technology Officer

Aptara Inc.
Falls Church, VA

        Pavan Arora, Vice President

Rambus Inc.
Sunnyvale, CA

        Dr. Martin Scott, Chief Technology Officer

eBay Inc.
San Jose, CA

        David London, Senior Director, US Government Relations

-END-

2

Appendix D
Summary of Positions of Interested Parties

The Commission held a public hearing for *Digital Trade 1* and *Digital Trade 2* on March 14, 2013, in Washington, DC. Appendix D of *Digital Trade 1* contains a summary of the views expressed to the Commission via testimony, written submissions, or both, received before the completion of that investigation in July 2013. The Commission also held a public hearing for *Digital Trade 2* on September 25, 2013, in Moffett Field, CA. This appendix contains a summary of the views expressed to the Commission via testimony, written submissions, or both, received after July 2013 in connection with *Digital Trade 2*. The views summarized are those of the submitting parties and not the Commission, and reflect only the principal points made by the participating party. In preparing this summary, Commission staff did not confirm the accuracy of, or otherwise correct, the information summarized. For the full text of hearing testimony, written submissions, and exhibits in connection with this investigation, see entries associated with investigation no. 332-540 at the Commission's Electronic Docket Information System (https://edis.usitc.gov).

Application Developers Alliance (ADA)[697]

In testimony at the Commission's hearing, Mr. Jon Potter, president of ADA, described his organization as representing more than 30,000 individual members and 150 corporate members, ranging from small mobile application (app) coders employed by companies of less than 50 people to large companies that service, promote, and benefit from the app industry. He explained that apps are software and related data that travel to and from customers on networks, and that the data associated with apps are stored on servers. Mr. Potter said that most app publishers are indifferent about who owns the network, who owns the servers, and where the network or the servers are located. He also stated that ADA members need robust and unrestricted networks at competitive prices so that customers have ready access to their data in markets across the globe.

Mr. Potter observed that the mobile app economy was reportedly born in 2008, when Apple opened its app store to iPhone users. Since that time, and with the introduction of the Google Play Store and other independent app stores, he said that the U.S. app economy has grown to support 725,000 jobs nationwide, including coders, quality testers, and project managers.

Mr. Potter stated that data must be accessible without limitation for the app economy to continue to grow and flourish. He said the ADA recognizes the legitimate concerns about government access to consumer data, but noted that businesses have an obligation to respect consumers and to be transparent about what consumer data are collected and how those data are managed and secured. He said that app developers need consumers to be comfortable using apps to share their thoughts, their interests, and to communicate with their contacts. Concerns that onerous government data practices might deter consumers from using apps has led ADA to work with the National Telecommunications and Information Administration, consumer groups, and industry groups to develop a new standard by which creators of mobile apps can communicate clearly and effectively with consumers about data-collection and data-sharing practices. Mr. Potter said that country-specific privacy and data localization regimes

---

[697] USITC, hearing transcript, September 25, 2013, 21–30.

should be harmonized in ways that maximize consumer benefits. He cited the successful negotiation of a United States–European Union (EU) safe harbor agreement that enables U.S. companies to do business in the EU as an example of what can be done to harmonize different data privacy regimes to ensure interoperability. He urged that this agreement be renewed, and recommended that the United States seek agreements similarly ensuring interoperability with other trading partners.

Mr. Potter described the ADA's concerns regarding app piracy. He said that app piracy is a particularly important issue because many of America's best creators are now app developers and publishers for the important creative entertainment side of the app economy. He recommended that governments act carefully when considering ways to thwart app piracy, observing that technological or policy solutions to cut piracy may do more harm than good. For example, he said that filtering technologies intended to block pirated apps may unintentionally create "back doors" that allow unfriendly governments to spy on users or let repressive regimes limit and/or block users' access to their own data.

Mr. Potter described the many benefits derived from the digital economy and outlined ways the digital economy supports U.S. and global economic growth. He said that the new business models that have grown out of the digital economy—such as app-based shared riding or room rental services and online music and video services that allow musicians and other creators to promote themselves directly to audiences on the Internet without the need to go through production and distribution intermediaries—can ultimately contribute to consumer welfare by creating new jobs, even though traditional jobs may be lost. He also stated that the outsourcing of some jobs, such as computer coding, helps create opportunities in other countries and may encourage other countries to open their markets to U.S. digital products.

Aptara, Inc.[698]

In testimony at the Commission's hearing, Mr. Pavan Arora, vice president of product and innovation of Aptara, Inc., stated that his company is a global organization that transforms book content into e-book formats for 9 of the top 10 publishers as well as many small, independent publishers, primarily in the United States. He noted that the U.S. e-book market has grown from less than one percent of overall trade book sales in 2002 to 23 percent in 2012. He also stated that while the United States now ranks as the largest e-book market, Europe is poised to overtake the United States in terms of e-book sales by 2017.

Among the issues Mr. Arora discussed in his testimony on the e-book industry were job creation, piracy, censorship, and globalization. He stated that the growth of the e-book market has led to an exponential growth in self-publishing. This, in turn, has facilitated significant growth in the number of independent authors who can now publish their work without going traditional publishing houses. He did not see this trend as having an adverse impact on large traditional publishers who, he said, could still find publishable authors by drawing from the pool of self-published authors. Mr. Arora said that sources report that about 90 percent of e-books

---

[698] USITC, hearing transcript, September 25, 2013, 213–21.

sold in Russia are pirated. He said that this piracy was not particularly problematic for his company's digital formatting operations, but he added that piracy concerns were being addressed by book publishers. Mr. Arora reported that his company had not experienced censorship of e-books because its operations focus primarily on English-language nonfiction works. He said that the time and costs of translating books from English into non-Latin-based languages, such as Arabic or Chinese, generally mean that translations of e-books that might be censored in some countries are simply not available in the local language of those markets. Finally, he stated that when an e-book is released it automatically becomes available globally and has an immediate global market, which has not been the case for print books. However, Mr. Arora also mentioned several factors that can constrain the availability and adoption of e-book reading in some markets. For example, he said the current short supply of e-readers that can track text from right to left is limiting the uptake of e-book reading in Arabic-reading countries. He also noted that in some European countries, e-books are considered licensed software and are thus subject to a higher value-added tax (VAT) than physical books.

BSA | The Software Alliance[699]

In a written submission, Mr. David Ohrenstein, director of global trade policy for BSA | The Software Alliance, notified the Commission of two recent BSA publications.

In its publication *The 2013 BSA Global Cloud Computing Scorecard*,[700] BSA ranks 24 countries using seven policy categories that measure the countries' preparedness to support the growth of cloud computing. The categories were data privacy; security; cybercrime; intellectual property rights; support for industry-led standards and international harmonization of rules; promoting free trade; and information and communication technology readiness and broadband deployment. Japan and Australia ranked first and second in 2013, unchanged from 2012. The United States ranked third in 2013, up from fourth place in 2012, while Germany ranked fourth in 2013, down from third place in 2012. The report cites another study that predicts that by 2015 cloud computing will generate as much as $1.1 trillion in annual revenue and account for nearly 14 million jobs worldwide.

In its publication *Powering the Digital Economy: A Trade Agenda to Drive Growth*,[701] BSA discusses the growth and benefits of digital trade, catalogues key barriers, and sets out a trade agenda for promoting the digital economy. Key findings from the report focused on three areas of needed action:

Modernize trade rules to enable digital commerce. The report recommends that trade agreements should ensure that data can flow across borders with few restrictions, and trade agreements should cover current and future innovative services.

---

[699] David J. Ohrenstein, director, global trade policy, BSA | The Software Alliance, written submission to the USITC, March 21, 2014.
[700] Available at http://digitaltrade.bsa.org/.
[701] Ibid.

Promote technology innovation. The report recommends that trade agreements should provide robust intellectual property protections and promote market-led, globally adopted technology standards, along with minimally burdensome technical regulations.

Ensure level playing fields. The report recommends that trade agreements strive to open government procurement and keep state-owned enterprises on a level playing field, and that the Information Technology Agreement be expanded.

eBay, Inc.[702]

In hearing testimony, Mr. David London, senior director of U.S. government relations for eBay, focused on the eBay subsidiary PayPal. He described PayPal as a company that lets people send and receive money online and, increasingly, in stores without having to share their financial information. He said that PayPal processes more than 7 million payments every day. It has more than 132 million active accounts in over 193 countries and regions, and it accepts payments in more than 26 currencies around the world. He said that cross-border trade accounts for about one-fourth of PayPal's total payments value, and that PayPal expects to process more than $20 billion in mobile payments in 2013. Mr. London's testimony drew on a 2013 Nielsen Co. report commissioned by PayPal—*Modern Spice Routes: The Cultural Impact of Economic Opportunity of Cross-Border Shopping*[703]—that was based on a survey of cross-border online shoppers in the six top online shopping markets: the United States, the United Kingdom, Germany, Brazil, China, and Australia.

Mr. London stated that cross-border online trade in the six top online shopping markets was expected to be an estimated $105 billion in 2013, with 94 million consumers regularly buying from overseas websites. He said that cross-border demand for online U.S. products was valued at an estimated $23 billion in 2013, and was expected to grow almost fourfold by 2018. Moreover, according to Mr. London, online merchants from the United States were the most popular among those surveyed, with 84 percent of Chinese cross-border customers buying from U.S. websites and their orders estimated worth an estimated $12 billion in 2013.

Mr. London said there are steps government can take to promote a healthy environment for technology-enabled small businesses. These steps include:

- Promote open development of remote mobile payments. He said that online cross-border trade via mobile devices has grown rapidly in importance and was valued at $36 billion in 2013, accounting for than one-third of the cross-border online trade that year. He also cautioned that thoughtful policy making is needed to ensure security and efficiency in the fast-growing and still evolving area of mobile payments.

---

[702] USITC, hearing transcript, September 25, 2013, 231–40.
[703] Available at https://www.paypal-media.com/assets/pdf/fact_sheet/PayPal_ModernSpiceRoutes_Report_Final.pdf.

- Ensure that a domestic presence is not required for digital trade in a given country, because the ability to move information and services across borders without the need to establish a domestic presence is essential to the global Internet framework.

- Promote innovative digital intermediaries by, for example, encouraging rights holders, intermediaries, and consumers in the Internet marketplace to work together to combat online piracy and counterfeit goods.

- Improve customs and shipping regimes, because issues with customs and shipping are often significant barriers facing Internet-enabled SMEs. He said that steps such as increasing the *de minimis* thresholds for levying duties and harmonizing shipping platforms would be particularly beneficial for small businesses that are engaged in cross-border trade.

- Recognize small Internet-enabled merchants in trade policy. He said that continued focus on promoting Internet-enabled trade will create additional opportunities for small businesses to access global markets.

IBM Corporation[704]

In hearing testimony, Ms. Anick Fortin-Cousens, IBM's program privacy officer for growth markets and director of corporate privacy, stated that her company is a globally integrated information technology company operating in more than 170 countries. Ms. Fortin-Cousens said that IBM relies on the ability to move data, including data pertaining to people, to individuals around the world without impediments. She stated that IBM has a strong interest in working with government leaders towards solutions to prevent, eliminate, or reduce impediments to cross-border data flows. She stated that IBM was the first company in the world to be certified under the Asia-Pacific Economic Cooperation (APEC) cross-border privacy rules (CBPR) system that was designed to facilitate data flows between the United States and the other APEC member economies through voluntary, enforceable codes of conduct.

Ms. Fortin-Cousens acknowledged the Commission's finding in *Digital Trade 1* that among the notable barriers and impediments to digital trade were divergent privacy and data protection laws. She added that many countries have cited privacy protection as a strong concern and their main reason for creating barriers to cross-border data flows. She outlined several of the different ways in which countries have implemented restrictions on cross-border data flows: by restricting the transfer of personal data to other countries; by requiring the express consent of individuals before their data can be transferred abroad; by establishing model contractual clauses that have onerous provisions; and by requiring the approval of a data protection body before data can be transferred abroad.

Ms. Fortin-Cousens discussed the concept of interoperability and the importance of establishing workable models for cross-border data flows based on voluntary but enforceable

---

[704] USITC, hearing transcript, September 25, 2013, 39–47.

accountability-based codes of conduct. She described interoperability as allowing countries to adopt different approaches to privacy, but with the objective of having data protection laws that are generally similar and that meet a certain threshold entitling them to mutual recognition by other countries. By providing an assurance that personal information, once collected, will receive the same level of protection regardless of where it is processed, she said that accountability-based systems can build trust among individuals, stakeholders, policymakers, and enforcement authorities. Ms. Fortin-Cousens discussed APEC's CBPR system as an example of certified accountability. Under this system, according to Ms. Fortin-Cousens, the APEC cross-border privacy rules work in conjunction with local laws. To participate in the CBPR system, she said, countries must have in place a privacy law that reflects the APEC privacy principles, and they must also have an enforcement authority. She stated that this system, like the Binding Corporate Rules that the EU recognizes as sufficient for cross-border transfers, provides credible evidence that participating organizations are trustworthy as regards privacy.

International Intellectual Property Alliance (IIPA)[705]

In a written submission, Mr. Michael Schlesinger, co-founder of IIPA, stated that his organization is a private sector coalition formed of trade associations representing U.S. copyright-based industries. He recommended that the Commission make further attempts to evaluate more comprehensively the contribution of copyright-intensive goods and services to digital trade for *Digital Trade 2*. However, he acknowledged the limited scope of publicly available data and the relative lack of disaggregated data points that would be necessary for such an analysis. His submission included several reports and papers.[706]

Mr. Schlesinger recommended that *Digital Trade 2* try to more accurately count the legitimate value added contributed by copyrighted works to the digital trade valuation. He cited findings from a study by Stephen Siwek that the "core copyright industries" (industries whose primary purpose is to create, produce, distribute, or exhibit copyrighted materials, including computer software, videogames, books, newspapers, periodicals and journals, motion pictures, recorded music, and radio and television broadcasting) now add over $1 trillion in value to the U.S. economy annually and account for almost 6.5 percent of U.S. GDP.

Mr. Schlesinger also recommended that *Digital Trade 2* fully examine the effects of notable barriers and impediments to digital trade on the copyright industries and the broader U.S.

---

[705] Schlesinger, written submission to the USITC, March 21, 2014.

[706] Mr. Schlesinger's written submission included the following documents: Stephen E. Siwek, *Copyright Industries in the U.S. Economy: The 2013 Report*, November 19, 2013; U.S. Department of Commerce, Economic and Statistics Administration and U.S. Patent and Trademark Office, *Intellectual Property and the U.S. Economy: Industries in Focus*, March 2012; Art Works and National Endowment for the Arts, *NEA Guide to the U.S. Arts and Cultural Production Satellite Account: Including a Blueprint for Capturing the Economic Value of Arts and Cultural Workers and Volunteers*, December 2013; IIPA Written Submission Regarding *2014 Special 301 Review: Identification of Countries under Section 182 of the Trade Act of 1974; Request for Public Comment and Announcement of Public Hearing*, February 7, 2014; Frontier Economics, *Estimating the Global Economic and Social Impacts of Counterfeiting and Piracy: A Report Commissioned by Business Action to Stop Counterfeiting and Piracy*, February 2011; David Price, *Sizing the Piracy Universe*, Net Names, September 2013.

economy. He said that the Commission should take into account the adverse impacts that copyright infringement over the Internet and consequent distortions in legitimate trade have on the growth of digital trade in copyrighted materials. His submission reported that Internet-based infringement continues to grow as Internet usage expands. His submission states that even in regions where legitimate distribution of content is advanced, the number of individuals involved in infringement has increased, the number of webpage views devoted to infringement has grown, and the absolute amount of bandwidth linked to infringement has risen. Mr. Schlesinger said that legitimate copyright industries face unfair competition from those who engage in digital piracy using illegal online services that are unencumbered by costs associated with either producing copyrighted works or obtaining rights to use them. He cited estimates of the commercial value of digitally pirated music, movies, and software at $30–$75 billion in 2010, growing to $80–$240 billion by 2015.

The Internet Association[707]

In hearing testimony, Mr. Markham Erickson, general counsel and partner, Steptoe & Johnson, stated that the companies he represents in The Internet Association have only recently begun to participate as stakeholders in international trade discussions. He noted that the Internet industry is relatively new, and until now Internet companies have largely been focused on establishing themselves in the U.S. market. He said that as they have started promoting their services globally, U.S. Internet companies now see the need to become more engaged participants in the U.S. trade policymaking process. Mr. Erickson stated that the dominance of U.S. firms in the global Internet space has led some other countries to impose protectionist regimes, often disguised as regulatory measures to protect data privacy or data security. He said that countries enact such protectionist regimes to allow their own domestic Internet companies time to become competitive with U.S. companies.

In his testimony Mr. Erickson spoke of the importance of an "innovation without permission culture," and he discussed some of the U.S. laws that embody this culture. He described section 230 of the Communications Decency Act as allowing U.S. companies that serve as intermediaries and conduits on the Internet to not be liable for the speech of third parties who use their systems. He further described the Digital Millennium Copyright Act as providing that Internet companies do not have to monitor or police their systems to look for copyrighted material, but they must remove any infringing content upon notification by copyright owners. Mr. Erickson recommended that the United States include such provisions in future U.S. trade agreements.

Mr. Erickson discussed some of his concerns with measures in place or being considered in important U.S. trading partners. He said that a forced localization measure being considered in Brazil would require that data transfers to that country be transferred via mirror or duplicate servicers located in Brazil, rather than the data being transferred directly from servers located in the United States. He also discussed problems of the regulation of content on the Internet in India, and Internet censorship and intellectual property theft in China.

---

[707] USITC, hearing transcript, September 25, 2013, 13–21.

Mr. Erickson also spoke about some of the regulatory challenges presented by new Internet technologies. He said that cloud computing presents unique challenges because while software might be located on a server in one country, customers may be in a different or in multiple countries. He said that the interoperability that is created by cloud computing may be prevented by country-specific regulations, having the effect that when customers travel to a different country they might not be able to access all of their cloud-based content due to local regulations. He also said that the United States should work to ensure that trade agreements allow for free cross-border flows because firms in sectors such as healthcare and financial services increasingly rely on cross-border data transfers.

Mr. Erickson also outlined some of the economic effects of digital trade. He said that the Internet can be economically disruptive and cause job displacement, but it can also be a source new job creation. He cited one report that said the Internet creates 2.1 jobs for every job it displaces. The new jobs are often jobs that did not exist prior to the Internet or that are not fully captured by economic data, such as the work of people who make a living selling items on eBay or people who are able to leverage the global exposure and audiences the Internet offers into entrepreneurial ventures or even careers as performance artists.

Motion Picture Association of America (MPAA)[708]

In hearing testimony, Mr. John McCoskey, executive vice president and chief technology officer of the Motion Picture Association of America (MPAA), stated that his association represents six of the world's largest producers and distributors of theatrical motion pictures, home entertainment, and television programing—specifically Disney, Fox, Paramount, Sony, Universal, and Warner Brothers. Mr. McCoskey stated that the U.S. film and television industry is constantly innovating to deliver its content where and how audiences want it. He said that there are now more than 400 unique online services around the world delivering full-length films and TV shows. He said that MPAA members are licensing their content to online retailers as well as to streaming, cloud, download, and video-on-demand platforms. About half of their revenue is generated from foreign markets. Mr. McCoskey said that MPAA places a high priority on securing both the legal and practical tools necessary to protect intellectual property rights in the digital age, and that he believes international trade rules should support a healthy online marketplace that has strong intellectual property protections, open markets, and freedom of expression.

Mr. McCoskey provided an overview of the significance of business-to-business (B2B) transactions by MPAA members, and recommended that the *Digital Trade 2* questionnaire address the B2B digital content market. He said that while many MPAA members have their own online platforms to reach potential customers, some are involved in licensing their digital content to other platforms via B2B relationships that the Commission should take into consideration.

---

[708] USITC, hearing transcript, September 25, 2013, 208–13.

Mr. McCoskey discussed the importance of physical digital products—in particular, digital cinema packs (DCPs). DCPs are hard drives onto which digital movies are securely encoded, replacing traditional film reels. DCPs are used to physically deliver digital movies to some movie theaters. Mr. McCoskey acknowledged that physically delivered digital products were outside the scope of *Digital Trade 1*, but he recommended that the scope for *Digital Trade 2* be expanded to include DCPs.

Mr. McCoskey also spoke about the impacts of censorship and piracy. He reported that problems with censorship faced by MPAA members often reflect cultural barriers in which a specific country denies entry to a particular film or type of films because of specific political, violent, or sexual content. He also said that piracy also remains a problem for MPAA members, although the extent of piracy varies significantly from country to country.

Mozilla[709]

In hearing testimony, Mr. Jim Cook, chief financial officer for Mozilla, said that the main product of this nonprofit company is its Firefox Web browser. Mozilla employs 900 people, and a further 25,000 volunteers contribute to Mozilla's open source software products. He said the Internet should be "more cared for than owned" and that his company's real mission is to enable users to be in control of their experience on the Internet. Mr. Cook cited a report that said that 80 percent of the top 10 global Internet companies are U.S.-based, while 80 percent of Internet users reside outside the United States. He said that the main foreign competitors to U.S. Internet companies are in China, and that the main focus of new economic competition has shifted to apps. Mr. Cook also noted the importance of the topic of the physical location of servers, particularly because the ability of companies to locate servers where they are needed is important to the continued growth of cloud computing and the app economy.

Mr. Cook spoke about the importance of user trust to the future growth of digital trade. He said that government and industry can make a difference in helping users to understand what happens to their data and how their data are used. He further described the economic impact of digital trade on the growth of the "sharing economy." He observed that peer-to-peer transactions based on mobile apps make up an increasing part of digital trade. Apps such as Uber, Lyft, Sidecar, and Airbnb contribute to the sharing economy by allowing people to monetize their personal assets or their excess capacity—such as a car or spare bedroom that they do not use all of the time—by renting them to others.

Mr. Cook also discussed the involvement of SMEs in digital trade. He noted the importance of venture capitalists to Internet-based SMEs. He said cloud computing can significantly benefit SMEs by allowing them to outsource many components of their business operations to cloud providers. However, he also observed that many small companies lack the resources and the maturity to compete internationally. Mr. Cook observed that the mobile payment industry, which includes many SMEs, may offer examples of small companies that have managed to overcome regulatory barriers.

---

[709] USITC, hearing transcript, September 25, 2013, 31–39.

Newegg[710]

In hearing testimony, Mr. Lee Cheng, chief legal officer and senior vice president of corporate development of Newegg, stated that Newegg is an online retailer of computer products, with nearly half of its 2,600 worldwide employees in the United States. The chief focus of Mr. Cheng's testimony was on lawsuits in recent years from patent holders alleging infringement by Newegg. According to Mr. Cheng, these lawsuits were broad, vague complaints largely based on end-of-life business method and software patents and often covering functionalities like an online shopping cart, payment, and search. He said that such legal challenges were particularly challenging given's Newegg's low margins and competitive market environment.

Mr. Cheng stated that online only digital sales are growing in large part because of the increasing popularity of mobile technologies. He reported that the growth in online sales continues to outstrip sales by traditional stores. Turning to international trade, he said that it is very difficult for foreign companies to become dominant online players in China because of the many restrictions that government imposes. For example, he said that it is difficult for foreign internet retailers operating in China to own key intellectual property assets, such as their Internet domain name. However, he stated that the "Made in America" is considered a mark of high quality in China that can make U.S. products highly competitive in the Chinese market.

Rambus[711]

In hearing testimony, Mr. Martin Scott, chief technology officer of Rambus, stated that his company is focused on research and development in many areas that support the hardware that makes digital trade possible. Mr. Scott said that frivolous and expensive patent litigation is bad for commerce and innovation, while noting that a more balanced view of legitimate patent rights is important and that legitimately enforced patent rights are good for consumers and businesses.

Mr. Scott stated that trade barriers were not high on his company's list of concerns because over the years Rambus has found ways to effectively conduct business with its customers globally. He reported that a shortage of available highly technically trained workers in the United States was an impediment to innovation-based companies such as Rambus, and stated that this shortage of highly qualified technical labor could be addressed though both domestic educational reform to produce a more skilled workforce and immigration reform to allow U.S. companies greater access to skilled workers abroad.

Mr. Scott noted that protecting intellectual property and maintaining data security are important goals for Rambus. He said that some of the hardware Rambus has developed, such as a layer of protection embedded on semiconductor chips, is an important component to securing data transmission that is the

---

[710] USITC, hearing transcript, September 25, 2013, 165–76.
[711] USITC, hearing transcript, September 25, 2013, 221–31.

backbone of digital trade. He stated that another security technology Rambus has developed is deployed in 75 percent of digital TV set-top boxes coming into the U.S. marketplace over the next year.

www.ingramcontent.com/pod-product-compliance
Lightning Source LLC
Chambersburg PA
CBHW080803180526
45168CB00006B/2309